Stratton Mountain
Country Club,
Stratton Mountain,
Vermont

GOLF® MAGAZINE GREAT GETAWAYS

THE BEST OF THE BEST THREE- AND FOUR-DAY GOLF TRIPS

EDITED BY TARA GRAVEL
INTRODUCTION BY ARNOLD PALMER

ABRAMS, NEW YORK

Introduction by Arnold Palmer   7
Preface by Tara Gravel   9

NEW ENGLAND

Massachusetts
The Berkshires 12
Cape Cod 14

Rhode Island
Newport 17

Vermont
The Equinox Resort,
Manchester Village 20

Bargain Tracks by
Big-name Architects 24

MID-ATLANTIC

New Jersey
Atlantic City 30

New York
Lake Placid 34
Long Island 35

Pennsylvania
Laurel Highlands 38

Virginia
Williamsburg 40
Virginia Beach 43

District of Columbia
Washington, D.C. 47

West Virginia
The Greenbrier 49

Major Venues
You Can Play 52

SOUTH

Alabama
Robert Trent Jones
Golf Trail 56

Florida
The Emerald Coast 61
The First Coast 64
Naples 67
Orlando 70

Georgia
Savannah 76
Sea Island 78

Louisiana
New Orleans 82

Mississippi
Northeastern Mississippi 84

North Carolina
Pinehurst and the
Sandhills 86

South Carolina
Kiawah Island 91
Myrtle Beach's
South Strand 94

Beat the Mile-high Blues 97

MIDWEST

Illinois
Chicago 100

Michigan
Northern Michigan 104

Minnesota
Northern Minnesota 110

North Dakota
The North Dakota
Golf Trail 114

Wisconsin
Kohler 117

College Courses That
Make the Grade 119

WEST

Arizona
Scottsdale-Phoenix 122
Tucson 129

California
Napa 134
San Francisco to
Pebble Beach 136
San Diego Area 139
Palm Springs 142

Colorado
Vail Valley 145

Nevada
Las Vegas 150
Lake Tahoe 153
Reno 156

Texas
Houston 160
San Antonio 162

**Utah to Montana,
Idaho, and Wyoming**
Salt Lake City 165
Salt Lake City to
Anaconda 166
Salt Lake City to
Sun Valley 167
Salt Lake City to
Jackson Hole 169

Play Ball! 144
The Shipping News:
Ship Your Clubs 171

 Gold and Silver Medal Resorts are indicated
throughout the book by these symbols.

CONTENTS

NORTHWEST

Idaho
Coeur d'Alene 174

Montana
Flathead Valley 176

Oregon
Bandon Dunes 179
Bend and Sunriver
Resort 184
Portland 187

Washington
Seattle 190

Trail Blazing:
GOLF MAGAZINE's
Top 10 Golf Trails 194

HAWAII

Maui 198
Lana'i 202
Oahu 206
Mauna Lea and
Mauna Lani 207

The Tipping Point 209

CANADA

British Columbia
Banff 212
Okanagan Valley 215

Ontario
Muskoka Golf Trail 218

Prince Edward Island 221

Code of the Road 223

CARIBBEAN & MEXICO

Caribbean
Barbados 226
Bermuda 229
Puerto Rico 232

Mexico
Los Cabos 235
Puerto Vallarta 237
Cancun 241

Crisis Management 243

EUROPE

Austria
The Alps 246

France
Biarritz 247

Ireland
Dublin 249

Italy
Emilia Romagna 252

Portugal
The Algarve 255
Estoril and Sintra 260

Scotland
St. Andrews and Fife 262

Spain
Costa del Sol 268

Perfect the Buddy
System 271

GOLF MAGAZINE'S "BEST OF" LISTS

Gold and Silver Medal Resorts	273
Top 100 Courses You Can Play	280
Top 100 Courses You Can Play (Ranked by State)	282
Thrifty 50 Courses	284
25 Best Golf Schools	291
Top 100 Courses in the U.S.	292
Top 100 Courses in the World	294
Golf.com User Ratings	296

| Index | 300 |

Hole 4 at Edgewood
Tahoe Golf Course,
Lake Tahoe, Nevada

INTRODUCTION

A wise man once said that golf, just like fishing, never happens in ugly places. If I had to choose what have been the best things about my 53-year career as a professional golfer and course designer, it wouldn't be the money or accolades or the seven major titles I've won. First would be the people I've met through this wonderful game, and second would be that I've been able to spend my career in some of the most beautiful places on earth.

In my early days on tour, well before I was successful enough to afford to fly commercial, let alone by private jet, we players caravanned from event to event, with the younger players relying on the old-timers for advice on the best hotels, restaurants, and entertainment. I know that this book seeks to be what those tour veterans were for us—a source of real inside information, a shortcut to getting the most out of any trip.

I'm especially pleased that some of my favorite places have made it into *Great Getaways*, from the Laurel Highlands in Pennsylvania, where I make my summer home in the town of Latrobe, to my winter residence, Bay Hill Club and Lodge in Orlando, where I host the PGA Tour's Bay Hill Invitational each March. I hope that someday you'll get to enjoy my favorite destinations, too, as well as some of the courses I've designed, more than a dozen of which are featured in this book. If you plan your golf trips with *Great Getaways* as your guide, it'll be like having a true expert by your side, pointing the way.

—Arnold Palmer

Hole 13 at Sunriver
(Crosswater), Oregon

PREFACE For avid golfers like you, a golf vacation is a pilgrimage, an affirmation of everything you love about the game. It's a chance to experience some of the best scenery in the world, to test your game on new fields of play, and to deepen your bonds with your favorite playing partners. Or maybe it's simply a chance to let loose playing 36 holes a day, with no baggage but your clubs and nothing on the line but a two-dollar Nassau.

Whatever your goals and desires as a traveler, GOLF MAGAZINE *Great Getaways* will help you fulfill them. In these pages you'll find more than 70 of the best golf destinations in the U.S., Canada, Mexico, the Caribbean, and Europe. And by the best, we don't mean the most expensive. While we've included golf Meccas where the greens fees will set you back a few bills, like Pebble Beach and Pinehurst, we've also focused on plenty of destinations for bargain-seekers, too.

Each getaway is broken into sections that make trip planning as easy as possible—Where to Play, Where to Stay, Where to Eat, Local Knowledge (other things to see and do), Getting There, and When to Go. We've also included more than 15 lists and travel tips—everything from GOLF MAGAZINE's 50 Best U.S. Courses for $50 or Less to guidelines on planning the ultimate buddy trip.

Golf is a game of beauty, camaraderie, and constant challenge, and at no time is this more evident than when you're leaving behind the "real world" to focus on the fun of the game. We hope that GOLF MAGAZINE's decades of travel experience and coverage, encapsulated here in *Great Getaways*, helps you get the most out of your many pilgrimages.

—Tara Gravel, Senior Editor, GOLF MAGAZINE

NEW ENGLAND

MASSACHUSETTS

RHODE ISLAND

VERMONT

THE BERKSHIRES
CAPE COD

NEWPORT

THE EQUINOX RESORT, MANCHESTER VILLAGE

THE BERKSHIRES
There's more to this northwestern corner of Massachusetts than the stately beauty of rolling hills. There is plenty of golf, including New England's finest course. The Berkshire Mountains in their October prime offer an unbeatable combination: rolling hills almost incandescent with the varied color of fall; postcard towns lofting church steeples and the chimney pots of rambling Victorian homes against the hills; and plenty of cultural activities to suit your taste.

WHERE TO PLAY

CRUMPIN-FOX CLUB
6,508 yards, par 72, 136/71.3
Greens fee: $70
413-648-9101, fox-golf.com

Crumpin-Fox (the name came from the discovery by construction crews of heaps of bottles made by Crump & Fox) was designed by Roger Rulewich in the town of Bernardston. It's a tight course, made treacherous by purling streams, shimmering ponds, and stands of woods. The eighth, a delicate 592-yard march along a fairway edged by water from beginning to end, is one to remember. Don't reach for more tees than you can grasp at this course and consider a round played to your handicap a fine effort.

WAHCONAH COUNTRY CLUB
6,567 yards, par 72, 126/71.9
Greens fee: $70
413-684-1333, wahconahcountryclub.com

Just east of Pittsfield, in Dalton, Wahconah was designed by Donald Ross disciple Wayne Stiles, who set the easy-going tone on the wonderfully wide, downhill first hole. Yes, the Housatonic River threads through the golf course, but it's mostly ornamental—you'll cross more by cart than by club. It's easy to have fun on this one. You don't need to crush the ball. You can make a mistake without making a mess. It's well groomed. The vibe is casual.

TACONIC GOLF CLUB
6,640 yards, par 71, 127/71.7
Greens fee: $150
413-458-3997

TOP 100 YOU CAN PLAY

Just south of Vermont in the tidy village of Williamstown, Taconic is owned by Williams College, which accounts for its Latin motto—*medio tutissimus ibis* (You will travel safest on a middle course)—a quote from Ovid printed on the scorecard. Taconic is regarded as the best public-access course in New England, a must-play even at this heavy price. Like Wahconah, it opens with an easy hole, a brief, straightaway par-five that yields an easy birdie. Taconic is not heavily bunkered, demands few forced carries, and isn't claustrophobically narrow, but the greens are slick, undulating beasts. Forget Ovid. Your motto should be: *Never leave the ball above the hole*.

WHERE TO STAY

Mount Greylock Inn, a perfectly manicured Victorian B&B within walking distance of Adams' main street, offers a scrumptious Saturday morning Sleepy Hollow breakfast. Rates from $84. 413-743-2665, mountgreylockinn.com •• The stylish Porches Inn, in North Adams, offers spa services. Rates from $125. 413-664-0400, porches.com

WHERE TO EAT

Gideon's is a lively, mid-priced restaurant serving New England and Mediterranean fare just a few blocks from MassMOCA in North Adams. 413-664-9449, gideonsrestaurant.com •• Jae's Inn in Adams serves inspired Japanese cuisine. 413-664-0100, jaesinn.com

LOCAL KNOWLEDGE

Mount Greylock, the state's tallest peak (3,491 feet) is the heart and soul of the Berkshires. Take a look from the summit. You can hike, drive, or bike to the top on Rockwell Road. The views stretch all the way to New York's Adirondacks. 413-499-4262, mass.gov/dcr/parks •• Tanglewood plays host to music ranging from classical to pop each summer and has been the summer home of the Boston Symphony Orchestra since 1937. 413-637-1600, bso.org •• The literary-minded can pay a visit to Arrowhead (413-442-1793, mobydick.org), the Pittsfield cottage where Herman Melville wrote *Moby Dick* and entertained colleagues, including Nathaniel Hawthorne. And Edith Wharton lived for a time at a spectacular estate, The Mount, in Lenox. 413-637-1899, edithwharton.org •• The Norman Rockwell Museum in Stockbridge, Rockwell's hometown, houses the seminal works of this American master. 413-298-4100, nrm.org •• The Clark Art Institute in Williamstown is home to national and international masterpieces, including some of Winslow Homer's depictions of New England. 413-458-2303, clarkart.edu •• MassMOCA in North Adams was built in a sprawling complex of converted factory buildings left vacant when the textile industry departed. Its huge spaces showcase contemporary art, from performances to interactive blends of sculpture, video, and audio. 413-662-2111, massmoca.org

GETTING THERE

The Berkshire area is a 45-minute drive southeast of Albany International Airport or a 90-minute drive northwest of Bradley International Airport in Hartford, Connecticut.

WHEN TO GO

Summer is peak season, but the fall foliage is at its best between mid-September and early November, depending on the weather.

CAPE COD
Any discussion about golf on Cape Cod should begin with a round of applause for the glaciers. When the last ice age drew to a close, those slowly melting monoliths receded in such a way that the uniquely shaped Cape was left in their wake. By 1900 this relatively small peninsula just 50 miles south of Boston was already home to seven courses. Today there are more than 50, making Cape Cod a veritable smorgasbord, rarely matched for the charm, quality, and variety of its layouts.

WHERE TO PLAY

WAVERLY OAKS GOLF CLUB
7,114 yards, par 72, 130/73.5
Greens fee: $85
508-224-6700, waverlyoaksgolfclub.com

This 27-hole Brian Silva design in Plymouth is the ideal starting point for any Cape Cod golf excursion. The fairways, despite being dotted with steep-faced bunkers, are some of the widest you'll encounter anywhere. Each hole presents its own risk/reward scenario. For example, Valley—the downhill, par-four 12th—is drivable if you want to challenge the bunker guarding the elbow of this subtle dogleg left. If you lay up, the Ross-inspired, inverted-saucer green makes even the shortest pitch a challenge.

PINEHILLS GOLF CLUB
Jones: 7,175 yards, par 72, 135/73.8
Nicklaus: 7,243 yards, par 72, 135/74.3
Greens fee: $60–$100
508-209-3000, pinehillsgolf.com

`TOP 100 YOU CAN PLAY`

On ideal terrain—sandy soil, pine groves, and glacial footprints ranging from esker ridges to large kettle depressions—Rees Jones and Jack Nicklaus have crafted versatile tests. Only four miles north of Cape Cod Bay, in Plymouth, the Jones layout can be breezy, which is why the designer built generous landing areas. However, good players are tempted at nearly every turn to cut the corner of an artfully sculpted bunker to gain advantage. By sculpting holes into glacial landforms and using the site's 60-foot elevation changes to dramatic effect, Jones established a unique identity for each hole. Nicklaus was blessed with similar terrain for his course. His fairways are tree-lined but generous and lead to large, challenging greens.

THE COUNTRY CLUB AT NEW SEABURY
Ocean: 7,131 yards, par 72, 133/75.7
Dunes: 6,340 yards, par 70, 122/69.5
Greens fee: $140–$175 (Ocean);
$100–$125 (Dunes)
508-477-9400

The Ocean course has long been one of New England's premier, if slightly schizophrenic, golf experiences. The par-five opener at this 1964 William Mitchell design in a development called New Seabury in Mashpee plays right down to Nantucket Sound, usually into the teeth of a coastal wind. The 4th is an outstanding par three that spans a small inlet, and while the remaining holes on this nine don't hug the shoreline, they remain exposed and subject to the elements. The Ocean's back nine is tree-lined, hilly, and totally inland. Although solid and enjoyable, the Dunes was considered a weak sister until a 2001 reconstruction that lengthened the yardage, rebuilt the greens, and added extensive waste and natural areas.

OLDE BARNSTABLE FAIRGROUNDS
GOLF COURSE

6,503 yards, par 71, 128/71.4
Greens fee: $40–$60
508-420-1141, obfgolf.com

Heading northwest out of Hyannis, the intrepid Cape traveler happens upon Olde Barnstable, which is operated by the town of Marston Mills. The course, which has hosted both U.S. Amateur and Mid-Amateur qualifiers, is loaded with first-rate, diverse golf holes, including the 196-yard 15th, which has a green set in a sandy waste area, Pine Valley–style, and the 18th, an uphill, 560-yard, double-dogleg par three with a green carved into a rocky knoll.

CAPTAINS GOLF COURSE

Port: 6,724 yards, par 72, 130/73.5
Starboard: 6,776 yards, par 72, 130/72.6
Greens fee: $35
508-896-5100, captainsgolfcourse.com

Opened in 1985 in Brewster, Captains fairly well invented the idea of upscale municipal golf. Its 36 holes are named for local sea captains. The land that Brian Silva inherited for the expansion of Captains helped make the new holes work individually and mesh with the originals. The par-four 16th on the Port course, for example, is a dogleg-right measuring 371 yards. The green's entire right side is shaped by a dramatic kettle hole; if the pin is back right, bold players must play over a corner of the kettle itself. The demanding par-three 5th on the Starboard course stretches 213 yards; a kettle on the left gives the putting surface a right-to-left tilt, allowing long-iron shots to bounce their way on.

CRANBERRY VALLEY

6,490 yards, par 72, 129/71.9
Greens fee: $55
508-430-7560, cranberrygolfcourse.com

Designed by Geoffrey Cornish and opened in 1974 in Harwich, Cranberry Valley is extremely enjoyable, with cute doglegs and heroic par threes, all flanked by the area's ubiquitous bogs.

CAPE COD NATIONAL GOLF CLUB

6,954 yards, par 72, 129/73.6
Greens fee: $105
508-432-5400, wequassett.com

Guests of the Wequassett Inn in Chatham are allowed to play this Brewster course, designed by Brian Silva and marked by glacially formed mounds, ridges, and hollows. Silva's retro look—blind shots, random bunkering—fits in well on a course where walking is encouraged and caddies are available. The par-three 6th is a redan that would make Seth Raynor proud, while the 7th—a short, uphill par four of 290 yards—plays blindly to a punchbowl green. The 17th is a 459-yard par four, whose fairway and putting surface are both guarded by the same enormous kettle hole; it plays more like a par five.

HIGHLAND LINKS

5,299 yards, par 72, 105/65.5
Greens fee: $16–$20
508-487-9201

Opened in 1892, this eccentric course in Truro is the oldest surviving layout on Cape Cod, and it remains one of the most exhilarating. Two years ago, the working lighthouse beside the 7th hole was moved inland (closer to the 7th tee) because its integrity had been threatened by beach erosion. Indeed, the nine holes at Highland Links have been rerouted and tinkered with many times. But the terrain here is so perfect for golf, it's virtually impossible to mess it up. The short ninth—a wind-ravaged pitch played across a tiny fjord to a minuscule green—has been recognized as one of the great par threes on earth.

WHERE TO STAY

On the elbow of the Cape in Chatham is the **Wequassett Inn Resort and Golf Club**, a splendid getaway with clapboard cottages spaced along a bluff overlooking the water. Guests have access to the otherwise private Cape Cod National Golf Club. Rates from $160. **800-225-7125, wequassett.com**

WHERE TO EAT

Ocean views and elegant "progressive New England" cuisine are the highlights of the Wequassett Inn's **Twenty Eight Atlantic**, where chef Bill Brodsky favors local, seasonal ingredients and an architectural presentation of his dishes. **508-430-3000, wequassett .com** •• You'll have your pick of fresh fish prepared in just about any international or Continental style—from Szechuan to Mexican— at the casual-but-upscale **Impudent Oyster** in Chatham. **508-945-3545** •• Set among the gardens and manicured lawns of the 300-year-old Chillingsworth Foster Estate in Brewster, the **Chillingsworth** restaurant (reservations required) serves sophisticated French and American cuisine flavored with locally grown herbs. Its more casual **Bistro** (reservations suggested) is set in the light and airy Greenhouse room. **508-896-3640, chillingsworth.com** •• For a mix of seafood (steamers, fried oysters) and more casual pub fare, such as burgers and sandwiches, try the **Chatham Squire** on Main Street, Chatham. **508-945-0945, the squire.com**

LOCAL KNOWLEDGE

You'll find trails, salt- and freshwater aquariums, guided walks, and nature tours at the **Cape Cod Museum of Natural History** in Brewster. **508-896-3867** •• President Kennedy, whose family owns a compound in Hyannisport, established the **Cape Cod National Seashore** in 1961, and visitors have been enjoying the 40 miles and more than 43,000 seaside acres ever since. **nps.gov/caco** •• You can find Cape Cod's dozens of museums and historical buildings, from the **Chatham Railroad Museum** to the **Edgartown Lighthouse** on Martha's Vineyard, at **attractionguide.com/cape_cod/**.

GETTING THERE

Cape Cod is about a 90-mile drive from Logan International Airport in Boston. The Cape's Barnstable Municipal Airport has connections through Logan, Newark International Airport in New Jersey, and LaGuardia Airport in New York.

WHEN TO GO

You'll get the best weather in the tourist-filled summer months, but November and April are traditionally great months for golf on the Cape for a number of reasons. Because the Cape juts into the Gulf Stream, it can be perfectly temperate when the rest of the Northeast is cold and dreary. Most courses offer discounted rates, and some private clubs open their doors to outside play.

NEWPORT

During the late 19th century, Newport was a summer playground for America's robber-baron elite, who built their summer "cottages" on its rocky ocean-side cliffs. Newport is still a blue-blood summer hot spot and home to one of the nation's most exclusive golf clubs, Newport Country Club, but today there are five great public courses within 40 minutes of downtown.

WHERE TO PLAY

ORCHARD COURSE AT NEWPORT NATIONAL GOLF CLUB

7,244 yards, par 72, 138/74.4
Greens fee: $125–$150
401-848-9690, newportnational.com

Just over the Newport Bridge and through downtown, this four-year-old design is the most difficult course in Rhode Island, with a daunting slope rating of 138. Architect Arthur Hills built all 18 tees with views of Rhode Island Sound, but the real drama comes on the mountainous, multitiered greens. Take the dogleg-left, 489-yard, par-four 17th, where the green slopes severely right to left. Approach shots are usually with a long iron from the right side, making the green extremely tough to hold.

Hole 9 at Newport National, Newport, Rhode Island

GREEN VALLEY COUNTRY CLUB

6,830 yards, par 71, 125/71.8
Greens fee: $45–$61
401-847-9543, greenvalleyccofri.com

Five miles north in Portsmouth, Green Valley sits in the middle of Aquidneck Island, where there are few ocean views but the breeze is constant. Farmer Manuel Raposa built this blue-collar country club on his family's property in 1957, and today his son Ron runs the course. The layout demands precision from the back tees. Thick groves of evergreens line most fairways and swallow errant tee shots. The most enjoyable hole is the 548-yard, par-five 17th, which plays downhill with the wind at your back to a large green with a single bunker standing on the right. Medium-length hitters don't often face a putt for eagle, but this hole offers a chance.

MONTAUP COUNTRY CLUB

6,513 yards, par 71, 128/72.6
Greens fee: $40
401-683-0955, montaupcc.com

Another family-run, laid-back track, Montaup opened in 1923 and plays along the rocky shores of Narragansett Bay in Portsmouth. The course is forgiving off the tee—misses are often playable from a parallel fairway. The test here comes on the greens, most of which are pedestal-style and slope from back to front. In the dry summer months, they can run as fast as 11 on the Stimp-meter, ensuring that even a solid ball-striking round can come undone on the putting surfaces.

EXETER COUNTRY CLUB

6,921 yards, par 72, 125/72.1
Greens fee: $32–$37
401-295-8212, exetercc.com

Twenty miles west of Newport in the rolling countryside of rural Rhode Island, the tiny town of Exeter has a church, a general store, a firehouse, and this golf course. Architect Geoffrey Cornish designed the course in 1969, and it's a mid-handicapper's heaven from the 6,406-yard white tees, with enough teeth for better players from the tips. Holes here usually narrow on approaches to greens that are often surrounded by bunkers. From the 576-yard par-five 2nd (530 yards from the whites), the charming town of Exeter is visible in the distance, but don't take your eye off the ball. The tee shot here is blind over a hill, so the course erected a rusty, 15-foot-high lookout post on the tee for golfers to climb to see if the coast is clear.

RESIDENT EXPERTS: BRAD FAXON AND BILLY ANDRADE

PGA Tour stars Brad Faxon and Billy Andrade grew up in Rhode Island, where their annual Charities for Children tournament has raised more than $4 million since 1990. The Ocean State duo offers you some pro tips for your trip.

THE GOLF

Faxon: "Rhode Island is better known for its private courses. Your best bet is to find someone who can get you on Newport Country Club or Wannamoisett. If you can't get on there, the best courses you can play are Newport National and Triggs Memorial."

DINING

Andrade: "Eating in Rhode Island is a sport unto itself. Three to try in Providence are Atwell's Avenue [Italian], 10 [steak and sushi], and Café Nuevo [European]."

Faxon: "Providence has probably got more good restaurants than any city its size. You can just walk up and down the street in Federal Hill, the Italian section, and you can't go wrong."

SIGHTSEEING

Andrade's must-sees for Newport: Tour the lavish, turn-of-the-century mansions. Check out the Tennis Hall of Fame. Go sailing!

TRIGGS MEMORIAL GOLF COURSE

6,897 yards, par 72, 126/70.5
Greens fee: $21–$36
401-521-8460, triggs.us

A trip to Rhode Island would be wasted without a round at Triggs in Providence, just a 45-minute drive from Newport. The Donald Ross design is the best layout in Rhode Island and, according to Ocean State native Brad Faxon, "one of Ross' best" in the country. Opened in 1932, the course had fallen into disrepair by the 1980s. But the current owners took over in 1990 and, armed with Ross' original plans, spent 15 years restoring the course to its former glory. The course sees more than 35,000 rounds a year, many of them in the five-hour range. But at $36 for a summer weekend round, Triggs is the best deal in the state.

WHERE TO STAY

If you want that high-life vibe, stay at **The Chanler at Cliff Walk**. Signature rooms feature private entrances, outdoor Jacuzzis and marble showers, and plasma televisions. Doubles from $695. **401-847-1300, thechanler.com** ●● There's a bed-and-breakfast on every corner in Newport, each with its own unique charm. **The La Farge Perry House**, the 19th-century home of stained-glass artist John La Farge, is the best. Its five rooms fill up fast, so book ahead. Doubles from $125. **877-736-1100, lafargeperry.com** ●● A clean and comfortable roadside motel only five minutes by car from downtown Newport, the **Harbor Base Pineapple Inn** is a solid option for bargain hunters. Doubles from $40. **401-847-2600**

WHERE TO EAT

In Newport, a restaurant is judged by the quality of its clam chowder. **The Mooring** is no longer allowed to enter its chowder for awards because it has won so many. 'Nuff said. **401-846-2260** ●● Overlooking the harbor, **22 Bowen's Wine Bar and Grille** is Newport's steak and seafood specialist. Try the lump crabmeat cocktail with spicy mustard followed by an eight-ounce filet mignon. **401-841-8884** ●● Established by a reformed pirate in the late 17th century, the **White Horse Tavern** is the oldest working pub in America, although "pub" is stretching it, as many consider this Newport's finest restaurant. **401-849-3600**

LOCAL KNOWLEDGE

Newport's grand mansions line Bellevue Avenue. The must-sees: Cornelius Vanderbilt II bought entire rooms from Italian palaces and sent them by steamship to build **The Breakers**. Coal magnate Edward Berwind modeled **The Elms** after an 18th-century French chateau at a cost of about $1.4 million ($30 million today). William Vanderbilt, Cornelius' brother, built **The Marble House** for his wife, Alva, using 500,000 cubic feet of imported marble. She divorced him three years later and kept the house. Silver heiress Teresa Fair Oelrichs fashioned **Rosecliff** after the Grand Trianon, the garden retreat at Versailles. **newportmansions.org**

GETTING THERE

You can drive to Newport in less than three hours from most places in the Northeast, and Providence's T.F. Green International Airport is just a 45-minute drive north from Newport on Interstate 95.

WHEN TO GO

Things get busy in the high summer, so try the spring and fall shoulder seasons for deals.

Hole 6 at Newport National, Newport, Rhode Island

THE EQUINOX RESORT, MANCHESTER VILLAGE Given its tranquil

Main Street setting in Manchester Village, it's hard to picture the Equinox Resort as a hotbed of radicalism. Set beneath the slopes of Mount Equinox, this stately Colonial resort has been celebrated for its great views and hearty food since Lincoln—Mary Todd, not Abe—slept here in 1863. But when it was known as the Marsh Tavern in the 1770s, this was a meeting place for the Green Mountain Boys, a band of revolutionary outlaws led by Ethan Allen. Back then, when someone raised a glass, it meant that a British soldier—or a raiding New Yorker—had been repelled. Today New Yorkers invade only on weekends, and a raised glass toasts a miracle birdie or a monster catch.

WHERE TO PLAY

GLENEAGLES GOLF COURSE

6,423 yards, par 71, 129/71.3
Greens fee: $88–$99
800-362-4747, equinox.rockresorts.com

When Equinox resort owner Louise Orvis was rejected from the all-male Ekwanok Country Club in 1927, she first got angry and then she hired its designer, Scotsman Walter Travis, to build the Equinox Links Club. In 1992 Rees Jones rerouted some holes and raised and refurbished the greens, and the course was renamed after the Equinox's sister hotel in Scotland. The result is an old-style course—testing but quirkily entertaining—that screams New England as it rolls through a hardwood-filled valley between the Taconic and Green Mountain ranges, with Manchester's First Congregational Church steeple peeking through the trees. Watch out for the elevated green on the 423-yard 13th hole—aptly named Volcano—which is perched 40 feet above the fairway and fronted by a slope steep enough to merit double-black-diamond status at any of the nearby ski resorts.

STRATTON MOUNTAIN COUNTRY CLUB

Lake: 3,325 yards, par 36
Mountain: 3,277 yards, par 36
Forest: 3,201 yards, par 36
Greens fee: $79–$99
800-787-2886, stratton.com

A 25-minute drive east of Manchester on Route 30, Stratton Mountain Ski Resort has three rollicking nines designed by Geoffrey Cornish along the base of the mountain. The Forest is a pretty but demanding test through the trees, but the Lake–Mountain combo is best. The Lake plays around a reservoir, with slick greens protected by flash-faced bunkers. The Mountain loop climbs into the hills before swooping back down with the dramatic, 621-yard 5th, the longest hole in Vermont. It twice demands a carry over a creek—on the second shot and on the approach to a narrow, elevated green guarded by three large bunkers. Take a deep gulp of mountain air and repeat, "Bogey is really par."

RUTLAND COUNTRY CLUB

6,134 yards, par 70, 125/69.7
Greens fee: $91
802-773-3254 (Call two days in advance for tee times.)

This semiprivate club is well worth the 45-minute trek north of Manchester on Route 7. The elevation changes are gentler than at Stratton, except on the greens, which are fast, small, and contoured. You'll need hot irons to strike here. The most engaging hole is the 365-yard 16th, which doglegs left uphill to a green overlooking Rutland and its three towering church steeples. It's the perfect place to pray for a birdie.

Hole 2 at Gleneagles
Golf Course, Manchester
Village, Vermont

Hole 2 at Stratton
Mountain Country
Club (Lake), Vermont

TATER HILL GOLF CLUB

6,396 yards, par 71, 130/71.1
Greens fee: $77
802-875-2517, okemo.com

Located 25 minutes east of Manchester on Route 11, Tater Hill—the highest course in Vermont—was recently renovated by Okemo Mountain Resort. The layout retains the former potato farm's charming stone walls and abundant flower beds. The holes from the original front nine run parallel to each other, with a few trees sprinkled in between. The newer back nine spices things up with hard doglegs and blind tee shots. Tater Hill doesn't rate as high as other area tracks, but it offers spectacular Green Mountain views and great grill-room panini.

WHERE TO STAY

The Equinox Resort's stay-and-play package offers unlimited golf with a cart at Gleneagles, accommodations, and use of the pool and fitness center. The cost is $229 per person per night on weekdays and $399 weekends. 802-362-3700, equinox.rockresorts.com

WHERE TO EAT

The Marsh Tavern in the Equinox is a cozy spot and serves hearty New England–inspired fare. The wine list rivals some of the finer restaurants on the Eastern seaboard. 866-346-ROCK, equinox.rockresorts.com •• Bistro Henry, a couple of miles west of Manchester on Routes 11 and 30, combines Italian, Asian, and French influences with local ingredients. Save room for the house dessert—an exceptional pear and blueberry crisp. 802-362-4982, bistrohenry .com •• If you're traveling with your significant other, Mistral's, which is about five miles west of Manchester, serves French–Continental cuisine in a romantic setting overlooking a waterfall on Bromley Brook. 802-362-1779 •• Stop in at Zoey's Deli in Manchester for huge sandwiches on freshly baked bread. If you eat there, the sandwiches are served with homemade potato chips and half-sour pickles. 802-362-0005, zoeys.com •• You can't leave Vermont without sampling a breakfast dripping

with real maple syrup. Stop by the Little Rooster Café on Route 7A between 7 A.M. and 11 A.M. for blueberry pancakes, waffles, and omelets. 802-362-3496

LOCAL KNOWLEDGE

You'll slip into vacation mode within minutes at the Equinox's elegantly rustic Avanyu Spa, where the offerings read more like a lunch menu than a treatment (the ingredients used include maple sugar and Green Mountain algae). The 80-minute "Spirit of Vermont" combines massage, reflexology, and the Japanese healing art of reiki. 866-346-ROCK, equinox.rockresorts.com •• The Equinox Preserve's 800 acres include miles of hiking trails—some of which go all the way to Canada—but if you're not one to risk a solitary encounter with Smokey or Bullwinkle, try the guided trek to Lake Equinox, which leaves the fitness center at 9 A.M. daily. 866-346-ROCK, equinox.rockresorts.com •• The U.S. Special Forces trained for desert driving in Iraq by retreating to Vermont and the Equinox Off Road Driving School. Ask for Eric Yohe, a retired investment banker who cut his teeth driving on the mean streets of New York City. 866-346-ROCK, equinox.rockresorts.com •• Falconer Rob Waite will teach you to handle and hunt with one of 15 Harris hawks in the

Equinox's British School of Falconry. The most requested bird is called Miss Piggy. Like her Muppet namesake, she's large and loaded with personality. 866-346-ROCK, equinox .rockresorts.com •• The motto at the Orvis Fly Fishing School is "Fish are like golf courses— they don't live in ugly places." Guides give lessons on trout-stocked Lake Equinox. 866- 346-ROCK, equinox.rockresorts.com •• Sprinkled throughout Manchester Village are dozens of major retail outlets—everything from Ralph Lauren to Movado. Don't miss the Orvis flagship store on Route 7A for deals on outdoor gear. 802-362-3750, orvis.com

GETTING THERE

Manchester is three hours by car from Boston and four hours from New York City. Several airlines fly into Bennington's William H. Morse State Airport and Rutland State Airport, each of which is about a 40-minute drive from Manchester. Albany International Airport, served by nine airlines, is a two-hour drive southwest.

WHEN TO GO

Summertime is lovely, but don't miss Vermont's peak foliage season between mid-September and early November, depending on the weather. Check vtonly.com or vtweb.com for predictions and updated reports.

BARGAIN TRACKS BY BIG-NAME ARCHITECTS

Americans love getting brand names at generic prices, and nobody relishes bargains more than the budget-conscious golfer. How about an A. W. Tillinghast track for 20 bucks? Or feasting on a Robert Trent Jones I-and-II combo for a mere $43? That's just $3 more than the average cost of a weekend round at a typical daily-fee, according to the National Golf Foundation. Several famous architects have been bullish on public golf, including America's most famous, Donald Ross, who would have liked this list: 19 bargain tracks—with an average greens fee of $30.58—built by the greats of American course design, including Ross himself.

BETHPAGE STATE PARK
Farmingdale, NY

Red: 7,297 yards, par 71, 148/76.6
Blue: 6,638 yards, par 72, 128/71.5
Greens fee: $29–$39
516-249-0707, nysparks.state.ny.us/golf

> TOP 100 YOU CAN PLAY
> TOP 100 IN THE U.S.
> TOP 100 IN THE WORLD

A.W. TILLINGHAST, 1935
Bethpage's four other courses benefited mightily from the Black's hosting of the 2002 U.S. Open. The Red is considerably less exacting than its imposing sibling, but it is less expensive, too. The Black these days costs out-of-state golfers $78; the Red is half the price. The Blue, designed by Tillinghast in 1935, was redesigned by Alfred Tull in 1960. The front nine is all Tillinghast and is as tough as any at this monument to public golf.

BUNCOMBE COUNTY GOLF COURSE
Asheville, NC

6,680 yards, par 72, 122/71.1
Greens fee: $36
828-298-1867

DONALD ROSS, 1927
This convivial muni may soon appear on the National Register of Historic Places. It's a period piece of Ross ingenuity, particularly the inventive, hilly back nine, which admirably stands the test of time. The stout, downhill par-three 18th hole features a wonderful sleight of hand, a greenside bunker that is almost hidden from the tee.

CACAPON RESORT STATE PARK
Berkeley Springs, WV

6,827 yards, par 72, 126/72.9
Greens fee: $27–$32
304-258-1022, cacaponresort.com

ROBERT TRENT JONES SR., 1974
At Cacapon Resort you'll discover a fine course by Trent Jones Sr. amid the foothills of West Virginia's Cacapon Mountain. This layout is muscular enough to host college conference championships, and the nearby parks offer enough stay-and-play packages to delight any coupon-clipper. One design quirk—the course sports a double green that is more than 100 yards wide.

FOREST MEADOWS GOLF RESORT
Murphys, CA

3,886 yards, par 60
Greens fee: $20–$31
209-728-3439, forestmeadows.com

ROBERT TRENT JONES JR., 1971
The Sierra Nevada Mountains and Stanislaus River Canyon provide a rustic setting for this charming but challenging executive course. One par five, four short par fours and 13 par threes —ranging from 102 to 207 yards—play around a lake, several ponds, towering pines and cedars, and subtle elevation swings. Forest Meadows is living proof that a short course does not necessarily mean shortcomings.

GRAYSBURG HILLS GOLF COURSE
Chuckey, TN

Knobs: 3,351 yards, par 36
Fodderstack: 3,483 yards, par 36
Chimney Top: 3,439 yards, par 36
Greens fee: $34–$40
423-234-8061, graysburghillsgolf.com

REES JONES, 1978, EDWARD LAWRENCE PACKARD, 1994

A picturesque valley framed by two ridges in East Tennessee offered Jones a natural backdrop for his sterling contribution to this exceptional 27-hole facility. These three loops could easily command a $100-plus greens fee elsewhere. Jones designed the Knobs and Fodderstack nines; Packard did the Chimney Top loop.

HYDE PARK GOLF CLUB
Jacksonville, FL

6,468 yards, par 72, 125/70.6
Greens fee: $22–$36
904-786-5410, hydeparkgolf.com

DONALD ROSS, 1925

This cozy Ross layout has grown up to be a northeast Florida favorite. Visitors will find ample reminders that length never made a golf course. The Jacksonville Open was staged here in the 1940s and '50s, and Ben Hogan once carded an 11 at the sixth hole, a 151-yard par three.

KEARNEY HILL GOLF LINKS
Lexington, KY

6,897 yards, par 72, 131/73.5
Greens fee: $23
859-253-1981, lfucg.com/parksrec/golf

PETE AND P. B. DYE, 1989

The thoroughbred of Lexington's muni system, Kearney Hill can beat up beginners. The charming countryside belies typical die-hard torment accentuated by rough and constant wind. Gary Player twice won Champions Tour events here.

LYMAN ORCHARDS GOLF CLUB
Middlefield, CT

7,011 yards, par 72, 129/73.2
Greens fee: $31–$45
860-349-1793, lymanorchards.com

ROBERT TRENT JONES SR., 1969

A 1,000-acre Colonial–era orchard offers strawberries in June, blueberries in July, peaches in August, and terrific golf all season. This 36-hole complex has long been considered among Connecticut's pay-and-play gems and is the only public RTJ Sr. facility in the state. Don't leave without gobbling down a piece of pie—there are 28 varieties of apples grown right on the property.

MACKENZIE GOLF COURSE AT HAGGIN OAKS
Sacramento, CA

6,991 yards, par 72, 125/72.7
Greens fee: $45–$50
916-481-4653, hagginoaks.com

ALISTER MACKENZIE, 1932

The discovery of Mackenzie's original plans helped guide the faithful transformation in 2001 of this upscale muni near Governor Arnold Schwarzenegger's office. Risk and reward, illusion, and an abundance of choice from tee to green are all hallmarks of this public-access reminder of Mackenzie's genius.

MARK TWAIN GOLF COURSE
Elmira, NY

6,857 yards, par 72, 130/73.6
Greens fee: $21
607-737-5770, ci.elmira.ny.us/golf

DONALD ROSS, 1939

This Depression–era Ross bequest near Corning could use some TLC, but its stout 6,887-yard frame remains fiendish when the greens firm up. The putting surface at the 230-yard, par-three 11th hole recently received the second tier called for in Ross's original plans.

MAYFAIR COUNTRY CLUB
Sanford, FL

6,382 yards, par 72, 117/69.7
Greens fee: $28–$33
407-322-2531

DONALD ROSS, 1924
Just 15 miles north of Orlando in bucolic Seminole County, this fine layout used to be owned by the New York Giants (the baseball Giants) before the team moved to San Francisco in 1958. With its mini-Magnolia Lane, ancient oaks, and Shaker simplicity, Mayfair once played host to golf's glitterati, including Walter Hagen and Gene Sarazen.

PENINSULA GOLF RESORT
Lancaster, KY

6,647 yards, par 72, 124/71.5
Greens fee: $30–$38
877-249-4747, peninsulagolf.com

PETE DYE, 1997
In the bluegrass half an hour south of Lexington, Peninsula offers enticing weekend packages and the stern challenges of a links-style track designed by Pete Dye. Most notable are its small, slippery greens and ball-swallowing bunkers.

RIDGEFIELD GOLF COURSE
Ridgefield, CT

6,444 yards, par 71, 123/70.9
Greens fee: $40–$45
203-748-7008, ctgolfer.com/directories/
public/ridgefield.html

GEORGE AND TOM FAZIO, 1976
Young Tom Fazio was working for his illustrious uncle George when he co-authored this tale of two nines, perched amid wetlands, with water in play on seven holes. Generosity off the tee on the front nine flips to an exacting driving stretch on the back, with a potentially ruinous Amen Corner at holes 13 through 15.

SANTA MARIA GOLF CLUB
Baton Rouge, LA

6,826 yards, par 72, 136/74.1
Greens fee: $23–$29
225-752-9667

ROBERT TRENT JONES SR., 1986
Santa Maria was a private club but went bust after only two years. The city of Baton Rouge snapped it up for a song in 1989 and made it public. With water in play on all but two holes, the course features the requisite RTJ opportunities for strategy, penalty, and heroism.

SHARP PARK GOLF COURSE
Pacifica, CA

6,299 yards, par 72, 119/70.6
Greens fee: $31–$35
650-359-3380, parks.sfgov.org

ALISTER MACKENZIE, 1931
This venerable muni track south of San Francisco may be no match for Mackenzie's nearby masterpiece Cypress Point, but it remains a strong challenge. Eleven of Mackenzie's original holes remain intact—but not, alas, the two-shotter that gave birth to his career: He entered a design-a-hole contest sponsored by *Country Life* magazine and won. Two similar holes were built here but have not survived the passage of time, but Sharp Park still provides numerous echoes of his design style.

SWOPE MEMORIAL GOLF COURSE
Kansas City, MO

6,274 yards, par 72, 132/70.9
Greens fee: $22–$27
816-513-8910
swopememorialgolfcourse.com

A.W. TILLINGHAST, 1934
"I count none but sunny hours," reads the weathered sundial at this cherished Tillinghast creation, which hosted the 2005 U.S. Women's Amateur Public Links. Swope Memorial is plenty challenging and has been spruced up in recent years. What it lacks in length, the course makes up for in history. The PGA Tour's Kansas City Open was contested here during the 1940s. Local legend Tom Watson is said to be a fan of the rolling layout.

SYCAMORE COURSE AT
EAGLE CREEK GOLF CLUB
Indianapolis, IN

6,646 yards, par 71, 137/72.2
Greens fee: $23–$25
317-297-3366, eaglecreekgolfclub.com

PETE DYE, 1974, TIM LIDDY, 2001

Site of the 1982 U.S. Amateur Public Links, this mainstay of the Indy golf scene has all the trappings of a modern club. Seven of Dye's holes were used for a second course, the Pines, and Tim Liddy crafted replacement holes for the Sycamore layout. The original's character, variety, and strong finish remain intact.

TRIGGS MEMORIAL GOLF COURSE
Providence, RI

6,522 yards, par 72, 128/72.9
Greens fee: $33–$35
401-521-8460, rigolf.com/trigs

DONALD ROSS, 1930

Good luck getting a tee time on this popular track in the heart of Providence. Ross was a longtime summer resident here and crafted a fine layout for his neighbors. Triggs Memorial is the only muni that has hosted the Rhode Island State Amateur. As a single, you'll stand a good chance of getting out on weekdays, but weekends are a tougher assignment, between afternoon tournaments and all the members (yes, members) who vie for times through a lottery system. Make the effort and you will be rewarded with a superb test of golf.

MID-ATLANTIC

NEW JERSEY

NEW YORK

PENNSYLVANIA

VIRGINIA

DISTRICT OF COLUMBIA

WEST VIRGINIA

ATLANTIC CITY

LAKE PLACID
LONG ISLAND

LAUREL HIGHLANDS

WILLIAMSBURG
VIRGINIA BEACH

WASHINGTON, D.C.

THE GREENBRIER

ATLANTIC CITY

With several excellent daily-fee courses opened in the past decade and a $7 billion renaissance plan, the slightly tacky but always charming seaside resort of Atlantic City in southern New Jersey is on the rebound. It was here that stressed-out city dwellers first came to stroll the nation's original boardwalk in 1870, taste the first batch of saltwater taffy in 1883, and collect picture postcards of the city's gaudy amusement piers. Now golf is a major drawing card. Most of the region's new and vintage courses, routed on sandy soil dotted with pines, resemble their exalted neighbor to the west, Pine Valley Golf Club. Because it's within driving distance of New York, Philadelphia, Baltimore, and Washington, D.C., whose combined citizenry represents one-third of the U.S. population, Atlantic City has the virtue of convenient access plus a mild maritime climate that makes year-round golf possible.

WHERE TO PLAY

BLUE HERON PINES GOLF CLUB

West: 6,777 yards, par 72, 132/72.9
East: 7,221 yards, par 71, 135/74.8
Greens fee: $54–$126
609-965-1800, blueheronpines.com

Opened in 1993, the club's West course was designed by Stephen Kay and is still among the area's best. Carved out of pines and hardwoods, Kay's creation is a classically styled parkland spread marked by clever, short par four. The straightforward front nine is reprised by a tougher back nine highlighted by the par-five 14th, its gaping fairway hazard inspired by Hell's Half Acre at Pine Valley. The East course, a Steve Smyers design unveiled in 2000, is a nearly treeless layout built to emulate a links, its playing surfaces kept firm and fast. The raised, tilted greens are slick, and large, oblong bunkers signpost the fairways and defend the greens. The facility hosted the U.S. Amateur Public Links Championship in 2003.

SHORE GATE GOLF CLUB

7,227 yards, par 72, 136/75.3
Greens fee: $49–$99
609-624-8337, shoregategolfclub.com

Named to GOLF MAGAZINE's 2002 Top 10 You Can Play list, this Ron Fream-designed fire breather, gouged from a thickly wooded, sand-based site, is a visually striking stage best played from a carefully chosen set of tees (there are five, starting at 5,284 yards). Fream's greens, most of them large, wavy, and undercut by swales, are as entertaining and unpredictable as the tee-to-green game. To survive, players must avoid numerous ponds, enormous waste bunkers, and vertical sand-flashed mounds alongside the fairways.

SEAVIEW MARRIOTT RESORT & SPA

Bay: 6,247 yards, par 71, 122/70.7
Pines: 6,731 yards, par 71, 128/71.7
Greens fee: $99–$129
609-748-7680, seaviewmarriott.com

The region's only full-service golf resort offers two very different layouts. The Bay course is a Donald Ross creation routed along the shores of Reeds Bay. Its vintage features—deep sand pits, high grassy mounds, and crowned or punchbowl greens—have been artfully restored. Although not long, the Bay, host to the ShopRite LPGA Classic, is no pushover when the wind blows. The Pines course, carved from a thick forest of pines and oaks, is a rolling, narrow layout that calls for accuracy off the tee. The demanding par-three 6th, fronted by a sandy wasteland, could pass for a hole at Pine Valley.

SAND BARRENS GOLF CLUB

North: 3,583 yards, par 36
West: 3,509 yards, par 36
South: 3,386 yards, par 36
Greens fee: $100–$125
609-465-3555, sandbarrensgolf.com

Although Sand Barrens was conceived as a parkland course, co-designers Michael Hurdzan and Dana Fry discovered a sizable layer of sand beneath the surface and changed the theme, shelving the manicured look for a more rugged style. Bent-grass greens at this 27-hole facility, among the Garden State's largest, require a sure touch—and a sense of humor. The riotously undulating, boomerang-shaped double green that serves No. 2 North and No. 4 West and stretches nearly 400 feet from end to end is a case in point.

MCCULLOUGH'S EMERALD GOLF LINKS

6,535 yards, par 71, 130/71.7
Greens fee: $40–$50
609-926-3900, mcculloughsgolf.com

Built on a closed landfill and opened in 2002, this Stephen Kay–designed muni features an 80-foot elevation change, plus variations of holes drawn from famous British and Irish courses.

THE LINKS AT BRIGANTINE BEACH

6,524 yards, par 72, 133/76.3
Greens fee: $39
609-266-1388, brigantinegolf.com

A windswept, Scottish–style links set on a barrier island, the course, established in 1927 and now owned by the city of Brigantine, is where pros tuned up for the British Open in the 1930s. There are bay views, native marshes, and tidal inlets that come into play on 14 holes.

WHERE TO STAY

Originally founded in 1912 as a private club, the **Seaview Marriott Resort & Spa**, located just north of Atlantic City in Galloway, is anchored by a Georgian Revival–style hotel overlooking Reeds Bay and has evolved into an elegant 36-hole getaway. The hotel, with 297 updated guest rooms, features fine dining in its window-walled main dining room and more casual fare in the Golf Grille. Celebrity guests? Actress and Princess Grace Kelly celebrated her 16th birthday at Seaview, and Bob Dylan reserved his room under the name "Justin Case." Seaview is home to the Faldo Golf Institute by Marriott, as well as an Elizabeth Arden Red Door Spa. Golf packages for two are available starting at $214 per night. **609-652-1800, seaviewmarriott.com** • • Want to stay on the boardwalk near the action? **Tropicana Casino and Resort**, a large hotel overlooking the beach, is the only casino property that markets a golf package. Rates from $58. **877-734-7702,**

tropicana.net • • In addition, the **Greater Atlantic City Golf Association** packages most of the courses above with several mid-priced hotels. Golf guide and reservations: **800-465-3222, gacga.com**

WHERE TO EAT

Just a few blocks south of the main casino drag in Atlantic City, the **Knife & Fork Inn** is a Prohibition–era institution serving up seafood and steaks. Don't miss the crab-and-corn chowder or the Kobe sirloin. **609-344-1133, knifeandforkinn.com** • • Try the **House of Blues Gospel Brunch** on Sundays. Right on the Atlantic City boardwalk. **609-236-5700, hob.com**

LOCAL KNOWLEDGE

Test Lady Luck—or play it safe with dinner and a show—at one of Atlantic City's 12 **casinos**, most of which are right on the beach. For a list, see **atlanticcitynj.com/visitors_casino.asp** • •

Get your laughs at the **Comedy Stop**, which has hosted more than 1,000 funny men and women since it opened in 2004 in The Quarter at the Tropicana. **609-822-7353, thecomedystop.com**

GETTING THERE

Atlantic City is about an hour's drive from Philadelphia and two hours from New York City. The Atlantic City International Airport is about 20 minutes from the city and has shuttles, taxis, and rental cars. **www2.sjta.com/acairport/**

WHEN TO GO

Golf courses are in prime condition from late May through October.

Hole 15 at Blue
Heron Pines Golf
Club (West), Atlantic
City, New Jersey

LAKE PLACID

Lake Placid is best known for the U.S. hockey team's "Miracle on Ice" at the 1980 Winter Olympics, but this town in upstate New York offers special moments on the turf, too. There's some fine golf here in the heart of the Adirondacks, a six-million-acre state park the size of neighboring Vermont.

WHERE TO PLAY

SARANAC INN GOLF CLUB

6,631 yards, par 72, 124/71.5
Greens fee: $45–$60
518-891-1402, saranacinn.com

Designed by Seymour Dunn at the turn of the 20th century, the course is set on the banks of Upper Saranac Lake, and although it stretches to just over 6,500 yards from the back tees, it plays much tougher than the scorecard says. Be sure to avoid the dramatic—and punitive—bunkers at the 423-yard 17th, where sand encircles mounds of dense fescue.

LAKE PLACID RESORT & GOLF CLUB

Links: 6,936 yards, par 71, 138/73.6
Mountain: 6,294 yards, par 70, 127/71.6
Greens fee: $55–$69 (Links); $35–$45
(Mountain), 518-523-4460, lpresort.com

On the lengthy Links course, the behemoth 618-yard 15th overlooks Mount Colden and Mount Marcy, the highest point in the state. The Mountain course makes for pleasant strolls but lacks the bite of its big brother.

WHITEFACE CLUB & RESORT

6,554 yards, par 72, 123/71.5
Greens fee: $55, 800-422-6757

The resort boasts a perilously narrow track dating back to 1898 and credited to John Van Kleek and Walter Hagen.

CRAIG WOOD GOLF COURSE

6,554 yards, par 72, 126/70.3
Greens fee: $42–$45
518-523-9811, northelba.org

This challenging layout on the edge of town has two distinct nines—one sits in the valley, the other in the woods—and spectacular views of the surrounding mountains.

WHERE TO STAY

Mirror Lake Inn Resort and Spa is a beautifully restored traditional building with rich mahogany interiors and is within easy walking distance of Main Street. Rooms start at $220. 518-523-2544, mirrorlakeinn.com ●● The Point is a luxurious mansion built in 1933 for William Avery Rockefeller. Rooms from $1,250 per night. 800-255-3530, thepointresort.com

WHERE TO EAT

Have lunch at the Lake Placid Pub & Brewery on Mirror Lake Drive, where the local brews have won presidential notice. Bill Clinton sampled the Ubu Ale during his visit in 2000. 518-523-3818, ubuale.com ●● The Cottage is a cozy spot for sunset cocktails and casual dining. 518-523-9845, mirrorlakeinn.com ●● End at least one day with dinner at the Great Adirondack Steak & Seafood Company on Main Street, which has its own in-house microbrewery. 518-523-1629, greatadirondacksteak andseafood.com

LOCAL KNOWLEDGE

You can relive Mike Eruzione's winning goal on the rink at Olympic Center or tour other sites of gold-medal glory. Every August, the rink hosts the annual Summer Ice Revue, featuring figure-skating stars. 518-523-1655, orda.org

GETTING THERE

Fly to Lake Placid Municipal Airport, a mile south of the village, or Adirondack Regional Airport, 16 miles west in Lake Clear.

WHEN TO GO

Peak golf season is from Memorial Day to Labor Day; you'll find deals in the spring and gorgeous fall foliage from September to mid-November.

LONG ISLAND
The east end of Long Island—home to members-only masterpieces such as Shinnecock Hills Golf Club, Maidstone Club, and National Golf Links of America—has just a handful of options for golfers who lack blue blood, but what is here is undeniably worth the trip. Montauk Downs is the only public-access, 18-hole facility in the 40-mile west-to-east stretch between the town of Riverhead, which serves as the gateway to the celebrity-studded Hamptons, and the region's iconic lighthouse at Montauk Point. It's a terrific course and a great place to start your tour of the Hamptons, because a new crop of enjoyable and challenging public tracks has sprung up on former farmland within a 60-minute drive of this venerable course.

WHERE TO PLAY

MONTAUK DOWNS

6,762 yards, par 72, 135/73.3
Greens fee: $34–$39 (New York residents),
$68–$78 (nonresidents)
631-668-5000, nysparks.state.ny.us/golf

Nestled between the Atlantic Ocean and Gardiners Bay, Montauk Downs counts as one of the best bargains in New York State, second only to Bethpage Black. In 1968 Robert Trent Jones Jr. and his son Rees completely redesigned what had been a lackluster private club to take advantage of rolling, tree-studded terrain punctuated by ponds and lakes and buffeted by strong winds. Today the course stretches close to 7,000 yards, and you'll feel every bit of it at holes like the uphill 452-yard ninth and, with its forced carry, the 213-yard 12th.

LONG ISLAND NATIONAL GOLF CLUB

6,838 yards, par 71, 132/73.6
Greens fee: $59–$129
631-727-4653, longislandnationalgc.com

This course, built by Robert Trent Jones Jr. in 1999, is just a 20-minute drive from Shinnecock Hills but a world away on the sleepiness scale. The double fairway shared by the 2nd and 3rd holes and the double green serving the 15th and 17th can be busier than New York's Penn Station at quitting time on a summer Friday—and more hazardous, as errant shots whiz in all directions. But the risks are rewarded. Case in point: The 466-yard 16th hole doglegs left to a green guarded by rough-covered mounds reminiscent of the Scottish Highlands. The finisher is a testing 590-yarder that slinks between strategically positioned bunkers.

THE LINKS AT SHIRLEY

7,030 yards, par 72, 135/74.6
Greens fee: $65–$80
631-395-7272, linksatshirley.com

Eighteen miles southwest of Riverhead, in the town of Shirley, the Links is a welcoming respite from the traffic and social congestion of the South Fork. It's also the best after-dark golf option on Long Island. Along with its championship course and double-ended driving range, the facility boasts a floodlit, 2,222-yard par-three track that stays open until 3 A.M. in the summer. Designed by Jeff Myers, Shirley has the longest, toughest finishing holes of any public layout in the area, with three par fours averaging about 460 yards, a 223-yarder, and an ulcer-inducing 549-yard closer backed by a lake.

ANOTHER NEW YORK GEM: BETHPAGE BLACK

`TOP 100 YOU CAN PLAY` `TOP 100 IN THE U.S.` `TOP 100 IN THE WORLD`

In the sleepy town of Farmingdale is Bethpage State Park, just 35 miles by car or a 60-minute train ride on the Long Island Rail Road from New York City's Penn Station, lies the beast that Tiger Woods slayed in the 2002 U.S. Open. Since you and everyone else want to play an open venue with a greens fee under $40, weekend tee times fill up faster than John Goodman at a New York hotdog stand. There are two ways to get on—first through a telephone reservation system, which begins accepting reservations from New York State residents (with a valid driver's license already logged into the system) at 7 PM seven days in advance of the desired tee time. Nonresidents can call two days in advance or show up to try for one of the early morning tee times that are given out on a first-come, first-served basis, which means getting to the course the night before, sleeping in your car, waking up before dawn to get a ticket outside the clubhouse, waiting hopefully for your number to be called, and then teeing off, most likely before 8 AM. Do whatever it takes, though, because renovation work by Rees Jones, the "U.S. Open doctor," has treated this patient extremely well. If you're not lucky enough to get on the heavily bunkered Black course, there are four more accessible layouts at the Park: the Blue (with its many elevation changes on the front nine) and the Red (with what may be the best closing hole of the five layouts) were designed—at least in part—by A.W. Tillinghast, who gets full credit for the Black course. The Yellow is the most straightforward of the quartet, while the Green is noted for its small putting surfaces. *Greens fee: $20–$25, 516-249-0707*

Hole 18 at Bethpage (Black), Long Island, New York

TALLGRASS GOLF CLUB
6,587 yards, par 71, 124/72.3
Greens fee: $45–$55
631-209-9359, golfattallgrass.com

In the North Shore town of Shoreham, Tallgrass was fashioned by architect Gil Hanse from a former sod farm. This might be Long Island's closest approximation to links-style golf outside Shinnecock Hills. The fairways are hard and fast, and the subtly contoured greens—some elevated, others hidden behind hogbacks—demand an array of approach shots from high floaters to running stingers. The most memorable hole is the deceptively difficult 384-yard 11th, where an imposing grass berm flanks the entire right side of the fairway and curls around the green to form a natural amphitheater. Serial slicers can only hope for a friendly bounce.

WHERE TO STAY
The charming **American Hotel** on Main Street in Sag Harbor has eight double rooms with sitting areas. Rates from $155. **631-725-3535, theamericanhotel.com** ●● East Hampton's **1770 House Restaurant and Inn**, built in the early 1800s as a private residence, has true country charm. Rates from $250. **631-324-1770, 1770house.com** ●● The Colonial-style **Huntting Inn** on East Hampton's Main Street is postcard-perfect inside and out. Rates from $295. **631-324-0410, thepalm.com/sitemain .cfm?site_id=31**

WHERE TO EAT
An outpost of the New York City-based, family-owned steakhouse chain, **The Palm**, located in East Hampton's Huntting Inn, is the perfect place for tender New York strip, but don't discount the lobster either. **631-324-0410, thepalm.com** ●● Hoping to spot Sara Jessica

Parker and Matthew Broderick? Try the tasty Italian fare—much of which is cooked in a wood-burning oven—at celebrity hotspot **Nick and Tony's** in East Hampton. **516-329-6666** ●● For martinis, sake, and delectable sushi, hit **Sen** on Sag Harbor's Main Street. **631-725-1774, senrestaurant.com/**

LOCAL KNOWLEDGE
Check out **The Stephen Talkhouse** in Amagansett, where the live music is the best on Long Island. You might even catch locals Billy Joel and Paul Simon. **631-267-3117, stephentalkhouse.com** ●● **Duck Walk Vineyards** in Water Mill has 14 fine labels for less than $20. The large patio is a favorite venue for live music on weekends. **631-726-7555, duckwalk.com** ●● On the village green in East Hampton you'll find **Home Sweet Home**, the residence of John Howard Payne, who wrote the song "Home Sweet Home" in

1822. The building's 18th-century feel has been preserved with antiques and an authentic windmill. **631-324-0713, east.hampton.com/ homesweet.home** ●● The **Parrish Art Museum** in the center of Southampton is a dramatic Italian–style building and home to a popular sculpture garden. Adults: $5, children: free. **631-283-2118, thehamptons.com/museum**

GETTING THERE
LaGuardia Airport and J.F.K. International Airport service the New York area and are about a two-and-a-half hour drive east of the North Fork and Montauk.

WHEN TO GO
Avoid the crowds that descend on the Hamptons and the North Shore from Memorial Day to Labor Day, and visit from September to early November, when the long grasses turn golden and the weather is still fine.

LAUREL HIGHLANDS

Set in the southwest corner of the state, 60 miles below Pittsburgh and a reasonable drive from New York, Philadelphia, Washington D.C., Baltimore, and Cleveland, Laurel Highlands is a scenic swath of 3,000-foot mountains, Revolutionary War–era forts and battlefields, restored inns and taverns, and timeless towns with names like Ohiopyle, Normalville, and Confluence. It's also where Arnold Palmer and Rocco Mediate learned the game. Woven through the countryside is enough top-notch public-access golf—including the highly rated Pete Dye–designed Mystic Rock course—to keep a golfer happy for many days.

WHERE TO PLAY

NEMACOLIN WOODLANDS RESORT

Mystic Rock: 7,471 yards, par 72, 149/77.6
Woodlands Links: 6,662 yards,
par 71, 131/73.0
Greens fee: $175 (Mystic Rock), $84
(Woodlands Links)
724-329-8555, nwlr.com

This GOLF MAGAZINE Silver Medal Resort features two outstanding 18-hole courses. The Links was built in the Laurel Mountains and features large greens. The terrain is naturally hilly, and the fairways are lined with glacial boulders and trees. There are several water hazards and sand bunkers incorporated into the course's design. Mystic Rock has water coming into play on 10 holes. With undulating greens perched on water's edge, giant boulders strewn in the rough, and Sahara–sized bunkers, count on playing nerve-crunching shots. Even though the fairways were cut out of the woods, they still afford generous landing areas.

SEVEN SPRINGS MOUNTAIN RESORT

Mountaintop: 6,454 yards, par 71, 131/71.7
Greens fee: $68–$72
800-452-2223, 7springs.com

This scenic mountain track dips and bends around a pine-dotted hillside with views of three different states. There are many uneven lies, tree-lined fairways, and tiered greens.

HIDDEN VALLEY RESORT

6,589 yards, par 72, 142/73.5
Greens fee: $32–$45
814-443-8444, hiddenvalleyresort.com

One of western Pennsylvania's most challenging tests, this tree-lined course offers plenty of elevation changes, dramatic views from a 3,000-foot summit, sweeping doglegs, and tricky par threes sited on plateaus. Water hazards (lakes, creeks, ponds, and streams) come into play on six holes.

WHERE TO STAY

Nemacolin Woodlands Resort has a few options: an English Tudor–style lodge, the opulent Chateau Lafayette, which is a recreation of the Ritz in Paris, and town houses. Guests receive discounted greens fees on Mystic Rock and the Links. Rates from $200. **800-422-2736, nwlr.com ● ●** **Hidden Valley Resort** offers golf packages, miles of hiking and biking trails, and a lake on its 2,000 acres. Rooms from $80. **800-458-0175, hiddenvalleyresort.com ● ●** A ski resort in winter, **Seven Springs** has plenty of summer sports to go with its golf course. Rates from $151. **866-437-1300, 7springs.com ● ●** The historic **Summit Inn**, built in 1907, has a wrap-around porch and a cozy lobby with a fireplace. Rates from $110. **800-433-8594, summitinnresort.com**

WHERE TO EAT

Nemacolin Woodlands has nine themed restaurants, from the refined Parisian–style **Lautrec** to the **Caddy Shack's** hefty burgers. **800-422-2736, nwlr.com ● ●** The **Stone House** in Chalk Hill is an early-19th-century inn with a broad menu of beef, seafood, pasta, and burgers. **800-274-7138, stonehouseinn.com**

LOCAL KNOWLEDGE

The charming downtown area of **Ligonier** (pronounced LIG-a-neer) has more than 60 boutiques and shops. **724-238-4200, Ligonier.com ● ●** The **Horizon Outlet Center** in Somerset, developed around an early 1900s Georgian mansion, has more than 50 shops. **814-443-3818, outletsonline.com ● ●** You

can go whitewater rafting, hiking, mountain biking, and fishing along the rushing, winding **Youghiogheny River**, known locally as "the Yough." Laurel Highlands River Tours & Outdoor Center: **800-4RAFTIN, laurelhighlands.com ● ●** Can a house change your life? It can if it's **Fallingwater**, architect Frank Lloyd Wright's sublime residential masterpiece, which is tucked in the woods near Nemacolin Woodlands. **724-329-8501, paconserve.org**

GETTING THERE

Laurel Highlands is about 60 miles southeast of Pittsburgh, 135 miles west of Harrisburg, and 180 miles east of Cleveland.

WHEN TO GO

Peak golf season runs from Memorial Day to Labor Day; you'll get deals in the spring and pretty fall foliage from late September to mid-November.

Hole 3 at Nemacolin Woodlands Resort (Mystic Rock), Laurel Highlands, Pennsylvania

WILLIAMSBURG
Colonial Williamsburg, the restored capital of pre–Revolutionary War Virginia and the nation's largest open-air living-history museum, underwent a $100-million makeover of its visitor center and hotels in 2001, the pet project of benefactor John D. Rockefeller Jr. and his wife, Abby. The couple spent nearly $80 million over four decades to reconstruct the 18th-century town, where George Washington, Thomas Jefferson, and other key leaders came of age politically. With more than 10 courses, including one that annually hosts an LPGA event, Williamsburg is one of the best places to play (literally) in history.

WHERE TO PLAY

GOLDEN HORSESHOE GOLF CLUB

Gold: 6,817 yards, par 71, 138/73.6
Green: 7,120 yards, par 72, 134/73.6
Greens fee: $155 (Gold); $99 (Green)
757-220-7696, goldenhorseshoegolf.com

TOP 100 YOU CAN PLAY   Gold

The Robert Trent Jones–designed Gold course was built in 1963 and treated to a $4.5 million facelift by his son Rees in 1998. Jones the younger, invited to nip and tuck his father's handiwork, provided better target definition; reconstructed bunkers, greens, and the trademark "runway" tees; and softened the course for the average player. It is, however, a long, difficult test from the tips, featuring a memorable quartet of watery par threes. The Green, laid out by Rees Jones in 1991, is a big spread that meanders across 250 acres of rolling, densely wooded terrain. Fairways are routed across ridges and tunneled through valleys, with water in play at six holes.

KINGSMILL GOLF CLUB & RESORT

River: 6,831 yards, par 71, 139/74.7
Plantation: 6,432 yards, par 71, 124/71.6
Woods: 6,659 yards, par 72, 139/72.5
Greens fee: $165 (River); $115 (Plantation); $140 (Woods)
757-253-3906, kingsmill.com

This GOLF MAGAZINE Silver Medal Resort features three regulation 18-hole courses and a 9-hole par-three course. The River, which hosted a PGA Tour event for 22 years and is now home to the LPGA Tour's Michelob ULTRA Open, has tight, tree-lined fairways and small greens. The signature 17th hole is a par three perched on the edge of the namesake James River. In 2004 Pete Dye renovated the green complexes, added tees, and redesigned the fairway bunkering on several holes. The shorter Plantation has water hazards in play on eight holes. The premium here is on iron play and putting the fast greens. The Woods, designed by Tom Clark and Curtis Strange, has open fairways and is easy to walk on the front nine, but the back nine is hilly; carts are recommended. Holes 12 and 15 share a green with a sand bunker in the middle. The par-three Bray Links has tight, tree-lined fairways, and small greens, and water comes into play on two holes. The longest hole on this course is 109 yards. This course is free, for hotel guests only.

THE COLONIAL GOLF COURSE

7,000 yards, par 72, 133/73.2
Greens fee: $35–$70
757-566-1600, golfcolonial.com

The Colonial is a traditional championship layout in an unspoiled natural setting. The course winds through hardwood forests and tidal marshes, completely devoid of housing. The 194-yard par-three 6th hole, affectionately referred to as the Abyss, requires a forced carry over Mill Creek Wetlands to a wide but shallow green, which is sloped and devilishly fast. The Colonial also has a large practice range and teaching facility, including a practice course with three regulation holes.

Hole 18 at Kingsmill
Resort (River Course),
Williamsburg, Virginia

WHERE TO STAY

 The post-colonial, Regency–style **Williamsburg Inn** feels more like a comfortable Virginia country estate than a commercial hotel. Its 62 rooms average 500 square feet and have large seating areas as well as beautifully detailed bathrooms. The front of the inn opens to the 173-acre Historic Area of Williamsburg, where the rumor of rebellion and war is everywhere. At the rear of the inn, French doors open onto a peaceful flagstone terrace shaded by tall oaks and elms. Rates from $319. **757-229-1000, colonialwilliamsburg.com ● ●**

 **Kingsmill Resort and Spa** Virginia's largest golf resort and a GOLF MAGAZINE Silver Medalist, sits on 2,900 acres along the historic James River and has more than 400 guest villas and suites, the Spa at Kingsmill, a 15-court tennis center, a full-service marina, six restaurants, and a state-of-the-art fitness center with a lap pool and racquetball courts. Rates from $129. **800-832-5665, kingsmill.com**

WHERE TO EAT

A Carrol's Bistro at 601 Prince George Street next to the historic area is known for its martinis and new American cuisine. The fabulous crab cakes are big and meaty. **757-258-8882. a-carrolls.com ● ●** The **Fat Canary** on Duke of Gloucester Street in Merchants Square shares space with the Cheese Shop and serves up yummy house salads and sinful deserts with in-season ingredients. Reservations are encouraged. **757-229-3333 ● ●** Kingsmill Resort & Spa's upscale **Bray Bistro** serves an indulgent brunch and a popular Chesapeake Bay Seafood Buffet on Sundays, while the resort's more casual **Regattas Café** serves wood-oven pizzas, steaks, and panini. **800-832-5665, kingsmill.com**

LOCAL KNOWLEDGE

No trip to Williamsburg is complete without time spent strolling the quaint streets of **Colonial Williamsburg's** 301-acre Historic Area, which has hundreds of restored and historically furnished buildings with costumed interpreters acting out life as it was in the 18th century. Adults: $19, children: $10. **757-229-1000, colonialwilliamsburg.com ● ●** **Busch Gardens Williamsburg**, designed like a 17th-century European village, is just three miles east of the historic area. There are more than 40 rides and roller coasters and eight stages for shows. Adults: $52, children: $45. **757-253-3350, buschgardens.com**

GETTING THERE

Three airports service Williamsburg, which is midway between Richmond and Norfolk on Interstate 64: Norfolk Airport, Newport News-Williamsburg Airport, and Richmond International Airport.

WHEN TO GO

Memorial Day to Labor Day is the high season, but mild temperatures, low prices, and gorgeous holiday decorations make fall and winter good off-season bets.

VIRGINIA BEACH

Even careful, competent golfers will struggle to avoid the sand at Virginia Beach. It is simply too vast, not to mention enticing. More than 35 miles of sugar shores make it one of the world's longest continuous pleasure beaches. A spacious three-mile-long boardwalk stitches together the hundreds of lively hotels, restaurants, taverns, and seafood shacks that give Virginia Beach, a—Ten! Hut!—military town, a throwback feel of a beach vacation shown on old family movie reels. Today some of the most powerful names in golf have enlisted to make Virginia Beach a top golf destination. And for a city where crew cuts will always outnumber dreadlocks, it's a great place to let your hair down.

Hole 5 at Signature at West Neck, Virginia Beach, Virginia

WHERE TO PLAY

THE SIGNATURE AT WEST NECK

7,010 yards, par 72, 135/73.8
Greens fee: $80
757-721-2900, signatureatwestneck.com

A wetlands property converted for residential and golf use, stately pines, lakes, and voluptuous mounds gives each hole at this Arnold Palmer design an appealing backdrop. But it's the lush landscaping that stands out. More than 100,000 fragrant flowers envelop numerous greens and fairways. If you stop to smell the roses here, you risk more than a two-stroke penalty for slow play—it could distract you into dunking your ball into water that comes into play on 13 holes. Five lakes seamlessly lap right into beach bunkers, one of Palmer's trademark design features. The course closes with two brutes, but the 544-yard par-five 4th offers ample reasons why this Signature is a keeper. The landing area for the tricky approach lurches around the water like a sailor on shore leave. Stout green defenses—bunkers, water, mounds—seem to have been designed not by Palmer but by the Pentagon.

HERON RIDGE GOLF CLUB

7,017 yards, par 72, 131/73.9
Greens fee: $59
757-426-3800, heronridge.com

Rolling hills, deft doglegs, and ample oak tree canopies make this Freddie Couples/Gene Bates design a shot-maker's pleasure. You risk a rinsing on 13 holes, where the only forms of water not in evidence are ice and steam. Lakes nestle in doglegs and front greens wrap around them; reed-studded marshes are positioned to snag dribbled drives; and some well-placed streams snag underclubbed approaches. From the tees, none of the water hazards seem particularly imposing, but they all hold round-wrecking potential. You'll need at least three good Freddy–style booms from the "Boom-Boom" tees on the torturous 554-yard 9th hole. Water to the left, out of bounds to the right, penal bunkers on the fairway and around the elevated green, the hole plays into the wind and golfers will be grateful to escape unscathed.

HELL'S POINT GOLF CLUB

6,766 yards, par 72, 130/73.3
Greens fee: $95
757-721-3400, hellspoint.com

The three sixes in the yardage total may be a diabolical coincidence, but this short Rees Jones layout can give golfers a devil of a time. The whisker-wide fairways pinched between the pines require golfers to be painstakingly precise or to wisely gear down with an iron off the tees on the short track that rewards such thoughtfulness. The 11th and the 15th are scenic par threes tee-to-green with teal-colored water. The lovely 341-yard par-four 17th has a fairway-hugging lake on the right that will shake souls of drivers prone to fades. The lake is buffeted by a wooden retention wall, which means that there is no room for error. A driver here offers just two results: safe or sorry.

BAY CREEK GOLF CLUB

Arnold Palmer Signature Course:
7,204 yards, par 72, NA
Jack Nicklaus Signature Course:
7,417 yards, par 72, 144/76.7
Greens fee: $65–$95
757-331-9000, baycreekgolfclub.com

Bay Creek—developed by the same corporation as the Signature at West Neck—is also decked out like a prom queen, with mini-Edens of roses, azaleas, and rhododendrons. But this windswept, bay-view gem with its emphasis on precise shot-making is no sweet-smelling sissy. It opens and closes with muscular par fives. A challenging trio of 11 through 13 has, in procession, a well-bunkered par 530-yard par five that is reachable with a helpful wind; a 171-yard par three over water that's all carry; and a 412-yard monster dogleg-right around a ball-devouring lake. This Amen Corner will result in many unanswered prayers. The Jack Nicklaus course, opened in 2005, romps along the dunes with whitecaps dancing in the distance. This course has potential to be designated one of Nicklaus' finest.

TPC AT VIRGINIA BEACH

7,432 yards, par 72, 142/75.8
Greens fee: $88–$128
757-563-9440, tpc.com

The glut of TPC courses has led to some justifiable bashing. They are too similar; they cost too much; they're gimmicky. Play this one, concocted by Pete Dye and Curtis Strange, and you'll gush: "They're great!" Fun and fair, the course does what all TPC venues should do—give amateurs a taste of what it's like to play where the big boys do. Ample and well-positioned waste bunkers on seven holes may tempt golfers to get gutsy with their drives, something they may regret. The 151-yard par-three 17th plays from an elevated tee that allows winds to create mischief with high iron shots. Water on the right can be avoided but only at the risk of playing into a cluster of deep bunkers. Like all of Dye's best, TPC mingles short holes like the tree-lined 343-yard 11th with brutes like the 498-yard par four closer. In this military town, this is one golf course that will always earn a crisp salute.

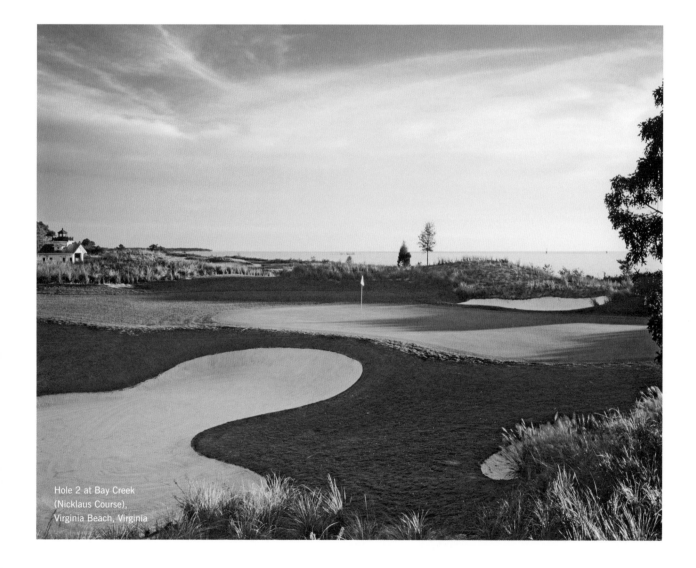

Hole 2 at Bay Creek
(Nicklaus Course),
Virginia Beach, Virginia

WHERE TO STAY

A posh new property built to take advantage of the brand-new $202 million Virginia Beach Convention Center, the **Hilton Virginia Beach Oceanfront** has a rooftop infinity pool 21 floors above the beach. That and the adjacent Sky Bar may make the rooms with the five-jet showers and 32-inch flat-screen TVs seem like a place to leave the clubs between piña coladas. Rates from $129. **787-213-3001, hiltonvb.com** • • The grand old dame of the beach since 1927, the **Cavalier Hotel** has hosted seven U.S. presidents over the years. In 1973 it opened the beachfront Cavalier Oceanfront. The hotels feature five restaurants and indoor and outdoor Olympic–size swimming pools. Rates from $75. **757-425-8555, cavalierhotel.com** • • The **Holiday Inn Surfside Hotel & Suites** rooms feature indoor jacuzzis, perfect for the aching muscles after a long day of golf. An indoor pool also soothes guests. Rates from $72. **757-491-6900, va-beach.com/surfside** • • The beach is lined with dozens of charming and moderately priced mom-and-pop hotels. Find these and other quaint accommodations from the **Virginia Beach Convention & Visitor's Bureau**. **800-822-3224, vbfun.com**

WHERE TO EAT

Mahi Mah's Seafood Restaurant and Sushi Bar is an elegant restaurant with the feel and fun of a down-home dive. Custom hot sauces on every table sizzle so much they make Tabasco seem like a weak sister. Oysters Mahi style is a rosemary-infused oyster stew served over French bread, and the succulent pan-seared crab cakes are superb. **757-437-8030, mahimahs.com** • • One of three can't-go-wrong restaurants crowded along the northern

shore overlooking the Rudee Inlet, **Rockafellers** has fresh seafood, steaks, chicken, and pasta here that are, like the view, both fulfilling and memorable. The barbecue shrimp wrapped in bacon will remind you of the best of the French Quarter. **757-422-5654, rockafellers.com** • • **One Fish Two Fish** sold itself short on the name. The menu features dozens of delicacies that swim. The fried catfish in lemon-jalapeño butter is great, but the fire-roasted pork chop is a true tongue tickler. **757-496-4350, onefish-twofish.com** • • When you've consumed so much seafood that your gills start craving something salsa-licious, fill up at one of **Guadalajara's** five Virginia Beach locations and you still won't spend more than $50. **757-433-0145, guadalajaravb.com**

LOCAL KNOWLEDGE

The Guinness World Records book named Virginia Beach as the "World's Longest Pleasure Beach," an apt description for the 35 contiguous miles of wide stretches of soft sand anchored by the three-mile-long **Virginia Beach Boardwalk**. Perfect for strolling or rolling, the boardwalk is studded with charming parks, playful statues, and great seafood restaurants and hotels offering balcony views of the mighty Atlantic. **Virginia.org** • • The **Oceana Naval Air Station (757-433-3131)** features jet observation parks that allow spectators to watch the Navy's most sophisticated aircraft taking off and landing. Oceana is one of just two master jet bases in the U.S. and the only East Coast station with both the F-14 Tomcat and the F/A18 Hornet fighters. Other Virginia Beach bases include the **Naval Amphibious Base Little Creek**, and the **Fleet Combat Training Center, Atlantic, Dam**

Neck. **nasoceana.navy.mil/** • • The **Virginia Aquarium & Marine Science Center** is one of the 10 most visited aquariums in the U.S. and features 800,000 gallons of water exhibits and live-animal habitats, 350 hands-on exhibits, and the state's only 3-D IMAX theater. **757-425-3474, virginiaaquarium.com** • • Don't think of the $12 ($5 return) fee to cross the **Chesapeake Bay Bridge-Tunnel** en route to Bay Creek as a toll: think of it as admission to a tourist attraction. The 17.6-mile engineering wonder connects Virginia's eastern shore to Virginia Beach and saves southbound motorists 95 mind-numbing miles. **757-331-2960, cbbt.com** • • Dozens of charter boats angle along the bridge's pilings like hungry gulls drawn to a big catch. Take a **deep-sea fishing excursion** for a chance to haul in a yellowfin tuna, marlin, amberjack, or wahoo. **800-822-3224, vbfun.com**

GETTING THERE

The Norfolk International Airport is a 20-minute drive from the oceanfront and offers close to 200 flights daily. The Newport News/Williamsburg International Airport is about a 50-minute drive from the oceanfront. **norfolkairport.com, nnwairport.com**

WHEN TO GO

Summers are splendid, so unless you want it to take 30 minutes to drive three blocks from your beachfront hotel, go in the shoulder seasons. Average highs in May, late September, and early October are a comfortable mid-70s, and the raucous crowds will be elsewhere…and so will those pesky hurricanes.

WASHINGTON, D.C.
Politicians often veer left or right, but if they stray too far from the middle, they'll lose. The same goes for golfers. Both politicians and golfers need a strong power game, but the best players in each sport know that finesse is crucial. And both understand that spin can ruin or save them. There's no shortage of notable private courses in our nation's capital—Congressional Country Club and TPC at Avenel to name two—but there is plenty of strong public-access golf too.

WHERE TO PLAY

EAST POTOMAC GOLF COURSE

Red: 1,311 yards, par 27
White: 2,505 yards, par 34
Blue: 6,599 yards, par 72
Greens fee: $22–$27
202-554-7660, golfdc.com

The district's most popular muni is practically in the shadow of the Washington Monument. We cannot tell a lie. The story of young George's throwing a silver dollar across the Potomac is a myth, but East Potomac Park is not to be missed—it's full of the city's famed cherry trees. Two courses, the Red and the White, are your basic nine-hole pitch-and-putts, but the Blue (completing the patriotic color scheme) is a regulation track with wide-open fairways as inviting as the low greens fee. Pace of play on the Blue is typically brisk, and you might get paired with the likes of former CNN anchor Bernard Shaw, a regular here. But no high finance, please. A placard beside the practice green bears the warning "No competitive putting on this green."

ROCK CREEK GOLF COURSE

4,715 yards, par 65
Greens fee: $19–$24
202-882-7332, golfdc.com

If you're looking for action, a good bet inside the Beltway is this short routing, which has seven par threes and eleven par fours, four of which measure less than 300 yards. The scorecard belies the challenge, particularly on the back nine, where the greens are small, the elevations deceiving, and the narrow fairways shouldered by woods as deep as recent parks department budget cuts. The four closing holes at Rock Creek make the best D.C. golfers sweat. You don't need to be long off the tee on the 368-yard 15th and 351-yard 16th, but with tree limbs jutting out from the sides, you must be as accurate as a Senate witness under oath. And if you can thread your tee ball to the minuscule green at the par-three 17th, hail to you.

LANGSTON GOLF COURSE

6,652 yards, par 72, 115/69.5
Greens fee: $21.50–$26.50
202-397-8638, golfdc.com

The most interesting of D.C.'s National Parks Service tracks is built on the site of an old city dump. Langston opened with pomp and circumstance in June 1939 as a nine-holer for black Americans. The man behind the course was Harold L. Ickes, FDR's progressive Secretary of the Interior. Today Langston is on the National Register of Historic Places. It's open year-round from sunup to sundown. In 1999 the course opened a second nine, which is notable for a pair of first-rate par threes: The 175-yard 13th reaches over the lake to a wide, bilevel green, while the 203-yard 15th plays uphill over a valley. Langston also offers the hairiest tee shot in the Beltway—a forced carry over Kingman Lake at the 538-yard 10th hole.

WHISKEY CREEK GOLF CLUB

7,010 yards, par 72, 137/74.5
Greens fee: $81–$97
888-883-1174, whiskeycreekgolf.com

Ernie Els consulted with designer Mike Poellot at this handsome track, which opened in 2000 in Ijamsville, Maryland, 45 minutes north of the capital. Named for a nearby stream used by bootleggers to float barrels of hooch into town during Prohibition, Whiskey Creek ambles through the countryside like a tipsy lobbyist. Boulders flank the tee box at the 402-yard 5th hole. The 547-yard 18th is the home hole in more ways than one, with the stone ruins of a German immigrant's farmhouse splitting the fairway.

P.B. DYE GOLF CLUB

7,036 yards, par 72, 140/74.2
Greens fee: $69–$89
301-607-4653, pbdyegolf.com

After it opened in 1999 in Ijamsville, the club drew fire from golfers who felt that the design was cruel and unusual. A few adjustments quelled the complaints without erasing the Dye touch (check the island green at the 169-yard 11th hole). P.B. had shaved the banks around the greens, à la Pinehurst No. 2, so that errant approaches funneled into collection areas. That proved too penal, so management let the grass grow. Today you can enjoy your round at P.B. Dye without getting too P.O.'d.

RASPBERRY FALLS GOLF & HUNT CLUB

7,191 yards, par 72, 134/74.3
Greens fee: $78–$98
703-779-2555, raspberryfalls.com

This Gary Player signature course in Leesburg, Virginia, is 15 minutes from Dulles airport, but once you set foot on this links-style gem you'll feel transported. How many modern courses host fox hunts? Civil War–style stone walls and a manorlike clubhouse contribute to the rustic setting. Player gave his stacked-sod bunkers nicknames that suggest their toughness: Grant's Tomb and Satan's Foxhole.

WHERE TO STAY

The Mandarin Oriental offers more than 400 serene rooms and luxury suites, as well as three happening restaurants, CityZen, Café MoZU, and the Empress Lounge, in downtown D.C. near the Jefferson Memorial. Rates from $385. **202-554-8588, mandarinoriental.com** • •
The hip, mod, boutiquelike **Hotel Helix**, just north of the White House in downtown D.C., has about 200 colorfully designed rooms and a complimentary "Bubbly Hour" every afternoon. Rates from $125. **202-462-9001, hotelhelix.com**

WHERE TO EAT

The list of accolades for **Galileo** is longer than John Daly off the tee—even on his best day. It is most known for its mention as one of the 10 best Italian restaurants in America by *Wine Spectator*. **202-293-7191, galileodc.com** • •
For authentic Mexican cuisine, head to **Lauriol Plaza**, which might have the strongest margaritas inside the beltway. Dine when the weather's nice, and ask to sit on the rooftop. **202-387-0035, lauriolplaza.com** • • Located across the street from the White House, the **Hotel Washington** restaurant lets you see the entire city without enduring one of those painful tours. Don't miss the crab-cake sandwich. **202-638-5900, hotelwashington.com**

LOCAL KNOWLEDGE

Chances are you're not visiting D.C. just for the golf but for an immersion in U.S. history and a visit to our nation's capital. For a list of all the memorials (from Jefferson to Lincoln), museums (the National Gallery of Art to the Air and Space Museum) and must-see attractions, visit seewashingtondc.net.

THE GREENBRIER

THE GREENBRIER The union between The Greenbrier, the premier establishment retreat, and Sam Snead, the supreme backwoods hustler, seemed like golf's equivalent of Julia Roberts and Lyle Lovett—a very odd match, albeit one that lasted more than 65 years, until Snead's death in 2002. When you visit this resort in White Sulphur Springs in the Allegheny Mountains of West Virginia, the marriage makes sense. Combining a welcoming hominess with a classy veneer, the stately getaway opened in 1778 and has hosted presidents, kings, and Andy Bean. The golf spans the centuries, too, from hickory shafts to the Ryder Cup. Be sure to raise a glass to Sam as you make your own history.

WHERE TO PLAY

GREENBRIER COURSE

6,675 yards, par 72, 135/73.1
Greens fee: $185 for hotel guests,
$350 for nonguests
800-453-4858, greenbrier.com

TOP 100 YOU CAN PLAY

Jack Nicklaus redesigned this 1924 Seth Raynor layout prior to the 1979 Ryder Cup. Length isn't the issue here. The keys are finding the fairways—which is no easy task on this tight, tree-lined design—and, more important, the proper side of the fairways, since sand and water keep a close watch over the greens. You can only attack the pins here from green-light angles. Three putts will be all too common if you don't find the right level on the multitiered greens. Slammin' Sam owns the course record—a tournament 59 in 1959.

OLD WHITE

6,783 yards, par 70, 136/73.6
Greens fee: $185 for hotel guests,
$350 for nonguests
800-453-4858, greenbrier.com

TOP 100 YOU CAN PLAY

The Greenbrier's first course, a 1913 Charles Blair Macdonald design with Seth Raynor updates, underwent a restoration in 2005 with the goal of bringing back some of the audacious bunkering and green complexes that have eroded over time. Now, as then, the fast, sloping greens and 12 varied par fours of this track are the hallmarks. Unlike the Greenbrier course, death here comes not with a bang but by a thousand nicks and cuts.

MEADOWS

6,795 yards, par 71, 129/72.8
Greens fee: $185 for hotel guests,
$350 for nonguests
800-453-4858, greenbrier.com

This is a diverse resort layout, thanks in part to its complex parentage, which contains elements of Raynor, Dick Wilson, and, more recently, Bob Cupp (Tom Fazio also made uncredited tweaks to two holes). The one constant has been the panoramic views of the Allegheny Mountains, making this a favorite for golf-is-a-walk-in-the-park types. Although it sports a few forced water carries, including the 188-yard island-green 2nd hole, the design features plenty of width off the tee and enough open greens to make it playable for golfers across the talent spectrum. That's for the best, since frustrated golfers wouldn't know which architect to blame.

OAKHURST LINKS

2,235 yards, par 35
Greens fee: $75
304-536-1884, oakhurst1884.com

Located three miles from The Greenbrier, this was the first golf club in the U.S.—established in 1884—and a must-see for history buffs and masochists alike. Visitors must navigate the layout using borrowed hickory-shafted clubs and gutta-percha balls (specially made in the U.K.) and without those modern wooden tees (the staff teaches you to make them from sand and water). The greatest hazard is the flock of sheep that tends the course. It all sounds quaint—until you make a 13 on a 322-yard par five. You may well leave thinking Old Tom Morris was the greatest golfer ever.

Hole 2 at the
Greenbrier, White
Sulphur Springs,
West Virginia

WHERE TO STAY

How good is the service at **The Greenbrier**? So good that both sides occupied the original hotel during the Civil War. Accommodations are on a modified American plan, which includes breakfast and dinner. The deluxe golf package runs through October and includes unlimited play, as well as breakfast and dinner. Rates range from $640 to $670 per day, per person, double occupancy. **800-453-4858, greenbrier.com**

WHERE TO EAT

The **Tavern Room** is The Greenbrier's most intimate dining option, with piano music and a wine list to cheer Greg Norman. **800-453-4858, greenbrier.com** • • Be sampled to death at **Sam Snead's**, where the resort staff will offer you samples of just about everything on the menu. **800-453-4858, greenbrier.com** • • The **General Lewis Inn** is another Lewisburg staple best known for its rainbow trout, sautéed, broiled, or blackened. **304-645-2600, generallewisinn.com**

LOCAL KNOWLEDGE

Learn how to use an SUV the way it was meant to be—not cruising to the mall and soccer practice but rather over the river and through the woods—at the **Greenbrier Off-Road Driving School**. Lessons from one to four hours start at $185. **800-453-4858, greenbrier.com** • • Golfers don't need to be sold on the allure of having a bird at one's beck and call. There are no eagles at the **Falconry Academy**, but you will find trained falcons and hawks. $85. **800-453-4858, greenbrier.com** • • Once part of the C&O railway, the 76-mile **Greenbrier River Trail** satisfies all active lifestyle needs. **Free Spirit Adventures** cares for hikers and bikers (**800-877-4749, freespiritadventures .com**). Kayakers can call the **Greenbrier River Company** (**800-775-2203, greenbrierriver .com**). Canoodlers, you're on your own. $30 per person access fee • • About 10 miles to the west lies **Lewisburg**, a quaint Southern town of art galleries and antique shops. It's also a National Register Historic District because a Civil War battle was fought in its city center.

304-645-2080, Lewisburg-wv.com • • The bones of the prehistoric three-toed sloth that Thomas Jefferson presented to Philadelphia's Philosophical Society were found at **Organ Cave**. Daily guided tours showcase the scientific and historical importance of the cave. $12.50 plus tax. **304-645-7600, organcave.com**

GETTING THERE

Fly into Greenbrier Valley Airport on U.S. Airways from Charlotte, Washington Dulles, and Pittsburgh; Delta flies here from Atlanta. Another option is Roanoke Regional Airport in Roanoke, Virginia, a 90-minute drive from the resort.

WHEN TO GO

The Greenbrier is in the Allegheny Mountains, but a temperate southern climate means you can play golf from April to November.

TOM WATSON'S TIPS

"I fell in love with it and started going there every year. Golf, off-road driving, fishing, shooting. I've done all of those things at The Greenbrier. It's a first-class spot. There's a genteel air about the resort."

The eight-time major winner on wrestling the Greenbrier's 456-yard, par-four No. 6: "The toughest par four from the back tee. It's an uphill second shot with a long iron to a green that's quartering from right front to back left. The back of the green is narrow and slopes away. There's no safe place to miss unless the pin is on the front, then you miss it short."

Hole 4 at Oakhurst Links, White Sulphur Springs, West Virginia

MAJOR VENUES YOU CAN PLAY

Most of us will never stroll on Amen Corner or challenge the fescue at Shinnecock Hills, but not every major championship venue is closed to the public. History buffs needn't know a member to walk in the spikemarks of Nicklaus, Snead, Trevino, Woods, and other champions. Here is our select guide to championship tracks where you can make your own history.

BETHPAGE STATE PARK (BLACK)
Farmingdale, NY

7,299 yards, par 71, 144/76.6
Greens fee: $78–$98
516-249-4040, nysparks.state.ny.us/golf

Everything you really need to know about Bethpage Black, the first municipal course to host a U.S. Open, is printed on a sign behind the first tee: "Warning—The Black Course is an Extremely Difficult Golf Course Which is Recommended Only for Highly Skilled Golfers." Locals often wait overnight in their cars to secure a tee time at this magnificent layout designed by A.W. Tillinghast and restored by Rees Jones in 1998. The Black is a walking-only test of stamina with wrist-fracturing rough and bunkers bigger than some Eastern European countries. Tiger Woods was the only man under par here at the 2002 Open.

TOP 100 YOU CAN PLAY	TOP 100 IN THE U.S.	TOP 100 IN THE WORLD

FRENCH LICK SPRINGS RESORT (HILL)
French Lick, IN

6,625 yards, par 70, 119/71.5
Greens fee: $20–$65
800-457-4042, frenchlick.com

Little has changed at this Donald Ross museum piece since its debut in 1920. It was here in 1924 that Walter Hagen won his second PGA Championship when his opponent, Long Jim Barnes, shanked his mashie-niblick approach to the final hole. Barnes three-putted four greens in the morning round, an easy thing to do on the slick, wildly contoured putting surfaces. The course length won't scare anyone, but the open, rolling landscape provides for stiff breezes and funky stances.

HERSHEY COUNTRY CLUB (WEST)
Hershey, PA

6,860 yards, par 73, 130/72.6
Greens fee: $52–$95
717-533-2464, golfhershey.com

The 1940 PGA Championship at Hershey saw a sweet finish: Byron Nelson made two late birdies to pip Sam Snead. The final hole back then (No. 5 in today's configuration) was a par three with the green almost at the front steps of chocolatier Milton Hershey's mansion. The West features five robust par fives on a heavily bunkered layout. No matter what you shoot, you won't leave with a sour taste in your mouth—the Hershey chocolate factory is next door.

KELLER GOLF COURSE
St. Paul, MN

6,566 yards, par 72, 128/71.7
Greens fee: $31–$44
651-766-4170, co.ramsey.mn.us/parks/golf

Two PGA Championships were held at Keller, but the winners—Olin Dutra and Chick Harbert—are not among the most famous golfers to tee it up at this muni. Jimmy Demaret, Ken Venturi, Sam Snead, and Ray Floyd all won PGA Tour events here. Gene Sarazen once made a 10 at the par-three 4th hole, a 150-yarder whose green is guarded by a gigantic tree. Legend has it that in the early 1930s, gangster John Dillinger was playing the par-five 12th (No. 3 then) when he heard the Feds were closing in. He picked up and hopped a freight train on the tracks alongside the hole. Put him down for a 5.

KEMPER LAKES GOLF CLUB
Hawthorn Woods, IL

7,217 yards, par 72, 143/75.9
Greens fee: $99–$139
847-320-3450, kemperlakesgolf.com

Resplendent in his Chicago Bears outfit, Payne Stewart birdied four of the last five holes to overtake a stumbling Mike "Radar" Reid and win the 1989 PGA Championship here. Now 25 years old, Kemper's layout embraces a mix of open prairie holes and narrow, forested ones. Most daunting, however, are the lakes. Eleven holes play across or around water, including the tough closing trio. If you're planning to play here, do it soon. Kemper Lakes is scheduled to go entirely private.

PEBBLE BEACH GOLF LINKS
Pebble Beach, CA

6,737 yards, par 72, 142/73.8
Greens fee: $425
800-654-9300, pebblebeach.com

A pilgrimage to Pebble isn't cheap, but it's worth it. Step onto the 17th tee and relive two of the most celebrated U.S. Open shots ever: Jack Nicklaus pin-seeking 1-iron in 1972 and Tom Watson's chip-in a decade later. Pebble Beach would be a must-play even if it weren't drenched in the history of five majors and Mr. Crosby's clambake.

`TOP 100 YOU CAN PLAY` `TOP 100 IN THE U.S.` `TOP 100 IN THE WORLD`

PECAN VALLEY GOLF CLUB
San Antonio, TX

7,010 yards, par 71, 131/73.9
Greens fee: $70–$90
210-333-9018, pecanvalleygc.com

Arnold Palmer never came closer to winning the only major that eluded him than at the 1968 PGA at Pecan Valley. Trailing clubhouse leader Julius Boros by one at the 447-yard closer, Palmer hooked his drive into deep rough. The King then lashed a 3-wood from 230 yards to 12 feet but missed the birdie putt. At age 48, Boros became the oldest major winner. After a facelift by Bob Cupp in 1998, Pecan Valley is a gem that winds through gnarled pecans and oaks and crosses Salado Creek nine times.

PGA NATIONAL GOLF COURSE (CHAMPION)
Palm Beach Gardens, FL

7,048 yards, par 72, 147/75.3
Greens fee: $139–$270
800-633-9150, pga-resorts.com

Birdies were as rare as spectators at the 1987 PGA Championship, when Larry Nelson battled the searing August heat and recorded the highest winning score in tournament history, just one under par. Our advice: Don't go in August. Holes 15 through 17 make up the infamous Bear Trap, named for Nicklaus, who redesigned the Champion in 1990. Save some ammo for the par-five 18th, where Lanny Wadkins and Seve Ballesteros hit heroic shots at the 1983 Ryder Cup.

PINEHURST RESORT & COUNTRY CLUB (NO. 2)
Pinehurst, NC

7,212 yards, par 72, 137/75.6
Greens fee: $245–$345
800-487-4653, pinehurst.com

At first blush, you might wonder what all the fuss is about at Ross's signature course. The topography is tame, the fairways are ample, and the hazards are few. Then you face the most frightening set of greens south of Shinnecock. On Sunday at the 1999 U.S. Open, John Daly hockeyed his still-moving ball and was slapped with a two-stroke penalty.

`TOP 100 YOU CAN PLAY` `TOP 100 IN THE U.S.` `TOP 100 IN THE WORLD`

SEAVIEW MARRIOTT RESORT & SPA
Absecon, NJ

Bay: 6,247 yards, par 71, 122/70.7
Pines: 6,800 yards, par 71, 132/73.0
Greens fee: $49–$129
800-932-8000, seaviewgolf.com

Snead captured the 1942 PGA Championship at Seaview just one day before he reported for duty in the Navy. Today a crazy quilt of holes makes up that PGA track. The windswept Bay course was designed in 1914 by Ross and Hugh Wilson and resurrected after a 1998 restoration by Bob Cupp. Snead's victory march took place over the front nine on the Bay and another nine holes designed by William Flynn, remnants of which are now scattered throughout Seaview's Pines course.

TANGLEWOOD PARK (CHAMPIONSHIP)
Clemmons, NC

7,018 yards, par 72, 140/74.5
Greens fee: $36–$46
336-778-6320, tanglewoodpark.org

In 1957 Robert Trent Jones Sr. created this long, viciously bunkered test in the heart of Tobacco Road, eight miles west of Winston-Salem. He toughened it for the 1974 PGA Championship, but sloping greens, wooded terrain, and 100-plus bunkers made it play more like a U.S. Open venue. Lee Trevino edged Nicklaus by a shot using a putter he found in the attic of his rented home. But the buzz that week was all about 62-year-old Snead, who tied for third. Since the PGA, the club has flopped the nines, but those abundant bunkers didn't go anywhere.

SOUTH

ALABAMA	ROBERT TRENT JONES GOLF TRAIL
FLORIDA	THE EMERALD COAST
	THE FIRST COAST
	NAPLES
	ORLANDO
GEORGIA	SAVANNAH
	SEA ISLAND
LOUISIANA	NEW ORLEANS
MISSISSIPPI	NORTHEASTERN MISSISSIPPI
NORTH CAROLINA	PINEHURST AND THE SANDHILLS
SOUTH CAROLINA	KIAWAH ISLAND
	MYRTLE BEACH'S SOUTH STRAND

ROBERT TRENT JONES GOLF TRAIL

Since the first course on the Robert Trent Jones Golf Trail opened in 1992, the circuit has transformed Alabama into one of the nation's top golf destinations. It's a place where quality courses and value prices intersect. Most of the commuting between sites can be done on virtual autopilot via interstate highways with 65-mile-per-hour speed limits. Sound like an ideal road trip for your favorite foursome? It is, although the trail spans almost 350 miles, from Hampton Cove in Huntsville, near the Alabama-Tennessee border in the north, to Magnolia Grove on the gulf shore in Mobile—10 venues and 432 holes later.

WHERE TO PLAY (NORTH TO SOUTH)

HAMPTON COVE

Highlands: 7,262 yards, par 72, 133/75.0
River: 7,667 yards, par 72, 130/76.0
Greens fee: $40–$55
256-551-1818, rtjgolf.com

Near Huntsville, the Highlands course incorporates links flourishes, particularly the bunkers. These are complemented by such distinctly non-Scottish features as Japanese black pines, crepe myrtles, oaks, dogwoods, and an old mule barn next to the 5th hole. The neighboring River course occupies a reclaimed soybean field in the flood plain of the Flint River. It capitalizes on natural elements, most notably some gargantuan black oaks, and in marked contrast to other Trail tracks, it involved very little earthmoving. It is also the only Trent Jones course with no bunkers.

THE SHOALS

Fighting Joe: 8,092 yards, par 72, 138/78.7
The Schoolmaster: 7,971 yards, par 72, 143/78.0
Greens fee: $40–$55
256-446-5111, rtjgolf.com

The Shoals lies between the Wheeler and Wilson dams on the Tennessee River. General Joseph "Fighting Joe" Wheeler, a hero of the Civil and Spanish-American Wars, got his nickname defending a wagon of pregnant women against the Indians. His namesake course delivers bruising blows from its 8,092-yard back tees, but don't let the inflated yardage discourage you. Architects Roger Rulewich and Bobby Vaughn toned down the Trail's trademark severe multilevel greens here. In a unique twist sure to influence even the friendliest Nassau, both nines finish with daring par threes—the 9th over water, the 18th over a ravine. The Schoolmaster was named for President Woodrow Wilson, who was known as "The Schoolmaster of Politics." Its tree-lined fairways roll along natural topography on the Tennessee River.

SILVER LAKES

Mindbreaker: 3,579 yards, par 36
Heartbreaker: 3,828 yards, par 36
Backbreaker: 3,846 yards, par 36
Greens fee: $40–$55
256-892-3268, rtjgolf.com

Almost laughably difficult, this Anniston/Gadsden complex—about two hours west of Atlanta—has the toughest golf on the Trail, with steep uphill approach shots on what seems like every hole. But Silver Lakes' appeal is not restricted to masochists. The course sits at the northwest edge of massive Talladega National Forest, and the setting is beautiful. The drive here, which includes a stint on sometimes-bucolic Highway 431 between Anniston and Gadsden, is a welcome change from the interstate driving that connects most Trail sites.

Hole 18 at the Shoals (Fighting Joe), Robert Trent Jones Golf Trail, Alabama

OXMOOR VALLEY

Valley: 7,292 yards, par 72, 135/73.9
Ridge: 7,055 yards, par 72, 140/73.5
Short: 3,660 yards, par 54
Greens fee: $40–$62
205-942-1177, rtjgolf.com

Although close to bustling Birmingham, Oxmoor Valley, which was built on reclaimed mining land, seems remarkably secluded. The more dramatic of the two courses is the Ridge, which was cut from the Shades Mountain segment of the Appalachian range. The Valley course is only slightly less daunting; although the altitude changes are more gradual, you still finish your round with the Assassin, a 441-yard uphill par four.

ROSS BRIDGE

8,191 yards, par 72, 135/78.5
Greens fee: $75–$100
205-949-3085, rtjgolf.com

The Robert Trent Jones Golf Trail at Ross Bridge is just two miles from Oxmoor Valley in Birmingham. A big, muscle-bound course, it reaches almost 8,200 yards from the back tees. The old parkland style course meanders through considerable elevation changes and around the Renaissance Ross Bridge Golf Resort. Ten holes play along the banks of two manmade lakes, connected by a spectacular waterfall dropping 80 feet between the 9th and 18th greens.

GRAND NATIONAL

Links: 7,311 yards, par 72, 135/75.1
Lake: 7,149 yards, par 72, 136/74.3
Greens fee: $40–$62
334-749-9042, rtjgolf.com

TOP 100 YOU CAN PLAY

Some of the bunkering, mounding, and even blasts of wind at the Links course will remind you of classic Scottish designs. But 600-acre Lake Saughahatche, which is incorporated into 32 of this Opelika complex's 54 holes, looks nothing like St. Andrews Bay. You will come to know it from all angles when playing the Lake—the aesthetic highlight of which is the 15th, a 230-yard par three with an island green.

CAPITOL HILL

Judge: 7,794 yards, par 72, 144/77.8
Senator: 7,697 yards, par 72, 131/76.3
Legislator: 7,323 yards, par 72, 126/74.1
Greens fee: $40–$62
334-285-1114, rtjgolf.com

TOP 100 YOU CAN PLAY

This Prattville complex has three full-sized—some say larger than life—layouts. The Judge features captivating views of the Alabama River's backwaters, with the Montgomery skyline as a backdrop on the elevated first tee. The layout is phenomenally difficult, with water in play on 14 holes. The mounding around the fairways on the Senator creates confusing perspectives as it separates the holes on this otherwise flat parcel of land. The more traditional Legislator weaves in and out of pine forest and along a bluff before it descends into a cypress swamp, which frames the six closing holes.

CAMBRIAN RIDGE

Sherling: 3,681 yards, par 36
Canyon: 3,746 yards, par 36
Loblolly: 3,551 yards, par 35
Greens fee: $35–$57
334-382-9787, rtjgolf.com

TOP 100 YOU CAN PLAY

Alabama's diverse, often nearly mountainous topography is on display at this Greenville complex. The Sherling course has the most precipitous elevation changes of the three. The Canyon is somewhat longer and shares Sherling Lake with the Sherling nine. The two are also linked by a double green at each nine's final hole, two par fours that entail steep forced carries over a ravine, followed by steep climbs to a green fronting the clubhouse. The Loblolly course is relatively flat, but still offers plenty of challenge.

HIGHLAND OAKS

Highlands: 3,892 yards, par 36
Marshwood: 3,812 yards, par 36
Magnolia: 3,699 yards, par 36
Greens fee: $40–$50
334-712-2820, rtjgolf.com

Anchoring the southeastern quadrant of the state in Dothan, Highland Oaks is home to some of the trail's longest holes. The Highlands course is comparatively wide and open but with some striking water hazards. Remember gasping the first time you saw a 600-yard par five? The 6th hole at Marshwood logs in at 701 yards. The Magnolia course is named for the profusion of these trees on the layout's higher elevations, which are reached by a 1,000-foot wooden bridge that crosses a marsh. The Short course is known for its tricky Bermuda greens.

MAGNOLIA GROVE

Crossings: 7,151 yards, par 72, 134/74.6
Falls: 7,239 yards, par 72, 137/75.1
Greens fee: $40–$62
251-645-0075, rtjgolf.com

The two full-sized par-72 courses at Magnolia Grove in Mobile traverse marshland, creeks, lakes, and a dense forest of pine and hardwoods, with surprising changes of elevation for land so close to the tidal plains of Mobile. The name of the Crossings course refers to the railroad tracks bisecting the layout, but that's hardly the most difficult crossing here. Facing the 17th hole's 220-yard carry over a marshy ravine, you may prefer to take your chances with a train. The up-and-down topography is perfectly suited to the pulpit greens so beloved by its architect, and the greens themselves are severely contoured. The Falls is a bit longer and slightly craggier, and it has more water. Design features include sprawling cloverleaf bunkers, the odd waterfall for which it is named, and multitiered greens.

Hole 17 at the Shoals (Fighting Joe), Robert Trent Jones Golf Trail, Alabama

WHERE TO STAY (NORTH TO SOUTH)

The 207-room **Marriott Shoals Hotel & Spa** in Florence, Alabama, is minutes from the Shoals courses. The hotel features 200 luxurious guest rooms, seven spacious suites, and a 6,000-square-foot European–style spa and salon. Rates start at $109 a night. **866-746-2560, shoalshotel.com** • • The 268-room **Renaissance Ross Bridge Golf Resort & Spa** is in Birmingham two miles from Oxmoor Valley and is home to the Ross Bridge course. Its design is reminiscent of the Banff Spring Hotel in Canada, and it has a 12,000-square-foot full service spa. Rates start at $169 a night. **800-593-6419, rossbridgeresort.com** • • The Auburn **Marriott Opelika Hotel and Conference Center at Grand National** is set on 2,000 acres replete with lakes, streams, and hundreds of species of old trees. Six hundred acres on Saugahatchee Lake are set aside for fishing, kayaking, and hiking. Rates start at $99 a night. **866-563-4389, marriottgrandnational .com** • • Montgomery **Marriott Prattville Hotel and Conference Center at Capitol Hill** overlooks the Senator course at Capitol Hill and has 90 luxury guest rooms and two eight-bedroom executive villas with pool tables, flat-screen televisions, and kitchens. Rates start at $139. **800-593-6429 marriottcapitolhill.com** • • The **Grand Hotel Marriott Golf Club & Spa** sits amid 550 quiet acres on Mobile Bay and is home to the Lakewood course. Rates start at $130 a night. **800-544-9933, marriottgrand.com** • • All the above hotels offer **Golf Trail packages**. For information call **800-949-4444** or e-mail **reservations@rtjgolf.com**, or visit **rtjgolf.com**.

WHERE TO EAT

Brock's in the Renaissance Ross Bridge Golf Resort & Spa specializes in steak and sushi, with a menu accented by local flavors. **205-949-3094, rossbridgeresort.com** • • In the Marriott Shoals Hotel & Spa, the casual **Bronzeback Café** pays homage to the area's bass fishing, while **Swamper's Bar & Grill** celebrates the area's rich musical heritage. For fine dining, try the hotel's revolving tower restaurant, which has amazing views of the Tennessee River. **866-746-2560, shoalshotel.com** • • Fifteen minutes west of Birmingham, in Bessemer, is **The Bright Star**, a family-run seafood restaurant known for its Creole and Southern–style snapper almondine. Look for the founder's sons at the host stand, and be sure to save room for their homemade desserts. **205-426-1861** • • **The Old Mill** in Dothan is a favorite of the locals, and reservations are encouraged on the weekends. The most popular item on the menu is the steak, but their burgers and other platters are just as tempting. **334-794-8530**

LOCAL KNOWLEDGE

In Montgomery visit the **Hank Williams Museum & Memorial**. The 29-year-old country music star was found in his Cadillac on New Year's Day 1953, dead of a coronary said to have been caused by high living. Days earlier a man named Cecil Jackson had rotated the tires on Williams' Cadillac; the car is now the centerpiece of the museum, which Jackson founded in 1999. Adults: $7, children: $2. **334-262-3600** • • In downtown Huntsville,

you'll find the **U.S. Space & Rocket Center** next to NASA's Marshall Space Flight Center. Skip the science-geek displays and head straight to the fun stuff—one of the original Gemini capsules and a mock-up of the International Space Station. Adults: $19, children: $13, under 6: free. **256-837-3400, spacecamp .com** • • For a different sort of driving pleasure, try **Barber Motorsports Park**, just east of Birmingham off Interstate 20. The museum and its racetrack opened in 2003; locals hope to attract world-class motorcycle races as companion events for NASCAR's Talladega 500. Adults: $10, children: $6, under 3: free. **205-298-9040, barbermotorsports.com**

GETTING THERE

Depending on how much of the trail you want to tackle, you can fly into, from north to south, Huntsville International Airport, Birmingham International Airport, Montgomery Regional Airport, or Mobile International Airport. **800alabama.com**

WHEN TO GO

There's no bad time to hit the trail, since Alabama—especially southern Alabama—is warm and sunny almost all year. By mid-March, temperatures are in the 60s and a sweater is usually enough cover in winter.

THE EMERALD COAST

For snowbirds who frequent the fairways of Palm Beach, Boca Raton, and Orlando, the Panhandle has been a hinterland—simply not on the map. That's because of a "Redneck Riviera" reputation as outdated as metal spikes and $500,000 PGA Tour purses. Sure, 15 years ago this 102-mile-long strip of land, which doglegs along the Gulf of Mexico from Pensacola to Panama City, was strictly a beer-and-burgers beach destination with a few drab courses. But the region—now dubbed "The Emerald Coast"—can compete with its posh Southern neighbors.

WHERE TO PLAY

SANDESTIN RESORT

Burnt Pine: 7,001 yards, par 72, 127/70.4
Greens fee: $165; 850-267-6500

Raven: 6,854 yards, par 71, 137/73.8
Greens fee: $89; 850-267-8155

Links: 6,710 yards, par 72, 124/72.8
Greens fee: $60; 850-267-8144

Baytowne Golf Club: 6,745 yards,
par 71, 127/73.4; Greens fee: $89

850-267-8155, sandestin.com

The 1994 opening of Rees Jones' semiprivate Burnt Pine pushed Emerald Coast golf beyond the ordinary. Demanding 12 carries over wetlands and lakes, the stern layout features undulating fairways and tiered greens, many guarded by pot bunkers. Towering pines line the front nine, while the back opens onto the bay. The 6,854-yard Raven, crafted by Robert Trent Jones Jr., could be Burnt Pine's polar opposite. Devoid of major mounding, with level greens and landing areas as broad as soccer fields, the Raven threatens par with strategic splayed bunkers and long stretches of wiry spartina grass, which border most fairways. The Links course and Baytowne Golf Club, both designed by Tom Jackson, are spunky and kind to the ego but less spectacular than their high-profile siblings. The 30-year-old Links twists and turns around 12 lakes, with five holes (8, 9, 13, 14, and 15) flirting with the bay. The most forgiving of Sandestin's quartet, the 6,745-yard Baytowne is heavily bunkered and lined with pines on the front but turns topsy-turvy on the back, with generous landing areas.

KELLY PLANTATION GOLF CLUB

7,099 yards, par 72, 144/74.2
Greens fee: $130
800-811-6757, kellyplantation.com

A driver and long iron up Highway 98 from Sandestin, Fred Couples and Gene Bates designed one of the Emerald Coast's most acclaimed layouts. Carved from a turpentine plantation, the course appears as affable and low-key as Couples himself. There are no doglegs or roller-coaster contours, and the fairway bunkers, while copious, are shallow. But this 1998 track can get cranky. The Bermuda rough is as tough as steel wool, and there's enough water to float an armada—15 lakes and the bay come into play on 10 holes.

REGATTA BAY GOLF COURSE

6,864 yards, par 72, 149/73.8
Greens fee: $89
850-337-8080, regattabay.com

If outfoxing erratic winds turns you on, play this Robert Walker production, which is heavily laced with wetlands. Fifty highly stylized bunkers—rife with capes and fingers—increase the challenge. The 191-yard 8th curls perilously around a lake on the left to a green defended by bunkers front and back. Stealth breezes tease well-struck irons on this dangerous one-shotter.

CAMP CREEK GOLF CLUB

7,159 yards, par 72, 145/75.1
Greens fee: $85–$125
850-231-7600, watercolorinn.com

Camp Creek, which has created a lot of buzz since its 2001 opening, lies six miles east of Seagrove Beach in a windblown, isolated landscape that conjures up Shinnecock Hills. Some liken it to red-hot Bandon Dunes, while others see hints of Torrey Pines and Pebble Beach. Designer Tom Fazio describes it as "a coastal dunescape golf course." One thing is certain: it doesn't look like Florida. The routing dips, rises, and swerves through seas of tall grass, yawning sand washes, and lakes bristling with birds and is all about elevation change. Fazio moved a million cubic yards of earth here. The immense greens undulate as severely as the fairways, and high-lipped bunkers form menacing clusters throughout the course.

WINDSWEPT DUNES

7,607 yards, par 72, 143/76.8
Greens fee: $56–$78
850-835-1847, windsweptdunes.com

Near the sleepy burg of Freeport, you'll find the Emerald Coast's newest links, Windswept Dunes. Each hole is framed by stark-white manmade dunes, which, thankfully, are more cosmetic than they are hazardous. The rolling layout, with huge, subtly contoured greens, marks the first Florida endeavor of Midwestern designer Doug O'Rourke.

Hole 4 at Sandestin
Resort (Raven Course),
The Emerald Coast, Florida

WHERE TO STAY

 Destin is a sport-fishing hub dominated by the 2,400-acre **Sandestin Golf & Beach Resort**, the largest Florida resort this side of Orlando. Sprawling between the sparkling Gulf and the sailboat-dotted Choctawhatchee Bay, this mega-playground—so big it has its own zip code, 32550—encompasses nearly 2,000 guest accommodations, from cottages to condos. Rates from $90 to $840. **800-622-1038, sandestin.com** •• Just down the road from Destin in Santa Rosa Beach, the chic **WaterColor Inn**, a boutique hotel with 60 rooms done in seashell tones, bunks golfers intent on tackling Camp Creek. Room rates from $250–$445. **850-534-5000, watercolorinn.com**

WHERE TO EAT

Sandestin's Village of **Baytowne Wharf** is a New Orleans–style cluster of 45 shops and 12 bistros. **800-277-9801, sandestin.com** •• At the dockside **Hammerhead's Bar & Grill**, potent quenchers such as the Category 5 Hurricane and Electric Lemonade erase bad memories of missed three-footers. **850-351-1997, sandestin.com** •• Marlin Grill

serves superb seafood, including the not-to-be-missed plank-grilled salmon in maple syrup sauce. **850-351-1990, sandestin.com** •• The cheery, French country–style **Another Broken Egg**, which starts stirring at 6 A.M., offers an infinite selection of robust omelets, such as the crabmeat-filled Floridian. **850-622-2050, sandestin.com** •• Sample the meaty crab cakes at the **Red Bar**, a lazy surfside haunt with a garage-sale motif in Grayton Beach on scenic Route 30A. **850-231-1008** •• In Seaside, a confection of a town of Victorian row houses fronted by white-picket fences (the setting for the movie *The Truman Show*), savor the hearty Old Florida oyster stew at **Bud & Alley's** or sip a sunset libation at the restaurant's open-air bar, perched above the Gulf. **850-231-5900**

LOCAL KNOWLEDGE

Going native on the Panhandle means getting serious about the grape. Not only do wine bars abound—10 lie within a 26-mile stretch between Destin and Rosemary Beach—but also wine shops, festivals, classes, tasting events, and dinners. At the annual **Sandestin Wine Festival**, which draws thousands of oenophiles

each April, $150,000 worth of vintage labels was sold in eight hours last year. **850-231-5900, sandestin.com** •• Golfers figure prominently in this exploding wine culture. Several wine bars, including **Courtyard Wine & Cheese (850-231-1219)** and **Cuvée Beach Cellar & Wine Bar Restaurant (850-650-8900, cuveebeach.com)** tune their televisions to the Golf Channel and ESPN. "If wine bars aren't the new 19th hole, they're the 20th hole," says Patrick Crumpler, manager of Cuvée Beach, which pours about 100 glasses a day, starting at 5 P.M. "Sometimes golfers have a cold one at the clubhouse—then finish up here."

GETTING THERE

To sample the best of Emerald Coast golf, fly to Fort Walton Beach and drive 20 miles east along Highway 98 to Destin, a sport-fishing hub dominated by the 2,400-acre Sandestin Golf & Beach Resort.

WHEN TO GO

You can avoid peak season (winter) crowds by hitting the courses in fall or late spring.

THE FIRST COAST

Most pilgrims to Rome pay homage at the Vatican and little attention to the venerable churches in its shadow. If golf in the U.S. has an equivalent, it is Florida's First Coast, which stretches from just north of Jacksonville to Daytona Beach 75 miles south, where NASCAR and Spring Break collide. The Vatican here is the Stadium Course at the TPC at Sawgrass, home of the Players Championship and headquarters of the PGA Tour. Pete Dye's celebrated course might be the best in the Jacksonville area; it is indisputably the best known. But visitors to northeast Florida will also find the work of other great architects too.

WHERE TO PLAY

AMELIA ISLAND PLANTATION
Oak Marsh: 6,580 yards, par 72, 136/72.3
Ocean Links: 6,108 yards, par 70, 128/69.3
Long Point: 6,775 yards, par 70, 135/73.0
Greens fee: $120–$160
888-261-6161, aipfl.com

A half-hour's drive north of Jacksonville International Airport, this sprawling resort on Amelia Island has three courses, two of which—Oak Marsh and Ocean Links—were designed by Dye and Bobby Weed, respectively. Oak Marsh opened in 1972 and showcases Dye characteristics that send middle handicappers reaching for Seconal. Dye's short holes can mar an otherwise spotless round, and there are several testers at Oak Marsh. Long Point is a beautiful Tom Fazio layout a couple of miles south on Highway A1A. This wonderfully schizophrenic design wanders from high dunes into marshland and back through forests. The signature hole is the 166-yard 15th, which precedes the eerily similar 158-yard 16th. The Atlantic Ocean to the right of both holes enters play only if you slice wildly.

THE CARD WRECKER: THE TPC OF SAWGRASS STADIUM COURSE, NO. 17, 132 YARDS, PAR 3

How could it be any other hole? The 17th is the shortest hole on the course and boasts the largest green, but it sure won't feel like it when you stand on the tee. No hole better illustrates the thin line between ecstasy and despair. We asked Ponte Vedra Beach resident Jim Furyk how to tread that line: "The 17th ought to be one of the most simple par threes in golf, but it's gotten into the head of every amateur on the planet," Furyk says. "It psyches them out before they've even hit their tee shot on the first hole. What you really need to do is eliminate the pin from your target focus and aim for the dead center of the green. Don't go for the edges because you're dying to say you aced or birdied it. Just forget it. Put it in the center of the green, get your two-putt, and live to brag about parring one of the most famous holes in golf."

THE TPC OF SAWGRASS

Stadium: 6,954 yards, par 72, 149/75.0
Valley: 6,864 yards, par 72
Greens fee: $214–$350 (Stadium);
$155 (Valley)
904-273-3235, tpc.com

TOP 100 YOU CAN PLAY
TOP 100 IN THE U.S. ⎫ Stadium
TOP 100 IN THE WORLD ⎭

An hour's drive south of Amelia Island on Interstate 95 or 50 minutes down coastal Highway A1A, Ponte Vedra is golf's answer to Malibu, California. Vijay Singh, David Duval, Jim Furyk, and Fred Funk are just a few of the Tour stars who live here. Their home club is the TPC, where the Stadium course, home to the Players Championship, is the most prized—and expensive— tee time on the First Coast. The course boasts one of the most notable closing stretches on the Tour, including the famed 132-yard island-green 17th. From the tips, the Stadium is too much of a course for most, but the second set of tees (6,514 yards) makes it an enjoyable facsimile of the Tour pro experience. The Valley opened in 1987 and still struggles for recognition in the shadow of its older sibling. Those who miss left get hammered here, with water in play on that side at almost every hole from the 3rd through the 14th. But Dye's cruelty is equal opportunity: Those who drift to the right off the tee get socked on the four closing holes.

SAWGRASS COUNTRY CLUB

East: 3,551 yards, par 36
South: 3,471 yards, par 36
West: 3,451 yards, par 36
Greens fee: $257
904-285-2261, sawgrasscountryclub.com

This private venue with three nines sits in Ponte Vedra across Highway A1A from the Sawgrass Marriott Resort, where you need to stay to get access. The course hosted the Players Championship from 1977 to 1981. Sawgrass relies less on traditional hazards than on the wind, which seems to come from every direction. This is no fun on the South's 6th, a 528-yard par five that snakes around a pond on the right and poses a ferociously tough approach over water to a green with a Himalayan ridge in the middle. The opening holes on the West are drier than the South nine, but the wind is no less troublesome, and even shots into short par fours can play several clubs longer. The fried-chicken sandwich in the clubhouse is a fine end to a challenging round.

WINDSOR PARKE GOLF CLUB

6,765 yards, par 72, 138/73.3
Greens fee: $40–$50
904-223-4653, windsorparke.com

A 10-minute drive west from Ponte Vedra Beach on J. Turner Butler Boulevard, this Arthur Hills design opened in 1990. Fairly forgiving overall, the course places occasional demands on accuracy. At the 363-yard 6th, the generous fairway sets up a nervy approach over water. The second shot at the 387-yard 9th hole appears to be all carry over a marsh, but there is actually a sizeable collection area short of the green. Beware a back-right hole location at the 141-yard 12th. A massive ridge bisects the green, and you'll need a parachute to stop your ball on the back. Windsor Parke has no holes that will remain seared in your memory, but it's an enjoyable respite from the experience of battling Mr. Dye.

HYDE PARK GOLF CLUB

6,468 yards, par 72, 122/70.8
Greens fee: $22–$38
904-786-5410, hydeparkgolf.com

If you want to squeeze in one more round before leaving town, this Donald Ross track is just 20 minutes south of the airport. It's also one of the least expensive Ross courses you'll find anywhere. A weekday round costs just $28, which is a fair indication that this isn't a high-end facility. However, you do get an opportunity to best Ben Hogan, for one hole at least. The 151-yard 6th, known as Hogan's Alley, is the most storied hole at Hyde Park, which hosted the Jacksonville Open in the 1950s. One year, Hogan carded an 11 here.

WHERE TO STAY

 The 1,350-acre **Amelia Island Plantation** on Florida's northernmost barrier island does a good job of catering to players, children, and everyone in between. There are three courses, a wonderful beach, bicycle paths, playgrounds, tree forts, and marked trails in sunken forests and salt marshes. Nice condo accommodations, good family-style restaurants, and excellent value. Rates start at $175. **888-261-6161; aipfl.com** ● ●

 The only way for non-TPC members to get access to the courses at Sawgrass is to stay at the **Marriott Sawgrass Resort & Spa**, set on 4,800 acres near the Atlantic beaches. There are 508 guest rooms—avoid rooms on the central atrium, which can get a bit noisy on weekends—and a new 20,000-square-foot spa. If you ask nicely, the staff might summon the now-retired sommelier, Ricardo Gracia, who invented the piña colada in 1954. And keep an eye on the Starbucks in the lobby, a favorite hangout of Vijay Singh. Rates start at $169. **800-457-4653, sawgrassmarriott.com**

WHERE TO EAT

The River City Brewing Company in downtown Jacksonville is a great joint for beer and American fare, with a large outdoor deck on the St. John's River. Stroll out on the river walk and you might see dolphins at play—the real thing, not the NFL team. **904-398-2299; rivercitybrew.com** ● ● **Café Italiano**, located in the Marriott Sawgrass Resort & Spa lobby, serves up great pasta dishes that seem as bottomless as a Pete Dye water hazard. **800-457-4653, sawgrassmarriott.com** ● ● **The Augustine Grill** at the Marriott Sawgrass Resort & Spa is more formal and expensive than the café, but you get what you pay for. Superb steaks and a great wine list make for a meat lover's paradise. **800-457-4653, sawgrassmarriott.com** ● ● A two-minute drive from the Marriott Sawgrass Resort & Spa in Ponte Vedra, the lagoon-side **Aqua Grill** has great seafood and steaks. **904-285-3017**

LOCAL KNOWLEDGE

Amelia Island Plantation isn't just renowned for its two golf courses. You can tackle a sport with a moving ball on one of 23 Har-Tru, fast-dry clay courts. There's also a **Racquet Park**, where the Women's Tennis Association holds the Bausch & Lomb Championships each spring. **888-261-6161, aipfl.com** ● ● At the Amelia Island Plantation **Nature Center**, set up a tour with one of seven staff naturalists to explore area beaches, flora, and fauna by foot or kayak. **888-261-6161, aipfl.com** ● ● Watch reenactments of Civil War times (no battles were fought here) at **Fort Clinch**, built in 1864 on Cumberland Sound, which separates Amelia Island from Georgia. The fort is part of a 1,086-acre state park with pristine beaches and sand dunes, trails, ponds, and salt marshes. There are also great views of the Amelia Island Lighthouse, the oldest structure on the island, built in 1839. **904-277-7274, floridastateparks.org/fortclinch** ● ● With U.S. Coast Guard–sanctioned captain **Mac Daniel** guiding you, the local flounder, which come out at night to feed, haven't got a chance. **904-277-3050, floundergigging.com**

GETTING THERE

Jacksonville International Airport is located 30 miles south of Amelia Island and 20 miles west of Ponte Vedra.

WHEN TO GO

You might want to avoid July and August, when the average daily high tops 90 degrees. Temperatures the rest of the year range from mid-60s to mid-80s.

> For more information on the courses and sites around Jacksonville, call 800-733-2668 or go to visitjacksonville.com. Packages are available at florida-golf.org.

NAPLES Naples has long teased golfers by claiming the highest number of courses per capita in the country—the truth is that most of the city's tracks are private. But the public-access courses here provide country-club quality at daily-fee prices. Toss in a vibrant nightlife scene and lush beachside retreats, and there's no better Gulf weekend for golfers.

WHERE TO PLAY

THE ROOKERY AT MARCO

7,180 yards, par 72, 143/75.1
Greens fee: $159, $149 for Marriott guests
239-793-6060, rookeryatmarco.com

Located on an estuary of Hammock Bay, the Rookery is prime roosting terrain for thousands of birds. To make Joe Lee's original 1991 design blend better with the environment, Bob Cupp Jr. recently replaced the turf between holes with acres of lakes and wetlands. The result means that water hugs 16 holes, but the fairways are generous enough to keep you dry most of the time. Vultures are the only birds you'd expect to see hovering over the finishing stretch of holes —which features forced carries over water four times, including one to the peninsula green on the 159-yard 16th.

Hole 7 at The Rookery
at Marco, Emerald Coast,
Florida

HAMMOCK BAY

6,912 yards, par 72, 134/73.4
Greens fee: $100–$155
239-394-4811, play.wcigolf.com

Designed by Peter Jacobsen and Jim Hardy, Hammock Bay is next to the Rookery and is routed around mangroves and coastal inlets. But forget the water hazards—this course gets its bite from huge expanses of white-sand dunes and coquina-shell waste areas. Beware the 170-yard 11th, which is all carry over shells and scrub to a green guarded by two pot bunkers. This course will turn private when its membership fills.

TIBURON GOLF CLUB

Black: 7,005 yards, par 72, 147/74.2
Gold: 7,288 yards, par 72, 137/74.7
Greens fee: $235 for Ritz-Carlton guests,
$250 for nonguests
239-593-2000, ritzcarlton.com

The PGA Tour stars who enjoy a Gold course rush each year at designer Greg Norman's Franklin Templeton Shootout follow two rules: Aim for the center of the fairway and keep it low around the greens. Both courses are known for stacked sod bunkers and pink-shell waste areas that abound around the greens.

NAPLES GRANDE GOLF CLUB

7,078 yards, par 72, 143/75.1
Greens fee: $160–$195
239-659-3718, naplesgrande.com

This five-year-old Rees Jones creation—open only to Edgewater Beach Hotel and Registry Resort guests—has so many water hazards the holes appear to float through the surrounding cypress and oak trees. But it's not just the aqua that puts a premium on accuracy over brawn. Devilishly tricky bunkers guard the corner of nearly every dogleg. The green at the 560-yard 16th is perched atop a 20-foot-high coral rock platform, but that's certainly not the first—nor even the most daunting—hazard you'll encounter on the hole. Water and a snakelike bunker on the left make for an interesting journey from the tee.

WHERE TO STAY

The **Ritz-Carlton** offers two options: Stay next to Tiburon at the Golf Resort or choose a 10-minute shuttle ride away at the Beach Resort. Rooms from $259. **239-598-3300, ritzcarlton.com** • • The **Marco Island Marriott** is on a gorgeous stretch of beach 25 minutes by car south of Naples. Rooms from $240. **800-438-4373, marcoislandmarriott .com** • • The **Edgewater Beach Hotel (800-821-0196, edgewaternaples.com)** and **Registry Resort (800-247-9810, registryresort .com)** are beachside properties with access to Naples Grande Golf Club. Rooms start at $133.

WHERE TO EAT

One of Naples trendiest spots, **Bistro 821**, serves up Asian-European–inspired dishes, such as duck ravioli and portobello "fries." **239-261-5821, bistro821.com** • • You can pair the casual but inventive Italian fare at **Pazzo** with a choice of more than 250 wines, including 30 or so served by the glass. **239-434-8494, pazzoitaliancafe.com** • • For the best dirty martini around—not to mention succulent seafood—head to **Kurrents** in the Marco Island Marriott. **800-438-4373, marcoislandmarriott.com**

LOCAL KNOWLEDGE

For those more into Gucci than golf, **Fifth Avenue South** boasts dozens of high-end boutiques and galleries. **fifthavenuesouth .com** • • For gifts created by local artisans, explore **Tin City**, a charming waterfront hodgepodge of casual restaurants and shops built on the site of a 1920s shellfish processing plant. **tin-city.com** • • A **wave-runner tour** through the Ten Thousand Islands reveals a side of Florida wildlife beyond spring break—including manatees, dolphins, and rare tropical birds. $130. **239-642-2359, marcoislandwatersports.com** • • The 24,000-square-foot, Bali–themed **Spa at Marco Island Marriott** is so hot that John Travolta and his wife, Kelly Preston, recently bought a condo next door to be close to its aquatic watsu massages. **239-642-2686, marcoislandmarriott.com**

GETTING THERE

Fort Myers International Airport is a 50-minute drive north of Naples on Route 75.

WHEN TO GO

Summer temperatures can sizzle. You'll avoid the snowbirds from October to the holiday season and then again after late February.

Hole 6 at The Rookery at Marco, Emerald Coast, Florida

ORLANDO

Putting up big numbers is not usually the goal in golf, but there are exceptions. There are big drives, of course, and the big money that usually comes to those who hit the biggest drives. And then there's Orlando, a city that can put up big numbers as few other golf destinations can. It is home to 451 hotels and motels with 110,000 rooms, 95 different attractions, approximately 4,300 restaurants, and 150 courses within a 45-minute drive of downtown. From perennial GOLF MAGAZINE Gold Medal Award Resorts, such as Grand Cypress and Walt Disney World, to a bevy of newer tracks, Orlando will keep your playing card full.

WHERE TO PLAY

VICTORIA HILLS GOLF CLUB

6,854 yards, par 72, 142/73.5
Greens fee: $45–$75
386-738-6000, arvida.com/victoriapark

The course is actually 35 miles north of Orlando in DeLand, a 45-minute ride on Interstate 4, but the course is well worth the journey. This Ron Garl design was formerly a cow pasture. The layout is part of the 1,859-acre Arvida Victoria Park residential community. Garl, a Florida native, has built an excellent course that runs through mature oaks and Floridian pines. Extremely fair in all respects, the layout unfolds over gently rolling hills and pine hammocks, with carries over sprawling waste bunkers required on some tee shots.

WALT DISNEY WORLD RESORT

Eagle Pines: 6,772 yards, par 72, 135/72.5
Osprey Ridge: 7,101 yards, par 72, 131/74.4
Palm: 7,010 yards, par 72, 138/73.9
Magnolia: 7,516 yards, par 72, 140/76.4
Lake Buena Vista: 6,749 yards, par 72, 133/73.0
Oak Trail: 2,913 yards, par 36
Greens fee: $38–$135
407-939-4653, disneyworld.disney.go.com

Osprey Ridge, by Tom Fazio, hopscotches from an Everglades-like wilderness to dense oak and pine forests to lagoons fringed by waste bunkers. Accented by long, sinuous mounds, Osprey Ridge is a superb, scenic test with a dramatic, watery finish. Beside it is Eagle Pines, a low-profile, minimalist layout by Pete Dye marked by concave fairways, native grasses, and topsy-turvy greens. Disney's traditional offerings are found at the Palm and Magnolia courses, both laid out by Joe Lee and both used as venues in an annual PGA Tour event. The sleeper is the Palm course, a narrow, tree-lined, shot-maker's track with plenty of water in play, especially on the back nine. The Palm's long par-four 18th, which calls for a long approach shot over water, has been ranked as high as the fourth most challenging hole on Tour. The Magnolia, longest of the Disney courses at 7,516 yards (par 72), has been host to the final round of the Disney tournament since 1971. With nearly 100 bunkers sprinkled around the course and water in play at 11 holes, this is a classic Florida test with plenty of driving room. For a shorter test, there's also Lake Buena Vista, a pleasant spread rated the easiest of the full-size courses. Last but not least is Oak Trail, a walkable 2,913-yard, par-36 layout designed for family play. A pushover it's not: According to head pro Kevin Weickel, Oak Trail has "small, challenging greens and two of the best par fives on property."

Hole 18 at Bay Hill Golf
Club, Orlando, Florida

GRAND CYPRESS RESORT

New: 6,773 yards, par 72, 72.2/122
North: 3,521 yards, par 36
South: 3,472 yards, par 36
East: 3,434 yards, par 36
Greens fee: $115–$180
877-330-7377, grandcypress.com

The two original nines opened in 1984, the North and South, remain the resort's best challenge. The East nine came on board in 1986, while the New course, a links-style track inspired by the Old course at St. Andrews, opened in 1988. All 45 holes were designed by Jack Nicklaus. A first-class practice facility features two ranges, a three-hole practice course, and a Golf Academy with GOLF MAGAZINE Top 100 Teachers Phil Rodgers and Fred Griffin.

GREG NORMAN SIGNATURE COURSE, RITZ-CARLTON GOLF CLUB

7,122 yards, par 72, 139/73.9
Greens fee: $185–205
407-393-4900, grandelakes.com

There's not a home in sight on this wide-open course, which Norman routed through a preserve in the Everglades headwaters, with lots of water, live oaks, cypress, palmettos, and pines providing the scenery. Trouble comes around the big contoured greens, which are surrounded by shaved banks, collection areas, and strategically placed hazards.

THE LEGACY CLUB AT ALAQUA LAKES

7,160 yards, par 72, 132/74.5
Greens fee: $70–$109
407-444-9995, legacyclubgolf.com

This Tom Fazio design is part of a residential community located just west of Interstate 4 in Longwood, 30 minutes north of downtown Orlando. Many of the natural habitats found on this former cattle ranch were incorporated into the layout. You'll pass around and over natural wetlands and possibly catch a glimpse of deer, black bear, bobcat, and wild turkey. Fazio incorporated a fairly open feel into the front nine, but the back requires more accuracy both off the tee and with approaches.

TIMACUAN GOLF AND COUNTRY CLUB

6,915 yards, par 71, 135/73.7
Greens fee: $55–$95
407-321-0010, golftimacuan.com

Mike Bender holds the course record of 62 at this Lake Mary course north of downtown. No surprise since he's a GOLF MAGAZINE Top 100 Teacher and runs the Golf Academy on site (the facility also has a lighted driving range open to 8 P.M.). Ron Garl did the original 1987 design, and Bobby Weed was brought in for renovation work after severe flooding in 1996. The front nine is wide open with good-sized greens, whereas the back has a more Carolina feel to it with numerous lakes and tighter fairways lined by tall pine trees.

Hole 17 at Eagle Pines
(Walt Disney World
Resort), Orlando, Florida

ORANGE COUNTY NATIONAL

Panther: 7,175 yards, par 72, 137/75.7
Crooked Cat: 7,277 yards, par 72, 140/75.4
Greens fee: $60–$150
888-727-3672, ocngolf.com

Orange County National is home to two very good courses—Panther and Crooked Cat. The former opened in 1997 and cuts through wetlands and lakes, especially on the 17th, a par three over water. A more links-style theme is found at Crooked Cat, with large bunkers stretching in all directions along many fairways. The facility is also home to the Phil Ritson Golf Institute.

MYSTIC DUNES

7,012 yards, par 71, 137/74.3
Greens fee: $75–$125
866-311-1234, mysticdunesgolf.com

You'll leave here talking about the severely undulated greens—and you'll either love them or hate them. Some are diabolical and hysterical at the same time (most notably the 6th and 8th), although they are kept at a fair speed. Add in shaved collection areas hugging most greens and a three putt may be a good effort. The overall layout is fun, with environmentally sensitive areas framing a number of holes. Stay out of the whiskey barrel bunkers on the linkslike front nine, and then avoid the oaks and pines on the back.

CHAMPIONSGATE

National: 7,128 yards, par 72, 133/75.1
International:
7,363 yards, par 72, 143/76.3
Greens fee: $68–$125
407-787-4653, championsgategolf.com

Greg Norman's two designs opened in October 2000. The National is more American in style, with larger bunkers and good-sized greens and fairways—everything is out in front of you. The International is by far the more challenging of the two, with high rough, more exposed holes, deeper bunkers, and more mounded dunes, all making it highly unpalatable if you play from the wrong tees. Don't be surprised to see some PGA Tour Pros here. ChampionsGate is home to the headquarters of David Leadbetter's Golf Academy.

BAY HILL CLUB & LODGE

7,267 yards, par 72, 140/75.3
Greens fee: $205, standard room
with golf starts at $440
888-422-9445, bayhill.com

Arnold Palmer's club, which opened in 1961 on the southwest side of town, is available to public play but only if you are staying at the Lodge. Time your stay around the PGA Tour's Bay Hill Invitational, usually scheduled around mid-March. Rates will be at their highest, but course conditions are optimal around tournament time.

TOP 100 YOU CAN PLAY

Hole 16 at Osprey Ridge
(Walt Disney World
Resort), Orlando, Florida

METROWEST GOLF CLUB

7,051 yards, par 72, 132/74.1
Greens fee: $58–$152
407-299-1099, metrowestgolf.com

One of the last designs of Robert Trent Jones Sr., Metrowest opened in 1987 just six miles southwest of downtown, close to Universal Studios. It's a local favorite because of its consistently superior conditions. Jones made the most of the 230 acres by creating plenty of roomy fairways, but extensive bunkering surrounds many of the large greens. The back nine is especially memorable thanks to a number of elevation changes, rare for the mostly flat central Florida landscape (check out the downtown skyline from the 13th and 14th tees).

NORTH SHORE GOLF CLUB

6,898 yards, par 72, 138/73.7
Greens fee: $50–$80
407-277-9277, northshore-golfclub.com

Florida-based designer Mike Dasher carved North Shore out of a wide-open cow pasture in which he created two distinct nines. The front is more open, and the back is loaded with oak trees and winds through more scenic marshland. The 417-yard 12th is North Shore's best and toughest hole—a par-four dogleg-right and a fairway lined with oak trees.

WHERE TO STAY

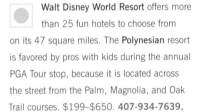 **Walt Disney World Resort** offers more than 25 fun hotels to choose from on its 47 square miles. The **Polynesian** resort is favored by pros with kids during the annual PGA Tour stop, because it is located across the street from the Palm, Magnolia, and Oak Trail courses. $199–$650. **407-934-7639, disneyworld.disney.go.com** ● ●

At **Grand Cypress Resort**, you can stay at the 700-plus room **Hyatt Regency** (check out the grotto pool and Hemingway's Restaurant), but you'll be a five-minute shuttle ride away from the courses. Stay at the **Golf Villas**, however, and you'll have a short walk to the golf facilities, including an expansive clubhouse that features a nice collection of memorabilia from Orlando–area PGA, LPGA, and Senior Tour players. $215–$450. **800-835-7377, grandcypress.com** ● ● There are two options—a Ritz-Carlton and a JW Marriott—and more than 1,500 rooms at **Grande Lakes Orlando**. Both hotels offer stay-and-play packages for the Norman Signature Course. The Ritz-Carlton also has a 40,000-square-foot spa. Rates from $249. **Ritz-Carlton: 407-206-2400, JW Marriott: 407-206-2300, grandelakes.com** ● ● The **Palms Resort**

and Country Club is just two miles south of Walt Disney World and is home to Mystic Dunes. Rooms start at $126. **877-747-4747, wyndham.com** ● ● Golfers who want to base themselves at ChampionsGate can stay at the 700-room **Omni Resort Hotel**. Rooms start at $239. **888-444-6664, omnihotels.com** ● ● Staying at the exclusive **Bay Hill Club & Lodge** is the only way to play the course that hosts Arnold Palmer's Bay Hill Invitational each spring. Rooms start at $204. **888-422-9445, bayhill.com**

WHERE TO EAT

After dinner at the **'Ohana** restaurant at Disney's Polynesian resort, you can relax on a man-made beach to ooh and aah at Disney's nightly fireworks show. **407-934-7639** ● ● Grownups can enjoy uninterrupted conversation and Asian-fusion fare at the the **California Grill** atop Disney's Contemporary Resort. Tom Lehman, a father of four, swears by the warm Valrhona chocolate cake with white chocolate ice cream. **407-939-3463** ● ● For the family that eats well together, there's the **Wolfgang Puck Cafe** in Downtown Disney West Side. **407-939-3463**

LOCAL KNOWLEDGE

If you have kids, the **Magic Kingdom** takes top priority over golf. Advanced planning will save you money (check out the length-of-stay and Park Hopper ticket options) and time (skip the long lines with Disney's Fast Pass, which gets you on certain rides at an assigned time). The Mickey's Philharmagic, a 3-D movie experience, is a must for any group, as are the mountains—Space, Splash, and Big Thunder. Adults: $63; children: $52. **407-934-7639, disneyworld.disney.go.com**

GETTING THERE

Dozens of national and international airlines, from AeroMexico to Zoom, fly into Orlando International Airport. **orlandoairports.net**

WHEN TO GO

Rates are cheapest in the summer, when the weather is the hottest. Prime time is January through April, when the roads are clogged with tourists and the green fees peak at full-fare. Sneak in around November and December and you'll find decent weather and middle-of-the-road rates both on the course and off.

SAVANNAH

SAVANNAH Each fall tourists flock to the "Hostess City of the South," drawn by Savannah's colorful past. The town is so lovely that General Sherman spared it during his Civil War march from Atlanta to the sea and bequeathed it as a gift to Abraham Lincoln. Today visitors take in Savannah's architecture and city squares decorated with fountains, statues, and cannonry. Until recently, however, golf has been an afterthought. Most golfers flying into Savannah's airport are bound for Hilton Head Island, a 40-minute ride across the South Carolina border. They don't know what they're missing.

WHERE TO PLAY

CROSSWINDS GOLF CLUB

6,512 yards, par 72, 132/71.1
Greens fee: $39–$47
912-966-0674, crosswindsgolfclub.com

Just five minutes from the airport, this well-conditioned track serves up five par fives and three drivable par fours. The course is hardly overwhelming—except from the tips—but a slope rating of 132 proves it's no pitch-and-putt. Late arrivals can enjoy a lighted par-three course.

CLUB AT SAVANNAH HARBOR

7,288 yards, par 72, 137/75.1
Greens fee: $115
912-201-2007
theclubatsavannahharbor.com

This resort layout, Savannah's golf centerpiece, sits on Hutchinson Island, a tiny spit of land in the Savannah River. The resort, which includes a Westin hotel, hosted the 2003 Liberty Mutual Legends of Golf, a Champions Tour event. You won't find many vacationers tackling this breezy, linkslike Bob Cupp–Sam Snead design from the tips. This well-varied test has excellent greens ranging in size from medium to enormous (the third is 17,000 square feet). The layout opens modestly, swings by tidal marshes midway through the round, and brings spires and steeples within the city's Historic District into view as it turns for home.

WILMINGTON ISLAND CLUB

6,715 yards, par 71, 133/72.5
Greens fee: $56
912-897-1615

Guests are welcome during the week and on weekend afternoons at this semiprivate Donald Ross design built in 1927 and renovated by Willard Byrd in the mid-1960s.

SOUTHBRIDGE GOLF CLUB

6,922 yards, par 72, 134/74.1
Greens fee: $36–$52
912-651-5455, southbridgegc.com

West of town, this little-known Rees Jones design has water on almost every hole, and Jones' narrow playing corridors wend their way through heavy forests.

WHERE TO STAY

The Westin Savannah Harbor Golf Resort and Spa is next to the Club at Savannah Harbor and offers Southern–style comfort with 403 guest rooms and expansive natural views. Rooms from $195. **912-201-2000, westinsavannah.com** • • The **Ballastone Inn** sits in the heart of the historic district. Rooms and suites at the 16-room bed-and-breakfast range from $215 to $395 per night and include full breakfast, afternoon tea, and a tempting selection of evening hors d'oeuvres. **800-822-4553, ballastone.com**

WHERE TO EAT

There's an inexpensive brunch at **Huey's on River Street (912-234-7385)**, and a pricier one at the **Hilton DeSoto**. **912-232-9000, hilton.com** • • Dinner options include the chic **Sapphire Grill**—continental cuisine with an urban flair. **912-443-9962, sapphiregrill .com** • • Classic southern in a more formal setting is on tap at **45 South (912-233-1881, thepirateshouse.com)**, **The Olde Pink House (912-232-4286)** and **Elizabeth on 37th. 912-236-5547, elizabethon57th.com** • • For simpler fare, duck into the **Sixpence Pub**; specialties include beef Guinness and shepherd's pie. **912-233-3151**

LOCAL KNOWLEDGE

Visit **Tybee Island**, a kitschy counter-culture community east of the city. **tybeeisland.com** • • History buffs will want to visit **Fort Pulaski National Monument**, a stronghold that was captured by Union troops during the Civil War. $3 per person. **912-786-5787, nps.gov** • • At **Land's End**, you'll find funky bars and restaurants, as well as a flat, broad expanse of sand that is every bit the equal of the beaches on Hilton Head.

GETTING THERE

Savannah/Hilton Head Airport is served by Delta, Air Tran, American Continental, Northwest, United, and US Air. **savannahairport.com**

WHEN TO GO

A subtropical climate and average highs that only drop as low as 60 (in January) mean you can play golf here all year long.

SEA ISLAND

Sea Island is where old-world gentility meets new-world order. This tranquil outpost halfway between Savannah, Georgia, and Jacksonville, Florida, has played host to everyone from Bobby Jones to 20 world leaders at 2004's G8 Summit. There are three courses at Sea Island, but as many as 10 designers get credit for them—each track having been altered at least once. Each offers its own challenges. "You have the variety of three courses that play three different ways," says island resident Davis Love III. "I don't think any of the courses favor one particular shot, but hopefully you possess a shot you can play in windy conditions!"

WHERE TO PLAY

SEASIDE COURSE

6,945 yards, par 70, 131/73.1
Greens fee: $170–$250
800-732-4752, seaisland.com

TOP 100 YOU CAN PLAY
TOP 100 IN THE U.S.

The first architects credited with this masterpiece are Harry S. Colt and Charles Alison in 1929; the most recent is Tom Fazio in 1999. What hasn't changed is the superb setting for one of the finest courses in the southeast. Fazio married the original Seaside nine with Joe Lee's later marsh-side holes to create a linkslike, lowland treasure that skirts St. Simons Sound. The fairways are hemmed by waste areas and deep, flash-faced bunkers that create an illusion of tightness. In fact, the landing areas are hard to miss. However, the greens are slick and guarded with mounds that repel sloppy approaches. Holes don't come much more beautiful than the 14th, which curls 407 yards alongside a marsh with views of the sound and the causeway bridge.

THE PLANTATION COURSE

7,058 yards, par 72, 135/73.9
Greens fee: $170–$200
800-732-4752, seaisland.com

In 1998 Rees Jones completed an extreme makeover on this course, which began as nine holes by Walter Travis in 1927. It is routed through thick forest—and around a few of the island's multimillion-dollar "cottages"—and is noteworthy for small greens protected by closely mowed mounds. The Plantation is rated the toughest of Sea Island's courses—but only if you compare slope and rating. In reality, Seaside is the hardest—but several of the par threes are knee-knockers when the wind kicks up off nearby St. Simons Sound. Holes 7, 11, and 15 require a carry over water and are devilishly bunkered to boot.

THE RETREAT COURSE

7,106 yards, par 72, 135/73.9
Greens fee: $170–$200
800-732-4752, seaisland.com

When Davis Love III was asked to explain the logic behind the 6th hole he designed at the Retreat Course, he reportedly replied, "Because people think I have no sense of humor." Golfers will get the joke when see the green at this 369-yard par four, which is as wide as the runway at nearby McKinnon Airport is long. That's the only quirk on an otherwise enjoyable course. Love joined his brother Mark in 2001 to redesign the former St. Simons Island Club, a five-minute shuttle ride from the Lodge. The Retreat is a charitable layout with generous fairways. The biggest threats to a good score are the trees that frame most holes and the greens, many of which are pinched on the approach by bunkers.

Hole 12 at Sea Island
(Seaside Course), Georgia

Hole 18 at Sea Island
(Seaside Course), Georgia

WHERE TO STAY

The $42-million **Lodge at Sea Island**, which is next to the Plantation and Seaside courses, opened in 2001 to complement the regal **Cloister Hotel**. Rooms from $650. **800-732-4752, seaisland.com** • • Sea Island Resort owns an exclusive hunting preserve, **Cabin Bluff**, about an hour south on Interstate 95 near the Intracoastal Waterway. It even has a unique six-hole golf course that Love Golf Design built, with alternating tees and pin positions, so it can play like an 18-holer. You'll need to bag the golden goose though. The fully staffed cabin costs $50,000 for a three-night stay. **800-732-4752, seaisland.com**

WHERE TO EAT

The Lodge has three restaurants. **The Terrace** overlooks the finishing hole of the Plantation Course and serves a terrific seafood chowder. The wood-paneled **Oak Room Bar** is modeled on the famous watering hole at New York's Plaza Hotel and has more than 40 whiskey selections. Try the bluepoint oysters topped with a cube of lemon gelée for a great appetizer. The **Colt and Alison Steakhouse** is semiformal—bring a jacket, hold the tie—and boasts a 700-bottle wine list. For lunch, try the **Davis Love Grill** at the Retreat clubhouse, which is decorated with memorabilia from Love III and his father. It also serves Georgia's best Caesar salad. **800-732-4752, seaisland.com** • • Take a five-minute drive to St. Simons Island for great crab cakes at **Barbara Jean's**, on the corner of Beachview and Mallory Streets. **912-634-6500, barbarajeans.com**

LOCAL KNOWLEDGE

Aside from the golf, there are other ways to get fired up at Sea Island. If you can't shoot par, hit the **Shooting School** instead. Classes are for beginners and crack shots. Lessons: $75 to $100, plus $30 per ammo round. Practice: $35 per round. Clays course: $150 • • Giddy up with **riding lessons** through marshland and on the beach. $20–$75 • • Kick up your heels in daily **ballroom boogie classes** with dance doyenne Audrey Wood. Free • • Tune up your game with GOLF MAGAZINE Top 100 Teachers Jack Lumpkin, Todd Anderson, and Gale Peterson at the **Golf Learning Center**. **800-732-4752, seaisland.com**

GETTING THERE

Sea Island is an 85-mile drive southeast from Savannah International Airport and a 70-mile drive north of Jacksonville International Airport. Delta, Southeast, and Atlantic Airlines fly into the regional Brunswick Golden Isles Airport 12 miles to the north.

WHEN TO GO

Late spring, summer, and early fall are the best times to experience warm, sunny weather. But you can get days in the 60s and 70s—as well as good winter rates—in November and December.

RESIDENT EXPERT: DAVIS LOVE

PGA Tour star Davis Love III grew up at Sea Island, designed one of its three golf courses, and lives nearby. Who better to provide the inside scoop on how to enjoy the local brand of southern comfort?

"My favorite hole on Seaside would have to be No. 13 because of the challenges and options it presents. You have to carry a tidal creek and avoid the marsh on the left and bunkers on the right. It can be a different hole every time you play it, depending on the wind."

"My company [Love Golf Design] redesigned the Retreat Course in 2001. With all the changes we made, my favorite hole is probably No. 6. It's a short par-four where long hitters can go for the green. But the real challenge is in the approach because the green is 14,000 square feet, with a deep swale through the middle."

"If I were staying at Sea Island, I probably wouldn't go anywhere else to eat. But if you're looking for local flavor, I enjoy Sweet Mama's in Longview Plaza for a quick and easy breakfast. Tacos del Mar a few doors down serves a great Tex-Mex lunch. And for dinner, you can't go wrong with the steak and seafood at Bennie's Red Barn on Frederica Road."

NEW ORLEANS
For Cajun food, jazz, and potent cocktails, New Orleans is Babylon on the Bayou. Now visitors have a reason to pack golf clubs with the Alka-Seltzer. Two courses designed by Pete Dye and former PGA champion David Toms are making a big splash in the Big Easy. With three fine tracks within 15 minutes of Bourbon Street—and two more a short drive away—golfers can squeeze in 36 a day and still be quaffing Hurricanes by sundown.

WHERE TO PLAY

CARTER PLANTATION
7,049 yards, par 72, 140/74.4
Greens fee: $75–$85
225-294-7555, carterplantation.com

Louisiana native David Toms and architect Glenn Hickey created this gem 45 minutes northwest of downtown in 2003. Like the gators that inhabit its water hazards, the course has bite, notably hefty par fives at the 13th and 15th holes.

TPC OF LOUISIANA
7,520 yards, par 72
Greens fee: $130–$155
504-436-8721, tpc.com

This Pete Dye course opened in 2004 on a reclaimed swamp just across the Mississippi and has plenty of punishment for the foolish. The course hosts the PGA Tour's Zurich Classic in late April. Be sure to try Chef Dwight Sherman's great seafood gumbo.

Hole 3 at Carter Plantation, New Orleans, Louisiana

AUDUBON PARK GOLF COURSE

4,189 yards, par 62, 104/61.6
Greens fee: $30–$38
504-212-5290, auduboninstitute.org

This executive course is only a short streetcar ride from town. Audubon opened in 1898 but recently underwent a $6 million renovation.

ENGLISH TURN

7,078 yards, par 72, 141/74.2
Greens fee: $155
504-391-8018, englishturn.com

This longtime PGA Tour stop, designed by Jack Nicklaus, is private but welcomes visitors on a limited basis. English Turn's best hole is the 15th, a 540-yard par five with water on the right and an island green that is neither big nor easy.

MONEY HILL GOLF AND COUNTRY CLUB

7,131 yards, par 72, 127/73.9
Greens fee: $100–$110
985-892-8250, moneyhill.com

This great Ron Garl–designed course an hour north of town is also private, but don't let that deter you. Call and politely ask for a tee time on a day when the football-crazy members are watching the Saints or LSU play. The concierge at many local hotels can also arrange a round.

WHERE TO STAY

If you want first-class accommodations, the **Ritz-Carlton Maison Orleans**, a French Quarter landmark, is for you. Rates from $269. **504-670-2900, ritzcarlton.com** • • The **Maison Dupuy** ain't as grand as the Ritz, but it's close to Bourbon Street. Rooms from $99. **504-586-8000, maisondupuy.com** • • **Carter Villas**, located at Carter Plantation, are great for foursomes. Doubles start at $99. **877-811-5295, carterplantation.com** • • A typical quaint bed-and-breakfast in the **French Quarter** starts at $85. **800-729-4640, historiclodging.com**

WHERE TO EAT

Recover from the night before over a café au lait and beignets (fried dough) at **Café du Monde** on Decatur Street. **800-772-2927, cafedumonde.com** • • Sample a Sazerac at the **Bombay Club** on Conti Street. Locals insist that the delicious $12 mix of rye whiskey, anisette liqueur, and Peychaud's bitters was the world's first cocktail. **504-586-0972, thebombayclub .com** • • Try **Bayona** for Great Cajun food, especially the roasted duck breast sandwich. **504-525-4455, bayona.com** • • The **Bourbon House** is a Bourbon Street staple. Sample the special: oysters raw on the half shell with caviar for $16. **504-522-0111, bourbonhouse .com** • • The best deal in town is **Acme Oyster House's** $8 Peace Maker Po' Boy, a fried shrimp and oyster sandwich with Tabasco–infused mayo. **504-522-5973, acmeoyster.com**

LOCAL KNOWLEDGE

Take a Mississippi paddleboat cruise on the **Cajun Queen** ($15) or board the **Creole Queen Dinner Jazz Cruise** ($53 with dinner; $30 for the cruise and music). **504-529-4567, neworleanspaddlewheels.com** • • Hook up with **Bourgeois Charters** for a Bayou fishing trip. Their guarantee: no catch, no pay. Otherwise it's $400 for two. **504-341-5614, neworleansfishing.com** • • Get up close and personal with a 'gator on a two-hour **guided tour of the Bayou**. $20. **800-467-0758, cajunpridetours.com** • • From late April to early May, more than 500,000 music fans attend the annual **New Orleans Jazz Festival** at Fair Grounds Race Course. Tickets are $25 in advance, $35 at the door. **504-522-4786, nojazzfest.com**

GETTING THERE

More than a dozen carriers fly into Louis Armstrong New Orleans International Airport. **flimsy.com**

WHEN TO GO

Summer is hotter than a new thriller from local celebrity writer Anne Rice, so lean toward spring or fall. August is hurricane season—and we don't mean the punchy local drink.

NORTHEASTERN MISSISSIPPI The thick grilled bologna and American cheese with mayo on white bread may—all by itself—be worth the trip to Old Waverly Golf Club in West Point, Mississippi. With treats you'll find nowhere else, the northeast part of the Magnolia State is gaining renown as a smorgasbord of fun food and surprisingly good golf. The "Mid-South" may never be confused with the Monterey Peninsula, but the golf is fun, the food is fine, and the local folks are warm and welcoming. Maybe that's why, despite worldwide adoration and untold riches, Elvis could never stay away for long. And he wasn't even a golfer.

WHERE TO PLAY

CHEROKEE VALLEY GOLF CLUB

6,761 yards, par 72, 128/72.2
Greens fee: $49
901-525-4653, olivebranchgolf.com

From the airport in Memphis, Tennessee, it's a 20-minute drive on Interstate 78 to Cherokee Valley, an entertaining, challenging place to work out the kinks at the start of your trip. The toughest hole is the serpentine 526-yard 8th, where a drive must flirt with a stately poplar tree. The 9th and 18th holes run uphill to greens backed by rough-covered slopes that require a deft touch with a lob wedge.

KIRKWOOD NATIONAL GOLF CLUB

7,129 yards, par 72, 135/73.6
Greens fee: $30–$40
662-252-4888, kirkwoodgolf.com

A half-hour south on Interstate 78, in Holly Springs, this course's short holes can lead to big numbers. The 6th is 209 yards uphill; the 12th plays 165 yards over a vast bunker; and the 132-yard 15th demands you land a high shot on a shallow green as lightly as a moth on a silk shirt. Local knowledge goes a long way here: You might shave 8 or 10 shots off your second time around.

MALLARD POINTE GOLF COURSE

7,004 yards, par 72, 131/73.8
Greens fee: $35
888-833-6477, mallardpointegc.com

Mallard boasts the motto "This Bird Has a Bite." This is evident at the 462-yard, par-four 9th, where the drive and approach shot are over deep jungle pits. "Two-tiered" does not do justice to the shelf on the 13th green—"two-storied" is more like it. If the pin is downstairs and your approach finds the upstairs level, consider leaving the pin in and trying to hit it, as the two-stroke penalty may be a more prudent play than the usual four-putt.

RIVER BEND LINKS

6,906 yards, par 72, 128/72.6
Greens fee: $45–$55
662-363-1005, riverbendlinks.com

From Mallard Pointe, it's an hour-long drive to a Scottish–style layout in Robinsonville, where, unusually, four par fives rate the easiest handicaps. Another quirk is that two of the par threes rank among the hardest holes. The 425-yard 18th features water on both sides like bowling-alley gutters.

COTTONWOODS COURSE AT GRAND CASINO

6,950 yards, par 72, 119/72.3
Greens fee: $89 for hotel guests
662-357-6078, grandcasinos.com

This Hale Irwin design has several hairpin curves, notably at the 232-yard 12th, where bunkers flank a humped green. A lake guards the island green at the 181-yard 16th and the right side of the 512-yard 17th, which makes for an intimidating closing stretch.

BIG OAKS GOLF CLUB

6,784 yards, par 72, 124/73.1
Greens fee: $39
662-844-8002, bigoaksgolfclub.com

From 250 acres of wetlands north of Tupelo, Tracy May crafted Big Oaks, where golfers, flora, and fauna share the wealth. Water Moccasin Point is an aptly named spot for the lethal 3rd tee, which demands a drive over a wall of trees—like clearing the back net at a driving range. The 17th is 221 backbreaking yards over water and bunkers that seem to have been created with mortars. Bogey here feels like birdie.

OLD WAVERLY GOLF CLUB

7,000 yards, par 72, 140/74.0
Greens fee: $94–$124 for hotel guests
662-494-6463, oldwaverly.net

Comparisons between Old Waverly and Augusta National are understandable. The willow oaks lining Old Waverly's stately driveway call to mind Magnolia Lane, and both courses have hosted memorable majors. One decided difference is that Old Waverly welcomes women members. Juli Inkster won the 1999 U.S. Women's Open on Bob Cupp's layout, helped by a magical bunker shot from a fried-egg lie to within a foot of the hole for par at the 7th. This 205-yard par three across a chasm to a plateau green is named Heather's Heaven for the late LPGA star and Old Waverly regular Heather Farr. The approach to the 18th is an all-time knee-knocker over water and a sheer-faced bunker to a green backed by a steep, rough-frosted hill.

NORTH CREEK

6,433 yards, par 72, 125/71.2
Greens fee: $20–$45
662-280-4653, golfnorthcreek.com

This semiprivate, links-style course designed by Tracy May has large, undulating greens that are well guarded by sand bunkers. The fairways are heavily mounded but fairly forgiving, with the exception of a couple of holes on the back nine.

WHERE TO STAY

Old Waverly in West Point has on-course cottages and villas from $110 to $480. **662-494-6463, oldwaverly.net** • • The **Grand Casino Tunica**, home to the Cottonwoods course, is the largest casino resort between Las Vegas and Atlantic City. Rates range from $39–$900. **662-363-2788, grandcasinos .com** • • **Kirkwood Cottages** in Holly Springs has quaint cottages and stay-and-play packages that start at $91, double occupancy, per night. **662-252-4888; kirkwoodcottages.com**

WHERE TO EAT

Como Steakhouse, located in a 120-year-old mercantile store, has a knack for cooking over open charcoal pots. The décor—photographs of local Mississippi blues artists—is just as enjoyable as the food. **662-526-9529** • •

Laws Hill Fish House has the best catfish in Holly Springs. **662-252-1500** • • The **Grand Casino** has plenty of dining options. **LB's Steakhouse** is known for its healthy portions of thick steaks and its vast selection of vintage wines. An evening at Murano's with Sicilian chef Gino Cipriano is authentic as you can get this side of the Mediterranean, especially if you ask to sit on the sidewalk café. Grab a quick burger or snack at **Delta Blues Café**. **800-946-4946, grandcasinos.com**

LOCAL KNOWLEDGE

It takes two hours to cross the state from Tunica to Tupelo, the birthplace of Mississippi's most famous son, **Elvis Presley**. On January 8, 1935, a tiny, two-room shack welcomed the future king of rock and roll. Seven bucks buys a quick spin through the museum (**662-841-1245, elvispresleybirthplace.com**), and you won't be charged for royalties when you hum "Heartbreak Hotel." To see how money changed a simple country boy, visit Graceland on your way back to the Memphis airport. **800-238-2000, elvis.com**

GETTING THERE

Fly into Memphis International Airport and work your way south. **memphisairport.org**

WHEN TO GO

Summers are steamy and winters can get chilly, so spring and fall are ideal times for golf.

For more information on Mississippi courses and sites, go to visitmississippi.org or mstourism.com.

PINEHURST AND THE SANDHILLS
A celebrated shrine that lives and breathes the game, Pinehurst holds a magnetic appeal for golfers. There's more tradition in the air and more magic in the ground here than at any other place this side of St. Andrews. Pinehurst was put on the map by the legendary No. 2 course at Pinehurst resort. It was there that designer Donald Ross made his home and unfurled his genius for building subtle, strategic courses playable by all types of golfers—or at least all those who can afford to stay at the resort and pay the No. 2's $375 greens fee. But the Carolina Sandhills—marked by the feathery longleaf pines and peaceful hills around Pinehurst, Southern Pines, and Aberdeen—is also possible on the cheap. Local stay-and-play operators offer packages at up to 75 percent less than major-resort prices. And you can still stroll through the quaint villages that haven't changed, give or take a couple of sports bars, since the days of Mr. Ross.

WHERE TO PLAY

PINEHURST RESORT

No. 1: 6,128 yards, par 70, 116/69.4
Greens fee: $160

No. 2: 7,217 yards, par 72, 137/75.6
Greens fee: $275–$375

No. 3: 5,682 yards, par 70, 115/67.2
Greens fee: $160

No. 4: 7,117 yards, par 72, 136/74.5
Greens fee: $250

No.5: 6,848 yards, par 72, 137/73.4
Greens fee: $160

No. 6: 7,008 yards, par 71, 139/74.4
Greens fee: $250

No. 7: 7,216 yards, par 72, 144/75.5
Greens fee: $250

No. 8: 7,092 yards, par 72, 135/74.2
Greens fee: $200–$250

800-ITS-GOLF, pinehurst.com

No. 2

No. 8

Well known for the last-putt victory by Payne Stewart in the 1999 U.S. Open, Pinehurst, established in 1895, offers eight outstanding courses and more holes than any other resort in the world. Ross designed the first four courses here, and each of the eight features defined cuts of rough along tree-lined fairways, numerous sand bunkers, and mature trees that come into play on nearly every hole. No. 1 is the most scenic. No. 2, ranked sixth on GOLF MAGAZINE's Top 100 Courses You Can Play in the U.S. and host to the 2005 U.S. Open, is a difficult test that requires great shot-making skills. The greens are contoured and not very large. Loosely played approach shots dive and roll into places that make par difficult to achieve. The best feature of No. 2 is its subtlety. It is never abrasive. You stand on every tee and know exactly where the drive should go. No. 3 is a typical Donald Ross design, featuring dome-shaped greens. When Rees Jones was walking through the woods in 1984 laying out the holes on No. 4, he came across several bunkers from a long-abandoned course. He ordered them restored, and today they sit on the 4th hole. No. 5 is very tight and has numerous out-of-bounds stakes lining its fairways. No. 6 is extremely long and has many elevated greens. No. 7 is a modern design laid out on undulating terrain with a lot of natural vegetation in play, along with well-maintained greens. No. 8, the Centennial course, which opened in 1996, is a traditional Fazio design traversing 125 acres of wetlands and freshwater marshes. The greens have some of the characteristics of those on No. 2 but are larger.

Hole 2 at Pinehurst
No. 4, The Sandhills,
North Carolina

PINE NEEDLES AND MID PINES

Pine Needles: 7,015 yards, par 71, 135/73.5
Mid Pines: 6,528 yards, par 72, 127/71.3
Greens fee: $140–$175
800-747-7272, pineneedles-midpines.com

TOP 100 YOU CAN PLAY

Business was roaring at Pinehurst resort by the 1920s, so the founding Tufts family expanded its empire and hired Donald Ross to design Mid Pines (1921) and Pine Needles (1928) on adjacent sites, a mile from downtown Southern Pines and four miles from the village of Pinehurst. At Pine Needles, you'll be walking fairways ruled by Annika Sorenstam at the 1996 U.S. Open and by Karrie Webb at the 2001 Open. At Mid Pines, you'll play a course once favored by smooth-swinging Julius Boros, the former PGA Tour star whose in-laws once managed and owned Mid Pines. Both courses will test every facet of your game. You'll find small greens with some of the shaping Ross was renowned for, although their contours are less severe than on Pinehurst No. 2. The par threes at Mid Pines and Pine Needles are varied; forced carries are few, but on longer holes you'll have to work the ball around towering pines.

TOBACCO ROAD GOLF CLUB

6,554 yards, par 71, 150/73.2
Greens fee: $59–$124
877-284-3762, tobaccoroadgolf.com

This course 20 miles north of Southern Pines, in Sanford, feels like a Scottish links without the sea views. There's no whipping wind or sod-faced bunkers, but the vast, wide-open design is reminiscent of golf's homeland. Course designer Mike Strantz built fairways 45 yards across in spots and surrounded them with heaving hillocks covered with tall, wispy love grass. Numerous carries over sandy waste areas and scrub vegetation, plus a handful of blind shots and roller-coaster greens, contribute to the 150 slope from the back tees. You may need to recharge your batteries after a loop around Tobacco Road, so kick back on the wrap-around porch overlooking the 18th green and put away a tasty barbecued pork sandwich. Styled after an old farmhouse, the club's main building, with its large, open fireplace and rustic antiques, is a great spot to replay your round.

THE PIT GOLF LINKS

7,007 yards, par 72, 133/73.4
Greens fee: $109
800-574-4653, pitgolf.com

Pinehurst native Dan Maples built the Pit two miles west of Aberdeen on a former sand quarry, altering the dramatic natural terrain as little as possible. Don't expect to see long, sandy stretches, however; the only quarry remnants on this lush, green layout are the mounds in and around some fairways and three lakes once used for washing sand. One huge lake comes into play on three holes, including the 199-yard 12th, which boasts an island green, and the 385-yard 13th, where you need a poke of 185 yards from the tips to clear the lake.

BAYONET AT PUPPY CREEK

7,021 yards, par 72, 134/74.0
Greens fee: $65
888-229-6638, bayonetgolf.com

Seventeen miles southeast of Aberdeen in Raeford, the Bayonet at Puppy Creek is as unusual as its name. (Owner Joe Poole attended the Citadel military academy, and Puppy Creek runs through the course.) What makes the layout unique? Instead of the evergreen forests ubiquitous in this region, clusters of oaks, red maples, and other deciduous trees frame the holes. It's a nice change of pace from punching out of the pines. The best hole on the Bayonet is the 422-yard 4th, where the second shot, from a downhill lie, must carry a lake to a peninsula green. Wise golfers lay up, wedge on in three, and try to one-putt for par. As a rule, the fairways are wide and the rough fairly tame, but if your game needs help, the Bayonet's 25-acre practice facility with short-game area is a good place to work out the kinks.

LITTLE RIVER FARM

6,956 yards, par 72, 135/73.4
Greens fee: $65
888-766-6538, littleriver.com

Heading back toward Pinehurst, about five miles from the resort, the rolling hillsides and sweeping vistas of Little River Farm are more reminiscent of the Kentucky countryside than the Sandhills. This is fitting, since the property used to be a horse farm and a harness-racing track. After the course debuted in 1996, golfers complained about the difficulty of Dan Maples' design, especially the 539-yard third hole, where a creek fronting the uphill green gathered approaches coming up short. In 2004 the owners built a more forgiving putting surface on a lower spot, making the hole, and the course, a more pleasant experience.

TALAMORE GOLF RESORT

6,840 yards, par 71, 140/73.2
Greens fee: $55–$95
910-692-5884, talamore.com

Talamore, on Talamore Drive in Southern Pines, opened in 1992 and attracted golfers with a novel idea: four llama caddies, led by a handler. The furry beasts proved more popular than Fluff Cowan in his heyday. Golfers and visitors snapped so many pictures that it slowed play, so the club retired the llamas to a pen near the 14th green. Don't be misled. This exquisitely maintained Rees Jones beauty didn't need the four-legged gimmicks. Cascading bunkers and severely undulating fairways are Talamore's trademarks. Down some Dramamine before reaching the 370-yard 10th, where a pod of five bunkers guards the right side of a roiling fairway. As on most holes at Talamore, distance with your driver is second to shot placement.

HYLAND HILLS GOLF CLUB

6,970 yards, par 72, 128/71.5
Greens fee: $49
888-315-2296, hylandhillsgolfclub.com

This course in Southern Pines owes its popularity to a lack of artificial features. What you see— a pretty, open, and inviting parkland course with elevated tees and greens—is exactly what you get. The course looks in places like an Augusta National wannabe, with meticulously manicured fairways and greens framed by azaleas and dogwoods. But numbers don't lie. The 138 slope and 69 course rating tacked to its 6,970 yards give away its forgiving nature. The real trouble lurks not on lightning-fast, multitiered greens (here they are gentle giants), but in the course's 57 strategically placed bunkers. Keep it straight to avoid playing Houdini all day.

Hole 14 at Pinehurst
No. 2, The Sandhills,
North Carolina

WHERE TO STAY

 The elegant **Pinehurst Resort**, known for its Southern hospitality and, of course, its eight courses, offers three different inns to choose from—the luxurious and historic Holly, the grand Carolina, and the more rustic Manor—as well as villas and condos. There are also a variety of golf packages that include the famed No. 2 course. Packages start at $225 a night. **800-487-4653, pinehurst.com** ● ●

 Owned and managed by the family of LPGA Master Professional, and GOLF MAGAZINE Top 100 Teacher Peggy Kirk Bell, Pine Needles and Mid Pines offer cozy accommodations, a satisfying dinner, friendly service, and top-of-the-line golf. The **Mid Pines Inn**, a rustic, three-story brick building, opened in 1921 (it has no elevators). **Pine Needles Lodge** (1927) is a series of 12 chalet-style lodges. There are also seven villas on site, perfect for groups of up to 17, along the 10th fairway at Mid Pines, and Pine Needles recently unveiled its Donald Ross Lodge, which can house as many as 16 visitors and sits within chipping distance of the driving range. Packages start at $100 a night. **910-692-7111, pineneedles-midpines.com** ● ● **Little River** in Carthage has modern condos priced well below the big resorts. Rates from $100. **910-949-4600, littleriver.com** ● ● **Talamore Villas** offer quiet, wooded ambiance just off Midland Road. Rates from $112. **910-692-1070, talamore.com** ● ● **Condotels** has units along Pinehurst Nos. 3, 5, and 6. Rates from $169. **800-272-8588, condotelsofpinehurst .com** ● ● For something cozier, try the **Magnolia Inn**, an 1896 Victorian bed-and-breakfast with claw-foot bathtubs in some rooms. Rates start at $85. **828-622-3543, mountainmagnolia inn.com**

WHERE TO EAT

Golfers love the **Barn (910-692-7700)** and the **Lob Steer (910-692-3503)** in Southern Pines. (Yes, the names say it all.) The 15-ounce rib eye at the Barn is a local favorite, and surf and turf at the Lob Steer is another sure bet. ● ● For a little more atmosphere, the **Pine Crest Inn (800-633-3001, pinecrestinn .com)** and **Magnolia Inn (800-914-9306, mountainmagnoliainn.com),** both in Pinehurst Village, offer fine Southern hospitality and cuisine—once you locate them. Olmsted designed the tiny village in 1895 in a wagon-wheel pattern, so you can find your way as easily as you lost it. Built in 1906, the Pine Crest Inn embodies the soul of Pinehurst, with a big porch and a quiet, softly lit dining room. A 12-ounce grilled pork chop is served with spicy fruit relish and sweet-and-russet-potato pie, and the 14-ounce rib eye comes smothered in Jack Daniel's sauce. The Magnolia Inn has a fun little pub and offers a less traditional, trendier menu. Pair the duck spring roll appetizer with one of the oft-changing seafood specials. ● ● Portuguese-born Frank Fernandes owns **Rosyln's**, at Midland Country Club, where you can get the best paella in North Carolina. **910-295-3241** ● ● If you're looking for a robust start before teeing off, try **Mac's Breakfast Anytime**. With restaurants in Aberdeen, Pinehurst, and Southern Pines, Mac's has cornered the early-morning market. They won't look at you funny if you order an egg-white omelet, but don't count out the full breakfast, biscuits and all. It'll get you ready to take on any course in town. **919-776-2715** ● ● The breakfast buffet in the **Carolina Dining Room** of the Pinehurst Hotel has the most decadent Southern–style spread you'll find anywhere. **910-235-8507, pinehurst.com**

LOCAL KNOWLEDGE

Stroll along the streets and browse the quaint shops of the **Village of Pinehurst**, founded in 1895 and planned in part by Frederick Law Olmsted, creator of New York City's Central Park. **villageofpinehurst.org** ● ● Night falls peacefully on the Sandhills, although **Brook's**, a comfy main-street hangout, has a pulse and isn't too loud for conversation. **910-692-3515** ● ● The best place to catch the big game on TV is at the **Broad Street Bar**, which has 30 screens and typical pub grub. **910-695-7077, broadstreetbar.com**

GETTING THERE

Raleigh-Durham International Airport is about an hour drive from Pinehurst, and Southern Pines. Moore County Airport is just a few miles away.

WHEN TO GO

The Appalachian Mountains shelter the Sandhills region, making the winters fairly mild, with average highs in the low-to-mid 50s from December through February. Spring warms temperatures up to the 60s by March, summers are hot and dry, and fall lasts well into November.

KIAWAH ISLAND

For two decades, Kiawah Island was half of a great golf resort. It always had the golf—five tracks, none better than the famed Ocean Course, the venue for the 1991 Ryder Cup—but the Kiawah experience ended when the last putt dropped and golfers had to shuffle off back to a sterile rented condo. With the recent opening of the Sanctuary, which is to hotels what Pete Dye's masterpiece is to golf courses, Kiawah Island can finally claim a place among America's great resorts. If things had been this comfortable in 1991, that Ryder Cup might not have gotten so ugly.

Hole 18 at Kiawah
Island (Ocean Course),
South Carolina

WHERE TO PLAY

THE OCEAN COURSE

7,296 yards, par 72, 152/78.0
Greens fee: $196–$305
843-266-4670, kiawahresort.com

TOP 100 YOU CAN PLAY

TOP 100 IN THE U.S.

TOP 100 IN THE WORLD

From the extreme back tees on every hole, the Ocean Course clocks in at almost 8,000 yards, but those who choose their tees wisely will enjoy a sublime experience on a track so majestic that score is almost irrelevant. One strong hole after another slithers through sand dunes and around fairway mounds that distort distance—a challenge amplified by the wind that whips across the eastern end of the barrier island.

OSPREY POINT

6,871 yards, par 72, 137/72.9
Greens fee: $185 for resort guests,
$205 for nonguests
843-266-4640, kiawahresort.com

Designed by Tom Fazio in 1986, the track weaves between maritime forests and saltwater marshes. Almost every shot here offers a safe option for the timid, so it isn't as punishing as it appears at first. The third hole is a great 175-yard par three across a marsh and through a brisk crosswind. A large ridge divides the green; land on the wrong side of it and two putts will feel like an ace.

TURTLE POINT

7,054 yards, par 72, 141/74.2
Greens fee: $185 for resort guests,
$205 for nonguests
843-266-4050, kiawahresort.com

Jack Nicklaus courses are an acquired taste. Too often the golf plays second fiddle to the housing that lines each hole. At Turtle Point, which opened in 1981, the homes are so close you can almost hear Rush Limbaugh on the kitchen radios. The best stretch comprises three fine oceanfront holes on the back nine, but they stand out not for their strength but because they are at odds with the rest of the property-lined layout. It's still a very enjoyable resort course, but playing here can feel like trespassing.

Kiawah Island (Osprey
Point), South Carolina

COUGAR POINT

6,887 yards, par 72, 134/73.0
Greens fee: $185 for resort guests,
$205 for nonguests
843-266-4020, kiawahresort.com

Gary Player designed this course in 1976, when it was known as Marsh Point. He returned 20 years later for an extreme makeover that retained the original routing and not much else. Despite a nice stretch of holes that skirt the Kiawah River, Cougar remains a distant fourth choice among visitors.

OAK POINT

6,759 yards, par 72, 140/73.8
Greens fee: $185 for resort guests,
$205 for nonguests
843-266-4100, kiawahresort.com

Located just off the island, Oak Point is an old Clyde Johnston design that received a recent facelift. Strictly for novices and families.

WHERE TO STAY

Despite its recent opening, the 255-room **Sanctuary** at Kiawah Island feels as if it's been around for generations. And that's the intent. It epitomizes Southern elegance, but it doesn't come cheap. Rooms start at $399. A resort charge of $25 a day covers tips everywhere except in the restaurants and the spa. **877-683-1234, thesanctuary.com** •• **Kiawah's villas** are still a popular option for foursomes. Rates start at $334 and golf packages are available. **800-654-2924, kiawahresort.com**

WHERE TO EAT

Jasmine Porch, the Sanctuary's casual restaurant, has the welcoming feel of a covered porch and serves fine low-country fare. **877-683-1234, thesanctuary.com** •• Upstairs from the Jasmine Porch, the **Ocean Room** is the hotel's more formal dinner restaurant. The New American cuisine is great. Jackets required for men. **877-683-1234, thesanctuary.com** •• A local favorite on nearby John's Island, **St. John's Island Café** is famous for down-home American food with a Southern flair, including hearty meatloaf and freshly baked bread. **843-**559-9090 •• **McCrady's**, Charleston's first tavern, was built in 1788 and serves fine French-American cuisine. **843-577-0025, mccradysrestaurant.com**

LOCAL KNOWLEDGE

At the **Preservation Society** on King Street, spend 75 cents on Lord Ashley Cooper's *Dictionary of Charlestonese*, a funny primer on the local accent that is part English, part Gullah. **843-722-4630, preservationsociety .com** •• **The Spoleto Festival** is Charleston's feast of opera, dance, and theater and runs from the end of May to mid-June. **843-722-2764, spoletousa.org** •• Enjoy a 60-minute **Golfers' Massage** at the Sanctuary's spa. You'll need to be peeled off the table afterward. $120. **877-683-1234, thesanctuary.com** •• Join the more than 800,000 people who annually visit **Fort Sumter**, a seminal Civil War site. Adults: $13, children: $7. **843-881-7337, nps.gov/fosu** •• Tour the **U.S.S. Yorktown** at Patriot's Point Naval Museum in Charleston harbor. The flight simulator defines the real meaning of "flier." Adults: $14, children: $7. **843-884-2727, patriotspoint .org** •• **Middleton Place** was an 18th-century plantation and is now a National Historic Landmark. Adults: $25, children: $30. **843-556-6020, middletonplace.org** •• **Magnolia Plantation and Gardens**, America's oldest man-made attraction, opened to the public the same year Abraham Lincoln was elected. The gardens are famed for an elaborate maze and a series of ornate bridges. Adults: $14, children: $8. **800-367-3517, magnoliaplantation.com** •• Twenty blocks long and lined with Palmetto trees, **King Street** in downtown Charleston is known as the home of more great antiques than the Champions Tour. Pick up a guide to the area at the Preservation Society. •• The **Palmetto Carriage Company's** one-hour buggy tour highlights Charleston's Southern charms at a leisurely Southern pace. Adults: $19, children: $8. **843-723-8145, carriagetour.com**

GETTING THERE

Kiawah Island is about 30 miles south of Charleston International Airport.

WHEN TO GO

You can play all year here, with average daily highs ranging from the high 50s in January to 89 in August.

MYRTLE BEACH'S SOUTH STRAND

Few golf destinations evoke more "been-there-done-that" than Myrtle Beach. And that's a shame, because nobody has been there and done it all. The 60-mile stretch known as the Grand Strand features 108 courses, 70,000-plus rooms, suites and condos, and more than 1,600 restaurants. Your stay-play-and-eat options are practically infinite. Storm the beach the smart way by choosing a manageable part of the Strand. The South Strand, marked by live oaks cloaked in Spanish moss, runs from Surfside Beach south to Pawleys Island. This is where neon signs, tourist traps, and all-you-can-eat chow halls give way to seafood shanties and boutiques that complement a languid landscape.

WHERE TO PLAY

CALEDONIA GOLF AND FISH CLUB AND TRUE BLUE

Caledonia: 6,526 yards, par 70, 140/72.1
True Blue: 7,062 yards, par 72, 145/74.3
Greens fee: $75–$140
800-483-6800, truebluegolf.com

TOP 100 YOU CAN PLAY

The Caledonia Golf and Fish Club is the South Strand's crown jewel. Eccentric architect Mike Strantz showed restraint with this traditional track set in reedy wetlands. The 383-yard 18th hole—one of the best closers in town—calls for a knee-knocking approach over a coastal lagoon to a green near Caledonia's wrap-around patio. Splashed approaches spark polite sighs from spectators, but a 9-iron to 10 feet might get you a round of applause. Across the road at Strantz's True Blue course—a.k.a. Golf's Heaven and Hell—the architect displays the diabolical streak that fed his rep as a maverick. True Blue's vast waste areas, scattered mounds, and oblique greens have polarized golfers since the course opened in 1998. Strantz tamed his beast in 2000, but the 145 slope from the black tees makes it one of Myrtle's toughest tracks.

TPC OF MYRTLE BEACH

6,950 yards, par 72, 145/74.0
Greens fee: $95–$140
843-357-3399, tpc.com

Another tough hombre, the Tournament Players Club of Myrtle Beach in Murrells Inlet, was designed by Tom Fazio, who clearly prefers beauty to brawn. But the TPC of Myrtle Beach showcases forced carries, tight fairways, and tricky approaches. The 17th is a 193-yarder that demands a tee shot over a pond to a peninsular green. The 538-yard 18th plays as a three-shotter from the tips and as a pure risk-reward challenge from the other four tees. Prince Creek bisects the fairway 300 yards out, forcing long hitters to think twice from the tee.

LITCHFIELD COUNTRY CLUB

6,752 yards, par 72, 130/72.6
Greens fee: $42–$100
800-882-3420, mbn.com

The Willard Byrd–designed Litchfield Country Club on Pawleys Island, one of the original eight courses on the Grand Strand, is an old-school stretch of narrow fairways, sharp doglegs, and small greens. At the 424-yard 11th, the fairway's sharp left turn and a shoebox-size green make four feel like a birdie. Litchfield finishes with a sweeping 406-yarder with a lagoon threatening drives and approach shots.

RIVER CLUB

6,677 yards, par 71, 125/72.2
Greens fee: $45–$107
800-882-3420, mbn.com

In 1985 Litchfield Beach & Golf Resort asked South Carolina native Tom Jackson to design a white-knuckle, championship-caliber course. Today River Club is still one of the area's better tests. Hazards—water, sand, or both—appear on all 18 holes. The layout plays much harder than its yardage suggests. Golfers from up north will feel at home on the slick, A-1 bentgrass greens—a novelty in the Carolina low country.

HERITAGE CLUB

7,005 yards, par 71, 144/74.8
Greens fee: $113
800-229-6187, legendsgolf.com

In 1985 developer Larry Young set out to create one of the South Strand's most scenic tracks on 600 acres along the Waccamaw River. Defying the decade's "more is better" theme, he sprinkled the Heritage Club with bunkers and mounding but let its 300-year-old live oaks and black lagoons play starring roles. For his greens, Young made like a 1980s-vintage Jack Nicklaus and built some of the southeast's most severely sloping surfaces. Architecture buffs ripped them as crazily severe, and a decade later Young smoothed them out.

PAWLEYS PLANTATION GOLF & COUNTRY CLUB

7,026 yards, par 72, 146/75.3
Greens fee: $135
843-237-6200, pawleysplantation.com

In 1988 the developers of Pawleys Plantation were looking for a big name to anchor their resort. They brought in Jack Nicklaus, who was then known for creating courses only scratch golfers could love. With a 146 slope from the back tees, the Golden Bear's layout will never be mistaken for a gentle resort course, but it's far more playable than some of his other 1980s tracks. From the 6,127-yard White Egret tees (130 slope, 70.8 course rating), it's fair and even fun.

WILLBROOK PLANTATION

6,704 yards, par 72, 127/71.8
Greens fee: $38–$100
800-882-3420, mbn.com

Willbrook Plantation is a 1988 Dan Maples design draped over the rolling terrain of two old rice plantations. History lovers enjoy the markers detailing the property's rich traditions; golfers appreciate the elevated tee boxes and gently breaking greens.

TRADITION CLUB

6,875 yards, par 72, 132/72.6
Greens fee: $65–$110
877-599-0888, traditionclub.com

Whereas Willbrook is open and watery, the nearby Tradition Club is tree-lined and relatively dry except for island greens on the par-four 7th and par-three 15th. This 1995 Ron Garl design is also graced with a tony clubhouse that will make you feel like a guest at a private club.

WACHESAW PLANTATION EAST

6,933 yards, par 72, 132/73.6
Greens fee: $125
888-922-0027, wachesawplantationeast.com

This Gary Player design hosted the LPGA's City of Hope Classic in 1998 and 1999. The 500-yard par-five 17th is a rendition of Augusta National's famous 13th hole, complete with a peninsula green fronted by a pond.

WHERE TO STAY

The Litchfield Beach & Golf Resort, a swanky, low-rise oceanfront property, is the preferred address for guests who need pampering. Rates from $99. **888-766-4633, litchfieldbeach .com** • • Pawleys Plantation offers one- to four-bedroom golf villas with living rooms, kitchens, washers and dryers, and outdoor patios. Some suites sport whirlpool tubs and high-speed Internet connections. Rates from $94. **800-367-9959, pawleysplantation.com** • • Hampton Inn Pawleys Island caters to the thrifty set. Rates from $49. **800-426-7866, hamptoninn.com**

WHERE TO EAT

For the freshest low-country catch, head to **Murrells Inlet (843-357-2007, murrellsinletsc .com)**, the self-proclaimed "Seafood Capital of South Carolina." The historic fishing village is home to more than 30 restaurants, most of which serve up fresh grouper, snapper, and crab. • • Local golfers recommend **Russell's Seafood Grille (843-651-0553)** at the inlet's southern end. The house specialties are grouper and mahi-mahi, served broiled, fried, blackened, or grilled. Across the street, the waterside gazebo at the **Hot Fish Club** is where the 20-something crowd goes to be seen. The atmosphere is "post-collegiate meets Jimmy Buffett." **843-357-9175, hotfishclub.com** • • After dinner, catch a local band at **Drunken Jack's (843-651-2044, drunkenjacks.com)** or the **Dead Dog Saloon (843-651-0664, deaddogsaloon.com)**, rustic watering holes with outdoor patios.

LOCAL KNOWLEDGE

Huntington Beach State Park has three miles of beach, a lagoon, a maritime forest, and salt marshes, all of which are home to about 300 species of birds. This is one of the prime bird-watching sites on the East Coast. **843-237-4440, southcarolinaparks.com** • • **Myrtle Beach State Park** also has prime wildlife habitats, as well as a butterfly garden and piers from which you can fish for flounder. **843-238-5325, southcarolinaparks.com** • • One of the largest reptile parks in the world, **Alligator Adventure** features live shows, albino alligators, and Utan, a 2,000-pound crocodile from Thailand, considered the largest in the U.S. **843-361-0789, alligatoradventure.com** • • You might think of Myrtle Beach as the home of kitsch. But you'll get your dose of high culture at **Brookgreen Gardens**, an outdoor sculpture garden with more than 550 works by American artists on display. **843-235-6000, brookgreen.org** • • The 26-acre **NASCAR Speed Park** lets you experience the excitement of NASCAR on seven challenging racetracks. There are also two miniature golf courses. **843-918-TRAK, nascarspeedpark.com**

GETTING THERE

Myrtle Beach is about 150 miles east of Columbia, South Carolina, and 200 miles south of Raleigh, North Carolina. Myrtle Beach International Airport is served by several airlines including US Air, Hooters Air, Continental, and Delta. **myrtlebeachairport.com**

WHEN TO GO

With average daily highs dropping only to 56 degrees in January and 215 sunny days a year, there's no bad time to visit Myrtle Beach. But golfers tend to avoid June through August, the high season for beachgoers, and prefer to visit in spring and fall. If you do visit in the winter months, bring a windbreaker and a sweater.

BEAT THE MILE-HIGH BLUES

Four tips to keep you healthy and fit from the runway to the fairway

A hard-core golf trip usually means stepping onto the first tee shortly after touching down, but arriving at Ballybunion nursing a hangover and a back stiffer than a vintage 1-iron can quickly turn your dream trip into a costly waste of time before you even change your shoes. GOLF MAGAZINE fitness expert Paul Hospenthal offers some tips on how to survive the not-so-friendly skies.

STAY HYDRATED.

It's tempting to open a beer on a flight, but alcohol and caffeine dehydrate you. Drink a four-ounce glass of water every 30 minutes. Take small sips. If you gulp it, you may pass the flight in the tiniest room on the plane.

GET IN THE ZONE.

To minimize jet lag, adjust your sleep pattern by a couple of hours in the two or three days before your flight. On the plane, set your watch for the new time zone and either snooze or stay awake to get into the new rhythm.

STAY LOOSE.

Cramped seats cause tightness and rounded shoulders. Side bends and leg stretches every hour will help. When you reach the course, stretch fully and twist at the waist while holding a club behind your neck.

MOVE IT.

Shake off that sluggish feeling and get your blood flowing with a brisk 15-minute walk around the terminal after you deplane. By the time you get to baggage claim, your clubs will be waiting and ready to go.

MIDWEST

ILLINOIS

MICHIGAN

MINNESOTA

NORTH DAKOTA

WISCONSIN

CHICAGO

NORTHERN MICHIGAN

NORTHERN MINNESOTA

THE NORTH DAKOTA GOLF TRAIL

KOHLER

CHICAGO

CHICAGO The Chicago area boasts about 200 public courses; they come in all shapes and sizes with one to fit every pocketbook and level of player. Of course, with so much else happening in the windy city, people don't think of it as a golf destination. They should. The late Chicagoan Joe Jemsek earned a reputation as America's "patriarch of public golf" for good reason. Jemsek was the first course owner to bring country-club quality to the public. Today the trend toward upscale daily-fee courses is so well established that it is almost impossible to imagine it wasn't forever thus.

WHERE TO PLAY

COG HILL GOLF AND COUNTRY CLUB

No. 1: 6,277 yards, par 72, 126/75.3
No. 2: 6,362 yards, par 75, 124/75.2
No. 3: 6,384 yards, par 72, 125/75.4
No. 4: 7,325 yards, par 72, 142/75.4
Greens fee: $41–$130
866-264-4455, coghillgolf.com

TOP 100 YOU CAN PLAY No. 4

Jemsek's vision of public golf lives on most vividly at Cog Hill—a four-course, 73-hole complex about 15 miles southwest of Chicago in the town of Lemont. No. 4, known as Dubsdread, has hosted the PGA Tour's Western Open since 1991. The 1964 parkland style course designed by Dick Wilson and Joe Lee allows you to drive the ball to generous fairways yet makes you work it into the greens around oak trees and bunkers. The No. 2 (Ravine) course's name comes from the ravines that front most of its greens. The No. 1 (Blue) and No. 3 (Red) courses share nearly the same design: They're more open than the others, and the terrain is not as undulating, but rolling hills can affect your lie.

PINE MEADOW

7,141 yards, par 72, 138/74.6
Greens fee: $95
847-566-4653, pinemeadowgc.com

Located on the property of St. Mary of the Lake Seminary in Mundelein, Pine Meadow has been wildly popular since it opened in the late 1980s. Regarded by locals as one of the top public layouts in Chicago's far northern suburbs, Pine Meadow is a pleasant course to play, thanks to its leafy scenery. But lurking behind the gentle, woodsy facade is a terrific layout that poses a stiff challenge yet rejects the principle of punishment for its own sake. Fairways are generous and most of the greens large, but there are plenty of hills, doglegs, and challenging pin placements.

HERITAGE BLUFFS PUBLIC GOLF CLUB

7,106 yards, par 72, 138/73.9
Greens fee: $25–$46
815-467-7888, channahonpark.org

Chicago-area golfers have been beating a path to this Dick Nugent design, located southwest of the city near Joliet, since it opened in 1993. The course provides a good challenge in a pleasant atmosphere at a very reasonable price. Owned and operated by the Channahon Park District, Heritage Bluffs has a full practice range, putting green, and short-game practice area.

THE GLEN CLUB

7,149 yards, par 72, 138/74.5
Greens fee: $125–$155
847-724-7272, theglenclub.com

TOP 100 YOU CAN PLAY

Located on the former Glenview Naval Airbase in the North Shore suburban town of Glenview, The Glen Club was developed by Kemper Sports Management, which hired Tom Fazio to transform formerly flat runways into idyllic fairways and greens with 40 feet of undulation, five lakes, a stream, and nearly 5,000 trees. On some holes, Fazio's earthmovers imparted a rolling North Carolina drawl to the naturally flat great Midwest.

Hole 2 at Cog Hill Golf and
Country Club (Dubsdread),
Chicago, Illinois

CANTIGNY GOLF CLUB

Lakeside: 3,437 yards, par 36
Woodside: 3,567 yards, par 36
Hillside: 3,394 yards, par 36
Greens fee: $185
630-668-3323, cantignygolf.com

This club, which opened in 1989, 30 miles due west of downtown Chicago, is in the 500-acre Cantigny Park in Wheaton. Robert McCormick, former editor and publisher of the *Chicago Tribune*, left the acreage in his will "for the recreation, instruction, and welfare of the people of the State of Illinois." The park has formal gardens, nature trails, and military and art museums. The Roger Packard–designed Woodside, Lakeside, and Hillside nines have received high praise. In 2000 the Woodside/Lakeside combination came in 50th on the list of GOLF MAGAZINE's Top 100 You Can Play.

VILLAGE LINKS

18 Hole: 7,208 yards, par 72, 136/74.7
9 Hole: 3,303 yards, par 36
Greens fee: $59
630-469-8180, villagelinksgolf.com

The Village Links of Glen Ellyn seems to be the best overall municipal golf facility in the Chicago area. With its 21 lakes and 96 bunkers, the David Gill–designed 18-hole golf course is big and strong enough to serve as host of U.S. Open and Western Open qualifying rounds. The nine-hole executive course caters to juniors and seniors.

ORCHARD VALLEY GOLF COURSE

6,745 yards, par 72, 134/72.8
Greens fee: $39–$59
630-907-0500, orchardvalleygolf.com

Operated by the Fox Valley Park District, Orchard Valley is another example of just how good municipal golf can be. Located about 40 miles west of downtown Chicago in Aurora, this is a course where excitement and fun reign. The first hole is a drivable par four for a power fader, but don't hit it straight through the fairway or you'll fall victim to a sand bunker that seems from the tee box to be oh-so-far-away. Architect Ken Kavanaugh gives players options from the tee between a safe bailout play that will make for a difficult second shot, or a tighter landing that will allow easier access to the green.

THUNDERHAWK GOLF CLUB

7,031 yards, par 72, 136/73.8
Greens fee: $76–$88
847-872-4295, lcfpd.org/thunderhawk

This course, designed by Robert Trent Jones Jr., is operated by the Lake County Forest Preserve District in Beach Park, about 45 miles due north of Chicago. The fairways are generous, but they transition suddenly to very thick native vegetation. Large, undulating fairways afford a wide variety of challenging pin placements. The 16th hole, a 578-yard par five, features a double fairway bordered by water on the right and bunkers on the left. The well-protected green is tucked back-right, demanding an accurate approach.

Hole 18 at Cog Hill Golf and Country Club (Dubsdread), Chicago, Illinois

HARBORSIDE INTERNATIONAL GOLF CENTER

Port Course: 7,164 yards, par 72, 132/75.1
Starboard Course: 7,166 yards, par 72, 132/75.0
Greens fee: $92
312-582-7837, harborsidegolf.com

Located 16 miles south of Chicago on the shores of Lake Calumet, Harborside is an extraordinary story of environmental reclamation. The center is owned by the Illinois Port Authority on a 458-acre former landfill. Dick Nugent of Kemper Lakes fame was hired, and he designed two treeless links courses, because the landfill was capped by a two-foot layer of clay and covered with a liner, making it impossible for trees to develop root systems. On Harborside, you can see the city skyline. If you play the Port course, you can try to match the only presidential hole-in-one in Chicago history. In 2001 Bill Clinton carded his first-ever ace on the 145-yard 6th hole (using a 9-iron). The facility also has a 58-acre practice area with short-game areas and putting greens.

BOLINGBROOK GOLF CLUB

7,104 yards, par 72, 130/73.7
Greens fee: $80–$95
630-771-9400, bolingbrookgolfclub.com

This championship track southwest of Chicago in Bolingbrook was designed by Arthur Hills. Opened in 2002, it features a parkland style layout with open fairways and undulating, fast, medium-sized greens (averaging 5,500 square feet). Water comes into play on 14 holes, and bunkers are plentiful.

WHERE TO STAY

If the nightly live musical acts aren't enough of a draw at **The House of Blues Hotel** on North Dearborn in downtown Chicago, the raucous, scrumptious Sunday gospel brunch will be. Package rates start at $229. **312-245-0333, loewshotels.com**

WHERE TO EAT

At **Lou Mitchell's** on West Jackson Boulevard, the hostess totes a Little Red Riding Hood–style basket of fresh doughnut holes, and you can choose between 19 types of omelets. **312-939-3111** •• **Ann Sather** on Belmont Avenue near Wrigley Field hits a home run with its hearty egg dishes and cinnamon rolls. **773-348-2378, annsather.com** •• Dig into an authentic deep-dish pizza at the original **Pizzeria Uno** on East Ohio. **312-321-1000, unos.com** •• Try the **ESPN Zone** on East Ohio Street for the killer Sudden Death Brownie dessert and the day's sports highlights. **312-644-3776, espnzone .com** •• Four and a half bucks buy you a cold Old Style at the **Cubby Bear** near Wrigley Field. **773-327-1662, cubbybear.com** •• Football

Hall of Famer **Mike Ditka** serves up steaks, chops, fresh fish, and cigars at his namesake restaurant. **312-587-8989; mikeditkaschicago .com** •• Hear history echo off the original 1890 tin ceiling at **John Barleycorn**. During Prohibition, this saloon operated with a front as a Chinese laundry; John Dillinger was a regular. **773-348-8899, johnbarleycorn.com** •• A great closer is dinner at **Harry Caray's** on West Kinzie Street, around the corner from the House of Blues. The Cubs' irrepressible broadcaster passed on to that big booth in the sky in 1998, but his love of food and drink lives. **312-828-0966, harrycarays.com**

LOCAL KNOWLEDGE

After a morning 18, you can do nine in the afternoon—nine innings, that is. The White Sox's **U.S. Cellular Field** boasts a new fan deck over center field, a perch best enjoyed with a Greg Luzinski Polish sausage slathered with grilled onions. Just inside Gate Three, you'll find batting cages and a guy with a radar gun. **312-674-1000, whitesox.com** •• At Grand Avenue station, take the "El" train's Red Line

northbound to the Addison stop and **Wrigley Field** to see the Cubs. **773-404-CUBS, cubs .com** •• The **Magnificent Mile** is a fun, if touristy, stretch of North Michigan Avenue, which includes the Art Institute of Chicago and the Lookingglass Theatre in the Water Tower Water Works building. **312-642-3570, themagnificentmile.com** •• Play the Chicago-themed mini-golf course at **Navy Pier**. **800-595-PIER, navypier.com** •• Visit the elephants and aardvarks at **Lincoln Park Zoo**. **312-742-2000, lpzoo.org** •• **Sears Tower** is North America's tallest building and offers panoramic views of four states from the 103rd floor. Adults: $12, children: $10. **312-875-9696, the-skydeck.com**

GETTING THERE

Chicago O'Hare International Airport is 20 miles northwest of downtown Chicago. **chicago-ord.com**

WHEN TO GO

Courses are in peak condition and temperatures are the mildest from late May to mid-October.

NORTHERN MICHIGAN

Consult five different sources and you will find five different lengths for Michigan's shoreline. But no matter how you measure it, the state has a lot of it—more than 3,000 miles by most estimates, making it second in length only to the shoreline of Alaska. Proximity to water is the main reason northern Michigan is a popular vacation area, but unlike in its more class-conscious East Coast counterparts—Cape Cod and the Hamptons—the golf in northern Michigan is highly accessible, fits a variety of budgets, and is highly rated, with five GOLF MAGAZINE Silver Medal resorts in the area.

WHERE TO PLAY

ARCADIA BLUFFS GOLF COURSE

7,300 yards, par 72, 143/75.1
Greens fee: $75–$180
800-494-8666, arcadiabluffs.com

TOP 100 YOU CAN PLAY

Arcadia Bluffs Golf Club probably has the best golf course sunset east of Pebble Beach. The clubhouse looks down on a landscape that tumbles toward the eponymous precipice, 180 feet above Lake Michigan. But land and sea didn't meet here quite as felicitously as at Pebble Beach—80 acres of forest had to be cleared and elevation changes were built by earth-moving equipment. One hole, the 16th, plays along the lake, but you can see the water from every hole, and there are plenty of elevated tees to enhance the vistas.

GRAND TRAVERSE RESORT

The Bear: 7,065 yards, par 72, 146/76.8
Spruce Run: 6,304 yards, par 72, 130/70.8
The Wolverine: 7,065 yards, par 72, 144/73.9
Greens fee: $95–$140 (The Bear, Spruce Run); $50–$90 (Wolverine)
800-236-1577, grandtraverseresort.com

This GOLF MAGAZINE Silver Medal Resort features three outstanding 18-hole courses with rolling and heavily bunkered terrain and myriad water hazards in the form of streams, creeks, and marshes. Both the Spruce, which has 1,100 spruce trees, and the Wolverine feature open front nines and tight back nines. The Bear, designed by Jack Nicklaus, hosts the annual Michigan Open and could be northern Michigan's most difficult track because of its narrow, tree-lined, terraced fairways and undulating greens.

FOREST DUNES

7,104 yards, par 72, 120/68.7
Greens fee: $75–125
989-275-0700, forestdunesgolf.com

TOP 100 YOU CAN PLAY

This semiprivate Tom Weiskopf design next to Huron National Forest in Roscommon captures the look of a true links. Weiskopf removed sand from two lakes to create nearly 20 acres of rolling "dunes." Framed by bracken, wildflowers, and tall red pines planted by work relief crews in the 1930s (the site had been a farm and orchard that failed because of depleted soil), the firm, fast course was created for purists who like to walk. The final three holes, which face into the prevailing breeze, are as good as anything Weiskopf has done. The 16th is a long par three that plays across a Hell's Half-Acre–style wasteland to a large green with an elephantine hump at its entrance. The 17th, 302 yards from the tips, is a brilliant short par four that parallels an old landing strip used by bootleggers to import Canadian whiskey during Prohibition. The 18th, Eagle Chance, is a 531-yard par five that proceeds from the dunes to a green perched above Lake Ausable. Match all square? Weiskopf built a 117-yard Bye Hole that plays over the lake to a convoluted green with a bunker in its center.

SHANTY CREEK

Cedar River: 6,989 yards, par 72, 144/73.6
Legend: 6,764 yards, par 72, 133/73.6
Schuss Mountain: 6,922 yards,
par 72, 127/73.4
Summit: 6,260 yards, par 71, 120/71.7
Greens fee: $120 (Cedar River, Legend);
$90 (Schuss Mountain); $54 (Summit)
800-678-4111, shantycreek.com

This GOLF MAGAZINE Silver Medal resort, while not directly on Lake Michigan, is just miles from Grand Traverse Bay in Bellaire. The Legend has panoramic views, exceptional greens, and rolling, tree-studded fairways with several water hazards. The course covers seven miles, making carts a requirement. Schuss Mountain is a championship layout with extra large greens and no parallel fairways. Shanty Creek was built on rolling terrain with many strategically placed trees. Lake Bellaire provides a scenic backdrop, and the third tee has such a striking setting that more than 21 weddings have taken place there. The Tom Weiskopf–designed Cedar River is linkslike by comparison to the Legends, but there is a good variety of landscaping, including hilly terrain, hardwoods, and pines.

BAY HARBOR GOLF CLUB

Links: 3,432 yards, par 36
Preserve: 3,378 yards, par 36
Quarry: 3,348 yards, par 36
Greens fee: $100–$199
231-439-4028, bayharborgolf.com

TOP 100 YOU CAN PLAY

Located in Bay Harbor, these layouts combine to form the longest coastline of any course in the U.S. There is diverse topography among the nines. The Links traverses high bluffs above Lake Michigan, the Quarry is surrounded by cliffs, and the Preserve is wooded. If you only have time for 18, play the Links-Quarry. You start high above the lake, and the water can be a distraction on several holes. The back nine turns into the quarry before returning toward the water for the final two holes. The most spectacular hole is the 17th—the Quarry's 8th. From the elevated tee, the green almost looks as though it sits in the water. Because of the change in elevation, a crisply struck tee shot seems to hang forever against the sky and water before falling to earth and (hopefully) finding the shallow.

BOYNE HIGHLANDS RESORT AND COUNTRY CLUB

Arthur Hills: 7,312 yards, par 73, 144/76.4
The Heather: 6,890 yards, par 72, 136/74.0
Donald Ross Memorial: 6,814 yards,
par 72, 136/75.5
The Moor: 6,809 yards, par 72, 135/74.6
Greens fee: $65–$134 (Arthur Hills,
The Heather); $60–$109 (Donald Ross
Memorial); $40–$79 (The Moor)
800-462-6963, boynehighlands.com

The most recent addition to this Silver Medalist resort is the Arthur Hills course, which features enormous sand traps and intimidating water holes. Every hole except the 10th on the Donald Ross Memorial replicates one of the design master's originals. The 10th copies the 14th at Royal Dornoch in Scotland, Ross' hometown. The Heather has a rural feel and wide, tree-lined fairways. The Moor, the favorite of summer-time resident and GOLF MAGAZINE Top 100 Teacher Jim Flick, features numerous doglegs and marshes, as well as water hazards on 11 holes. All the courses were built at the base of a valley in Harbor Springs.

LAKEWOOD SHORES

Blackshire: 6,898 yards, par 72, 125/75.0
Gailes: 6,954 yards, par 72, 138/75.0
Serradella: 6,806 yards, par 72, 124/72.3
Greens fee: $62 (Blackshire, Gailes);
$35 (Serradella)
800-882-2493, lakewoodshores.com

TOP 100 YOU CAN PLAY

Lakewood Shores is less than a mile from Lake Huron just outside Oscoda. The water is not visible, but its presence is discernible, especially at the Gailes. Most U.S. courses that are advertised as links are links-style at best, cosmetically resembling the seaside courses of Great Britain and Ireland. But gorse, fescue, and heather do not a links make. The Gailes is a true links. It plays fast and firm, and every shot gives you at least two options. The Blackshire is built in the Pine Valley tradition, although the course also evokes a different Pine—Pinehurst. Serradella is a gorgeously landscaped parkland track with few water hazards, wide fairways, and more than 50,000 flowers.

Hole 6 at Treetops
Sylvan Resort (Jones),
North Michigan

TREETOPS SYLVAN RESORT

Premier: 6,832 yards, par 72, slope 136/73.6
Masterpiece: 7,060 yards, par 71, 144/75.5
Signature: 6,653 yards, par 70, 140/72.8
Tradition: 6,467 yards, par 70, 122/70.3
Greens fee: $87–$115 (Premier, Masterpiece,
Signature); $68 (Tradition)
989-732-6711, treetops.com

Treetops, about an hour inland in Gaylord off Interstate 75, is well worth the detour from the coast. All four courses are laid out on hilly terrain, with many elevated tee boxes. The Masterpiece, with its small, fast greens and narrow, tree-lined fairways designed by Robert Trent Jones Sr., is the most difficult layout. The Premier and the Signature courses, designed by Tom Fazio and GOLF MAGAZINE Top 100 Teacher Rick Smith, respectively, have more forgiving, although still tree-lined, fairways and larger greens. The Tradition was designed on gently rolling, wooded land for players who like to walk; carts aren't allowed but caddies are available. Smith also has an exceptional golf academy on site.

Hole 6 at Marquette
Golf Club (Greywalls),
North Michigan

MARQUETTE GOLF CLUB

Greywalls: 6,828 yards, par 72, 144/73.0
Heritage: 6,260 yards, par 71, 124/70
Greens fee: $85–$125
866-678-7171, marquettegolfclub.com

Architect Mike DeVries grabbed the rugged Greywalls site, in Marquette, by the shoulders and shook loose 18 distinctive challenges in a rough-and-tumble layout. The result is a distinctive course that made GOLF MAGAZINE's 2005 Top 10 You Can Play list. DeVries used the exposed granite here as jagged hazards alongside the fairways and as aiming points behind greens. Views of Lake Superior greet you on the first tee, and everything that follows—from the approach on the 579-yard par-five 1st hole to the forested, downhill, saddle-shaped 18th fairway—lives up to the lake's name. The less spectacular but wholly enjoyable Heritage has a flat front nine and hilly back nine; the 15th tee overlooks the lake.

WHERE TO STAY

Grand Traverse Resort sits on 900 acres in the northwest corner of Michigan's Lower Peninsula along the shores of Lake Michigan's East Grand Traverse Bay. It's just a 10-minute drive from Traverse City's Cherry Capital Airport and has more than 400 rooms in the Hotel and Tower and 190 condominiums. Rates start at $139. **800-236-1577, grandtraverseresort.com** ● ●

 The Inn at Bay Harbor on Lake Michigan is a waterfront Victorian–style hotel, where you can nap on a hammock, play croquet, or enjoy a game of chess on an oversize board with two-foot-high pieces—all within feet of Little Traverse Bay. Rooms start at $115. **888-229-4272, bayharbor.com** ● ● Though not directly on Lake Michigan, **Shanty Creek**, a GOLF MAGAZINE Silver Medalist, is just a few miles from Grand Traverse Bay. Options include the Lodge at Cedar River's 85 luxury suite condominiums, guest rooms overlooking Lake Bellaire at Summit Village, or villas and condos at Schuss Village at the foot of Schuss Mountain. Rates from $55. **800-678-4111, shantycreek.com** ● ●

 Boyne Highlands Resort, a GOLF MAGAZINE Silver Medalist, is just across Little Traverse Bay from Bay Harbor and three miles inland from the coastal town of Harbor Springs. Options include everything from rooms at the Main Lodge to cottages and town houses. Rates from $72. **800-462-6963, boynehighlands.com** ● ●

 Treetops Resort lies just off Interstate 75, about an hour inland in Gaylord. Its 252 guest rooms are spread throughout the Lodge and Inn, as well as in chalets and condos. Rates from $99. **989-732-6711, treetops.com** ● ● Nearly all the great golf development in Northern Michigan has been to the west. The notable exception is the 80-room **Lakewood Shores**, a no-frills resort just outside the quiet town of Oscoda. Rates from $68. **800-882-2493, lakewoodshores.com**

WHERE TO EAT

The restaurant and lounge **Trillium** occupies the top floors of the Grand Traverse Resort's tower, 16 stories up. From here, you can sample North Woods specialties while you look out over the bay and the Bear golf course. **800-236-1577, grandtraverseresort.com** ● ● Northern Michigan's foodies make a pilgrimage to the **Rowe Inn** in Ellsworth, where French regional cuisine blends seamlessly with local specialties. **231-588-7351, roweinn.com** ● ● **Tapawingo**, another fine restaurant in Ellsworth, features local cuisine prepared by chef/owner Pete Peterson, who has on occasion been asked to cook for the White House and heads of state. **231-588-7971, tapawingo.net** ● ● In Petoskey, cozy **Chandlers**, which is almost like

a California bistro, is a great place to sip a glass of wine and relax. In the summer you can sit on the patio, and if it's cool, you can watch the chef prepare your meal from your table. **231-347-2981**

LOCAL KNOWLEDGE

In early July, Traverse City pulls out all the stops with its **National Cherry Festival**. There's a main stage with live music, plenty of good food, sports competitions, and parades. **213-947-4230, cherryfestival.org** ● ● At the tip of the Lower Peninsula, where it nearly meets the Upper Peninsula, Lake Michigan becomes Lake Huron, forming a strait. **Mackinac Island** sits at this confluence of land and water, which is why the British used the island as a fort. A popular tourist destination, the island is unique for its lack of motorized transportation. Once you reach the island by ferry, you can explore by foot, bicycle, or horse-drawn buggy. **mackinac.com**

GETTING THERE

Cherry Capital Airport in Traverse City is served by more than 30 airlines. **tvcairport.com**

WHEN TO GO

Peak golf season falls during peak tourist season: The area is abuzz with visitors from Memorial Day to Labor Day.

NORTHERN MINNESOTA

NORTHERN MINNESOTA Long a popular destination for fishing in the summer and deer and duck hunting in the fall, northern Minnesota in the past decade has begun to draw golfers with top-notch courses. The area around Lake Mille Lacs and the many lakes near Brainerd have developed into a hotbed of family-style resorts that offer outstanding courses, as well as fishing, water sports, hiking, and camping. The focal points are Brainerd and the nearby summer town of Nisswa, about 150 miles north of the Twin Cities.

WHERE TO PLAY

THE CLASSIC COURSE AT MADDEN'S ON GULL LAKE

7,102 yards, par 72, 143/75.0
Greens fee: $90–$105
800-642-5563, maddens.com

No trip to the Brainerd would be complete without a stop at the Classic. Its name is appropriate—it is one of the finest daily-fee courses in Minnesota and ranks with top private clubs in both natural beauty and challenge. Designed by Scott Hoffman, who has worked as the superintendent for the other family-style courses at Madden's Resort since 1975, the course opened in 1997. The Classic melds tall hardwoods and pines with creeks and ponds, which come into play on 13 holes. Each hole is separate, flowing effortlessly into the next. There is quiet solitude here, interrupted only by the chirping of birds.

GRAND VIEW LODGE

Deacon's Lodge: 6,964 yards, par 72, 126/71.7
Preserve: 6,601 yards, par 72, 140/72.8
The Lakes Nine at the Pines:
3,414 yards, par 36
The Woods Nine at The Pines:
3,460 yards, par 36
The March Nine at The Pines:
3,423 yards, par 36
The Garden: 2,502 yards, par 35
Greens fee: $60–$106
800-432-3788, grandviewlodge.com

TOP 100 YOU CAN PLAY

Deacon's Lodge opened in Brainerd in 1999 and is hailed by many as Arnold Palmer's best design. The course is set among lakes, wetlands, and beautiful forest. The feel, thanks to numerous waste bunkers, is similar to that of Pine Valley. The Preserve opened in 1996 and offers rolling hills, 14 elevated tees, 75 feet of elevation changes, and 40 acres of wetlands. Golf in Brainerd began with the Pines' three nines. The Marsh plays around a vast marshland area. The resort's signature hole is the Lakes' 7th, a 152-yard, par three with a tee shot over water to a green framed by large timbers. The Lakes' 5th, a 356-yard par four, requires a blind approach shot over water to the green. Most of the greens on the Pines' three nines are large.

THE LEGACY COURSES AT THE CRAGUNS

Legacy Walk: 6,879 yards, par 72, 149/74.4
Bobby: 6,755 yards, par 72 , 145/74.0
Greens fee: $59–$109
800-272-4867, craguns.com

These parkland-style courses in Brainerd are situated in a naturally wooded marshland area, so water frequently comes into play. Narrow, undulating fairways favor the shot-maker, meaning that placement is essential to a good score. The greens are always well maintained and play very true. Man-made waterfalls along the course add a pleasing aesthetic.

RUTTGER'S BAY LAKE LODGE

Lakes: 6,774 yards, par 72, 131/72.2
Lodge Nine: 2,285 yards, par 34
Greens fee: $19–$49
800-450-4545, ruttgers.com

Located in Deerwood, the charming well-kept Lakes Course has 10 holes that make good use of the site's two lakes, Goose and Bass. The greens are large, and the hilly fairways are tree-lined, giving the course a north woods flavor. The signature hole is No. 18, a 233-yard par three that requires a tee shot over water to a slightly elevated, double-tiered green. The Lodge Nine was the first resort course in Minnesota. From its rough-hewn beginnings in 1920, it has evolved into an excellent course for beginners or experienced players who wish to work on their short game.

IZATY'S GOLF & YACHT CLUB

Black Brook: 6,867 yards, par 72, 140/74.2
Sanctuary: 6,646 yards, par 72, 134/72.6
Greens fee: $59–$69
800-533-1728, izatys.com

Located in Onamia, both layouts are routed through acres of natural water and marsh hazards, deciduous trees, and wildflowers, with plenty of railroad ties, pot bunkers, and undulating greens accenting the designs. The Minnesota PGA Championship was played on the Sanctuary from 1992 to 1994. The most challenging hole is No. 2, a 604-yard par five. Black Brook's signature par-three 14th hole sits hard on Lake Mille Lacs.

WHERE TO STAY

 A perennial GOLF MAGAZINE Silver Medal Resort, **Grand View Lodge** offers charming North Woods accommodations, from cabins on Gull Lake to fairway villas. Rates from $174. **800-432-3788, grandviewlodge.com** • • With 1,000 acres along Gull Lake, great views abound from the cozy, cabin-style rooms at **Madden's on Gull Lake**. Packages start at $165. **218-829-2811, maddens.com** • • There are more than 200 accommodation options at **Craguns Resort on Gull Lake**, from lakeside and hilltop cabins to lake-view hotel rooms. Rates from $99. **800-272-4867, craguns.com** • • The family-run **Ruttger's Bay Lake Lodge**, opened in 1898, offers villas, course-side condominiums, lakeside cottages, and lodge rooms, starting at $90. **800-450-4545, ruttgers.com** • • Just 90 minutes from the Twin Cities on Lake Mille Lacs, **Izaty's Golf & Yacht Club** has a full-service marina, as well as lodge, cabin, villa, and town-house accommodations. Rates from $66. **800-533-1728, izatys.com**

WHERE TO EAT

Everything from the soups to the desserts is homemade at **Iven's on the Bay**, a Brainerd Lakes institution known for its seafood and martini bar. **218-829-9872, ivensonthebay .com** • • Everyone can find something to enjoy at **Ernies on Gull Lake**, which has salads, sandwiches, burgers, seafood, and dishes with Italian and Cajun flare. **218-829-3918, erniesongull.com** • • The **Timberjack Smokehouse and Saloon** in Pequot Lakes is serious about its smoke, using special woods and seasonings on its chicken, ribs, and seafood. **218-568-6070, timberjacksmokehouse.com**

LOCAL KNOWLEDGE

Fishermen flocked to the Brainerd area long before golf was on the map here. The lakes are full of walleye, crappie, small- and large-mouth bass, perch, and northern pike. See **brainerd .com** for a list of fishing guides. • • You can cruise the lakes on a rented boat even if you're not up to catching dinner. See **brainerd.com** for

rental shops. • • Nearly every town here has a statue of local icon Paul Bunyan; you can bike, hike, or rollerblade through 14 of them on 57 paved miles of the 100-mile-long Paul Bunyan Trail. **paulbunyantrail.com**

GETTING THERE

The destination is served by Highway 2 and Interstate 35 and commuter flights from Minneapolis-St. Paul International Airport. **mspairport.com**

WHEN TO GO

Memorial Day to Labor Day is peak season. Course conditions and foliage are at their peak and crowds are virtually non-existent in the fall, especially on weekdays.

Hole 2 at Madden's
on Gull Lake (Classic),
Brainerd, Minnesota

THE NORTH DAKOTA GOLF TRAIL

Two things will stand out on your first trip to western North Dakota, just as they did for Lewis and Clark 200 years ago—first, the savage, rugged beauty of the Badlands, and second, the appalling lack of cellular-phone service. (While building Fort Mandan, Lewis is said to have heaved his BlackBerry into Lake Sakakawea.) "NoDak" is home to some pretty fantastic (and wildly cheap) golf. Whether you're on the 20-course Lewis and Clark Golf Trail (lewisandclarkgolftrail.com) or cherry-picking its best three tracks on the roughly 500-mile Triple Challenge from Bismarck to Medora to Williston, as detailed here, you'll be doing plenty of driving. Here are a few tips. Budget at least four days for this Old West adventure. Don't tell your cardiologist about the steak fondue dinner. And lay off the Fargo jokes—that's eastern North Dakota.

WHERE TO PLAY

HAWKTREE GOLF CLUB

7,085 yards, par 72, 137/75.2
Greens fee: $60
888-465-4295, hawktree.com

THRIFTY 50

A mere 15 minutes from the airport, in Bismarck, Hawktree is a bucolic track with few trees and wide-open vistas. As at Montana's acclaimed Old Works Golf Course, the bunkers are filled with black coal slag. You'll see a few historical tokens along the way, giving architect Jim Engh's topsy-turvy design a distinct sense of place. An old broken-down wagon has been left to rot in the long grass to the right of the second green, and a pair of rusted windmills stands guard over the 4th and 14th holes. Myrtle Beach it's not. The downhill, 164-yard 3rd hole is one of the prettiest par threes you'll ever see without water, with its recessed sliver of green framed by thick rough.

BULLY PULPIT GOLF COURSE

7,166 yards, par 72, 133/75.4
Greens fee: $50
800-633-6721, medora.com

Bully Pulpit is in Medora, a two-hour drive west of Bismarck on Interstate 94 (take Exit 27). When architect Michael Hurdzan heard about Bully Pulpit, he says he "had no interest in going someplace you can't get to." When he got there, he was so struck by the scenery—towering buttes, jaw-dropping chasms, and bright-orange "burning" rock—he cut his fee to make sure he got the job. The result is a terrible beauty that made GOLF MAGAZINE's Top 10 You Can Play in 2004. The back nine gives Bully its true swagger. A mammoth wall of soft, brown rock—a gateway to the Badlands—backdrops the green of the par-five 11th hole. Before long, you're playing through surreal spires and majestic buttes.

THE LINKS OF NORTH DAKOTA

7,092 yards, par 72, 128/75.1
Greens fee: $50
701-568-2600, thelinksofnorthdakota.com

THRIFTY 50

Red Mike, named for a notorious 19th-century horse thief who was buried there, is in Ray, a four-hour drive west and north of Bismarck. Yes, that's a very long haul, but then it's a long trip to Scotland, too. From the gnarly, Pro V1–filled rough to the views of Lake Sakakawea, Red Mike is a pure links experience, inland style. Architect Stephen Kay moved very little earth on the bluffs overlooking the lake. There is no water to hit into, just native grasses and 82 bunkers. You'll feel a sense of pride and wonder here—pride that you put in the drive-time necessary to find the place and wonder that such a track exists in central nowhere.

WHERE TO STAY

The **Best Western Ramkota Hotel** in Bismarck is close to downtown and provides access to Hawktree, Riverwood, and Prairie West. Rates from $74. **701-258-7700, ramkota.com** •• In Medora the **Badlands Motel**, the **Bunkhouse**, **Rough Riders Hotel**, and **AmericInn** are less than a five-minute drive from Bully Pulpit. The AmericInn offers the most updated amenities; the Bunkhouse the most modest. Rates range from $60 to $95. **800-633-3444, americinn .com** •• The **El Rancho Motor Hotel** in Williston is just 25 minutes from the Links of North Dakota. Rooms are $54.95, double-occupancy, and include refrigerators. **888-452-3706, elranchomotel.net**

WHERE TO EAT

Good aromas abound at the classy **Bismarck Bistro**, where the menu features such eccentric fare as a sautéed Montana ostrich. **701-224-8800** •• At 6 P.M. at the **Pitchfork Steak Fondue** at 3422 Chateau Road, Medora, the chef starts slapping hundreds of rib eye steaks

onto, yes, pitchforks, before he cooks them in giant vats of boiling vegetable oil. Diners at this open-air, cafeteria-style setup sit at picnic tables on a covered terrace overlooking the Badlands. **800-633-6721, medora.com** •• For the less adventurous, downtown Medora also has **Maltese Burger**, **Badlands Pizza Parlor** and the **Marquis de Mores Ice Cream Parlor and Medora Fudge Depot**. **800-633-6721, medora .com** •• In Williston the **El Rancho Motor Hotel** dining room and coffee shop serves breakfast, lunch, and dinner. Try the walleye—right out of Lake Sakakawea—and homemade pie for dessert. **888-452-3706, elranchomotel.net**

LOCAL KNOWLEDGE

Rent a mountain bike at **Dakota Cyclery Mountain Bike Adventures** on Main Street and 3rd Avenue, Medora. **701-623-4808, dakotacyclery.com** •• Learn about Harold Schafer, inventor of Glass Wax and a patron of Medora, at the **Schafer Heritage Center and Sheila Schafer Art Gallery**, open daily 10 A.M. to 6 P.M. (admission is free). **800-633-6721** ••

Make your own teddy bear at the new **Teddy's Bear** shop on Main and 3rd Avenue in Medora. **701-623-1503** •• Saddle up for a trail ride at the **Medora Riding Stables**. $17 per hour, ages 6 and up. **800-633-6721** •• Don't miss the **Medora Musical** in the Burning Hills Amphitheater. The old meat-packing town of Medora was left for dead until Harold Schafer restored it in the early 1960s. The Medora Musical celebrates its 40th anniversary this season. The outdoor amphitheater fits naturally into the walls of a ravine. The show is clean family entertainment, and kids will appreciate the invitation to sing along with the on-stage band, the Coal Diggers. Adults: $75, children: $55. **800-633-6721, medora.com**

GETTING THERE

The Bismarck airport has direct flights from Denver, Minneapolis, and Las Vegas.

WHEN TO GO

The height of summer—June through August—to early fall is the best time for golf.

SECOND-TIER TRACKS

It's a big state—break up the driving with a quick 18 on one of these lesser-known courses:

Prairie West Golf Course

Prairie West in Mandan features scenic, environmentally sensitive grasses off the fairways for the native ducklings, geese, and other critters. The pretty 506-yard, par-five 6th hole is protected by water to the left and a channel in front of the green. *6,681 yards, par 72, 127/71.6, Greens fee: $20, 701-667-3222*

Riverwood Golf Club

The opposite of wide-open Hawktree, Riverwood Golf Club in Bismarck is so long (6,888) and tight—the fairways are lined with cottonwood trees—you'll want to use anything you can hit straight off the tee. *6,888 yards, par 72, 132/73.2, Greens fee: $30, 701-222-6462*

Heart River Municipal Golf Course

Heart River in Dickinson is a tale of two nines. The front, built in 1983, is flat; the original nine (now the back) is chock-a-block with water and trees. *6,734 yards, par 72, 114/71.2, Greens fee: $18, 701-225-9412*

Souris Valley Golf Club

A half-hour outside Minot, Souris Valley features fairly open fairways and the Souris River on eight holes. The adjacent Jack Hoven Wee Links nine-holer is for kids 12 and under and costs only $1, $5 for an adult accompanied by a child. *6,759 yards, par 73, 125/72.5, Greens fee: $19, 701-857-4189*

Painted Woods Golf Course

Painted Woods is a cute nine-holer just off Highway 83, 35 miles north of Bismarck in Washburn. *5,958 yards, par 72, 108/67.0, Greens fee: $15, 701-462-8480*

Hole 12 at
Whistling Straits
(Straits), Kohler,
Wisconsin

KOHLER
It's been more than a decade since Wisconsin first made a significant blip on golf's radar. In 1996 Tiger Woods walked to the tee at Brown Deer Golf Course and struck the first blow of his professional career, at the Greater Milwaukee Open. Woods hasn't been back since, but the Badger State returned to the spotlight in August of 2004, when the PGA Championship was played on one of the four courses that are part of plumbing magnate Herb Kohler's American Club near Kohler, 50 miles north of Milwaukee. Vijay Singh won the championship at Whistling Straits, which, with its sister club, Blackwolf Run, constitutes Wisconsin's best double act since Laverne and Shirley.

WHERE TO PLAY

BROWN DEER GOLF COURSE

6,759 yards, par 71, 132/72.6
Greens fee: $77–$84
414-352-8080, browndeergolfclub.org

This county course in Milwaukee is worth a stop on your way to or from the airport, since it has hosted the Greater Michigan Open since 1994. It's the PGA Tour's second-shortest venue (only Indian Wells at the Bob Hope Chrysler Classic is shorter). Designed in 1929 by George Hansen, Brown Deer is like the players who tend to win here—solid but unspectacular. The roster of GMO champions features more workhorses—Kenny Perry, Jeff Sluman—than showy thoroughbreds. Brown Deer has generous fairways and gentle doglegs but no shortage of subtle trouble.

BLACKWOLF RUN

River Course: 6,991 yards, par 72, 148/74.4
Meadow Valleys: 7,142 yards, par 72, 144/74.6
Greens fee: $189–$214
800-344-2838, destinationkohler.com

TOP 100 YOU CAN PLAY
TOP 100 IN THE U.S.

Both of these Pete Dye courses are part of the American Club, which is less than five minutes away. The River is about as bucolic as golf gets, particularly the salmon leaping in the namesake Sheboygan near the elevated tee at the 419-yard 5th hole. The plunge from tee to fairway here is as steep as the climb to the putting surface, where a perilous slope to the right makes for a near-impossible up-and-in. At Meadow Valleys, Dye used slopes and bunkers to distort distance and depth perception. According to one veteran ranger, the 565-yard 4th generates more gripes about unfair hole locations than any other hole. This is no surprise—the putting surface is as small and wrinkled as a raisin. The 458-yard 18th has a quirky touch: two greens.

WHISTLING STRAITS

Straits: 7,362 yards, par 72, 151/76.7
Irish: 7,201 yards, par 72, 146/75.6
Greens fee: $325 (Straits); $53–196 (Irish)
800-344-2838, destinationkohler.com

TOP 100 YOU CAN PLAY
TOP 100 IN THE U.S. } Straits
TOP 100 IN THE WORLD

TOP 100 YOU CAN PLAY Irish

This property in Sheboygan was flat before Dye shaped enough bluffs and hills to give a fair imitation of seaside Ireland. The resulting Straits course might one day compete with the Ocean course at Kiawah Island as Dye's enduring masterpiece. The walking-only track is a daunting test hard on the cliffs above Lake Michigan. The dominant feature, after the views, is the bunkering—there are several hundred bunkers, from the bee-sting-sized variety to gaping wounds. The 18th hole is a strenuous par four of 489 yards. Opt for an aggressive line off the tee, and you'd better have 270 yards left in the tank to clear a big grassy ravine. The huge green is nearly cross-shaped, which cynics might suggest is a coy hint at a crucifixion. The Irish suffers from its proximity to the Straits but, like all four of the Kohler courses, has earned a place on GOLF MAGAZINE's Top 100 You Can Play. The 160-yard 6th is a sandy version of Dye's famous island green at the TPC of Sawgrass, with the dance floor perched in the middle of a gargantuan bunker. The closing stretch is typically brutal Dye. The 15th and 16th holes are parallel two-shotters measuring more than 470 yards each, and the lay-up area on the 558-yard finisher is the width of a goose's neck.

WHERE TO STAY

 The epicenter of Kohler, Wisconsin, a "garden community at industry's gate," is **The American Club**. The red-brick, slate-roofed lodge, originally built as a dormitory for immigrant workers, was transformed in the 1980s into a world-class hotel, its interior courtyards graced by themed gardens and the guest-room bathrooms decorated with Kohler's prettiest fixtures. (You may never want to leave the shower!) There's also a Kohler Waters Spa that has a glass-enclosed rooftop deck with a whirlpool, fireplace, and lounge. Rates from $109. **800-344-2838, destinationkohler.com**

WHERE TO EAT

Biro Restaurant and Biro Wine Bar on New York Avenue in Sheboygan serves upscale, European–inspired cuisine. The restaurant is more intimate, with 36 seats, while the more casual Wine Bar specializes in tapas. **920-451-0333, kitchensofbiro.com** •• **Il Ritrovo** and **Trattoria Stefano** on 8th Street in Sheboygan

are owned by the same purveyor. The more casual Il Ritrovo features wood-fired pizzas and has an adjoining Italian specialty store and deli, whereas Trattoria Steffano serves authentic Italian specialties in a romantic setting. **920-803-7516** •• You can't go wrong with a meal at any of the American Club's 10 dining establishments; they range from the casual pub-style **Horse and Plow** to the award-winning **Immigrant Restaurant**, which serves contemporary cuisine in six rooms decorated in the style of early Wisconsin settlers. **800-344-2838, destinationkohler.com**

LOCAL KNOWLEDGE

At the **Miller Brewing Company** In Milwaukee, you can see how brews are made and sample the finished product. It's a nice place to wash down the Milwaukee and Kohler combo, which has some of the finest public-access golf you'll find between Bethpage Black and Pebble Beach. **414-931-2000, millerbrewing.com** •• The annual **Kohler Food & Wine Experience**

is held each October and includes a weekend of culinary demonstrations, food and wine seminars, and tastings. **destinationkohler.com** •• The **Kohler Design Center** is free and open to the public daily and offers renovation advice from design professionals as well as factory tours. **destinationkohler.com**

GETTING THERE

From Milwaukee's General Mitchell Airport, a 20-minute drive brings you to Brown Deer. From there, it's an hour-long cruise north on Interstate 43 to the village of Kohler and the American Club.

WHEN TO GO

High season is Memorial Day to Labor Day. If you play Whistling Straits in the spring or fall, expect better hotel rates, but also plenty of fog. It can be so dense you might not see the greens, even on par threes.

COLLEGE COURSES THAT MAKE THE GRADE

Colleges aren't just for toga parties; they also have subsidized golf. These schools let post-grads like you play, too. Your honor, professor.

ARIZONA STATE
THE KARSTEN GOLF COURSE
Tempe, AZ
7,026 yards, par 72, 132/74.1
Greens fee: $37–$89
480-921-8070, asukarsten.com
Alums include Phil Mickelson, Billy Mayfair, and Paul Casey.

DUKE UNIVERSITY
WASHINGTON DUKE
Durham, NC
7,127 yards, par 72, 139/74.5
Greens fee: $85
919-681-2288, washingtondukeinn.com
A well-bunkered romp through the Carolina pines.

NEW MEXICO STATE UNIVERSITY
NMSU GOLF COURSE
Las Cruces, NM
7,044 yards, par 72, NA
Greens fee: $25
505-646-3219, nmsu.edu/~golf
This three-time host of the NCAA Championships has huge greens and expansive fairways.

OKLAHOMA STATE UNIVERSITY
KARSTEN CREEK
Stillwater, OK
7,285 yards, par 72, NA
Greens fee: $250
405-743-1658, karstencreek.net
Cowboy alums include Scott Verplank and Charles Howell III.

PURDUE UNIVERSITY
BIRCK BOILERMAKER
West Lafayette, IN
Kampen: 7,333 yards, par 72, 145/76.5
Ackerman Hills: 6,436 yards, par 72, 124/70.3
Greens fee: $28–$45
765-494-3216, purdue.edu/Athletics/golf
You'll need a boilermaker after battling Pete Dye's waste bunkers.

UNIVERSITY OF ARIZONA
ARIZONA NATIONAL
Tucson, AZ
6,785 yards, par 71, 146/72.4
Greens fee: $65
520-749-3636, arizonanationalgolfclub.com
Jim Furyk and Annika Sorenstam are both former Wildcats.

UNIVERSITY OF WISCONSIN
UNIVERSITY RIDGE GOLF COURSE
Verona, WI
6,888 yards, par 72, 142/73.2
Greens fee: $36–$69
800-897-4343, universityridge.com
The namesake "ridge" gives this Robert Trent Jones course its bumpy, rolling character.

WEST

ARIZONA

SCOTTSDALE-PHOENIX
TUCSON

CALIFORNIA

NAPA
SAN FRANCISCO TO PEBBLE BEACH
SAN DIEGO AREA
PALM SPRINGS

COLORADO

VAIL VALLEY

NEVADA

LAS VEGAS
LAKE TAHOE
RENO

TEXAS

HOUSTON
SAN ANTONIO

UTAH TO MONTANA, IDAHO, AND WYOMING

SALT LAKE CITY
SALT LAKE CITY TO ANACONDA
SALT LAKE CITY TO SUN VALLEY
SALT LAKE CITY TO JACKSON HOLE

SCOTTSDALE-PHOENIX

There's nothing else like desert golf. If you've played only where the grass is lush, the trees are tall, and the sand is all in the bunkers, you can't fathom the difference. Every golfer should feel the odd mix of fear and exhilaration you get looking from an elevated tee over a cactus-filled gully to that small patch of grass you *have* to hit—or else. Home to 200 golf courses and more than 40 PGA Tour players, the Scottsdale-Phoenix area was the epicenter of the 1990s course-building boom. Fairways lurk behind practically every cactus and you'll find everything from target-style desert courses to lush, parkland-style tracks.

WHERE TO PLAY

BEAR CREEK GOLF COURSE

Bear: 6,832 yards, par 71, 118/71.7
Cub: 3,500 yards, par 59
Greens fee: $20–$49
480-883-8200
bearcreekgolfclubarizona.com

Southeast of Phoenix, in the East Valley on Riggs Road, lies the Bear Creek Golf Course. Both courses, created by Nicklaus Design with Jack Nicklaus' son-in-law Bill O'Leary serving as the designer, have a wide-open links feel, with wind a factor in the afternoon. Keep the ball low and you can run up approach shots through openings on every hole.

THE BOULDERS

South: 6,726 yards, par 71, 140/73.6
North: 6,811 yards, par 72, 137/73.9
Greens fee: $75–$290
866-397-6520, theboulders.com

TOP 100 YOU CAN PLAY South

These outstanding, scenic Jay Morrish–designed courses about 30 minutes north of downtown Phoenix hopscotch over arroyos and around cacti. The courses are continually alternated, allowing one to be kept private while the other is used by Boulders Resort guests. The natural desert terrain frames the fairways and in many cases, shows up in the middle too, so accuracy is a must.

GRAYHAWK GOLF CLUB

Talon: 6,973 yards, par 72, 143/73.6
Raptor: 7,135 yards, par 72, 143/74.1
Greens fee: $50–$225
480-502-1800, grayhawkgolf.com

TOP 100 YOU CAN PLAY Talon

Just northeast of Scottsdale, Grayhawk opened in 1994 and regularly hosts CBS announcers Peter Kostis (a GOLF MAGAZINE columnist) and Gary McCord, as well as young hotshots Aaron Baddeley and Paul Casey. Grayhawk was Phil Mickelson's backyard until he moved to Southern California. His memorabilia still festoon Phil's Grill, the laid-back 19th hole. Both courses have ample rough between their wide-open fairways and the desert beyond. The Talon, designed by David Graham and Gary Panks, features extremely large and undulating elevated greens and panoramic views of the McDowell Mountains and Phoenix Valley. Tom Fazio's Raptor course once hosted Tiger Woods' charity tournament. Its closing hole—a 521-yarder with an approach over a large lake—isn't made any easier by the gallery watching from Phil's Grill.

THE RAVEN GOLF CLUB AT VERRADO

7,258 yards, par 72, 132/73.8
Greens fee: $159
623-388-3000, ravenatverrado.com

This two-year-old raven flies high 30 miles west of Phoenix in the sleepy town of Buckeye, but you'd better be wide awake when you tackle this track by John Fought and Tom Lehman. The designers chiseled an option-laden layout in the foothills of the White Tank Mountains. Holes skip around scrub-filled ravines and down rock-encrusted slopes. The Raven is a healthy trek from downtown, but the Phoenix skyline vistas from the 494-yard 18th remind you that civilization isn't that far away.

TALKING STICK GOLF CLUB

North: 7,133 yards, par 70, 125/73.8
South: 6,833 yards, par 71, 129/72.7
Greens fee: $120–$170
480-860-2221, talkingstickgolfclub.com

Ben Crenshaw and Bill Coore routed both courses in the East Valley's Salt River Pima-Maricopa Indian Community. The links-style North is a refreshing minimalist design that features wide fairways void of trees, strategic bunkering, native grasses, and unobstructed views. The greens are open, the fairways wide, and the roughly carved bunkers look as if they've been there for hundreds of years. The South course features subtle elevation changes, fingered bunkers, and a heavily treed landscape full of native cottonwoods and hardwoods.

TPC SCOTTSDALE

Stadium: 7,216 yards, par 71, 138/74.6
Desert: 6,423 yards, par 70, 119/69.9
Greens fee: $238 (Stadium); $60 (Desert)
888-400-4001, tpc.com

Tom Weiskopf and Jay Morrish built the Stadium specifically to host the PGA Tour's Phoenix Open (now the FBR Open). The Stadium is a spacious layout fringed by saguaro cacti and mesquite trees, with a broad view of famed Pinnacle Peak to the north and the McDowell Mountains to the east. This course can be a substantial challenge because of the strategically placed mounds and bunkers. The Stadium has a desert ambiance, but the natural terrain doesn't come into play. The 162-yard 16th hole was the scene of one of Tiger Woods' most memorable—and loudest—career moments: an ace in front of a thunderous, beer-fueled gallery in 1997. The giant practice facility here is frequented by about 30 PGA Tour pros, including Tom Lehman and Steve Jones. At the shorter, target-style Desert, errant shots are likely to trickle into desert shrub, but the course offers the same dazzling views of the McDowell Mountains as the Stadium.

THE CARD WRECKER: TPC OF SCOTTSDALE (STADIUM COURSE) NO. 17, 332 YARDS, PAR 4

One of the game's greatest risk/reward par fours, you can attack this heavily contoured green from the tee, but the penalties for failure are severe. Andrew Magee aced this hole at the 2001 FBR Open by ricocheting his ball off the putter of Tom Byrum, who was standing on the green while playing in the group ahead. How will you master it? We asked the co-architect Tom Weiskopf how to play it:

"This hole gives the player plenty of options. The lure for the big hitter is to try driving the huge green, the reward being an eagle putt. The risk for the errant drive is water left of the green and swale to the right. We also rewarded the shorter hitter, letting him use his short-game expertise to handle the bold contours of the green. The exciting aspect to this hole is that so many things can happen—there are so many different ways to play it."

Hole 15 at Grayhawk
(Raptor Course),
Scottsdale, Arizona

TROON NORTH GOLF CLUB

Monument Course:
7,028 yards, par 72, 147/73.3
Pinnacle: 7,044 yards, par 72, 147/73.4
Greens fee: $75–$295
480-585-7700, troonnorthgolf.com

TOP 100 YOU CAN PLAY

The desert frequently comes into play on the Monument, which opened in 1990 to become the town's most popular track, but the course is not a target course. Co-designer Tom Weiskopf (with Jay Morrish) won the British Open at Royal Troon in 1973 and built Postage Stamp, the 140-yard 16th, as a nod to the famously tiny 8th green at this year's British Open venue. Weiskopf's Pinnacle is a worthy companion to the Monument. Built around dramatic granite boulders and striking elevation changes, The Pinnacle features a more traditional desert layout with tighter landing areas, spectacular carries over desert washes and views of Pinnacle Peak.

VISTAL GOLF CLUB

7,013 yards, par 71, 126/72.6
Greens fee: $39–$44
602-305-7755

This facility, built by the Thunderbirds, a local civic organization that sponsors the PGA Tour's FBR Open at the TPC Stadium Course each January, sits at the base of Phoenix's South Mountain State Park and includes an 18-hole regulation course and a 9-hole short course. The 18-hole layout was created by PGA Tour Design Services Inc., with consultations by pros Tom Lehman, Billy Mayfair, and Howard Twitty. The routing takes advantage of views of the downtown skyline. On the 1st and 10th tees, you can use the Bob (Bank One Ballpark, home of the 2001 world champion Arizona Diamondbacks) as a target.

TOM LEHMAN'S FAVORITE SCOTTSDALE ATTRACTIONS

Scottsdale resident and 2006 Ryder Cup captain Tom Lehman names his favorite spots about town.

PUBLIC COURSES: **The Raven at Verrado.** "I'm biased because I helped design it, but it's a fun course. The **Raptor Course** at Grayhawk is tough, and I like challenging courses. I won Tiger Woods' first tournament on that course—it had a $1 million purse. The **TPC of Scottsdale** (Stadium Course) is one of the best of the TPC courses. The 15th hole is great, a par five with an island green. Classic risk-reward."

FAVORITE HOLE: The **17th at TPC of Scottsdale** (Stadium Course), a short par four. "It's reachable off the tee and looks so benign that it makes you step up and hit driver. It's tricky because the fairway gets narrow, but the only way to play the hole is aggressively, because the fairway is narrower for the lay-up shot than for the drive. There's a bunker 50 yards short of the green—aim right over it with a draw. Get it up there where you can chip or pitch and take your chances."

EAT AT: **Z-Tejas.** "It's an upscale place with Southwestern and Mexican food. I get the Voodoo Tuna, which is spicy ahi tuna, or the Diablo Chicken, which is like a fettuccini Alfredo only kicked up a notch and with red sauce instead of white. I go to **Flo's Hong Kong Market** probably four times a week when I'm home, and they know to bring me the usual: the Spicy General Flo's. It's a chicken thing that'll make you sweat. There's a place called **Fleming's** in D.C. Ranch, where my wife and I split a steak and have a beer and watch the sunset. And **Frank & Lupe's** is a little hole in the wall in the middle of Scottsdale that has great Mexican food."

STAY AT: **The Royal Palms Resort and Spa.** "This is awesome if you want to go way upscale. The **Hermosa Inn** is not quite as expensive. Both are more intimate, casita-type hotels with personalized service. Farther north is the **Fairmont Scottsdale Princess**, which is a nice place—a bit bigger but in the middle of all the golf."

TAKE THE FAMILY TO: **Rawhide.** "It's an Old West–themed place in North Scottsdale with donkey and horse rides, train and stagecoach rides, and a six-gun theater with Wild West plays and shootouts."

Make sure you pack sunscreen and your credit card. "Scottsdale is not cheap. Shorts, a T-shirt, and some sandals and you don't need much else, except for going out to dinner," says Lehman.

VISTA VERDE GOLF COURSE

7,219 yards, par 72, 144/73.3
Greens fee: NA
480-471-2710

Arizona's newest public-access course was slated for a soft opening in early 2006. It was so new at press time that they don't have a phone number and had not decided on greens fees. The best way to gain access is to stay at Resort Suites and ask the golf concierge to arrange your tee time on this gently rolling track by the Tonto National Forest.

WE-KO-PA GOLF CLUB

7,225 yards, par 72, 136/73.0
Greens fee: $70–$195
480-836-9000, wekopa.com

TOP 100 YOU CAN PLAY

A 20-minute drive east of downtown on Fort McDowell Yavapai Nation land you will find this Scott Miller design, which opened in 2001 and has since catapulted to must-play status, thanks to its incomparable scenery and to holes that zigzag artfully through canyons, over ridges, and down mountain slopes. Free of water restrictions, We-Ko-Pa (from the Yavapai phrase for "Four Peaks Mountain") has wide fairways and big greens but also more than a few reminders of the desert. A 50-foot-high boulder rises like a tombstone in the fairway of the 566-yard 10th, while a small wall fronting the green at the 605-yard 8th mirrors the shape of the Red Mountains in the distance.

WHIRLWIND GOLF CLUB

Devil's Claw: 7,027 yards, par 72, 129/72.6
The Cattail: 7,218 yards, par 72, 132/73.4
Greens fee: $80–$170
480-940-1500, whirlwindgolf.com

Whirlwind is on the other side of South Mountain, just one minute off Interstate 10 within the Gila River Indian Community. When you see one of the mini-funnel clouds spring up on the desert floor, you'll appreciate the name. The straightforward and enjoyable Devil's Claw course by Gary Panks is framed by wild grasses, mesquite, saguaros, and great views of the Santan and Estrella Mountain ranges. Panks' second, slightly more challenging course, the Cattail, is a lush, green oasis with more water features (including three man-made lakes) than its counterpart.

WILDFIRE GOLF CLUB

Faldo Championship:
6,846 yards, par 71, 127/71.6
Palmer Signature:
7,145 yards, par 72, 135/73.3
Greens fee: $70–$205
888-705-7775, wildfiregolf.com

Nick Faldo's 2002 design at Wildfire, which is northeast of Scottsdale, lacks the sweeping grandeur of We-Ko-Pa, but more than 100 bunkers—106 to be exact, but who's counting?—make for a claustrophobia-inducing layout. The 341-yard 8th hole typifies the style of an architect who played with laserlike accuracy. A 150-yard-long bunker inhabited by the loneliest cactus in Arizona guards the right side, while two bunkers nip the fairway like a Victorian corset 250 yards off the tee. From there it's just a wedge to a green guarded by a phalanx of five more bunkers. The Palmer course has generous fairways lined by native brush and cacti and large, undulating green complexes ringed by bunkers. Gorgeous Camelback Mountain serves as the backdrop for the signature hole, the 415-yard 6th.

WHERE TO STAY

The Boulders Resort & Golden Door Spa in Carefree gets its name from the 12-million-year-old, precariously perched geological formations on its 1,300 Sonoran Desert acres. You can choose among casitas, suites, and one- to three-bedroom villas. There's also a 33,000-square-foot Golden Door Spa. Rates from $199. **866-397-6520, theboulders.com** ••

Every casita-style room at the **Four Seasons Resort Scottsdale at Troon North** has a balcony or patio overlooking the desert. The resort's Cowboy Campfires—nighttime stories of the Old West from a cowboy crooner—almost match the entertainment value of the two courses. Rates from $295. **866-888-6540, fourseasons.com/Scottsdale** ••

The sprawling-yet-elegant **Fairmont Scottsdale Princess**, next to the TPC Stadium Course, has more than 800 rooms, from suites to villas to casitas, at rates starting from $225. **800-257-7544, fairmont.com/scottsdale** ••

The McDowell Mountains backdrop the lushly landscaped **Hyatt Regency Resort & Spa at Gainey Ranch** in Scottsdale, which has a 2.5 acre water playground and 400-square foot rooms with balconies and patios. Rates from $195. **800-233-1234, hyatt.com** ••

The Phoenician pampers golfers with complimentary 10-minute pre-round back massages near the first tee, and the resort's Centre for Well-Being provides golf yoga classes for those in need of deep relaxation. Rooms from $225. **800-888-8234, thephoenician.com** •• Frank Lloyd Wright consulted on Phoenix's grandest hotel, the **Arizona Biltmore Resort & Spa**. One round of golf (with breakfast) costs $258 a night (double occupancy). **800-950-2575, arizonabiltmore.com** •• The sprawling **JW Marriott Desert Ridge Resort & Spa** is home to the Faldo and Palmer courses at Wildfire Golf Club. The hotel and convention center has 950 rooms (with 81 suites), nine restaurants, a two-story Southwest-themed spa, four acres of swimming pools, and a 20,000-square-foot Desert Botanical Garden. Rates from $239. **800-835-6206, desertridgeresort.com** •• The **Sheraton Wild Horse Resort & Spa** has 500 rooms and an Adji Spa featuring treatments influenced by Native American rituals. There is also a Cultural Heritage Center, an equestrian center, and the Wild Horse Pass Casino. Rates from $350. **602-225-0100, wildhorsepassresort.com**

WHERE TO EAT

Lefty gave his name to Phil's Grill at **Grayhawk Golf Club** and helped plan the menu. It's the premier public-access 19th hole in the state, thanks to tasty prime-rib sliders, massive margaritas, and mounds of Mickelson memorabilia. **480-502-1700, grayhawkgolf.com** •• **Mastro's Ocean Club Fish House** at Kierland Commons serves up fresh fish flown in daily and memorable martinis. **480-443-8555, mastrosoceanclub.com** •• For affordable Mexican food, few rival **Garduño's** near the Hyatt Regency Scottsdale. **480-607-9222, margaritafactory.com**

LOCAL KNOWLEDGE

Horse lovers will be hot to trot at the **Scottsdale Arabian Horse Show** held each February at WestWorld. **480-515-1500, scottsdaleshow.com** •• Play your own war games with **Desert Storm Hummer Tours**. You get rugged 4x4 action in the mountains east of Scottsdale. **866-374-8637, dshummer.com** •• The classic-ride gazing is terrific at the annual **Barrett-Jackson Collector Car Auction** at WestWorld each January. **480-421-6694, barrett-jackson.com** •• Get a high-speed thrill in a racecar at the **Bob Bondurant School of High Performance Driving**. **800-842-RACE, bondurant.com** •• The **Phoenix Suns** shocked the sages in 2005 by reaching the Western Conference finals. Catch them in action. **602-379-SUNS, nba.com/suns**

WHEN TO GO

If you can stand temperatures consistently above 100 degrees, reduced green fees abound in Phoenix during the summer months. Plus you may even get a cart with cool mist machines or mango-scented iced towels that feel and smell better than a birdie. But if you don't buy the "dry heat" theory, you can also find discounts at various Arizona courses during peak season from January through April. If you're planning a trip in early fall, beware of overseeding, where courses are shut down for two to three weeks as the fairways are changed from a relatively heat-resistant strain of grass to one more receptive to the slightly cooler winter temperatures. This takes place anywhere from mid-September to mid-October, so call ahead and plan accordingly.

For more information, call 800-805-0471 or visit experiencescottsdale.com.

TUCSON

Tucson is one of the desert game's capitals. On the northern edge of the high Sonoran Desert, the city is laid back, beautiful, and off the beaten track, though just an hour and 15 minutes from Phoenix Sky Harbor International Airport. Climate and topography work in Tucson's favor. The city is only 60 miles from the Mexican border, but the temperature is usually about 10 degrees cooler than in the state capital. The area features a huge variety of cacti, which dot the mountainsides and washes. (Warning: Don't brush up against them or you'll be pulling spines out of your backside for a week.)

Hole 15 at the Gallery
Golf Club (North),
Tucson, Arizona

WHERE TO PLAY

ARIZONA NATIONAL

6,785 yards, par 71, 146/72.4
Greens fee: $55–$165
520-749-3519
arizonanationalgolfclub.com

This Robert Trent Jones Jr. layout on the northeast side of town opened in 1996 and was originally called the Raven at Sabino Springs. It's another mountainside layout in the mold of Gallery North, if not as sublime. Since this is home to the University of Arizona's nationally ranked golf teams, the clientele is young and casual. As for the golf, it's superb if a bit gimmicky (the championship tee on 18, for instance, perches 200 feet above the back tee). The course meanders up the Santa Catalinas and overlooks the valley, offering spectacular views. Nine natural springs provide more water features than you usually see in Tucson—including a spring on the 12th hole that supported a Hohokam Indian village about 1,000 years ago.

THE GALLERY GOLF CLUB

North: 7,412 yards, par 72, 142/74.0
South: 7,315-yard, par 72, 140/73.9
Greens fee: $175
520-744-4700, gallerygolf.com

About 20 minutes north of Tucson in the Tortolita Mountains, the Gallery Golf Club's spectacular North course, a John Fought–Tom Lehman design, winds around natural rock outcroppings. As the course climbs from Ruelas Canyon up Dove Mountain, you'll find yourself gawking at the views of bare hilltops above, miles of saguaro-studded desert floor below, and the mesquite and multihued rocks everywhere in between. You're snapped back to reality on holes like the 4th and 8th, both par fours, and the par-five 16th, which all call for long drives over gullies. But forced carries are the exception. The South course was designed by Fought to contrast with the North. Although not as imposing as its sibling, South is sublimely beautiful, laid out in a forest of saguaro mixed with ironwood, mesquite, and palo verde trees, which make each hole a secluded enclave. The Gallery is private, but you can play as a visitor until the membership fills up. The courses are open on alternate days, so check ahead. You can also buy a package that allows a foursome to stay at a course-side *casita*—a cozy two-bedroom cottage with a kitchen and a whirlpool tub.

GOLF CLUB AT VISTOSO

6,952 yards, par 72, 147/72.1
Greens fee: $169
520-797-9900, vistosogolf.com

Just north of town, this Tom Weiskopf design is so smartly crafted that a high-handicapper can easily manage his game from the correct set of tees. Much of the course is secluded and wild, rich with jackrabbits, hawks, roadrunners, and lizards. Weiskopf excels at building risk-reward holes, and there are plenty at Vistoso, including the aptly named 2nd, Double Cross, a 530-yard dogleg-right that tempts you with a dangerous shortcut to the green. On the back nine, there's the 14th, Risky, a bifurcated 350-yarder that asks you to choose between playing it safe or going for the green over trees. Average golfers have a chance here, provided they're able to resist temptation.

TUCSON NATIONAL

Catalina: 7,262 yards, par 73
Sonoran: 6,552 yards, par 70
Greens fee: $65–$180
520-297-2271, tucsonnational.com

The Catalina course at Tucson National hosts an annual PGA Tour event, the Chrysler Classic, and for that reason—as well as for its famous water-guarded 465-yard 18th hole—it's a worthy side trip. Tom Lehman designed the National's new course, the Sonoran, which opened in December 2005.

VENTANA CANYON GOLF CLUB

Canyon: 6,819 yards, par 72, 140/72.6
Mountain: 6,898 yards, par 72, 147/73.0
Greens fee: $225
520-299-2020
thelodgeatventanacanyon.com

These tough and inventive Tom Fazio tracks are two of Tucson's best circuits. The front nine of the Mountain features one of the most photographed holes in the country, the 107-yard 3rd, which offers a panorama across the Sonoran Desert to Mexico. The back tees are set on a 50-foot-high mesa, with a dramatic drop to the green on a lower mesa. The back nine of the Canyon, which winds through Esperro Canyon, is indelible—particularly the 336-yard 10th, which incorporates Whaleback Rock, a geological formation that does indeed look like the back of a black whale. The rock chokes the left side of the fairway and the long, narrow green. The 503-yard, dogleg-right finishing hole wraps up this surreal test with a green backed by a shimmering artificial waterfall. The courses are open on alternating days, and you don't have to be a resort guest to play them.

WESTIN LA PALOMA RESORT

Canyon: 3,534 yards, par 36
Ridge: 3,554 yards, par 36
Hill: 3,463 yards, par 36
Greens fee: $195–$205
520-742-6000, westin.com/lapaloma

These three Jack Nicklaus–designed loops are also at the north of town. The courses provide sweeping views of Tucson, and Nicklaus balanced narrow fairways with his trademark racetrack-like banking, which keeps wayward tee shots in play. La Paloma is no pushover, however. "This was among the first dozen or so courses Jack designed, and one of his first desert courses," says Westin director of golf Dan LaRouere. "He created holes by taking a plastic mat out into the scrub and smacking balls to where he thought the fairways and greens should be."

Hole 9 at Tucson National (Sonoran), Tucson, Arizona

Hole 10 at the Gallery
Golf Club (South),
Tucson, Arizona

GREEN VALLEY

A 40-minute drive south of Tucson, in the cooler, clearer climate around Green Valley, several developments offer some challenging golf. The **San Ignacio Golf Club** (Greens fee: $30–$69; 520-648-3468; sanignaciogolfclub.com), designed by Arthur Hills in the mid-1980s, is a 6,704-yard high-desert layout with plenty of elevated tees to offer expansive views of the narrow and unforgiving fairways. Dave Bennett laid out the tight 6,610-yard **Canoa Hills** (Greens fee: $40–$69; 520-648-1880; tucsongolf.com) through a small canyon; the course rewards golfers who can hit it straight and control distance. **Canoa Ranch Golf Club** (Greens fee: $35–$59; 520-393-1966; canoaranchgolfclub.com), a new course designed by Lee Schmidt and Brian Curley, may be the best of the bunch. The 6,549-yard design has lots of elevation, so it's terrific for playing near sunset for great views of the Kitt Peak National Observatory

across the valley. Set within a retirement community, Canoa Ranch is beautiful and cheap and has a lively, convivial restaurant, Grill on the Green. Finding a hotel is tricky in this area, but the Inn at San Ignacio offers private suites. If you're a history buff, make a side trip to **Tubac Golf Resort** (Greens fee: $45–$75; 520-398-2211; tubacgolfresort.com). Its 6,533-yard course, designed by Red Lawrence in 1959, is nothing special, but Tubac, originally a hacienda built on land granted by the Spanish crown in 1789, is a mile from a 300-year-old Spanish pueblo that has become a thriving artists' colony with more than 90 galleries, boutiques, and studios. In the late 1950s, Bing Crosby and a group of Tucson businessmen bought the 500-acre property and turned it into a golf resort while preserving the original buildings. Lush fairways and tall cottonwood trees evoke the look of old Tucson.

WHERE TO STAY

 But you could do worse than to stay at another famed resort in the northern foothills, **Loew's Ventana Canyon**, hailed by *Architectural Digest* as "the first environmentally conceived resort in North America." It also offers great amenities: tennis, swimming, hiking, horseback riding, and a spa. Rooms from $129. **520-299-2020, loewshotels.com** ● ●

 The charming and rustic **Lodge at Ventana Canyon** is affiliated with the Ventana Canyon Golf Club. Rooms from $89. **the lodgeatventanacanyon.com, 800-828-5701** ● ●

 In order to play at La Paloma you must stay at the **Westin La Paloma**. One of Westin's best hotels, it features an Elizabeth Arden Red Door Spa, tennis, swim-up bars, and the nouvelle cuisine of the Janos restaurant. Rooms from $140. **520-742-6000, westin .com/lapaloma**

WHERE TO EAT

Loews Ventana Canyon has Arizona's only AAA five-diamond restaurant. The **Ventana Room** (*ventana* mean "window" *en Español*) overlooks the Sonoran Desert, Rincon Mountains, and

the lights of Tucson in the distance. Chef Philippe Trosch pairs French technique with Southwestern seasonings. **520-299-2020, loewshotels.com** ● ● **El Charro Mexican Cafe** is not just the oldest family-operated Mexican restaurant in the country, but it's also one of the best. **520-622-1922, elcharrocafe.com** ● ● Pair a little live country-western with your Mesquite-grilled steak, seafood, ribs, chicken, and wild game at the **Last Territory Steakhouse & Music Hall**. Closed Mondays. **520-544-1738** ● ● **Janos Restaurant** serves French-inspired Southwestern cuisine in contemporary setting with gorgeous views of downtown Tucson. Extensive wine list, too. **520-615-6100, janos.com** ● ● **Fuego** isn't just a fun place to visit for its patio happy hour or Sinatra-themed Sundays; chef Alan Zeman serves bold, innovative cuisine including oysters, seafood, ostrich, and mesquite grill. **520-886-1745, fuegorestaurant.com**

LOCAL KNOWLEDGE

The **Pima Air & Space Museum** is home to one of the largest aircraft collections in the United States and features two Space Exploratorium

exhibits. **520-574-0462, pimaair.org** ● ● The **Tucson Sidewinders**, the Triple-A affiliate of the Arizona Diamondbacks, play about 72 home games from April through August in Tucson Electric Park. **520-325-6026, tucsonsidewinders.com** ● ● You can't visit Tucson without cycling, hiking, or horseback riding through the mountains. Visit **Saguaro National Forest (520-733-5158, nps.gov/ sagu/)** or hike to the freshwater pools in **Sabino Canyon (520-749-2861, sabinocanyon.com)**.

GETTING THERE

Tucson International Airport accepts flights from 10 carriers, including Delta, American, Continental, Northwest, and United. **tucsonairport.org**

WHEN TO GO

January through April is the high season, but you'll still have great weather and course conditions from October through December (ask courses about their overseeding schedule). Rates bottom out in the summer, with average temps hitting 105 from June to August—about 10 degrees cooler than Phoenix.

NAPA
Vineyards far outnumber golf courses in Napa and Sonoma, but a handful of solid tracks provide a memorable diversion from the more serious business of wine tasting.

WHERE TO PLAY

FOUNTAINGROVE GOLF & ATHLETIC CLUB

6,439 yards, par 72, 128/69.1
Greens fee: $100
707-579-4653, fountaingrovegolf.com

Heading north in Sonoma County, you'll come to the town of Santa Rosa and this design by California native Ted Robinson. Opened in 1985, it's available to guests of the nearby 124-room Fountaingrove Inn. The layout cuts through secluded glens and hillsides full of wild turkey and deer. Few of the holes parallel each other, and good-sized greens are protected by deep bunkers. Elevation changes often dictate club selection.

NAPA GOLF COURSE AT KENNEDY PARK

6,704 yards, par 72, 131/72.7
Greens fee: $31–$41
707-255-4333, playnapa.com

Just a few minutes north of Chardonnay, this course was designed by Bob Baldock and Jack Fleming and opened in 1968. As the only municipal course in the area, Napa handles plenty of golfers—about 55,000 rounds a year. It also hosts the city championship each September. Water is in play on 16 holes, but you only have to carry it twice—on the 486-yard, par-five 8th and the 527-yard, dogleg-left 18th.

SILVERADO RESORT

North: 6,900 yards, par 72, 134/73.1
South: 6,685 yards, par 72
Greens fee: $155–$175
707-257-5460, silveradoresort.com

This 1,200-acre property in Napa features two courses designed by Robert Trent Jones Jr. and hosted a Champions Tour event from 1989 to 2002. Before that, it was home to the PGA Tour's Kaiser International and Anheuser-Busch Golf Classic. The North is the more traditional, longer, and more challenging of the two. There's no easy start here, whether it's on the 436-yard opener or on the 418-yard 10th. Bring your driver—you'll use it often. The South, which hosted the Champions Tour event, demands more accuracy. Hilly terrain often means uneven lies and frequent changes in elevation. Packages start at $320 per night, based on double occupancy, including greens fee and accommodations.

SONOMA GOLF CLUB

7,103 yards, par 72, 137/75.2
Greens fee: $160
707-996-0300, sonomamissioninn.com

This 1928 Sam Whiting–Willie Watson creation was once described by Sam Snead as the best-designed course he had ever seen. Snead was especially fond of the 7th, which has water on the right, bunkers left and right of the green, and some 220 yards between you and the hole. In fact, except for the 142-yard 17th, all of the par threes at Sonoma play to more than 200 yards. The course is affiliated with Sonoma Mission Inn Resort, known for its luxurious spa treatments. You have to be a guest to play the course.

VINTNER'S GOLF CLUB

5,858 yards, par 68, 121/66.3
Greens fee: $45–$85
707-944-1992, vintnersgolfclub.com

This is not an executive course—its longest hole is 530 yards and the greens are pretty slick. The course sits just down the street from the Domaine Chandon vineyard, where visitors can taste a selection of sparkling wines.

WHERE TO STAY

Sonoma Golf Club is open only to guests of the **Fairmont Sonoma Mission Inn Resort**, which is known for its luxurious spa treatments and hot mineral springs. Rates from $359. **707-938-9000, sonomamissioninn.com** • • The 124-room, redwood-and-stone **Fountaingrove Inn** in Santa Rosa on the historic Fountaingrove Ranch property offers access to the Fountaingrove Golf & Athletic Club. Rates from $119. **800-222-6101, fountaingroveinn.com** • • Originally a Spanish land grant, the 1,200-acre **Silverado Country Club & Resort** is nestled among the vineyards of Napa Valley and offers golf packages for its two courses and accommodations in private cottage suites that surround secluded courtyards and pools. Rates from $160. **800-532-0500, silveradoresort.com**

WHERE TO EAT

The **Girl and the Fig** in Sonoma serves Provence–inspired local seafood, game, and seasonal produce. **707-938-3634,** thegirlandthefig.com • • There's plenty of delicious fare to choose from at the buzzing **Zin Restaurant and Wine Bar** in Healdsburg, where juicy zinfandels make up more than half the wine list. Don't miss the chicken dumplings special, paired with a bottle of Limerick Lane Zinfandel. **707-473-0946, zinrestaurant .com** • • Intricate, artistic preparations, inspired pairings, and a James-Beard–award-winning chef (Thomas Keller) make Yountsville's **French Laundry** one of the hottest (and toughest) reservations in the world. Call after 10 A.M., two months before the reservation date (use a phone with automatic redial). **707-944-2380** • • Among the special offerings at Healdsburg's **Cyrus**, which was named by *Food & Wine* as the best wine-country restaurant in 2006, are artisanal cheeses, champagne and caviar, and a Sonoma-centric wine list. **707-433-3311,** cyrusrestaurant.com • • Elegant simplicity, as well as fresh local ingredients, define the four-star **Santé** at the Fairmont Sonoma Mission Inn. **707-938-9000, sonomamissioninn.com**

LOCAL KNOWLEDGE

The main reason to visit Napa and Sonoma—way ahead of the golf—is to tour the local vineyards and wineries. Sure, you can rent a car and drive yourself, but you're going to taste too, so a guided tour or limo is often the safest bet. Both **California Wine Tours (800-294-6386, californiawinetours.com)** and **Napa Valley Wine Country Tours (707-226-3333, winecountrylimos.com)** offer a range of options. If you're going solo, visit napasonoma.com to map your path.

GETTING THERE

Napa Valley and Sonoma are about an hour and a half north of San Francisco by car.

WHEN TO GO

High season is from May through October, but it's possible to play here year-round, since winter temperatures rarely drop below the 50s.

SAN FRANCISCO TO PEBBLE BEACH

Pebble Beach, America's greatest public-access golf course, is less than a three-hour drive from one of its best munis, the newly refurbished Harding Park in San Francisco, the site of a 2005 WGC-American Express Championship. These beacons of public golf are connected by the legendary Pacific Coast Highway, and there are a handful of other fine courses worth a stop along the way.

WHERE TO PLAY

HARDING PARK GOLF COURSE

6,845 yards, par 72, 126/72.8
Greens fee: $125–$138
415-750-GOLF, harding-park.com

For many years, Harding Park was the Marilyn Monroe of golf courses—a beautiful creation left to crumble slowly before our eyes. Former UGSA president Sandy Tatum eventually stepped in, spearheading a $16 million renovation that resurrected the tree-lined 1925 design by William Watson, which overlooks Lake Merced. Harding Park finally got its props in October of 2005, when it hosted the PGA Tour's WGC-American Express Championship. The 440-yard 18th shows how far this once-bedraggled muni has come. The new tee stands on what was a parking lot, and the green occupies the site of the old practice green. The result tests even the hardiest golfers.

PRESIDIO GOLF COURSE

6,477 yards, par 72, 136/72.2
Greens fee: $42–$96
415-561-4661, presidiogolf.com

As at Harding, the best holes on this San Francisco muni come back-to-back—the 12th, a killer par four of 453 yards that rates toughest on the course, and the 13th, a 175-yard bully shielded by a nasty old-coast live oak in the middle of the fairway. It's a one-two punch worthy of San Fran's cinematic cop Dirty Harry. Couch potatoes had best think twice about walking this hilly course.

HALF MOON BAY GOLF LINKS

Old Course: 7,090 yards, par 72, 135/75.3
Ocean Course: 6,712 yards, par 72, 125/71.8
Greens fee: $155–$170
650-726-4438, ritzcarlton.com

Located less than an hour south of Harding Park and close to the quaint town of Half Moon Bay, the two tracks at the Ritz-Carlton at Half Moon Bay are an ideal way station on the road to the Monterey Peninsula. The Old Course was designed by Arnold Palmer and Francis Duane in 1973 and redesigned by Arthur Hills in 1999. Truthfully, this track is a one-hole golf course, although that one hole—the 418-yard cliff-top closer—is among the finest in California. Hills sought a Scottish feel in designing the Ocean Course in 1997, and while the effect doesn't quite rise to that level, he did a better job than you'd expect. The water views are constant, but you'll wait until the 16th hole before the Pacific comes into play.

PASATIEMPO GOLF CLUB

6,439 yards, par 70, 138/71.9
Greens fee: $150–$197
831-459-9155, pasatiempo.com

TOP 100 YOU CAN PLAY

Dr. Alister MacKenzie is undoubtedly best remembered as the architect of two of the world's finest courses: Augusta National and Cypress Point. Not far north of Cypress in Santa Cruz is Pasatiempo, which he designed in 1929 and where he lived, alongside the 6th fairway, until his death in 1934. Pasatiempo (the name is Spanish for "passing of time") is a masterpiece of strategic bunkering, and that's where you're most likely to come undone. MacKenzie said that the 395-yard 16th hole was the best two-shotter he ever designed. Architect Tom Doak is now restoring the course to its former glory. You'll so enjoy the challenges at Pasatiempo that you won't even notice that it ends on a par three.

PEBBLE BEACH GOLF LINKS

6,737 yards, par 72, 142/73.8
Greens fee: $425–$450
800-654-9300, pebblebeach.com

TOP 100 YOU CAN PLAY

TOP 100 IN THE U.S.

TOP 100 IN THE WORLD

To step onto the first tee at Pebble Beach is to risk an anticlimax. Golfers know the course so intimately from television that it can seem less dramatic in person. As an annual stop on the PGA Tour, this isn't a course that steps into the major spotlight only every decade or so. Telecasts often lavish attention on Pebble's closing holes, but the real magic is to be found on the front nine. The most spectacular series of holes you'll find anywhere are Nos. 5 through 8, which are on the promontory between Stillwater Cove and the Pacific Ocean. The truth is that Pebble Beach is entirely a second-shot golf course. You can survive misses with your driver, but misfiring on your approach shots will make it a very long day. You won't be writing about the opening few holes in your postcards home, but beware the deep cross bunker in the fairway on the 2nd. Caddies call it the Yao Ming bunker after the 7-foot-6 Rockets center entered it in 2004 and disappeared from view. For most golfers, Pebble is all about the final two holes. Who doesn't want to try recreating Tom Watson's chip-in from the 1982 U.S. Open or Jack Nicklaus' 1-iron that clattered against the flagstick a decade earlier? That's the charm of Pebble: a mixture of familiarity, history, and superb golf.

SPYGLASS HILL

6,862 yards, par 72, 148/75.3
Greens fee: $300–$330
800-654-9300, pebblebeach.com

TOP 100 YOU CAN PLAY

TOP 100 IN THE U.S.

TOP 100 IN THE WORLD

Don't be fooled by the 62 that Phil Mickelson shot at Spyglass Hill last year—this Robert Trent Jones Sr. course has been flat-out nasty since it opened in 1966. Spyglass Hill is ranked No. 49 on our Top 100 Courses in the U.S. Although Spyglass gets overshadowed by its neighbors Pebble Beach and Cypress Point, there's no overlooking its unmatched blend of beauty and brawn. The 595-yard first hole offers jaw-dropping ocean views from the crest of a fairway lined with towering Monterey pines, while Nos. 2 through 5 romp through dunes and ice plant. The rest of the course is thickly forested, and the difficulty in walking is matched only by the difficulty in scoring.

Hole 18 at Pebble Beach Golf Links, Pebble Beach, California

LINKS AT SPANISH BAY

6,821 yards, par 72, 146/74.1

Greens fee: $240–$270

800-654-9300, pebblebeach.com

TOP 100 YOU CAN PLAY

Located off 17-Mile Drive around the corner from Pebble Beach, the Links at Spanish Bay, designed by Tom Watson and Sandy Tatum in connection with Robert Trent Jones Jr., approximates an authentic Scottish links, with Pacific mist wafting across rumbled fairways and the sound of a kilted bagpiper pacing the terrace of the Inn at Spanish Bay at dusk. Low handicappers may grumble when seemingly good drives carom into sand pits, but the bunkers here cater impartially to the amusement of all. The course is ranked 46th on GOLF MAGAZINE's Top 100 Courses You Can Play in the U.S.

WHERE TO STAY

San Francisco is only seven square miles, so drop anchor in the heart of the action atop Nob Hill at the landmark **Fairmont Hotel**, where Tony Bennett first sang about leaving his heart. Rates from $299. **415-772-5000, fairmont.com/sanfrancisco** • •

 The **Ritz-Carlton at Half Moon Bay**, home to the Old and Ocean Courses, has 261 deluxe guest rooms, most with ocean or coastal views, and a spa with an oceanfront yoga studio, a coed candlelit Roman mineral bath, and a whirlpool tub on an ocean bluff. Rates from $235. **650-712-7000, ritzcarlton.com** • •

 Pebble Beach Resort has three lodging options, two of which are GOLF MAGAZINE Gold Medalists. There are 269 rooms in the Inn at Spanish Bay, all of which feature gas-operated fireplaces, posh marble bathrooms, and spacious balconies. The Lodge at Pebble Beach, near the Links, has luxurious rooms with guest rooms, most with working fireplaces, marble dressing areas, and oversized baths. Just off the first and second holes of the Links course, the private-estate-style Casa Palmero has just 24 rooms and suites. Rates from $505. **800-654-9300, pebblebeach.com**

WHERE TO EAT

In the lower level of the Fairmont, **The Tonga Room** has San Francisco's best happy hour, with exotic cocktails (beware the Bora Bora Horror!), a monster buffet chock full of spare ribs, Shanghai noodles and pork buns for less than $20, plus the crowd-pleasing indoor "thunderstorm" on the half-hour. **415-772-5000, fairmont.com/sanfrancisco** • • For tasty cocktails and pan-Asian fare in a trendy setting, try **Betelnut** on Union Street in San Francisco. **415-929-8855, betelnutrestaurant.com** • • The **Half Moon Bay Brewing Company** serves delectable seafood, burgers, and microbrews in an oceanfront setting. **650-728-BREW, hmbbrewingco.com** • • For Sunday brunch (or a hearty lunch or dinner), hit the waterfront patio of the historic **Moss Beach Distillery** in Moss Beach, between Pacifica and Half Moon Bay off Highway 1. Keep a lookout for the Blue Lady, the lovelorn resident ghost. **650-728-5595, mossbeachdistillery.com** • • Just about every golfer who has played Pebble Beach Golf Links visits **The Tap Room**, behind the 18th green, for a post-round celebration. The walls are lined with celebrity photos and priceless golf memorabilia. **831-625-8535, pebble beach.com** • • The opening in 1995 of **Roy's**, its tantalizing Eurasian fare some of the tastiest food on the Monterey Peninsula, makes the Inn at Spanish Bay a culinary hotspot. **831-647-7423, pebblebeach.com**

LOCAL KNOWLEDGE

Tour the infamous former federal penitentiary on **Alcatraz Island**, now a national park, in San Francisco Bay. **nps.gov/alcatraz** • • Every first-time visitor to San Francisco needs to hoof it across the **Golden Gate**, one of the world's most beautiful bridges. **goldengatebridge.org** • • Head to **Fisherman's Wharf** for lunch—yes, it's a tourist trap, but you can't go wrong with the breadbowl seafood chowder at any of its many restaurants. Stroll over to **Ghirardelli Square** afterward for confections from the famous chocolate maker. **fishermanswharf.org** • • Learn about the creatures—from sharks to starfish—that dwell in and around the Pacific at the **Monterey Bay Aquarium**. Adults: $22, Children: $20, under 3: free. **831-648-4888, mbayaq.org** • • Browse the shops, galleries, restaurants, pubs, and attractions on **Cannery Row** in Monterey, the former sardine cannery made famous by John Steinbeck's 1945 novel *Cannery Row*. **831-372-9323, monterey.com**

GETTING THERE

San Francisco International Airport is served by more than 20 carriers. **flysfo.com**

WHEN TO GO

April to October is the peak season for golf.

SAN DIEGO AREA California is famous for many things, including its valleys. There's Death Valley with its merciless heat, San Fernando Valley with its contributions to 1980s teenage jargon, and Silicon Valley, home to cutting-edge technology. Add to that list Titanium Valley, located just north of San Diego and home to more than 30 golf-equipment manufacturers. With fantastic year-round weather (average temperature 70 degrees) and 44 public golf facilities, golfers have more choices than area native Phil Mickelson has with a wedge in his hands.

WHERE TO PLAY

AVIARA GOLF CLUB

7,007 yards, par 72, 144/75.0
Greens fee: $195–$215
760-603-6900, fourseasons.com/aviara

Opened in 1991, this Arnold Palmer design is part of the Four Seasons Aviara, a GOLF MAGAZINE Gold Medalist resort in Carlsbad, close to La Costa. The course is laid out on a hilly piece of land. Knowing the pin positions ahead of time will increase your birdie chances on the large greens. Three challenging downhill holes round out the front nine, while a flatter back nine makes its way through a hilly valley. Aviara is also home to the Aviara Golf Academy and GOLF MAGAZINE Top 100 Teacher Kip Puterbaugh.

THE AULD COURSE

6,855 yards, par 72, 135/73.4
Greens fee: $75–$95
619-482-4666, theauldcourse.com

This John Cook and Cary Bickler collaboration in the heart of the Otay Valley meanders through original creeks and wetlands, offering a natural setting like no other in the area. Only 100 of the 280 acres here are used for golf; the rest are part of a 500-acre reserve. Views of south San Diego Bay and the Coronado Islands are highlights. Featuring pronounced changes in elevation, undulating yet generous fairways, and friendly bent-grass greens, the Auld Course was not designed to severely punish errant shots. Although the greens do not have sharp breaking tiers, their slope and shape allow for pin positions sure to test your shot-making ability.

BARONA CREEK GOLF CLUB

7,088 yards, par 72, 140/74.5
Greens fee: $80–$110
619-387-7018, barona.com

Deployed like a blanket over the hillsides and valley in the Southwest corner of the Barona Indian Reservation in Lakeside, Barona Creek was built with very little earth movement. This natural-looking Gary Roger Baird design consists of wide-open, gently rolling fairways and spacious, undulating, bent-grass greens, and bunkers filled with soft, snowy-white sand. Several old oaks scattered on the course give this layout a rustic flavor.

THE ENCINITAS RANCH GOLF COURSE

6,587 yards, par 72, 127/71.2
Greens fee: $60–$80
760-944-1936, jcgolf.com/Encinitas.htm

Opened in March 1998, this course is 20 miles north of downtown via Interstate 5. Owned by the city of Encinitas and managed by JC Resorts, this daily fee golf facility includes two natural water hazards, 61 bunkers, dramatic changes in elevation, and undulating fairways covering 175 acres of land. This track is a fun course with beautiful panoramic views. The Pacific Ocean is visible from some holes, and a noticeable sea breeze comes into play in the late morning and early afternoons.

THE GRAND GOLF CLUB

7,054 yards, par 71, 136/74.0
Greens fee: $145–$175
858-792-6200

Grand Del Mar gets the local vote for the most beautiful course in San Diego. This Tom Fazio design is carved through the hills and canyons of Carmel Valley, only four miles east of the Del Mar coastline and just minutes from the famous Del Mar Race Track. Created to challenge the advanced player but also to provide a relaxing round of golf for the beginner, this layout follows the natural contours of the land with holes running atop hills and along canyons filled with native vegetation. In addition to menacing bunkers, chaparral-laden ravines, and strategically located pines, sycamore and California pepper trees are also used to defend the rolling fairways and greens.

LA COSTA RESORT & SPA

North: 7,021 yards, par 72, 141/74.9
South: 7,004 yards, par 72, 140/74.8
Greens fee: $165–$195
760-438-9111, lacosta.com

La Costa is home to the World Match Play Championship reserved for the world's top 64 golfers. The Dick Wilson–Joe Lee layouts are similar in design. The fairways are generous but scattered with trees. The elevated greens putt true and are well bunkered. Both courses have water hazards coming into play on several holes. The terrain is flat and easy to walk, but you must hire a caddie if you walk.

MADERAS GOLF CLUB

7,115 yards, par 72, 145/75.6
Greens fee: $155–$195
858-451-8100, maderasgolf.com

Designed by Johnny Miller and Robert Muir Graves, Maderas is near the city of Poway, three miles east of the Interstate 15 corridor. Maderas is snugly tucked in the hills and canyons neighboring the upscale Heritage Estates development. The Old Coach Road, which leads to the club entrance, was a path followed by the stagecoach that ran between Ramona and San Diego in the late 1800s. Maderas combines spectacular landscaping with strategic golf design to produce a thrilling course that flows calmly through the terrain. The planting of more than 170 oak trees and 40 acres of native wildflowers has only enhanced the natural beauty of the site.

THE RIVERWALK GOLF COURSE

Mission: 3,153 yards, par 36
Friars: 3,230 yards, par 36
Presidio: 3,397 yards, par 36
Greens fee: $95–$105
619-296-4653, riverwalkgc.com

Built on land previously home to the Stardust Country Club, where the PGA Tour's San Diego Open was held in the 1960s, Riverwalk is in the heart of Mission Valley, just a few minutes from the San Diego International airport off Interstate 8. Designed by Ted Robinson, the three nines are not extremely demanding in length, but small and well protected greens, combined with ponds and waterfalls that come into play on 13 of the 27 holes, add to the challenge.

TORREY PINES MUNICIPAL GOLF COURSE

North: 6,874 yards, par 72, 130/73.2
South: 7,607 yards, par 72, 143/78.1
Greens fee: $140–$205
800-985-4653, torreypinesgolfcourse.com

TOP 100 YOU CAN PLAY
TOP 100 IN THE U.S.
┤ South

Fifteen miles south of Carlsbad on coastal Interstate 5, you'll find San Diego's most famous golf destination, Torrey Pines, on the headlands high above the Pacific. This top-rated municipal course has 36 holes and hosts the PGA Tour's Buick Invitational every February. The North is more scenic but less demanding than the longer South, which ranks 41st on GOLF MAGAZINE's Top 100 You Can Play. The South is wide open but requires long drives, sometimes into a stiff sea breeze. The South is the paradigm of a modern championship course, with no weak holes and a handful that might scare the bejesus out of the world's best players on a breezy day—which is why it was chosen for the 2008 U.S. Open.

WHERE TO STAY

The Four Seasons Aviara has 329 rooms and 44 suites set amid rolling valleys above the Pacific. It is home to the Aviara Golf Academy and Golf Magazine Top 100 Teacher Kip Puterbaugh. Rates from $395. **760-603-6800, fourseasons.com/aviara** ● ●

The Lodge at Torrey Pines is a 175-room hostelry that embodies the region's early 1900s Craftsman–style architecture, its shingle and sandstone-bluff exteriors designed to blend the building into the coastal landscape. Spacious guest rooms, most with balconies, have granite-topped bars, leather chaise lounges, and Stickley furniture. The Lodge offers guaranteed advance tee times on the Torrey Pines' North and South courses. Rates from $325. **858-453-4420, thelodgeattorreypines.com** ● ● Located near Lakeside, in the pretty Barona Valley 30 minutes from downtown San Diego, **Barona Valley Ranch Resort & Casino** was built by the Barona band of Mission Indians. Rates start at $119. **888-722-7662, barona.com** ● ● **La Costa Resort & Spa** is a full-service luxury resort situated on 400 rolling acres of scenic coastal terrain. It is home to the North and South courses, a top-notch spa, and Deepak Chopra's Chopra Center, and it has a complete tennis program and 511 guest rooms. Rates from $225. **800-854-5000, lacosta.com**

WHERE TO EAT

Chef Bruce Logue has imported regional Italian cuisine via Mario Batali's Babbo, where Logie spent three years, to **Vivace** at the Four Seasons. Some highlights: hand-cut pastas, crispy *branzino* with peas and prosciutto in a Roman carrot sauce, and a thyme-basted guinea hen with summer squash caponata. **760-603-3773, fourseasons.com/aviara** ● ● The Zagat guide has rated **Pamplemousse Grill** (across from the Del Mar Fairgrounds) the best restaurant in San Diego for three years. The wine cellar stocks more than 700 wines to go with the New American–Continental cuisine. **858-792-9090, pgrille.com** ● ● The **Donovan's Steak House** motto, "all prime, all the time," is all you need to know about this La Jolla establishment. **858-450-6666, donovanssteakhouse.com** ● ● Casual but scrumptious, **The Fish Market** (also across from the Del Mar Fairgrounds) serves up fresh-caught fish and has an extensive raw bar. **858-755-2277, thefishmarket.com**

LOCAL KNOWLEDGE

The **TaylorMade Performance Labs at the Aviara Golf Academy** have a Motion Analysis Technology System that uses nine cameras to capture your swing in 3D, as well as your club speed, launch angle, and ball-spin rate. A $350 session includes analysis and instruction by a PGA professional, a personalized custom fitting for driver, fairway woods, irons, hybrids, and a putter, as well as a CD with a moving 3D image of your swing. **800-433-7468, fourseasons.com/aviara**

GETTING THERE

Fly into San Diego International Airport, about 30 miles south of Carlsbad and 20 miles south of Torrey Pines. **san.org**

WHEN TO GO

It's sunny and mild all year here, although there will be a few more rainy days from December through March.

Hole 13 at Barona Creek, San Diego, California

For more information on the golf courses in the San Diego area, visit the Web site of the San Diego Convention and Visitors Bureau (sandiego.org).

PALM SPRINGS
Palm Springs attracts less attention than it did when Frank, Dino, and the rest of the Rat Pack prowled the town, but for golfers this desert retreat is hotter than ever. Move in any direction, and you'll stub your spikes on a new course, from exclusive private tracks to municipal courses that will welcome you with open arms. Toss in the one of the toughest course in America, the abundant year-round sunshine of the Coachella Valley, and some white-knuckle off-course thrills, and your buddies will proclaim you the new chairman of the board.

WHERE TO PLAY

DESERT WILLOW GOLF RESORT (FIRECLIFF)
7,056 yards, par 72, 138/73.6
Greens fee: $55–$130
800-320-3323, desertwillow.com

Owned by the city of Palm Desert, Firecliff and its sister course—Mountain View—are among the nation's most expensive munis, but it's money well spent. The kaleidoscope of desert flora plantings and gorgeous bunkering by architects Michael Hurdzan and Dana Fry help this design meld into the landscape—so much so that Firecliff became the only course ever featured on the cover of *Smithsonian* magazine. Mountain View has wider fairways, fewer forced carries, and smaller greens, but both share marvelous par-five finishers.

ESCENA GOLF CLUB
7,173 yards, par 72, 130/74.2
Greens fee: $45–$105
760-778-2737, escenagolf.com

When it opened in November, this layout by Nicklaus Design was the first new public course built within the Palm Springs city limits in 20 years. Besides being a half hour closer to Los Angeles and the Palm Springs Airport than some of the tracks in Palm Desert or La Quinta, Escena (Es-SEE-Na) is a fun-to-play frolic that offers ample fairways, speedy but not unfair greens, bunkers that won't destroy a 15-handicapper, and enough water hazards and elevated greens to test the single-digit crowd.

LA QUINTA RESORT & CLUB (MOUNTAIN)
6,756 yards, par 72, 140/74.1
Greens fee: $150–$190
760-564-7686, laquintaresort.com

`TOP 100 YOU CAN PLAY`

In 1980 this established resort became the launch pad for public golf in Palm Springs, when Pete Dye designed the Mountain and Dunes courses here. A full generation on and they're better than ever. The Mountain track has one of the game's most memorable back nines, especially the stretch from Nos. 14 through 16. The 14th calls for a drive over a barranca followed by an all-carry approach to a three-tiered green. No. 15 is a reachable 524-yard par five with a green that button-hooks into a secluded cove, while 16 is a par three that plunges downhill to a green amid rocky desert scrub.

THE CARD WRECKER: PGA WEST STADIUM COURSE NO. 17, 168 YARDS, PAR 3

Pete Dye didn't want to replicate his island green from Sawgrass in the desert but was talked into it. This hole is longer than its Florida counterpart by 30 yards and has a much larger green. We asked Lee Trevino—who famously had a hole-in-one here in the 1987 Skins Game—how to ace this test.

"It's a knuckle-cruncher because none of the water hazard is lateral. If you hit in the water, you've got to drop at a closer tee and try again. There's a 99 percent chance you're going to make 5 or more from that lower tee. Normally, the hole is a 7-iron for me, though I made the ace with a cut 6-iron. In any conditions, do not shoot at the flag. Go to the dead-center of the green, as Jack Nicklaus would do. You'll have an 18-foot putt in either direction. The firmness of the green is the key to the hole. If there's wind and the green is firm, it's damn near impossible. You've got to hit the front of the green and pray like hell it doesn't run into those rocks."

MARRIOTT'S SHADOW RIDGE RESORT

7,006 yards, par 71, 134/73.9
Greens fee: $65–$165
760-674-2700, golfshadowridge.com

Nick Faldo's first U.S. design opened in 2000 and, although he had plenty of help from architects Lee Schmidt and Brian Curley, it was Faldo's fondness for the famed Australian Sandbelt courses around Melbourne that led to the creation of some of the most stylish bunkering in the desert. These bold hazards straddle the line between playable and punishing, but they are always strategically placed, which makes for a true reflection of the Faldo playing style. The practice facility is Tour-standard and the views of the Santa Rosa Mountains are eye-popping.

PGA WEST STADIUM COURSE

7,266 yards, par 72, 142/73.0
Greens fee: $55–$235
800-742-9378, pgawest.com

TOP 100 YOU CAN PLAY

In the mid-1980s the best players on the PGA Tour refused to return to the Stadium Course, whining that it was too difficult. Well, Pete Dye's West Coast answer to the TPC at Sawgrass is laughing all the way to the bank, because every golfer who comes to town still lines up to play it. Technology has defanged the course for the pros since its big-hair heyday, but for the rest of us the Stadium Course remains relentless in its assault, thanks to insanely deep bunkers, moguls that resemble Vail ski slopes, and forced carries over water and desert. Long after you leave you'll remember the stirring mountain backdrops, the 19-foot-deep bunker guarding the green at No. 16 and the treacherous island green at No. 17. Sure, playing here is an exhausting—and often deflating—experience, but the numerous thrill-seeking opportunities and the prospect (however remote) of passing the most demanding test west of the Mississippi make the Stadium Course an essential stop.

WHERE TO STAY

J.W. Marriott Desert Springs Resort & Spa is a striking modern hotel at the foot of the Santa Rosa Mountains. Rates from $129. **800-228-9290, desertspringsresort.com** ● ●

The Grande Dame of the Desert since 1926, **La Quinta Resort & Club** features superior dining, a spa, tennis, and the best access to the three PGA West courses, as well as its own two fine tracks. Rates from $115. **800-598-3828, laquintaresort.com** ● ● The town's newest, hippest hotel, **The Parker Palm Springs**, is in revitalized downtown Palm Springs. They don't offer golf packages, but the concierge can make arrangements with many of the region's best private courses in addition to resort layouts. Rooms start at $205 per night. **760-770-5000, theparkerpalmsprings.com**

WHERE TO EAT

Fine desert dining gets no better than at **Azur** at La Quinta Resort & Club. The coconut-butter poached Maine lobster and espresso-cocoa-rubbed prime beef filet will take the sting out of any double bogey. **760-777-4835, laquintaresort.com** ● ● For the perfect post-round pit stop, try **Beer Hunter Sports Pub & Grill** in La Quinta, which serves up 46 TVs. **760-564-7442, thebeerhunter.com** ● ● **Arnold Palmer's Restaurant** in La Quinta is just what you'd expect from the King: it's a crowd pleaser with all-American entrees such as pot pie and mac and cheese, plus a practice putting green to smooth your stroke between courses. **760-771-4653, arnoldpalmers.net**

LOCAL KNOWLEDGE

Take your trip to new heights courtesy of **Nostalgic Warbird & Biplane Rides**, where a decorated Marine Corps major will take you up in a restored vintage plane. **800-991-2473, nostalgicwarbirdrides.com** ● ● The world's largest rotating tram cars at **Palm Springs Aerial Tramway** will ascend more than 8,000 feet in the air. **888-515-TRAM, pstramway .com** ● ● It took an Irish rock band (U2) to best capture the ethereal beauty of the Southwest. Visit the **Joshua Tree National Monument** an hour from downtown. **760-367-5500, joshua .tree.national-park.com** ● ● Dedicated to the restoration and preservation of America's legendary fighters and bombers, **Palm Springs Air Museum** has one of the world's largest collections of WW II airplanes. **760-778-6262, air-museum.org** ● ● **Living Desert Wildlife and Botanical Park** is a major family attraction with all kinds of critters. **760-346-5694, livingdesert.org**

GETTING THERE

Palm Springs is about a 110-mile drive east of Los Angeles. Twelve carriers fly to Palm Springs International Airport. **760-318-3800, palmspringsairport.com**

WHEN TO GO

Average daily highs head into the 100s June through August, so late fall, early spring, and winter are the best times for golf.

PLAY BALL!

Combine America's two greatest pastimes by teeing it up at these courses within home-run distance of some legendary ballparks

FENWAY PARK
GEORGE WRIGHT GOLF COURSE
6,357 yards, par 70
Greens fee: $20–$49
617-361-8313

This Donald Ross course five miles from downtown Boston is named after a 19th-century baseball legend. The tiny greens will have you asking, "Who's my daddy?"

YANKEE STADIUM
VAN CORTLANDT PARK GOLF COURSE
6,122 yards, par 70
Greens fee: $40–$50
718-543-4595, americangolf.com

Babe Ruth used to play here, but 20 years ago the country's oldest municipal course was a fearsome, crime-ridden place. Things have been cleaned up a lot since then. Expect to go extra innings to finish your round on a weekend.

CAMDEN YARDS
MOUNT PLEASANT GOLF COURSE
6,726 yards, par 71
Greens fee: $16–$28
410-254-5100, bmgcgolf.com

This muni is one of the best values in Baltimore. The hilly terrain offers more uneven lies than a steroid user testifying on Capitol Hill.

WRIGLEY FIELD
OLD ORCHARD COUNTRY CLUB
6,053 yards, par 70
Greens fee: $31–$73
847-255-2025, oldorchardcc.com

Located 10 miles from the Chicago loop, this tough track is as well conditioned as the Wrigley infield. As Ernie might say, "Let's play 36."

BANK ONE BALLPARK
PAPAGO GOLF COURSE
7,068 yards, par 72
Greens fee: $28
602-275-8428

There are three great Phoenix courses within six miles of BOB, but the Raven and the Legacy charge skybox ticket rates. Play all day on Papago's heaving greens for the price of a nosebleed seat.

ROGER CLEMENS RECOMMENDS
Roger Clemens owns seven Cy Young Awards and a 5 handicap. We asked for his favorite away-game courses. Here are five that you can play.

ANAHEIM
STRAWBERRY FARMS GOLF CLUB
Greens fee: $95–$145
949-551-1811, strawberryfarmsgolf.com

BALTIMORE
BULLE ROCK
Greens fee: $145
410-939-8887, bullerock.com

CLEVELAND
STONEWATER GOLF CLUB
Greens fee: $82
440-461-4653, stonewatergolf.com

KANSAS
IRONHORSE GOLF CLUB
Greens fee: $70
913-685-4653, ironhorsegolf.com

TORONTO
GLENN ABBEY GOLF CLUB
Greens fee: $235
905-844-1800, clublink.ca

VAIL VALLEY

VAIL VALLEY As befits one of the most affluent communities in North America, the quality of life in the Vail Valley is high—very high. The collection of restaurants and art galleries tucked into the faux-Tyrolean buildings in pedestrian-only Vail Village is exceptional. Yet despite its prosperity, Vail Valley isn't stuffy and there's just enough golf for a great getaway. The Valley is pricier than most summer golf destinations—green fees are high because the season is short, and because Vail is Vail—but reasonably priced accommodations are available.

WHERE TO PLAY

CLUB AT CORDILLERA

Summit: 7,380 yards, par 72, 135/74.0
Valley: 7,005 yards, par 71, 139/72.4
Mountain: 7,413 yards, par 72, 140/75.3
Short: 1,252 yards, par 27
Greens fee: $150–$205
970-926-2200, cordillera.rockresorts.com

You must be a guest at the Lodge & Spa at Cordillera, a GOLF MAGAZINE Silver Medalist, to play here. The most dramatic of Cordillera's four courses is the Summit, which was designed by Jack Nicklaus over the mountain ridges that tower above the Vail Valley at an elevation of 9,000 feet. The course is designed in a loop, which affords stunning views of the surrounding mountains. The tee box on the 18th reaches the highest point on the course, and this downhill par four rewards both the big hitter and everyone who takes in the scenery. The Tom Fazio–designed Valley has mountain desert terrain consisting of natural ravines decorated with sage and junipers. The Hale Irwin–designed Mountain, at 8,200 feet, provides enough hazards length to test the most experienced player's shot-making abilities, plus quite a few difficult-to-read greens. The Dave Pelz Short Course is the first attempt by GOLF MAGAZINE Top 100 Teacher Pelz to design a course that integrates his short-game teaching techniques and practice philosophy. Each hole is less than 130 yards but features challenging shots and tight bunkering.

COTTON RANCH GOLF CLUB

6,980 yards, par 72, 130/72.9
Greens fee: $65–$85
970-524-6200, cottonranchgolfclub.com

Fourteen holes of this Pete Dye design are situated on the floor of the beautiful Cottonwood Valley in Gypsum; the other four are atop a mesa serviced by a vertical lift. The "mesa holes" are lined with native sage, piñon, and cedars, offering a target golf experience similar to desert courses. On all 18 holes, players have to navigate streams, ponds, native wetlands, and a fair share of bunkers. The greens are medium-sized, undulating, and fast.

EAGLE RANCH GOLF COURSE

7,575 yards, par 72, 136/74.1
Greens fee: $69–$99
866-328-3232, eagleranchgolf.com

This course in Eagle, designed by Arnold Palmer and opened in 2001, is a prairie links-style layout that lies at the foot of the Sawatch Mountains in the Brush Creek Valley. Palmer has never concerned himself with trying to design difficult courses, especially when creating facilities for vacationers. That's not to say this course is easy. The 9th (498 yards) and 18th (478 yards) are demanding par fours that play together, on either side of a lake, and finish at sister greens separated by a beach bunker with sand washing into the water. One of the most picturesque holes is the 182-yard 5th, a par three that drops from an elevated tee box built into the side of a hill. The green borders a lake, front and right, and a bunker waits behind the green to catch thinly struck shots. Be ever aware of the wind here, which you may not be able to feel from the tee box.

Hole 17 at Cordillera
(Mountain Course),
Vail Valley, Colorado

RED SKY GOLF CLUB

Greg Norman Course:
7,580 yards, par 72, 137/72.7
Tom Fazio Course:
7,113 yards, par 72, 136/72.1
Greens fee: $175–$225
970-477-8425, redskygolfclub.com

TOP 100 YOU CAN PLAY

The aspen groves that predominate in the area comprise hundreds of trees, but they share a common root structure, making them a single organism. The magnificent Norman course shares a similar unity. There are astonishing shots to be tried, especially from the tips, which are surprisingly playable for a high single-digit handicapper. But while you won't soon forget knocking a hybrid onto the green of the downhill 283-yard par-three 16th, the strongest impression will be how the design hangs together. A weak or silly or showy hole is nowhere in evidence. The views from almost 8,000 feet will drop your jaw, but the layout demands that you keep your head on straight. The equally aesthetically pleasing Fazio course has a majestic, if split, personality. The desertlike canyon front nine gives way to a lush, aspen-dominated inward half, with the transition between the two taking place on the 231-yard par-three 10th, one of the most heroic one-shotters in the world. Fazio's wavy greens prove the design's most interesting element, full of ridges and tiers. The path to the greens is a touch less intimidating and hazardous than at the Norman, but the fact that each course ends on a majestic, reachable, risk-reward downhill par five only underscores the fact that these fraternal twins form a top-class brotherhood.

SONNENALP GOLF CLUB

7,100 yards, par 71, 138/72.3
Greens fee: $70–$160
970-477-5371, sonnenalp.com

Located 13 miles west of Vail Village in Edwards, this superb sagebrush-lined links by Bob Cupp and Jay Morrish is framed by alpine meadows, native grasses, and lakes and streams. The greens are lightning fast.

BEAVER CREEK GOLF COURSE

6,784 yards, par 70, 140/71.0
Greens fee: $80–$165
970-845-5775, beavercreek.com

This high-altitude (8,500 feet), exceptionally scenic, compact out-and-back design by Robert Trent Jones Jr. is dotted with fanciful mansions and rewards finesse and control, not power. Beaver Creek flows throughout the course, affecting your shots on several holes, and there's a 500-foot drop in elevation from the highest point to the lowest. Beware the narrow, treacherous opening holes.

THE CARD WRECKER: RED SKY GOLF CLUB, NORMAN COURSE NO. 4, 565 YARDS

It begins with an "I'm the king of the world!" tee shot from across the street that can hang in the air for 10 seconds to an angled fairway below, followed by a thought-provoking lay-up or adrenaline-inducing whack at a small, tricky, well-bunkered green.

Greg Norman on how to play it: "The first obstacle is negotiating a dramatic downhill tee shot to a narrow, sloping fairway with trouble left and right and a prevailing right-to-left wind. Precision is vitally important, especially if you have any thoughts of going for the green in two. The second shot is equally difficult, as a boundary fence runs the length of the hole on the right side, and seven bunkers lurk on the left. I played the grand opening round with John Elway, Dan Marino, and Mike Shanahan and lipped out for a double eagle. So good scores can be found, but a big number is very much a possibility if you don't exercise caution."

VAIL GOLF CLUB

7,024 yards, par 71, 121/70.8
Greens fee: $99
970-479-2260

The oldest course in town is a flat, friendly, tree-lined muni crisscrossed by Gore Creek. Beaver ponds come into play on a number of holes. The medium-sized greens are undulating and moderate in speed.

WHERE TO STAY

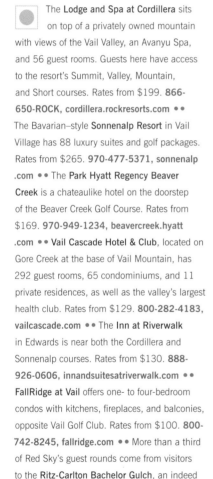

The **Lodge and Spa at Cordillera** sits on top of a privately owned mountain with views of the Vail Valley, an Avanyu Spa, and 56 guest rooms. Guests here have access to the resort's Summit, Valley, Mountain, and Short courses. Rates from $199. **866-650-ROCK, cordillera.rockresorts.com** •• The Bavarian–style **Sonnenalp Resort** in Vail Village has 88 luxury suites and golf packages. Rates from $265. **970-477-5371, sonnenalp .com** •• The **Park Hyatt Regency Beaver Creek** is a chateaulike hotel on the doorstep of the Beaver Creek Golf Course. Rates from $169. **970-949-1234, beavercreek.hyatt .com** •• **Vail Cascade Hotel & Club**, located on Gore Creek at the base of Vail Mountain, has 292 guest rooms, 65 condominiums, and 11 private residences, as well as the valley's largest health club. Rates from $129. **800-282-4183, vailcascade.com** •• The **Inn at Riverwalk** in Edwards is near both the Cordillera and Sonnenalp courses. Rates from $130. **888-926-0606, innandsuitesatriverwalk.com** •• **FallRidge at Vail** offers one- to four-bedroom condos with kitchens, fireplaces, and balconies, opposite Vail Golf Club. Rates from $100. **800-742-8245, fallridge.com** •• More than a third of Red Sky's guest rounds come from visitors to the **Ritz-Carlton Bachelor Gulch**, an indeed ritzy yet rustic lodge in the "Parkitecture" style and the latest example of Ritz's shift toward geographically specific luxury. Rates from $195. **970-748-6200, ritzcarlton.com**

WHERE TO EAT

The Ritz-Carlton Bachelor Gulch's fine dining restaurant, **Remington's**, features "gourmet mountain cuisine," which is, thanks to new chef Richard McCreadie, worth every penny. Two words: elk tenderloin. **970-748-6200, ritzcarlton.com** •• **Juniper** serves sophisticated American cuisine in a lively setting. On a warm evening, request a table on the raised patio overlooking the Eagle River. **970-926-7001, juniperrestaurant.com** •• **The French Press** has the best breakfast in Vail Valley, and it's just a few miles from Red Sky Ranch. **970-926-4740** •• The **Sapphire Restaurant & Oyster Bar's** Asian-influenced American cuisine is best evidenced by the brilliant tuna nachos appetizer. **719-476-2828, sapphirerestaurant.com**

LOCAL KNOWLEDGE

Outdoor activity is the Vail Valley's reason for being, and the water is where the most fun can be had. Kayak the Colorado River with the friendly folks at **Colorado River Center**, who can even get beginners down the mild rapids in one piece—and smiling. **888-759-4005, coloradorivercenter.com** •• After disembarking from your kayak (or car, if you're water-phobic), grab a cold beer and some great fries at a true piece of Americana, the **State Bridge Lodge**. Concerts Saturday and Sunday nights bring 'em in from all over; the Dixie Chicks and others played here before hitting the big time. **970-653-4444, statebridgelodge.com** •• Fishermen, cast your lot with **Fly Fishing Outfitters**. **800-595-8090, flyfishingoutfitters .net** •• Take a trek without your clubs around glorious **Booth Creek** in Vail, whose 50-foot waterfall would make Donald Trump envious. Use your 3-iron as a walking stick if it'll make you feel better. •• Hike from the Ritz-Carlton and you can take along its in-house Labrador retriever, Bachelor. •• Window-shoppers, dawdlers, and latté sippers should spend an afternoon in **Vail**, which is in the midst of a $1 billion (yes, *billion*) upgrade financed by a combination of public and private funds.

GETTING THERE

Fly into Vail/Eagle County Airport, which is served by Delta, Northwest, United, US Air, Continental, and American, or drive two hours from Denver International Airport. **eaglecounty.us**

WHEN TO GO

The dry Vail Valley sees about 300 sunny days a year, but the months of October through April get pretty chilly. High temperatures range from the low 60s in May, to the high 70s in August and high 60s in September.

LAS VEGAS
Sin City is less sinful than it used to be. No longer just a haven for hopelessly optimistic gamblers and washed-up lounge acts, most of the major resort casinos now make almost half their profits on non-gaming entertainment. MGM Mirage Resorts—whose 12 Las Vegas properties include most of the best-known hotels on the Strip—has helped transform the desert oasis into a destination for families. Golfers get their due, too. Staying at an MGM hotel gets you through the gate of the most famous—and formerly the most exclusive—course in town, Shadow Creek.

WHERE TO PLAY

SHADOW CREEK GOLF CLUB

7,239 yards, par 72
Greens fee: $500
866-260-0069, shadowcreek.com

TOP 100 YOU CAN PLAY
TOP 100 IN THE U.S.
TOP 100 IN THE WORLD

Shadow Creek is golf's Brigadoon—even casual fans of the game have heard of this mythical oasis in the desert, but precious few have actually laid eyes on it. For years it was open only to high rollers at Vegas impresario Steve Wynn's Mirage casino, and now that it is open to guests at all MGM Mirage properties, the price tag is $500. The course, opened in 1989 and designed by Tom Fazio, offers not a hint of the surrounding desert—the only sand you'll see is in the bunkers—and conjures more of a Carolina feel with tree-lined corridors and elevation changes. But what you get for your $500 is one great hole built upon another until you reach a show-stopping Vegas finale at Nos. 17 and 18.

PRIMM VALLEY GOLF CLUB

Lakes: 6,945 yards, par 71, 135/73.3
Desert: 7,131 yards, par 72, 135/74.2
Greens fee: $85–$155
800-386-7867, primmvalleygolfclub.com

This MGM Mirage–owned property is 40 minutes south of the Strip along Interstate 15, about one mile over the California border, and features two Tom Fazio–designed courses. The Desert is one of the more enjoyable outings in the area. There are only a few memorable holes—and none that make you stand back in awe—but it's a solid test that won't sour your mood before you hit the No Limit Hold 'Em tables. The lush Lakes opened to widespread acclaim in 1997. The layout is littered with water hazards that come into play on 11 holes and sports more trees than seems reasonable this side of Shadow Creek. The Lakes track won't bust you off the tee—the driving lines are fairly forgiving—but the second shots will make or break you. Beware who you get paired with on the first tee here: there's often a "mega pot" outing at Primm, and getting caught in that may be the biggest hazard here.

BALI HAI GOLF CLUB

7,002 yards, par 71, 130/73.0
Greens fee: $175–$325
888-427-6678, balihaigolfclub.com

Located right on the Strip in the shadow of the Mandalay Bay casino, Bali Hai was designed by Lee Schmidt and Brian Curley in 2000 and is known for its South Seas tropical feel and Augusta white sand bunkers. The course does come with one unusual hazard—the overhead traffic from McCarron International Airport next door—but if you want a quick 18 holes before dashing back to the tables, there is no more convenient location. Bali Hai is operated by Walters Golf, which has an affiliation with the MGM Mirage resorts to ease passage for resort guests onto its four courses, which also include Royal Links, Stallion Mountain, and Desert Pines.

LAKE LAS VEGAS RESORT

Reflection Bay: 7,261 yards, par 72, 138/74.8
The Falls: 7,250 yards, par 72
Greens fee: $255–$275
877-698-4653, lakelasvegas.com

TOP 100 YOU CAN PLAY

This GOLF MAGAZINE Gold Medal Resort 17 miles east of the Strip has two public courses. Opened in 1998, Jack Nicklaus' Reflection Bay ranks 54th on GOLF MAGAZINE's Top 100 Courses You Can Play. Routed around arroyos, water hazards, and the Hyatt Regency, it is a strategic masterpiece that demands three of its architect's celebrated attributes: a high fade, pinpoint accuracy, and on-course smarts. Fairways here are generous and the bunkering stern, but much of the course's bite comes around the greens. Five holes play along the lake. Nicklaus benefited from the superior piece of property here with Reflection Bay, while Weiskopf's blank canvas for the Falls, which opened in 2002, was little more than a rocky mountain and its barren foothills. This course is not unlike its architect: often entertaining, sometimes exasperating, and always in danger of derailing into something just plain goofy. The layout looks as if its roots owe more to dynamite than to fertilizer. The front nine plays down in the flats and could put you to sleep save for the 7th, a serpentine par five requiring a tee shot through a rock-walled alley and a delicate approach over an arroyo to a shallow green. This is not the place to gamble. Wait for your thrills on the back nine, an exhilarating ride that rises and falls like a stack of chips at the high rollers table.

Hole 17 at Shadow Creek,
Las Vegas, Nevada

WHERE TO STAY

MGM-Mirage can claim the best-known resorts on the Vegas Strip, including the MGM Grand, the Mirage, Bellagio, Luxor, Monte Carlo, Treasure Island, and New York, New York. Staying at any one of these properties will get you access to Shadow Creek Golf Club. Reservations—and information on their many promotions—can be obtained through **mgm-mirage.com** ● ● For the ultimate high-rollers experience, **Skylofts** at the MGM Grand is the way to go. These duplex penthouses come with a butler, complimentary limousine service, and a free bar—three elements that make you feel like a player. One-bedroom lofts range from $800 to $1,500 per night. **877-646-5638, skyloftsmgmgrand.com** ● ●

 Lake Las Vegas comprises three golf courses and as many hotels, all anchored around the largest privately owned lake in Nevada. Julia Roberts, John Cusack, Catherine Zeta-Jones, and Billy Crystal filmed the 2001 flop *America's Sweethearts* at the Morocco–inspired **Hyatt Regency at Lake Las Vegas**, which emerged with its fine rep intact. The Hyatt's real stars are the Pacific Rim cuisine at Japengo restaurant and the Moroccan marinated chicken at Café Tajine. Rooms start at $149. **888-591-1234, lakelasvegas.hyatt.com** ● ● The property's hotel-casinos also include a swanky new **Ritz-Carlton**, which offers

ultra-private suites atop the Pontevecchio bridge. Rooms start at $199. **800-241-3333, ritzcarlton.com** ● ● The condo suites at **MonteLago Village** are ideal for larger groups, shopaholics, and chocoholics. Browse the jewelry, original art, and designer duds in shops along cobblestone streets. Studios start at $129. **866-564-4799, montelagovillage.com**

WHERE TO EAT

Mix, atop the hotel at Mandalay Bay, is superstar chef Alain Ducasse's Las Vegas highlight. Feast on white truffle dishes on the outdoor terrace 64 stories above the Strip. **877-632-7800, mandalaybay.com** ● ● **Sensi** is located at the Bellagio and combines superb Italian and Asian cuisine. **877-234-6358, bellagio.com** ● ● The first chef to win three consecutive Michelin stars has landed at the MGM Grand. **L'Atelier de Joel Robuchon** serves up French cuisine. Almost as enjoyable as the food is watching the military precision of the staff preparing it. **702-891-7358, mgmgrand.com**

LOCAL KNOWLEDGE

Cirque Du Soleil has two shows in Las Vegas that are among the most engaging acrobatic spectacles ever mounted on a stage. **O** takes place in a massive water tank at the Bellagio, while **Ka** at the MGM Grand will have you

spending most of the show wondering how much the astonishing stage hydraulics must have cost. These are two shows you don't need to be traveling with kids to enjoy. **cirquedusoleil.com** ● ● If you want to get up close and personal with the stars of the World Poker Tour, the best bet is the poker pit at the **Bellagio**, where such stars as Phil Ivey and Chip Reese ply their trade. Just remember the golden rule from the movie *Rounders*—if you don't spot the sucker at the table within 30 minutes, it's you. **bellagio.com** ● ● For the ultimate rush in Vegas, try **Insanity** at the Stratosphere. You'll be spinning from an arm atop the tower at three G's, ending up facing directly down 100 floors to the Strip below. **insanityride.com**

WHEN TO GO

If your golden rule is not to play golf when the temperatures exceed your worst-ever score, abandon it for Las Vegas. Hotel and golf fees in summer are often a fraction of the usual prices. You can only play one round per day—teeing off in the early morning—but it will cost you a lot less. Temperatures are mildest from November to April.

INSIDER'S GUIDE: ERICK LINDGREN

We asked the World Poker Tour star and golf nut how you can act like a pro when setting your on-course wager in Las Vegas, and how to collect if you win:

"If you are going to bet with a stranger, set your match as you normally would but only do it for nine holes and bet smaller than normal. This will at least force him to hustle you for a decent

period of time (yes, there are hustlers out here, and no, I'm not one of them) and you can judge his ability. Collecting debt is a tricky thing. Often the wagers are large enough that you can't expect to get paid immediately. This requires some trust if you allow him to owe you. Most everybody is honest enough to pay as long as they have the money. If they don't have the money, I wish you lots of patience and good luck."

LAKE TAHOE
With some of the sweetest air and most scenic eye candy in the nation, the two-state Tahoe and High Sierra region is one great golf venue. The area, straddling California and Nevada, has across-the-board appeal, thanks to the variety of golf-course designs and mountain-and-forest topography. Unparalleled outdoor recreation plus nightlife and gambling on the Nevada side add to the attraction. Then there's Lake Tahoe itself. Any description of fewer than 10,000 words is insufficient to relate its grandeur and beauty. It is the third deepest lake in North America, its water nearly 99 percent pure—virtually the same as distilled. It's said that a dinner plate can be seen some 75 feet below the surface. Ringed by snow-capped peaks in the 10,000-foot range, this 22-mile-long, 12-mile-wide inland sea 190 miles east of San Francisco is one of the choicest playgrounds in the West.

WHERE TO PLAY (NEVADA SIDE)

EDGEWOOD TAHOE GOLF COURSE
7,445 yards, par 72, 144/75.5
Greens fee: $200
775-588-3566, edgewood-tahoe.com

There are only about 10 courses in the U.S. that are true scenic treasures, where the beauty of the surroundings exceeds the test of golf. Edgewood Tahoe in Stateline is one of them. At 6,200 feet above sea level, this stunner, designed by George Fazio on a former cattle ranch in 1968 and updated by nephew Tom in the mid-1990s, hosts the annual American Century Championship, a celebrity golf event. Stretched across an open meadow and cut through pine forests, Edgewood Tahoe was designed to provide a stern examination, but the drop-dead gorgeous setting takes the sting out of high scores. Finishing holes, banked along the lake, are breathtaking. Caddies are available.

CLUB AT GENOA LAKES
7,263 yards, par 72, 132/73.7
Greens fee: $50–$120
775-782-4653, genoalakes.com

A John Harbottle–Peter Jacobsen design set along the Carson River in Genoa, this course is a nature lover's paradise, with mature trees, wetlands, and water on 14 holes. Several of the holes climb into hills; the rest roll beside the shady river. The Sierra Nevada provides a dramatic backdrop.

DAYTON VALLEY GOLF CLUB
7,218 yards, par 72, 140/75.1
Greens fee: $75–$95
775-246-7888, daytonvalley.com

Flat and windswept, this Arnold Palmer–Ed Seay creation in Dayton is all there right in front of you—no blind shots, nothing tricky. There's plenty of water, with several forced carries, notably on the par threes. It's a lot of work, but fun work. It's also a first-stage PGA Tour qualifying site and a big-time test from the tips at yards.

LAKERIDGE GOLF COURSE
6,715 yards, par 71, 130/71.8
Greens fee: $45–$100
775-825-2200, lakeridgegolf.com

A long-time area favorite located within Reno city limits, this hilly Robert Trent Jones design (1969) is known for its signature island green at the long par-three 15th, which drops 120 feet from tee to green. Great mountain and city views.

Hole 16 at Edgewood
Tahoe Golf Course,
Lake Tahoe, Nevada

WHERE TO PLAY (CALIFORNIA SIDE)

GOLF CLUB AT WHITEHAWK RANCH

6,927 yards, par 71, 133/72.6
Greens fee: $95–$125
530-836-0394, golfwhitehawk.com

A consensus must-play, this pristine and serene Dick Bailey design 45 miles north of Truckee has it all—alpine air, skyscraper pines, five lakes, lots of streams, sprawling meadows, and a morning fog that clings to the fairways like gray cotton candy. Whitehawk is roomier than other mountain courses—you'll be able to hit a driver here and you'll need it, too.

DRAGON AT GOLD MOUNTAIN

7,077 yards, par 72, 147/74.2
Greens fee: $75–$130
800-368-7786, dragongolf.com

Glorious, fun, and woodsy, this semiprivate spread in Clio by Robin Nelson winds through the mountains, providing something different at every hole—splendid views, towering pines, rock outcrops. It's tricky, too, requiring both knowledge and heart. The Dragon makes a statement and keeps you off balance as it climbs and plunges. Six sets of tees, starting at 4,611 yards, enhance playability. The Nakoma clubhouse, originally designed by Frank Lloyd Wright in the 1920s for another club, anchors Gold Mountain.

COYOTE MOON GOLF CLUB

7,177 yards, par 72, 138/74.1
Greens fee: $150
530-587-0886, coyotemoongolf.com

Debuted to immediate acclaim in 2000, this Brad Bell–designed course meanders through the Sierra Nevada foothills in Truckee. A stand-alone track, it rolls through 250 acres of pines without a single house to disturb the view. A very fair test with few forced carries and great conditioning.

WHERE TO STAY

If you like the natural setting of Tahoe without the noise, smoke, and clatter of the casinos, check out **Embassy Suites** in South Lake Tahoe on the California side. It's a nice, quiet place only minutes from all the action. Rates from $123. **877-497-8483, embassytahoe .com** •• Both **Caesar's Tahoe** and **Harveys** have packages that include Edgewood Tahoe. Rates from $109. Web site bookings only for golf packages: **golfthehighsierra.com**

WHERE TO EAT

Evan's American Gourmet Café in South Lake Tahoe serves seafood specialties with an eclectic blend of seasonings and pairings. **530-542-1990, evanstahoe.com** •• For tasty lakefront dining and fun cocktail specialties, try the California cuisine at the **Riva Grille Restaurant on the Lake** in South Lake Tahoe. **530-542-2600, rivagrill.com**

LOCAL KNOWLEDGE

Put it all on black at one of Tahoe's 11 **casinos.** For a complete list and descriptions, see **laketahoeconcierge.com** •• Try **Action Watersports** at Timber Cove Marina for parasailing, sailboat cruises, and boat and Jet Ski rentals. **530-544-5387, action-watersports.com** •• **Tahoe Paddle & Oar** in Kings Beach has a large selection of kayaks and canoes for rent, as well as guided tours on Crystal Bay. **530-581-3029, tahoepaddle .com** •• Looking for a faster ride? **Tahoe Whitewater Tours** will take you down one of five Sierra rivers. Rates start at $45. **530-581-2441, gowhitewater.com** •• At **Squaw Valley Stables,** you can ride horseback through the site of the 1960 Winter Olympics. One hour starts at $29. **530-583-7433, squawvalleystables.com**

GETTING THERE

Lake Tahoe is 198 miles from San Francisco, 100 miles from Sacramento, and drivable on Highways 50 and 89. Nine carriers fly into Reno Tahoe International Airport, including Northwest, America West, Continental, United, and Delta. **renoairport.com**

WHEN TO GO

Summer is peak season. Great deals can be had in the fall and spring shoulder seasons, particularly in April, October, and November.

For more information on the region, contact the Reno-Sparks Convention & Visitors Authority (888-HIT-RENO, playreno.com) or Lake Tahoe Visitors Authority (800-AT-TAHOE, virtualtahoe.com).

RENO

Glitzy resorts and stratospheric greens fees give Las Vegas a lock on golf's high rollers, but for most players eyeing a Nevada road trip, Reno is the better bet. The values are good, the weather is great, and the thin mountain air allows for lots of ego-boosting drives. With dozens of quality courses clustered a short drive from downtown casinos, and others in the mountains just outside the city, you can clean out your buddies on the links by day and lose it all back at the tables that night.

WHERE TO PLAY

RESORT AT RED HAWK

Lakes Course: 7,140 yards, par 72, 134/72.9
Greens fee: $50–$100
775-626-6000, resortatredhawk.com

The avian theme—holes have names like Falcon's Run and Heron's Nest—is alive and well at Reno's most immaculate public course. But Robert Trent Jones Jr. made sure that birdies would remain scarce, mining his design with more than 100 bunkers and putting water in play on half the holes. Red Hawk is perched at nearly 5,000 feet, so its yardage isn't as daunting as it appears on paper. But there's no denying the heft of the par-three 17th, a 241-yard blast over a lake, or the testy 434-yard par-four 18th, where the wind works against you and a big cottonwood tree helps guard the green. Red Hawk also has a private course, the Hills course, designed by Hale Irwin, which sets aside a handful of tee times for the public. Don't tell the members we said so, but the Lakes is actually the better track.

WOLF RUN GOLF CLUB

7,100 yards, par 72, 133/73.1
Greens fee: $45–$75
775-851-3301, wolfrungolfclub.com

Depending when you play it, Wolf Run, the home course of the University of Nevada, can feel like two different courses—a docile animal in the morning or a monster in the wind-whipped afternoon. Elevation changes play a huge role here. So does course knowledge, which helps on a number of risk-reward par-fours. The 412-yard 4th looks simple on the scorecard but leaves you muddling whether to lay up or attempt a carry over wetlands 226 yards out. The fairways are wide and forgiving, and the course is burdened by a couple of forgettable holes. But the par threes are nifty, and Thomas Creek, which wanders through the course, can seem like the Mississippi when the winds at this Wolf begin to howl.

LAKERIDGE GOLF COURSE

6,715 yards, par 71, 130/71.8
Greens fee: $45–$100
775-825-2200, lakeridgegolf.com

LakeRidge is the handiwork of Robert Trent Jones Sr., who couldn't have imagined back in 1970 how technology would transform the game. This is a course of throwback touches that draws little defense from length. It protects itself instead with doglegs, ancient oaks, and bunkers designed to deceive the eye. Many of the holes have small, elevated greens, but not the signature par-three 15th, which plummets from a skyscraper tee box to an island green. The green is enormous, but as your playing partners pause to admire the postcard view and a gallery gathers from the groups behind you, the target gradually begins to shrink. By the time you hit, it looks no larger than a speck in a wind-blown lake.

OLD GREENWOOD

7,518 yards, par 72, 149/75.8
Greens fee: $100–$170
800-754-3070, oldgreenwood.com

Jack Nicklaus' design sits in the high Sierras, a half-hour drive on the interstate from Reno but a world away in its terrain. This is alpine golf, in 8,000 feet of altitude, with tall pines shadowing every shot. Although not as sadistic as some early Nicklaus courses, Old Greenwood punishes misplaced drives by forcing you to shape your approach shot or execute a long and awkward carry over water. The par-five 6th is a splendid siren: it tempts you to try reaching it in two despite the watery risk that you'll take a 10. Old Greenwood is part of a resort development, so you'll see some houses. But the setting is serene, and even when you're standing in the heart of the fairway it feels as if you're wandering through the woods.

D'ANDREA GOLF CLUB

6,849 yards, par 71, 133/72.2
Greens fee: $45–$105
775-331-6363, dandreagolf.com

D'problem most players face at D'Andrea is d'constant elevation change. Designer Keith Foster was handed a hilly plot to work with, and rather than bulldoze it into oblivion, he opted to go with the lay of the land. As a result, getting up and down at D'Andrea often means going from tee to green. The character of the course is apparent from the first hole, a steeply sloped par four that requires two extra clubs on the approach. But it's even clearer when you reach No. 3, a nosebleed par three that drops severely to a tricky tiered green. Conditions at D'Andrea are firm and fast, and the views are superb of downtown Reno and the Sierra Nevada looming just beyond. Foster did well with what he was given. And his flair for design comes through in places, like the par-three 6th, a long-iron over water with a green fronted by a high stone wall. Its nickname is "aces and eights" in honor of the numbers that come into play.

WHERE TO STAY

Casinos are never quaint, but the **Siena Hotel Spa & Casino** comes close. Rooms from $100. **775-327-4362, sienareno.com** • • With 817 rooms, **El Dorado** is big and bustling. Rooms start at $45. **800-879-8879, eldoradoreno .com** • • Big-name entertainers, ranging from the Spinners to Don Rickles, perform at John Ascuaga's **Nugget**, where rooms start at $132. Well, they were once big names, anyway. **800-648-1177, janugget.com**

WHERE TO EAT

The **Liberty Belle Restaurant** offers rare prime rib and even rarer slot machines. Some 200 of them make up the restaurant's slot machine museum. Stored behind glass, they include the Liberty Belle, the late 1800s precursor to the modern slot. **775-825-1776, liberty bellereno.com**

LOCAL KNOWLEDGE

Water is bad for golfers but great for kayakers. **Truckee River Whitewater Park** at Wingfield Park features a half-mile whitewater kayak course. **775-334-2414** • • At the **Wilbur D. May Museum** you'll find Egyptian scarabs, Eskimo scrimshaws, and other cool and curious items collected by the wealthy world traveler. Adults: $5, children: $3. **775-785-5961, maycenter.com**

GETTING THERE

Nine carriers fly into Reno Tahoe International Airport, including Northwest, America West, Continental, United, and Delta. **renoairport.com**

WHEN TO GO

Reno is a year-round town, but peak season is summer. Starting around May, greens fees and hotel rates go up, all of which makes April a good time to make the trip. The weather can be cool, but perfectly playable. And the golf costs roughly half of what it does in summer.

Hole 16 at the Resort
at Red Hawk (Lake),
Reno, Nevada

HOUSTON

Houston...we have solved the problem! America's space capital is also one of its great golf towns, but the glut of out-of-this-world courses makes narrowing the field more daunting than a moon walk. These courses will turn any buddy trip into a blast.

WHERE TO PLAY

REDSTONE GOLF CLUB

7,422 yards, par 72, 138/75.8
Greens fee: $115–$130
281-459-7820, redstonegolfclub.com

Redstone's new Tournament Course, designed by Rees Jones and David Toms, hosted its first PGA Tour Shell Houston Open in 2006. (Redstone's other course, which previously hosted the event, has gone private.) If you opt to play from the tips, the shortest par five you'll face is 564 yards long. If you move up a set of tees, you'll still face plenty of challenges with tough bunkers, water hazards and greens that have more curves than Jennifer Lopez. Access to the private course—which was unanimously well received by Tour pros—is available for guests of the Houstonian Hotel.

MAGNOLIA CREEK

England: 3,664 yards, par 36
Ireland: 3,680 yards, par 36
Scotland: 3,669 yards, par 36
Greens fee: $48–$59
281-557-0555, magnoliacreekgolf.com

Golfers with a lot of imagination (and a bad fake accent) can pretend they're playing Scottish links golf at this 27-hole facility just south of town. There's one lone tree on the entire property—a pine in the center of the 6th on the Scotland course—but plenty of knolls, waist-high grass, and wind off the Gulf of Mexico. And polish your Texas wedge. Many greens have severe collection areas.

Hole 4 at Blackhorse
Golf Club (North),
Houston, Texas

BLACKHORSE GOLF CLUB

North: 7,301 yards, par 72, 130/75.0
South: 7,171 yards, par 72
Greens fee: $69–$89
281-304-1747, blackhorsegolfclub.com

Peter Jacobsen and GOLF MAGAZINE Top 100 Teacher Jim Hardy designed the two tracks here. The North course demands sharp iron play to avoid the jailhouse bunkers protecting the greens. The South is more treelined and less testing, but you'll still need plenty of stick to carry a marsh on the 213-yard 17th. Both courses are routed around wetlands—water is in play on 19 of the 36 holes—and you seldom will have a level stance.

CYPRESS WOOD GOLF CLUB

Cypress: 6,909 yards, par 72, 134/74.4
Creek: 6,937 yards, par 72, 124/72.0
Tradition: 7,220 yards, par 72
Greens fee: $40–$55
281-821-6300, cypresswood.com

You'll need to maneuver the ball like Astros ace Roger Clemens at Cypress Wood's three courses, just 15 minutes away from Bush Intercontinental Airport. Dense woodlands help to create tight chutes that place a premium on driving accuracy. The Tradition course—known for its exhausting bunkers and heaving greens—recently reopened after an extensive renovation.

WHERE TO STAY

You'll love the old-time baseball motif and the fact that there are plenty of restaurants within walking distance of the **Inn at the Ballpark**. Rooms from $89. **866-406-1520, innattheballpark.com ● ●** The **Alden-Houston**, built in 1924, boasts all modern conveniences. Rooms from $155. **832-200-8808, alden hotels.com ● ●** The **Houstonian's** guests have access to Redstone's private course. There's also gourmet dining at the **Manor House** and **Olivette**. Rooms from $185. **877-348-8800, thehoustonian.com**

WHERE TO EAT

El Tiempo Cantina's fajitas come with combinations of steak, chicken, shrimp, and lobster and are almost as tasty as the margaritas. **713-807-1600, eltiempocantina .com ● ●** In a town known for barbecue, **Goode Company Barbeque's** is superb. **800-627-3502, goodecompany.com ● ●** The **Strip House's** mammoth cuts of beef—like a 32-ounce double-cut strip steak—and their 24-layer chocolate cake are sure to fill you up. **713-659-6000**

LOCAL KNOWLEDGE

Boldly go where a few million have gone before and visit the inside of a space shuttle at the **Space Center Houston**. **281-244- 2100, spacecenter.org ● ●** The battleship **U.S.S. Texas**, which fought in World War I and World War II, is open for tours in nearby La Porte. **281-479-2431, tpwd.state.tx.us ● ●** Hear some live country music and two-step

the night away at **Blanco's**. **713-439-0072, houstonredneck.com/blancos.html ● ●** Catch a Houston Texans' game at **Reliant Stadium**. **832-667-2000, houstontexans.com**

GETTING THERE

Most carriers service Houston's two airports, George Bush Intercontinental and William Hobby International. Rental cars with GPS are smart in this sprawling city (available from Hertz and Avis).

WHEN TO GO

Course conditions peak in the fall through the early spring.

SAN ANTONIO
Hilly San Antonio, the country's ninth largest city, not only has an abundance of great public courses, but a mild climate, a less-hurried feel than Houston or Dallas, and a vibrant Mexico-centric culture. Add kid-magnet attractions such as SeaWorld and Six Flags Fiesta Texas, historical jewels such as the Alamo and Spanish Mission Trail, and the alluring limestone canyons and cool streams of the Texas Hill Country, and you have a fine alternative to better-known golf meccas. A San Antonio primer: The region is neither pool-table prairie nor piney Deep South. Expect rolling fairways, Bermuda grass everywhere, and plenty of different looks, from woods to plains to quarries.

WHERE TO PLAY

PECAN VALLEY GOLF CLUB
7,010 yards, par 71, 131/73.9
Greens fee: $70
210-333-9018, pecanvalleygc.com

A $5.5 million renovation by architect Bob Cupp to J. Press Maxwell's 1963 design attracted the 2001 U.S. Amateur Public Links Championship and restored this jewel to its former luster (it hosted the 1968 PGA Championship). Salado Creek winds among huge, gnarly oaks—one is 800 years old—their branches shrinking the fairways. The mighty 2nd, a 453-yard uphill par four, is probably the best hole in town. Walkable and free of fairway housing, the city's best players flock to this pure-golf sanctuary.

LA CANTERA GOLF CLUB
Palmer: 6,926 yards, par 71, 142/74.2
Resort: 7,021 yards, par 72, 134/72.5
Greens fee: $125–$140
210-558-4653 (Resort); 210-558-2365 (Palmer Course), lacanteragolfclub.com

Famous for its hallelujah tee shots from 80-foot quarry walls and roller-coaster scenery (Six Flags's 16-story Superman Krypton Coaster looms nearby), the original Resort course, a 1995 Tom Weiskopf–Jay Morrish work, hosts the PGA Tour's Valero Texas Open. Even more stunning is La Cantera's Palmer course, with its breathtaking hilltop views of the city and holes cut beside deep ravines and limestone cliffs. Fun and fair, this is thrill-packed golf with a matching price tag, but the course and magnificent Westin resort are worth the splurge.

HILL COUNTRY GOLF CLUB
Oaks: 3,438 yards, par 36
Creeks: 3,429 yards, par 36
Lakes: 3,502, par 36
Greens fee: $125–$145
210-520-4040, hillcountry.hyatt.com

Arthur Hills' seductively subtle design intrigues better players and deserves, if not requires, two rounds to appreciate it. Blind shots and overhanging trees have you always thinking shot placement. Unobtrusive housing and a restful ranch setting perfectly complement this exceptional Hyatt Regency Resort compound.

SILVER HORN GOLF CLUB

6,922 yards, par 72, 134/79.9
Greens fee: $55–$65
210-545-5300, silverhorngolfclub.com

Like Pecan Valley, this Randy Heckenkemper design is not about awesome, cliff-hanging golf, just intelligent holes. It quietly attracts the low-handicapper crowd with Tour-like par fours, speedy rounds, and great conditioning. Walkable and mature, Silver Horn is better than many overhyped rivals.

CEDAR CREEK GOLF COURSE

7,158 yards, par 72, 132/73.4
Greens fee: $26–$30
210-695-5050

Among the nation's better munis, Cedar Creek, opened in 1989, is caviar golf on a fajita budget. Steep ravines, waterfalls, and multitiered greens make this ample course the equal of some area resorts at one third the price. Hard to walk, very popular, and, alas, somewhat slow.

REPUBLIC GOLF CLUB

7,007 yards, par 71, 131/73.5
Greens fee: $35–$49
210-359-0000, republicgolfclub.net

Downstream from Pecan Valley and 10 minutes from the Alamo, Republic is a new pure-golf experience with big, fast greens and secluded oak-lined holes. No encroaching homes, no glitz, just inviting fairways and impenetrable woodsy rough in a beautiful river flood plain. From the hacienda clubhouse to the eco-mindful use of replanted trees and recycled water, Republic's owners got everything right.

QUARRY GOLF CLUB

6,740 yards, par 71, 128/72.4
Greens fee: $75–$90
210-824-4500, quarrygolf.com

Architect Keith Foster, known for creative natural layouts, carved a treeless, links-style course from this turn-of-the-century limestone quarry. Busy, plenty of water, truly unique. Trendy shopping and a movie theater just up the hill. Some people adore this place; others are ho-hum.

BANDIT GOLF CLUB

6,928 yards, par 71, 130/72.7
Greens fee: $40–$50
888-923-7846, banditgolfclub.com

Twenty minutes outside San Antonio in New Braunfels, Foster has created another demanding layout with more than two miles of creek, big elevation changes, sharp doglegs, and 13 water holes. A good bargain and close to factory-outlet heaven.

GOLF CLUB OF TEXAS

7,022 yards, par 72, 135/73.1
Greens fee: $55
210-677-0027, thegolfcluboftexas.com

A sprawling, windy course located on historic Briggs Ranch 20 miles west of town. Less hilly than other area courses, good service, plus a Texas-shaped water hazard. Yee-haw.

WHERE TO STAY

 The **Westin La Cantera Resort** promotes golf packages starting at $329, including accommodations, unlimited golf, and breakfast. **210-558-6500, westinlacantera.com** • •

 The **Hyatt Regency Hill Country Resort** offers a one-night golf package priced at $290 for one player ($350 for two) that includes accommodations, unlimited golf with cart and range balls, full breakfast, and complimentary valet parking. **800-233-1234, hillcountry.hyatt.com**

WHERE TO EAT

So much Mexican food, so few belt notches. Try the muy fancy **El Mirador** on Saint Mary Street for delectable lobster tacos. **210-225-9444** • • **La Calesa (210-732-6017, lacalesa.com)** and local faves **Los Barrios (210-732-6017)** and **Mi Tierra (210-225-7262, mitierracafe.com)** are more casual, but just as tasty. • • **Aldino** serves fine northern Italian cuisine. **210-340-0000, aldinos.com** • • **Craig's Sauté and Grill**, in Sequin, serves creative Pacific Rim delights. **830-303-3553** • • **Le Reve** is a dressy French splurge. **210-212-2221** • • **The Liberty Bar** offers unpretentious home-grown grub. **210-227-1187, liberty-bar.com** • • **Casbeer's Center Bar and Grill** (good burgers) frequently offers jazz, blues, and roots music. **210-732-3511, casbeers.com** • • Head to the **Laboratory Brewing Company** for cervezas, tamales, and music. **210-824-1997**

LOCAL KNOWLEDGE

Try **Gruene Hall** for well-known Texas acts. **830-629-5077, gruenehall.com** • • Don't miss seeing the **Spanish Mission Trail (210-932-1001, nps.gov/saan)** and, of course, the **Alamo**, a tourist cliché but also an awe-inspiring monument. **thealamo.com** • • The **McNay Art Museum (210-824-5368, mcnayart.org)**, which is traditional, and **ArtPace (888-212-9247, artpace.org)**, which is modern, both have large, inspiring collections.

GETTING THERE

San Antonio International Airport is within a three-hour flight of most of the continental U.S.

WHEN TO GO

Average daily highs never drop below the low 60s in winter but can reach highs into the 100s in July and August. Spring and fall are best for golf.

Visit the San Antonio Convention and Visitors' Bureau Web site for a list of other attractions. 800-447-3372, sanantoniocvb.com.

SALT LAKE CITY

SALT LAKE CITY Never thought you'd win a long-drive contest? Now you can, with a golf road trip of more than 1,500 miles. Head west but bypass the crowded courses in Arizona, Nevada, and California. Make your way to Salt Lake City and then head north on Interstate 15 and keep going. And going. The drives out here are measured in miles, not yards, and they take you to some of the most beautiful places—and courses—in the country. Keep going until you reach such cities as Butte, Montana; Sun Valley, Idaho; and Jackson Hole, Wyoming. Although ski runs outnumber golf holes here, and national parks get most of the summer visitors, you'll find a handful of high-altitude layouts surrounded by dramatic landscapes that you won't encounter anywhere else. A visit to all three cities in one trip (a journey that would require a full day of driving between stops) means one of three things: You have plenty of time on your hands, you have a coffee maker in your car, or you're a golf writer being paid to rack up some serious miles. Whatever your category, each city offers so many diversions that a little golf can provide a break from your tourist itinerary.

Hole 15 at Sun Valley Resort, Sun Valley, Idaho

GETTING THERE

If you're flying out to these parts, odds are you'll be routed through Salt Lake City. You can hop a small plane from there to regional airports in the Sun Valley, Jackson Hole and Butte areas. Do it that way, however, and you'll miss some terrific drives, with views of eye-popping scenery and plenty of wildlife.

WHEN TO GO

Late summer through late autumn, before the first snowfall, is prime for three- and four-day jaunts to any one of these destinations.

Want more information? Go to visitmt.com, visitsunvalley.com or jacksonholenet.com.

SALT LAKE CITY TO ANACONDA

The drive north between Salt Lake City and Butte gives you plenty of time to contemplate swing changes. The trip clocks in at six hours, with the midpoint coming at Idaho Falls, where you can grab some lunch and check out the famed waterfalls of the Snake River.

WHERE TO PLAY

OLD WORKS GOLF COURSE

7,705 yards, par 72, 133/76.0
Greens fee: $29–$44
406-563-5989, oldworks.org

THRIFTY 50

Cross into Montana and you'll weave through the Beaverhead and Deer Lodge National Forests before taking Interstate 90 west to Anaconda, home to the only U.S. course that sits atop an Environmental Protection Agency Superfund Cleanup site, although the copper mines and smelters that made Anaconda famous are long gone. Jack Nicklaus transformed this wasteland more than a mile above sea level into a golfer's Eden. The Golden Bear preserved the history of the old smelter by building the front nine around Anaconda's old Upper Works—the original ore-smelting facility—and the second nine on land that housed the Lower Works. Brick flues, slurry chutes, and granite slabs from the old mill still stand, as do remnants of the Upper Works, which sit adjacent to the third fairway. Old Works has also grabbed attention for using black slag, a byproduct of the copper-smelting process, in bunkers rather than traditional white sand.

FAIRMONT HOT SPRINGS RESORT

6,741 yards, par 72, 107/68.6
Greens fee: $29–$39
800-332-3272, FairmontMontana.com

On your way in or out of Anaconda, stay and play at the Fairmont Hot Springs Resort on Interstate 90, 17 miles east of Anaconda and 15 miles west of Butte. The resort's Lloyd Wilder–designed course is more fun than fearsome. It's also a bargain. Lodge guests are eligible for a discounted greens fee.

WHERE TO STAY

When Old Works opened in the late 1990s, it was hailed as a breakthrough for Anaconda and the surrounding community. But the small, rustic mining town still struggled to succeed as a golf destination, largely because of its lack of accommodations. A 30-room lodge at Old Works is in the bidding stages. Until then, a few small motels in Anaconda welcome golfers:

The Trade Wind (406-563-3428) is only $59 per night and the Vagabond Motel (800-231-2660, vagabondmt.com) is just a 5-iron or two from Old Works. ●● Fairmont Hot Springs Resort on Interstate 90, 17 miles east of Anaconda and 15 miles west of Butte, has two hot-springs pools, the Mile High Dining Room, Springwater Café, and Whiskey Joe's lounge. 800-332-3272, FairmontMontana.com

LOCAL KNOWLEDGE

Walk through the old mining town of Anaconda, founded in 1883, and stop at the Anaconda Visitor Center Complex (406-563-2400) in the middle of town to get your bearings; then visit both the old City Hall, which now houses Copper Village Museum (406-563-2422) and shops and the historical and beautiful Washoe Theater (406-563-6161).

SALT LAKE CITY TO SUN VALLEY

The drive from Salt Lake City to Sun Valley will take about five hours, most of it on fast-moving Interstates 84 and 15, until you reach Idaho Highway 75 at Twin Falls. There you'll head north to Sun Valley on local routes. This part of Idaho is renowned as a ski mecca and a hangout for celebrities. Ernest Hemingway is buried in the neighboring town of Ketchum, but these days you might spot Demi Moore, Bruce Willis, Arnold Schwarzenegger, or snowboarding aficionado David Duval strolling around town.

WHERE TO PLAY

SUN VALLEY RESORT GOLF COURSE

6,892 yards, par 72, 140/72.2
Greens fee: $89–$145
208-622-2251, sunvalley.com

Sun Valley Resort opened its doors in 1936. Two years later it unveiled a course designed by William Bell amid the pine forests near Bald and Dollar Mountains. The layout, redesigned in 1980 by Robert Trent Jones Jr., wraps around Trail Creek and changes elevation dramatically. This is five-star scenery. A trio of par threes is what you will remember most. The 5th, at 120 yards, is the shortest hole at Sun Valley, but your uphill tee shot must carry Trail Creek and a large bunker to reach a severely sloped green. A new back tee at the par-three 15th stretches this downhill devil to 244 yards, with a vertical drop of 75 feet. Finally, the 197-yard 17th plays over a large pond that doubles as a goose sanctuary. When the hole is cut on the front-right of the green, you'll have but 20 feet between the water's edge and the cup.

ELKHORN RESORT

7,214 yards, par 72, 135/74.2
Greens fee: $155
800-355-4676, elkhornresort.mb.ca

Also in Sun Valley, Elkhorn Resort's 29-year-old layout is one of the few design collaborations between Robert Trent Jones Sr. and son Robert Jr. The course struggled to maintain its upscale status, but new owners brought in management Troon Golf, who proscribed a massive redesign in 2005. The front nine is hilly, and the back nine has water hazards coming into play at least seven times. In 1993, the club hosted the Nike Boise Open, one of the SGA National qualifiers, and the Idaho Tournament of Champions. Nonmembers can play after 2 P.M., but you must make tee-time reservations three days in advance.

BIGWOOD GOLF CLUB

6,904 yards, par 72, 117/70.5
Greens fee: $29–$49
208-726-4024
bigwoodatthunderspring.com

You'll get some serious bang for your buck at the nine-hole Bigwood Golf Course just north of Ketchum. Designed by Robert Muir Graves, Bigwood uses multiple tees that help make two loops of the layout a good day's work. There are bunkers aplenty and magnificent views of nearby Bald Mountain.

WHERE TO STAY

Sun Valley Resort is the opposite of Anaconda when it comes to accommodations. The resort is a village unto itself with a total of 509 rooms at the Sun Valley Lodge and Sun Valley Inn, as well as resort-owned apartments, cottages, and condominiums. Rates from $109. **800-786-8259, sunvalley.com**

WHERE TO EAT

Favorites at Sun Valley Resort include **Gretchen's (208-622-2144)** in the Sun Valley Lodge, the **Ram Restaurant (208-622-2225)** in Sun Valley Village, and Sunday brunch at the chic **Lodge Dining Room (208-622-2150)** in the Sun Valley Lodge. **800-786-8259, sunvalley.com ● ●** In downtown Ketchum, stop by Hemingway's former haunt, the **Pioneer Saloon**, still famous for its steaks and spirits. **208-726-3139, pioneersaloon.com**

LOCAL KNOWLEDGE

Throughout spring, summer, and fall, Sun Valley offers a jam-packed activities menu—you can even cool off with a whitewater ride on the nearby Salmon or Payette Rivers. **The River Company** offers day-long rafting trips, with a stop for lunch, on the Salmon River. **208-788-5775, therivercompany.com**

Hole 17 at Sun Valley Resort, Sun Valley, Idaho

SALT LAKE CITY TO JACKSON HOLE

You can take divergent routes to complete the five-hour trek from Salt Lake City to Jackson Hole, where the Jackson Hole Golf & Tennis Club and Teton Pines Country Club & Resort stand in the shadows of the towering Grand Teton Mountains. For the best combo of scenery and speed, try Interstate 80 east out of Salt Lake City to Evanston, Wyoming, then follow the Wyoming and Utah Highway 89 signs to Afton, toward Yellowstone and Grand Teton National Parks. If there's no hurry, wet a fly and see how many fish you can hook in an hour on the Salt River. It's a slow go from Afton up the Hoback Canyon, where the Snake River meanders from Jackson and Jenny Lakes. Upon reaching Jackson Hole, head to the north side of town near the Gros Ventre River.

WHERE TO PLAY

JACKSON HOLE GOLF & TENNIS CLUB

7,168 yards, par 72, 130/72.3
Greens fee: $78–$135
307-733-3111, JHGTC.com

Originally owned by the Rockefeller family, the course has garnered international renown for its awe-inspiring views of the Grand Tetons. Opened in 1963, the club hosted the 1988 U.S. Men's Public Links Championship and the 1993 U.S. Women's Public Links. Designed by Bob Baldock, the course was redesigned by Robert Trent Jones Jr. in 1973. Jones' best move was building the 530-yard 11th hole around a big bend in the Gros Ventre River. The design tempts you to bite off as much as you can chew, rifling a driver down the left side and over the waters of the river to a dogleg-left fairway.

TETON PINES COUNTRY CLUB & RESORT

7,412 yards, par 72, 131/74.7
Greens fee: $55–$75
800-238-2223, tetonpines.com

Just west of Jackson Hole rises this pristine, country-club-quality course, which was designed by Arnold Palmer and Ed Seay. Sprawled at the base of the Grand Tetons—6,200 feet above sea level—Teton Pines features water on all but two holes. The 634-yard 7th is a three-shot torture track that requires an approach over a large lake to a wide, shallow green. But the four memorable finishing holes at Teton Pines typically dominate the post-round rehashes.

WHERE TO STAY

Teton Pines Resort features every amenity imaginable, and fishermen will be delighted to discover that they can cast a fly right off their verandahs into a pond or stream from several lodging units. A Jack Dennis fly-fishing school sits between the 18th green and the clubhouse. Rates from $500. **800-238-2223, tetonpines .com** • • **The Snake River Lodge & Spa,** affiliated with the Jackson Hole Golf & Tennis Club, is the only premier lodge and full-service spa in Teton Village at the base of Jackson Hole Mountain Resort. Rates from $129. **866-975- ROCK, snakeriverlodge.rockresorts.com**

WHERE TO EAT

Be sure to stop in at **GameFish** restaurant at the Snake River Lodge & Spa, which offers new American cuisine in an elegant Western setting. **866-975-ROCK, snakeriverlodge.rockresorts .com** • • Outside the Snake River Lodge you'll find wild game entrees and great burgers at the **Alpenrose**. **307-733-3242, alpenhoflodge .com** • • **The Mangy Moose** is a popular watering hole in the village. **307-733-4913, mangymoose.net** • • Before departing Jackson Hole, stop by the **Million Dollar Cowboy Bar and Saloon**, where you can sit on a saddle at a bar embedded with old silver dollars. Take advantage of one of the 50 different beers and "cowboy cocktails" available to toast your new status as a long-drive champion. **307-733- 2207, milliondollarcowboybar.com**

LOCAL KNOWLEDGE

Ride the Snake River with **Jackson Hole Whitewater** through rapids dubbed Big Kahuna, Lunch Counter, and Rattlesnake. **800-700- RAFT, jhww.com** • • Tour one of the **50-plus art galleries** in downtown Jackson Hole. And don't be surprised if you catch a glimpse of local landowners Harrison Ford and Vice President Dick Cheney. **307-733-3326, jacksonholenet.com** • • The 40-mile-long Teton Range, which has eight peaks over 12,000 feet, including the 13,770-foot Grand Teton, is what makes **Grand Teton National Park** one of our nation's scenic treasures. Hit the park to camp, mountain bike, horseback ride, hike, or fish its streams and more than 100 alpine lakes. **307-739-3300, nps.gov/grte**

THE SHIPPING NEWS: SHIP YOUR CLUBS

There are places where golfers expect to queue—the parking lot at Bethpage Black, the first tee at Pebble Beach—but at least those occasions promise an immediate reward. Lost luggage offices in airports promise only the company of equally angry travelers. In April 2005 alone, more than 255,000 disgruntled passengers filed reports about lost or damaged bags. Perhaps it's time to start skipping the hassle by shipping your sticks ahead. Here are three options for your next trip.

	FedEx 800-463-3339 fedex.com	Luggage Concierge 800-288-9818 luggageconcierge.com	Golf Bag Shipping 866-744-7427 golfbagshipping.com
Sample shipping cost (all prices for round-trip shipping)			
New York to Orlando			
5-day ground	$26.54	$63.41	n/a
2-day air	$168.36	$185.37	$108.00
Dallas to Myrtle Beach			
5-day ground	$25.54	$63.41	n/a
2-day air	$168.36	$185.37	$108.00
New York to London			
International Shipping	$629.36	$400.00	$298.00
Advance notice required	None	48 hours	5 days
Home pick up?	Yes	Yes	Yes
Insurance included?	Yes, up to $100	Yes, up to $1,500	Yes, up to $100 (domestic), $1,000 (international)

NORTHWEST

IDAHO

MONTANA

OREGON

WASHINGTON

COEUR D'ALENE

FLATHEAD VALLEY

BANDON DUNES
BEND AND SUNRIVER RESORT
PORTLAND

SEATTLE

COEUR D'ALENE
The postcard-pretty Idaho panhandle is prime golf territory, with miles of sparkling lakes set against the evergreen Selkirk, Cabinet, Coeur d'Alene, and Bitterroot Mountains. The 25-mile-long Lake Coeur d'Alene is the star of its famous namesake course, but there are plenty of hidden golfing gems in the Gem State.

WHERE TO PLAY

INDIAN CANYON GOLF COURSE
6,255 yards, par 72, 126/70.7
Greens fee: $20–$25
509-747-5353, spokaneparks.org

It's less than five minutes from the Spokane airport to this hilly track where Ben Hogan made one of his few aces at the short fourth. Try the Canyon Burger in the clubhouse, but don't expect to finish it. This belly buster is piled high with ham, bacon, cheese, lettuce, and onion and ought to be served with a surgeon general's warning.

CIRCLING RAVEN GOLF CLUB
7,189 yards, par 72, 140/74.5
Greens fee: $69–$79
800-523-2464, golfcirclingraven.net

This 2003 Gene Bates design winds through wetlands and around railroad tracks, and sports a sparkling back nine. The par-three 13th is Circling Raven's nastiest; when the pin is tucked in the back right it measures a bruising 270 yards. Forget the ravens—vultures could circle this killer hole.

THE COEUR D'ALENE
6,735 yards, par 71, 119/71.1
Greens fee: $200–$250
800-935-6283, cdaresort.com

`TOP 100 YOU CAN PLAY`

Water views abound, and so is the pampering. Players are ferried from the hotel to the course via mahogany water taxi and massaged on the practice tee. A water taxi also shuttles players to and from the famous floating 14th green. Bunker rakes pop magically out of the ground; restrooms, too, are underground. The design has some hiccups—the 307-yard fourth hole, is followed by two par threes, but it is white-glove golf at its finest.

THE CARD WRECKER: COEUR D'ALENE NO. 14, 100 TO 175 YARDS

This is the Incredible Hulk of island greens: 5 million pounds complete with trees and bunkers, floating on concrete blocks moved by a computer-controlled cable pulley system. Its 15,000 square feet might sound generous, but it is surrounded by the vast blue lake Coeur d'Alene, across which golfers—feeling either elated or deflated—are ferried by mahogany boat. About 50,000 pellets drown here each year.

Four-time PGA Tour winner Chip Beck won the 1992 Merrill Lynch Shootout here and says that you have to aim for the core to score: "Use a club you can make a normal swing with and play a good solid shot to the middle, accepting that you might have to make a longer putt. It is most important to hit a full, solid shot and not let details like the water and the boats affect you." Easy for him to say....

HIDDEN LAKES GOLF RESORT

6,923 yards, par 71, 136/72.9
Greens fee: $61
888-806-6673, hiddenlakesgolf.com

Moose sightings are common, and the eponymous lakes are easy to find, too, with water in play on 16 holes. A non-aqua challenge is found at the 18th, where golfers are forced to shape their tee shots around a lone pine.

ESMERALDA GOLF COURSE

6,249 yards, par 70, 108/68.7
Greens fee: $23–$27
509-487-6291, spokanegolf.org

"Easy Essy" opened in 1956 and hosted the country's first Senior Open in 1957. With its big greens and tall trees, it's a pleasant place to kill time before putting your clubs back in the travel cover.

WHERE TO STAY

 Hit your dates right at **Coeur d'Alene Casino Hotel** and you might see a big-name act or a title fight. Packages start at $179 to $219 a night based on double occupancy. **800-523-2464, cdacasino.com** • • Views, amenities, and convenience make the 18-floor, waterfront **Coeur d'Alene Resort Hotel** worth considering for your HQ. Rooms start at $99 and go as high as $449 for the 180-degree postcard-view suite. Packages, including golf and accommodations, start at $179. **800-688-5253, cdaresort.com**

WHERE TO EAT

Beverly's restaurant at the Coeur d'Alene hotel serves a terrific orange roll—a sweet, unique dinner roll with a Krispy Kreme yum factor. **800-523-2464, cdacasino.com** • •

Venture downtown to **Moon Time** on Sherman Avenue. Ask for the salmon cakes, which don't appear on the eclectic menu. **208-667-2331, wedonthaveone.com** • • Sandpoint has been named one of the top 10 small towns in America. There you'll find **Ivano's**, renowned for its pasta dishes and wine list. **208-263-0211**

LOCAL KNOWLEDGE

Kokanee isn't just the name of a local brew; it's a kind of salmon in Lake Coeur d'Alene. See Jeff Smith at **Fins & Feathers** tackle shop and guide service. **208-667-9304, fins1 .com** • • The Moyie River is the best whitewater rafting spot you've never heard of. Book a day trip with **River Odysseys West**. Cost $84. **800-451-6034, rowadventures.com** • • Fifteen miles north of Coeur d'Alene on U.S. Route 95, **Silverwood** theme park features

two wooden roller coasters, plus a double-corkscrew gut-check billed as the nation's first upside-down ride. $33. **208-683-3400, silverwoodthemepark.com**

GETTING THERE

Spokane International Airport is about a 45-minute drive west of Coeur d'Alene.

WHEN TO GO

Courses are in prime shape from high summer (June to August) to early fall.

FLATHEAD VALLEY

FLATHEAD VALLEY Ready to shed the suit, unloosen the tie, and live out a Western vacation fantasy along the lines of *City Slickers*, with a few pleasurable rounds in place of a dusty cattle drive? There is perhaps no better place in the nation for home-on-the-range hospitality, exceptional value, and genuine mountain splendor than Montana's Flathead Valley. Enclosed by more than a million acres of federal wilderness, the valley's collection of public courses—nine facilities, including a 36-hole complex and three 27-hole layouts—are all within 45 minutes of one another. They are among the least heralded and most breathtaking courses in the American West. Two of the courses are routed along the shores of Flathead Lake, the largest and cleanest freshwater lake west of the Mississippi. Others are carved from birches and pines and crossed or flanked by rivers. Fairways serve up sweeping views of the Mission and Swan mountain ranges.

WHERE TO PLAY

EAGLE BEND GOLF CLUB

Championship: 6,711 yards, par 72, 124/71.0
Greens fee: $41–$75
406-837-7310, golfmt.com

Site of 1994 U.S. Amateur Public Links Championship, this 27-hole track in Bigfork sits on the north shore of Flathead Lake. The original 18 was given a boost with opening of Jack Nicklaus-designed Lake Nine in 1995. Generally the best-conditioned course in the valley, Eagle Bend offers fine lake, mountain, and river views, a 3,425-yard nine course, plus an excellent practice facility.

BIG MOUNTAIN GOLF CLUB

7,015 yards, par 72, 121/72.5
Greens fee: $35–$51
406-751-1950, golfmt.com

THRIFTY 50

Located in Kalispell 10 miles north of the lake, this course was built by the design team of Andy North and Roger Packard. The front nine, routed on a former potato farm, is marked by rolling mounds, native grasses, and wildflowers. The back nine wanders through tall ponderosa pines near Stillwater River. It's the region's longest course.

WHITEFISH LAKE GOLF CLUB

South: 6,563 yards, par 71, 122/70.5
North: 6,604 yards, par 72, 118/69.8
Greens fee: $36–$44
406-862-5960, golfwhitefish.com

Montana's only 36-hole complex offers a pair of mature, well-bunkered layouts lined with birches and pines. South Course is slightly tougher; roomier North Course has fine views of Whitefish Lake and the Big Mountain's ski trails. Both layouts are served by the cozy Log Clubhouse Restaurant and Lounge.

BUFFALO HILL GOLF COURSE

Championship: 6,584 yards, par 72, 118/71.1
Cameron Nine: 3,001 yards, par 36
Greens fee: $30–$51
406-756-4530, golfbuffalohill.com

Solid 27-hole muni in Kalispell on former buffalo grazing site is a sleeper, especially given newly rebuilt greens. The Championship is a hilly, tree-lined layout marked by numerous doglegs and narrow fairways. The Cameron Nine is sporty and lots of fun.

MEADOW LAKE

6,694 yards, par 73, 124/70.9
Greens fee: $29–$52
406-892-8700, meadowlake.com

This gorgeous resort course in Columbia Falls north of Kalispell is a heavily wooded layout nestled in a valley, with four lakes and a stream in play on many holes. The fairways are hilly and isolated from one another. The small, fast greens are elevated and some are double-tiered. The course has spectacular views of Glacier National Park.

POLSON COUNTRY CLUB

Eighteen: 6,964 yards, par 72, 123/72.5
Olde: 3,188 yards, par 36
Greens fee: $28–$35
406-883-8230, polsoncountryclub.com

A former private club dating to mid-1930s traces the south end of Flathead Lake's shoreline. The lake comes into play on one hole on the Eighteen and three holes on the Olde. Four additional ponds come into play on seven holes. The large, undulating greens are usually in good shape and have above-average speed.

MISSION MOUNTAIN COUNTRY CLUB

6,479 yards, par 72, 115/70.1
Greens fee: $20–$35
406-676-4653, golfmontana.net/
missionmtn.htm

This lushly manicured semiprivate layout 14 miles south of Flathead Lake in Ronan has very large greens and excellent views of the Mission Mountains. The back nine is the more scenic than the front nine. A lake and a stream come into play on four holes.

VILLAGE GREENS GOLF COURSE

6,401 yards, par 70, 117/69.3
Greens fee: $33
406-752-4666, montanagolf.com

Flat, moderately challenging course in Kalispell, known for its well-groomed greens, is a walker's delight. Water hazards come into play on six holes.

GLACIER VIEW GOLF CLUB

5,161 yards, par 69, 88/61.4
Greens fee: $29
406-888-5471, golfmontana.net/
glacierview.htm

Located at the gateway to Glacier National Park in West Glacier, this friendly, family-oriented layout is perhaps the region's most scenic track. The tree-lined fairways are flat and provide generous landing areas. The Flathead River flows on two sides of the course, but it does not come into play. There are two ponds that can come into play on five holes if you hit extremely errant shots.

WHERE TO STAY

Big Mountain Resort offers rooms at the Hibernation House hotel, as well as several condominium and villas options. Rates from $70. **800-858-5439, stayatbigmountain.com** • • **Meadow Lake Resort** in Columbia Falls offers fairway-side condos and rooms in its inn, plus golf packages. Rates from $95. **800-321-4653, meadowlake.com** • • **Grouse Mountain Lodge** in Whitefish, about 45 minutes from Glacier National Park, has 145 accommodation units, including 12 family-style lofts. Rates from $99. **877-862-1505, grousemountainlodge.com**

WHERE TO EAT

Bigfork, a lakeside town known for its art galleries and cherry orchards, has some of the state's best restaurants in a three-block area. Don't miss **La Provence**, a hot spot serving superb French-Mediterranean cuisine. **406-837-2923, bigforklaprovence.com** • • For lakeside dining, try the **Launch (406-837-5720)** or the **Swan River Inn (406-837-2328, swanriverinn.com)** • • The **Bulldog Pub** in Kalispell re-creates an Irish pub atmosphere and serves great steaks. **406-837-9914, bulldogpub.net** • • Lively bars with good menus include **Moose's Saloon (406-755-2337, moosessaloon.com)** in Kalispell and the **Garden Bar (406-837-9914)** in Bigfork.

LOCAL KNOWLEDGE

The one-million-acre **Glacier National Park** is an alpine trophy case of toothy spires, massive glaciers, more than 200 lakes, and 700 miles of hiking trails. **406-888-7800, nps.gov/glac** • • Take a leisurely drive on **Going-to-the-Sun Road**, a 52-mile highway that traces the crest of the Continental Divide as it winds through Glacier National Park. You'll see cascading waterfalls, mile-thick glaciers, and impressive rock spires. **406-888-7800, nps.gov/glac** • • Paddle, raft, or float some of the Flathead's **219 miles of wild and scenic rivers**. There's also fly fishing for trophy trout in the area's blue-ribbon streams. Other off-course pursuits include mountain biking, hot-air ballooning, hay rides, horseback riding, kayaking, sailing, and even llama trekking. **406-756-9091, fcvb.org** • • Small-stakes **poker games** are still legal in Montana's saloons, notably in the Old West town of Kalispell. **montana.casino city.com/Kalispell**

GETTING THERE

Glacier Park International Airport in Kalispell is served by America West, Big Sky Airlines, Northwest, Horizon Air, and Delta. **406-257-5994, glacierairport.com**

WHEN TO GO

Flathead Valley courses are open from mid-April through October, but prime time is late June through mid-September. Spring and fall are less crowded and slightly less expensive, but the weather can get iffy by mid-October.

For a golf guide, tee times, and lodging reservations, contact Flathead Valley Golf Reservations: 800-392-9795, golfmontana.net. For more general information, contact Flathead Convention & Visitor Bureau: fcvb.org, 406-756-9091.

BANDON DUNES

Seasoned golf travelers know that the number of high-end amenities offered by a resort is too often in inverse proportion to the quality of the golf courses. All the spas and tennis courts and equestrian facilities in the world don't compensate for mediocre golf. At Bandon Dunes, the opposite approach has carried the day. There are no bells and whistles: It is about golf the way Bali is about beaches. And with three of GOLF MAGAZINE's Top 100 Courses in the U.S. on site, it's the greatest one-stop shop you'll find anywhere.

WHERE TO PLAY

PACIFIC DUNES

6,633 yards, par 71, 138/72.6
Greens fee: $75–$240
888-345-6008, bandondunesgolf.com

- TOP 100 YOU CAN PLAY
- TOP 100 IN THE U.S.
- TOP 100 IN THE WORLD

Pacific Dunes opened in 2001 and already is ranked No. 2 on GOLF MAGAZINE's best public-access courses in the U.S., behind only Pebble Beach. At 6,633 yards, Pac Dunes is a bantamweight by modern standards, but the reality is that yardage means nothing here. Does it matter what the book says when you're facing a shot from an uphill lie into the teeth of a howling gale? There are some quirks here—two greens at No. 9 and consecutive par threes at Nos. 10 and 11—but the entire package falls together seamlessly. Among the best holes are the 13th, a par four that teeters along the dunes for 444 yards, No. 16, short (338 yards) but about as treacherous as Benedict Arnold, and the 17th is a 208-yard par three, where the Redan–style green can either funnel balls toward the hole or act like a roulette wheel, swinging them around the surface before dropping them off the back. The strength of Pacific Dunes doesn't lie in any one spectacular hole; it is in the plethora of options that are presented throughout.

THE CARD WRECKER: PACIFIC DUNES NO. 16, 338 YARDS, PAR 4

The last time you faced this much potential heartbreak from something so short was when your grade-school crush told you to take a hike. We asked architect Tom Doak how to survive the second-shortest hole on his course: "The green is protected by a deep hollow front right and bunkers behind. The hollow is the card wrecker: From down there you're playing off a bare lie to a shelf of green 20 feet above you. Leave it short and the ball may come back to you. Some players try to drive the green, figuring they'd rather be in the hollow with their first shot than with their second. You can drive out to the left and play a short running approach shot, maybe even with your putter, but for most players it's best to lay back and leave a full wedge shot. You may not be able to hold the green, but you'll wind up in the back bunker playing back into the wind and into the slope of the green. Or maybe on the "off ramp" of grass which runs between the bunkers. I often aim for that ramp myself—that's why I built it! I've seen people make 4 from the hollow in front, but they were either really good or really lucky."

Hole 11 at Bandon
Dunes (Pacific Dunes),
Bandon, Oregon

BANDON DUNES

6,732 yards, par 72, 142/73.9
Greens fee: $75–$240
888-345-6008, bandondunesgolf.com

TOP 100 YOU CAN PLAY
TOP 100 IN THE U.S.
TOP 100 IN THE WORLD

This was first course at the resort when it opened in 1999, and was designed by Scotland's David McLay Kidd. The course was rightly hailed as one of the world's finest, and despite the ever-lengthening shadow cast by Pacific Dunes, it remains one of the most enjoyable tracks you'll ever play. The layout starts with a gentle par four and gradually picks up steam. Bandon Dunes is masterfully bunkered with deep, sod-walled affairs that simultaneously goad aggressive players into intemperate plays and steer higher handicaps toward conservative plays. Perhaps the best hole here is No. 16, a superb par four of 363 yards. From the tee it seems an awfully long carry to reach the upper tier of the fairway to avoid a blind second shot (it isn't), and on the approach you can't help but be intimidated by the gorse, a bunker, and the Pacific Ocean backdrop.

BANDON TRAILS

6,765 yards, par 71, 130/73.4
Greens fee: $75–$240
888-345-6008, bandondunesgolf.com

TOP 100 YOU CAN PLAY
TOP 100 IN THE U.S.
TOP 100 IN THE WORLD

Ben Crenshaw and Bill Coore are the most accomplished double act in golf course architecture since Bobby Jones and Alister Mackenzie created Augusta National. Their joint designs include some of America's greatest modern courses, including Sand Hills, Cuscowilla, and Kapalua's Plantation Course. We feel the need to say all that before admitting this: Bandon Trails is the black sheep in this family of courses. To be fair to Crenshaw and Coore, they were handed the least impressive property of the three, set inland from the coastline and dunes. And they did a decent job with what they had. But it's just that—a decent resort course. When you walk off Pacific Dunes or Bandon Dunes, you're conditioned to expect something more than what you get here: ho-hum terrain, where too many tee shots funnel into the same divot-riddled collection areas, and greens that are borderline unfair. For each intriguing hole that combines the potential for agony and ecstasy in equal measure (the drivable 321-yard eighth, for example), there is one that just has you shaking your head—such as No. 14, a 325-yard par four with a green so small and unyielding that caddies will recommend you aim to miss it. Bandon Trails is always going to suffer from shadow syndrome, never quite earning the same level of acclaim as its siblings. It's still a pretty enjoyable trot in many respects, but it's just not in the same league as the rest of the golf you'll find here. That's why you should play it first in the rotation.

THE SHEEP RANCH

888-345-6008, bandondunesgolf.com

Known to a select few as "Area 51," the Sheep Ranch isn't a conventional course. Tom Doak laid out 13 holes on the bluffs atop the Pacific. Then again, they're not really holes but more like a series of greens and tee boxes. Drop a ball, choose the destination, and begin a journey that takes you back to the way the game must have been played centuries ago. When you're done, pull the gate behind you. That's if you can persuade the powers-that-be to let you get out there in the first place. No harm in asking, right?

WHERE TO STAY

The Lodge at Bandon Dunes is about as simple as golf resorts get—good food and drink and located close to the courses. There are just 19 single rooms and 2 four-bedroom suites in the Lodge. Rooms here are $150 through April, $180 May through October. A suite is $1,500 a night in high season. Rooms in the nearby cottages start at $280 in high season. **800-742-0172**

WHERE TO EAT

The Gallery at the Lodge serves up great local seafood and steaks. The bone-in cowboy rib eye is as daunting a challenge as the courses. **888-345-6008, bandondunesgolf.com • • McKee's Pub** has all the warmth of a Scottish highland hostelry and is the perfect spot for pub grub while reliving the round. **888-345-6008, bandondunesgolf.com • • Lord Bennett's** in

Bandon has great steaks and ocean views to match, with prices that won't crimp your style. **541-347-3663 • • The Crows Nest Lounge** in the Old Town Mall has decent food, even if the service is spotty. **541-347-9331**

LOCAL KNOWLEDGE

Bandon is a walking-only resort so a caddie is a smart investment—and not just as a sherpa for your golf bag. His intimate knowledge of the subtleties of the three tracks will save you from more big numbers than a crooked accountant. That's a good return on the $50 fee. • • Take a sunset tour of the **Cape Blanco Lighthouse** with the keeper, including climbing the tower to the lantern room. $35. **541-332-2750 • • Shore Acres State Park** boasts a Monterey pine that is listed on the National Big Tree Register (who knew there was one?). It's 95 feet tall with a 74-foot crown spread. **541-888-4902 • •** The

hazards at **West Coast Game Park Safari** seven miles south of Bandon have even more bite than the courses: lions, snow leopards, and panthers. $13. **541-347-3106**

GETTING THERE

Alaska Airlines flies into North Bend Airport four times a day from Portland. The flight is one hour. The resort is 25 minutes from the airport down Highway 101. Driving time south from Portland is four and a half hours.

WHEN TO GO

If you can get there in April, the weather might be sketchy, but you'll get a relative bargain: greens fees are $75 to $130 for guests, $100 to $175 for nonguests. June through September have the highest number of sunny days.

BEND AND SUNRIVER RESORT A leisurely three-hour drive southeast of Portland, Oregon, smack in the middle of the Beaver State, the city of Bend anchors a region that rivals any in the country for its fine combination of public-access golf and off-course activities. The undisputed king of central Oregon golf remains the Sunriver Resort, a perennial GOLF MAGAZINE Gold Medalist. A quick drive south of Bend, this sprawling oasis has been pampering guests for 35 years. It offers plenty for kids to do, superb accommodations, and delicious food. Best of all, there are three stellar golf courses.

WHERE TO PLAY

SUNRIVER RESORT

Crosswater: 7,683 yards, par 72, 150/76.9
Meadows: 7,012 yards, par 71, 128/72.8
Woodlands: 6,880 yards, par 72, 131/73.0
Greens fee: $60–$160
800-962-1769, sunriver-resort.com

TOP 100 YOU CAN PLAY

Crosswater, ranked 34th on GOLF MAGAZINE's Top 100 You Can Play, is just a two-minute drive from the resort. Essentially flat, this walkers' delight calls for 11 forced carries over the Deschutes and Little Deschutes Rivers (hence the course name) and has plenty of length, measuring a whopping 7,683 yards from the tips. Your round may be observed by elk, deer, and osprey, while your lost balls—and you will be sure to lose some on this tough layout—may be collected by river otters. The solid Meadows sits directly behind the resort, with a driving range that faces the facility's private airport and the Cascade Mountains beyond. Renovated in 1999 by John Fought, Meadows hosted the 2002 U.S. Women's Amateur Public Links Championship, the first USGA championship held at Sunriver. The resort's namesake provides the water hazard on seven holes, while the 536-yard 17th and 467-yard 18th offer dramatic views of the Cascades. The Woodlands offers the most diverse terrain of Sunriver's three layouts. This Robert Trent Jones Jr. design rises and falls over natural topography, with the back nine a bit tighter than the front.

WIDGI CREEK

6,903 yards, par 72, 134/71.9
Greens fee: $49–$85
541-382-4449, widgi.com

Get a little closer to towering Mount Bachelor at Widgi Creek, a lovely but tight track on the western outskirts of Bend. Tall ponderosa pines lining each fairway make you feel you're playing down narrow chutes, and the greens have some of the funkiest slopes you'll encounter around here or anywhere else. That muted roar from behind the 14th green and 15th tee comes from the Deschutes River flowing 100 feet below. Play here and then drive up to Mount Bachelor for lunch at Scapolo's Bistro.

LOST TRACKS GOLF CLUB

7,003 yards, par 72, 124/71.8
Greens fee: $40–$75
541-385-1818, losttracks.com

Just north of Sunriver but still south of Bend, you'll find Lost Tracks. This layout, opened in 1996, was designed by owner Brian Whitcomb, vice president of the PGA of America. He crafted a memorable venue with more doglegs than in your average kennel. Some are 90-degree turns. Playing such severe doglegs can get frustrating, but there's relief in the fantastic mountain views from the tees and fairways.

EAGLE CREST

Ridge: 6,927 yards, par 72, 128/72.7
Resort: 6,673 yards, par 72, 128/70.8
Mid Iron: 4,160 yards, par 63
Greens fee: $40–$65
541-923-GOLF, eagle-crest.com

Four miles away, Eagle Crest—a resort with three walkable courses—enjoys a different microclimate from that of Bend or Sunriver. That means a longer golf season. Warm weather arrives earlier in the year here and leaves later. The Ridge, designed by John Thronson, is fairly straightforward, with large greens that break predominantly toward a nearby butte. For lunch, try the surprisingly good hot dogs in the pro shop. The Resort is the oldest of the trio and was crafted by Gene "Bunny" Mason. The standout hole: the 481-yard 2nd, which cuts through a canyon as it twists left and then right to a smallish green. But the Mid Iron is the resort's newest and most intriguing course. This tough, immaculate Thronson design features nine par threes (the longest is the 188-yard 10th) and nine par fours (ranging from the 259-yard 17th to the 398-yard 4th). Be sure to check out the 18-hole putting course next to the Ridge Course. It comes complete with rough, trees, bunkers, and even elevation changes, and at $8 for adults and $4 for children, it's a steal.

ASPEN LAKES

7,302 yards, par 72, 135/75.4
Greens fee: $40–$56
541-549-4653, aspenlakes.com

Aspen Lakes is William Overdorf's only design in Oregon. Overdorf worked his magic on a beautiful piece of property just outside the town of Sisters. It's hard to beat this track for natural beauty, with ponderosa pines and views of mountains almost everywhere you look. There's a refreshing variety of holes; perhaps the only downside of the routing is that the 462-yard 9th and the 583-yard 18th holes finish a half-mile hike from the clubhouse. But the course, which calls for few forced carries, is in such great shape that you won't mind the walk.

Hole 2 at Sunriver
(Crosswater), Oregon

BLACK BUTTE RANCH

Big Meadow: 6,850 yards, par 72, 125/71.3
Glaze Meadow: 6,574 yards, par 72, 122/70.7
Greens fee: $40–$65
800-399-2322, blackbutteranch.com

Just west of Sisters looms Black Butte Ranch, first developed as a tennis haven when it opened in 1969. Its original course is Big Meadow, a 33-year-old Robert Muir Graves design that's fair to players of all skill levels. Glaze Meadow, a Mason design that debuted in 1979, is a classic shotmaker's course. There's more water in play than on Big Meadow, and several holes are isolated in dense woods.

QUAIL RUN GOLF COURSE

3,512 yards, par 36
Greens fee: $24–$40
800-895-GOLF

The toughest tee time in the area might be at Quail Run, a nine-holer situated 15 minutes south of Sunriver. This 12-year-old layout is popular for both its affordability and quality. It offers solid, no-frills golf.

WHERE TO STAY

 Sunriver is to outdoor nuts what Scotland is to whisky hounds. There is no shortage of mind-clearing activities, from biking on a 30-mile network of trails to ice skating in the winter and a ropes course in the summer, all set amid winding rivers and Ponderosa Pines. Essentially one big, beautiful meadow, the 3,000-plus acres on which Sunriver sits hosted the Paiute Indians as late as 1813, when the first Europeans arrived. The resort, built in the mid-1960s and spruced up by new owners over the past decade, offers accommodations ranging from comfy rooms in the lodge to six-bedroom homes. There are three restaurants, a cozy spa, and three distinct courses. Rates from $149. **800-962-1769, sunriver-resort.com**

WHERE TO EAT

Sunriver resort has four restaurants. The elegant **Grille at Crosswater** and the more casual **Meadows** restaurant and **Owl's Nest** pub all serve Northwest–influenced fare. **800-962-1769, sunriver-resort.com** •• The **Deschutes**

Brewery and Public House in Bend serves tasty sandwiches, pasta, and burgers. Pair the roasted garlic burger with one of the brewery's seasonal ales. **541-385-8606**

LOCAL KNOWLEDGE

Get the real lay of the land at the **High Desert Museum and Lava Lands**, both off Interstate 97 between Bend and Sunriver. The spectacular topography you'll see there will give you some insight into the terrain you've been treading. **541-382-4754, highdesertmuseum.org** •• Cool off by white-water rafting down the Deschutes. Hop in with **Sun Country Tours**, which has been running trips for 25 years. One run down the rapids may convince you to head back to the golf courses. **800-770-2161, suncountrytours.com** •• Sunriver resort's **Race & Ace Challenge** happens every May, when the area's unique climes are ideal for slalom racing in the morning on nearby Mount Bachelor, followed by an 18-hole shotgun scramble at Sunriver in the afternoon. A sunset feast and awards ceremony on the lodge's great lawn caps the day.

GETTING THERE

Sunriver is a fairly long but gorgeous three-and-a-half-hour drive southeast from Portland through the mountains and high desert. It's a two-and-a-half-hour drive east of Eugene and a 45-minute drive south of the Redmond Airport, to which you can make a connection through Portland, Seattle, and San Francisco.

WHEN TO GO

The dry high-desert climate means plenty of sunny days in the summer. Average highs range from the mid-60s to high 80s from May through October.

> For more information, contact the Central Oregon Visitor's Bureau. 888-350-8017, visitcentraloregon.com.

PORTLAND

PORTLAND In the early part of the 20th century, Portland boasted more golf holes per capita than any other city in the nation. (A caffeine capital, it currently boasts the most double lattes.) In recent decades, population has outstripped course development as folks have been drawn to the laid-back lifestyle, multitude of outdoor sports, and high livability of what is variously known as the Rose City, River City, and Puddletown. But golf around Portland is still accessible and excellent, especially since a construction boom during the 1990s brought a handful of great courses on line. You can easily play 36 holes a day in the late light of summer, and then relax in—or outside of—a lovely, quirky city bustling with microbreweries, coffee houses, tasty ethnic dining, and homegrown music.

WHERE TO PLAY

PUMPKIN RIDGE

Ghost Creek: 6,839 yards, par 71, 139/73.8
Greens fee: $50–$150
888-594-4653
pumpkinridge.nemexinc.com

TOP 100 YOU CAN PLAY

A world-class layout even before Tiger won his third U.S. Amateur title here, Ghost Creek harkened the start of upscale public golf in Northwest. On numerous holes, a mysterious stream gobbles golf balls like Halloween candy. But Bob Cupp's well-groomed treat is still worth the sometimes scary price. The club's Witch Hollow course is open only to members.

HERON LAKES

Great Blue: 6,902 yards, par 72, 140/73.2
Greenback: 6,608 yards, par 72, 124/71.4
Greens fee: $40 (Great Blue); $32 (Greenback)
503-289-1818, heronlakesgolf.com

The Great Blue course is Robert Trent Jones Jr.'s unflappably challenging links-style course laid out in riverside lowlands with views of Mount Hood. The three watery finishing holes alone would be worth the green fee. Great Blue hosted the U.S. Amateur Public Links Championship in 2000. The 6,608-yard Greenback course is a typical early Trent Jones Jr. design with elevated, bunker-framed greens, a handful of forced carries, and an easygoing demeanor.

LANGDON FARMS

6,931 yards, par 71, 125/73
Greens fee: $20–$40
503-678-4653, langdonfarms.com

John Fought and Bob Cupp partnered on this farm-themed layout 15 miles south of city in Aurora. Langdon plows through a pastoral Willamette Valley setting with recessed fairways that run like canyons between high grassy mounds. Most of the greens are elevated on one or two sides, resulting in large collection areas at the base. The greens are undulating, mostly large, and tough to read. Several greens are tiered, and some have a ridge in the center, with the back sloping away from you.

Hole 8 at Pumpkin
Ridge (Ghost Creek),
Portland, Oregon

OREGON GOLF ASSOCIATION COURSE

6,559 yards, par 72, 132/71.4
Greens fee: $50
503-981-6105, oga.org

This Bill Robinson design, which opened in 1996, boasts a great variety of holes, a couple of reachable par fives, a huge double green, and some of the finest putting surfaces in the region.

THE RESERVE VINEYARDS & GOLF CLUB

South: 7,196 yards, par 72, 134/74.5
North: 6,852 yards, par 72, 135/73.5
Greens fee: $88
503-649-2345, reservegolf.com

This club with a wine-maker theme has two distinctive designs. The longer, tougher John Fought–designed South course is like a bold cabernet. It runs through mature stands of trees, naturally rolling terrain, and testing golfers with more than 110 bunkers. The Bob Cupp–designed North, like a crisp chardonnay, is open and linkslike, but sly. It feels as if you are closer to the coast than you really are.

WHERE TO STAY

The **Heathman Hotel**, an elegant old Portland favorite, features original artwork by regional painters, the French-accented Heathman Restaurant, a tea court, and evening jazz in the lobby lounge. Rates from $159. **800-551-0011, heathmanhotel.com** • • The **Paramount Hotel**, a European-style hostelry in heart of downtown, offers summer specials. Rates from $139. **800-426-0670, portlandparamount.com** • • The **Silver Cloud Inn** is a nice budget hotel in the Northwest district with easy freeway access. Rates from $109. **800-205-6939, silvercloud.com**

WHERE TO EAT

Upscale restaurants such as **Wildwood** and **Lucy's Table** attract diners to the trendy Northwest district. **503-248-9663, wildwoodrestaurant.com** and **503-226-6126, lucystable.com** • • **Typhoon** serves up the most varied and creative Thai menu this side of Bangkok at its two downtown locations. **typhoonrestaurants.com** • • **Jake's Crawfish** House on SW 12th Avenue has been purveying fresh fish and exemplary service for 100 years. **513-226-1419** • • **Hot Lips Pizza's** four locations proffer highly original pies made with local, organic ingredients. **hotlipspizza.com** • • **Clay's Smokehouse** Grill on Division Street turns out the best ribs in town. **503-235-4755**

LOCAL KNOWLEDGE

The **McMenamin brothers** are famous for their string of microbreweries in combination with vintage movie theaters (Mission Theater, Bagdad Theater), concert venues (Crystal Ballroom), and unique hotels. Their **Kennedy School** bar is located a converted grade school; check out the Detention Room cigar bar. Their Edgefield complex even has a short "pub course," where you can stop at cozy bars between golf holes. **mcmenamins.com** • • Both **Tom McCall Waterfront Park** and the **Oregon Zoo** host open-air concerts. Portland's **Washington Park** is abloom with roses in summer, has a tranquil Japanese Garden, and owns the best views over downtown with Mount Hood in distance. **Mount Tabor Park** is an old volcano cone grown over with huge, lovely firs. **portlandonline.com/parks** • • Pick up a bottle of pear brandy from **Clear Creek Distillery** on 23rd Avenue. **503-248-9470, clearcreekdistillery.com** • • Peruse 250 booths for original crafts at **Portland Saturday Market** on West Burnside Street. **saturdaymarket.org** • • Motor through **Columbia Gorge National Scenic Area** to Multnomah Falls, 35 miles west. Hoof it to top of falls and then recover your strength with huckleberry pie in the lodge. **fs.fed.us/r6/columbia/forest/**

WHEN TO GO

Portland's courses are always lush and green from the ample rainfall, but summer weather is reliably sunny and warm. Autumn delivers crisp days, changing leaves, and often plenty of sunshine through October. In winter and early spring, locals slog around the fairways in knee-high clamming boots fit with golf spikes. Bring plenty of Gore-Tex outerwear if you visit between November and May.

SEATTLE

No matter where you live, chances are there's a little piece of Seattle in your backyard in the form of a Starbucks coffee shop. Happily, the ubiquitous java joints give way to other draws in the Emerald City: microbeers, a thriving art scene, and the vibe of a city with a small-town feel. Golf is also beginning to compete with pub-hopping as a pastime. Six courses have opened in the last 15 years, including three terrific bargains. Spectacular views are the norm in Seattle, with twin-peaked Mount Rainier rising to the south, the Olympic Range to the north, and Lake Washington and Elliott Bay flanking the city. The area's cluster of affordable courses (all under $60) lies across Elliott Bay, west of the city in an area locals call the Peninsula, less than an hour's drive around the Sound. (Take the Bremerton ferry from Pier 52 for exceptional views.)

WHERE TO PLAY

GOLD MOUNTAIN GOLF COMPLEX

Olympic: 7,073 yards, par 72, 134/73.5
Greens fee: $35–$63
360-415-5432, goldmt.com

TOP 100 YOU CAN PLAY

THRIFTY 50

First stop is in Bremerton at the Olympic Course at Gold Mountain, which hosted the 2006 U.S. Amateur Public Links Championship. The front nine of John Harbottle III's design is a pleasant stroll through the forest; the back is a Stairmaster workout, highlighted by the 357-yard 15th, which curls left around a lake to a tiny peninsula green.

MCCORMICK WOODS GOLF COURSE

7,040 yards, par 72, 134/74.3
Greens fee: $29–$55
800-323-0130, mccormickwoodsgolf.com

At this Jack Frei design in Port Orchard, local knowledge goes a long way. The 575-yard dogleg-left ninth begs you to cut the corner off the tee. Bad idea. The smart play is to a plateau on the right to avoid a steep downhill lie in the rough for your next shot, which is over water. On the back nine, take one step off the fairway and you're in thickly forested Bigfoot territory. On the 432-yard par-four 15th, aim at the left peak of Mt. Rainier and don't try to cut the corner—there's a lake beyond it, obscured by reeds. After the round, try Mary Mac's in the clubhouse for fine seafood.

TROPHY LAKE GOLF & CASTING

7,206 yards, par 72, 137/74.3
Greens fee: $45–$59
360-874-8337, trophylakegolfclub.com

Trophy Lake Golf & Casting completes the Peninsula's hat trick of good, budget-friendly golf. Ten minutes south of McCormick, the John Fought design stretches through groves of Douglas fir and around wetlands. Weigh your options off the tee here. For example, at the 547-yard 7th, a cavernous bunker splits the fairway in two. Go right to find an 80-yard wide section of short grass, but you'll have two full shots left to the green. The 30-yard-wide low road on the left brings the green into play—and the dense trees.

Hole 1 at Newcastle
(Coal Course), Seattle,
Washington

GOLF CLUB AT NEWCASTLE

Coal Creek: 7,024 yards, par 72, 152/74.7
China Creek: 6,632 yards, par 71, 129/72.3
Greens fee: $150
425-793-4653, newcastlegolf.com

Back to the Seattle mainland, 20 minutes southeast of the city is the Golf Club at Newcastle. Opened in 1999, it's the priciest public course in the state (cart is extra). You do get your money's worth, with an oak-paneled locker and restrooms with heated seats for frigid mornings. Newcastle features two 18s: Coal Creek, the better of the two, and the much easier China Creek, which has beautiful skyline vistas but less memorable holes. Bob Cupp teamed up with local boy Fred Couples to design Coal Creek, which plays like a links course with uneven lies, gusting wind, and thick fescue. On the 438-yard 3rd, the temptation is to aim right at the hole but Columbia Tower, Seattle's tallest building, is the smart line.

WASHINGTON NATIONAL GOLF CLUB

7,304 yards, par 72, 141/75.6
Greens fee: $52–$94
253-333-5000
washingtonnationalgolfclub.com

Wild tee shots are forgiven, but the charity stops there on this John Fought design. The 635-yard par-five 14th can easily take four shots to reach, each shot facing its own set of hazards—a 10-foot deep waste bunker winds across the fairway twice before giving way to a group of bunkers that protect the green.

DRUIDS GLEN GOLF CLUB

7,146 yards, par 72, 140/75.2
Greens fee: $40–$70
253-638-1200, druidsglengolf.com

You'll find a touch of Ireland in the Pacific Northwest at Druids Glen, which you'll leave remembering the par threes. Three of the four are carries over water. The 206-yard 16th is the highlight; a lake horseshoes around the green to catch shots that miss the three bunkers on each side.

Hole 8 at Newcastle
(Coal Course), Seattle,
Washington

WEST SEATTLE GOLF COURSE
6,725 yards, par 72, 124/71.6
Greens fee: $23–$31
206-935-5187, seattlegolf.com

Solid, inexpensive golf can also be had at West Seattle Golf Course, just south of downtown. Built by H. Chandler Egan in 1939, it's one of the best inner-city munis in the country and host of the annual Seattle Amateur Championship. Egan gained fame for reshaping Pebble Beach in 1928 into today's masterpiece. At West Seattle, Pacific views have been substituted by the city skyline, which dominates the course. While it will never be confused with Pebble, West Seattle does share one trait with the famed links: a weekend round here can surpass five hours. The difference is that you can show up here during the week and zip around much quicker, and it will cost you only $23. The skyline of Seattle makes a hell of a backdrop, even if it ain't Stillwater Cove.

WHERE TO STAY
The **Alexis Hotel** is a hip boutique property close to Pike Place Market. Rates from $155. **866-356-8894, alexishotel.com** • • The **Pensione Nichols** has 10 rooms, four bathrooms, and two suites with views of Elliott Bay. Good for buddy trips. Doubles are $110, suites: $195. **206-441-7125** • • The **Westin Seattle's** twin towers are a landmark. Try to get a bay-view room. Doubles from $199. **800-228-3000, westin.com**

WHERE TO EAT
Tom Hanks and Meg Ryan put the romantic **Dahlia Lounge** on the map in *Sleepless in Seattle*. If you're sneaking rounds on a family vacation, your wife will forgive you after dinner here. **206-682-4142, tomdouglas.com** • • **Ivar's Acre of Clams** is a good seafood place

to stuff yourself without emptying your wallet. **206-624-6852, ivars.net** • • Every table at **Maximilien**, which is tucked away in Pike Place Market but worth the search, has a bay vista, if you ever look up from your plate. **206-682-7270, maximilienrestaurant.com** • • From wild sturgeon to jumbo prawns, **McCormick & Schmick's** has everything that used to swim. **206-623-5500, mccormickandschmicks.com** • • Every big city has a great steakhouse, and Seattle's is the **Metropolitan Grill**, or Met, as the locals call it. Every cut of corn-fed Nebraska beef is dry aged and grilled over mesquite charcoal. **206-624-3287, themetropolitangrill.com**

LOCAL KNOWLEDGE
Washington wines are increasingly popular, but Seattleites still pride themselves on the old malt and hop. Brew styles to look for (ranging from light to dark) are hefeweizen, pale ale, amber ale, porter, and stout. Try the Brewer's Rack at **The Pyramid Alehouse** on First Avenue South, across from Safeco Field, to sample five five-ounce beers of your choosing for $6 ($3 at happy hour). **206-682-3377, pyramidbrew.com**

WHEN TO GO
It rains less in Seattle than most people think—about 37.5 inches annually, which is drier than New York City, Atlanta, and Washington, D.C. But when it's not raining, the skies are often overcast. Summers, particularly from the last half of July through the first half of August, are warm, dry, and sunny. Fall is also a good time to visit, with mild temperatures during the day until the rainy season starts in early October.

TRAIL BLAZING
GOLF MAGAZINE's Top 10 Golf Trails

1 | ALABAMA
ROBERT TRENT JONES GOLF TRAIL
Started in the late 1980s, this trail was first out of the chutes. There are 300 holes—many exceptional—on nine sites, all designed by Jones Sr. The courses are well spaced, well run, and well priced (around $50 each).
Best Course: Capitol Hill (The Judge)
You won't forget: Fighting Joe, the trail's newest "heavyweight" (8,072 yards from the tips), which will take a few rounds out of you.
Average cost to play: About $450 (including five rounds and four nights lodging)
800-949-4444, rtjgolf.com

2 | LOUISIANA
AUDUBON GOLF TRAIL
This collection of 10 rock-solid, environmentally friendly courses—named after the naturalist John Audubon—runs through the Bayou...and beyond. The trail boasts unique designs by David Toms, Hal Sutton, Steve Elkington, Pete Dye, and more.
Best Course: Carter Plantation
You won't forget: Trying to make contact the morning after knockin' 'em back on Bourbon Street.
Average cost to play: About $325 (including three rounds and three nights)
866-248-4652, audubontrail.com

3 | BRITISH COLUMBIA, CANADA
VANCOUVER ISLAND GOLF TRAIL
Vancouver Island is about beaches, boating, whale watching, salmon fishing, and soul-soothing golf. Away-from-it-all tracks, such as Storey Creek in Campbell River (home to salmon the size of small children) and Morningstar in Parksville, make the government-sponsored trail a true adventure.
Best Course: Bear Mountain
You won't forget: Reeling in the biggest flippin' Chinook salmon you've ever seen at Painters Lodge.
Average cost to play: $625 (including six rounds and six nights)
888-465-3239, golfvancouverisland.ca

4 | TENNESSEE
BEAR TRACE
A Jack Nicklaus Signature course for $59? Try five of them at that price or less (with cart) on this thoughtfully conceived pathway to golfing glory. The Bear Trace is a peaceful, laid-back, and incredibly priced compilation of some of Nicklaus' best work.
Best Course: Ross Creek Landing
You won't forget: Hunkering down in your rocking chair, sipping a cool beverage, and divvying up the dough on "The Porch"—a staple at every track on the trail.
Average cost to play: $475 (including five rounds with cart, breakfast, and four nights)
866-770-2327, beartrace.com

5 | PRINCE EDWARD ISLAND, CANADA
PRINCE EDWARD ISLAND GOLF TRAIL
Many regard this maritime province Canada's best golf destination. Play these courses (there are five on the trail, which is owned and operated by Rodd Hotels), stroll along the beaches, and cruise through quaint fishing villages, and you'll see why.
Best Course: The Links at Crowbush Cove
You won't forget: The Malpeque Bay oysters. No pepper, no lemon, no sauce: just open the oyster, kiss it off the shell, and crush it on the palate.
Average cost to play: $729 (including five rounds, one hour lesson, and four nights' lodging at Rodd Hotels).
800-565-7633, rodd-hotels.ca

6 | ARKANSAS
NATURAL STATE GOLF TRAIL
Why this trail? Them thar hills are mighty fine to look at—and play golf in, too. Eight well-positioned sites and 10 of the best courses in the "Natural State" make for a fine trek.
Best Course: Big Creek
You won't forget: Taking a ride on the Duck (a WW II–era amphibious vehicle) in Hot Springs and then slurping spaghetti at Belle Arti.
Average cost to play: $400 (including five rounds with cart and four nights)
866-2-GOLF-AR, naturalstategolftrail.com

7

SCOTLAND
THE JAMES BRAID GOLF TRAIL (HIGHLANDS LOOP)

The James Braid Golf Trails of Scotland (there are six total) feature the courses of one of the game's most prolific architects. Play courses such as Brora, Nairn, Golspie, and Boat of Garten, and you'll fall in love with this surreal, strangely forlorn region of mountain and sea.

Best Course: Brora

You won't forget: Playing golf around the sheep at Brora.

Average cost to play: Approximately $800 (including five rounds and four nights lodging)

011-0845-2255-121, toscotland.com

8

NORTH CAROLINA, VIRGINIA, AND SOUTH CAROLINA
THE MAVERICK GOLF TRAIL

This wild and woolly six-course feast features the work of Mike Strantz. Strantz (a.k.a. "The Maverick") has sculpted daring pieces of art—i.e., True Blue, Caledonia, and Royal New Kent—that are an absolute scream to play.

Best Course: Caledonia? Tobacco Road? Close call.

You won't forget: Cleaning the sand out of your orifices and the "love" grass from your hair after playing the visually stunning Tobacco Road Golf Club.

Average cost to play: $810 (including six rounds, five nights, breakfast, and maps)

877-284-3762, maverickgolftrail.com

9

IDAHO
IDAHO GOLF TRAIL

Idaho, christened with rocky cathedrals, clear blue lakes, fantastic resorts, and world-class golf, doesn't get the acclaim it deserves. Six keepers, including staples like Sun River and Coeur d'Alene Resort, make up the trail.

Best Course: Circling Raven

You won't forget: White-water rafting down the Payette River.

Average cost to play: $972 (including six rounds and six nights' premium lodging)

800-844-3246, idahogolftrail.com

10

MICHIGAN
ARTHUR HILLS MICHIGAN GOLF TRAIL

Includes 12 of Hill's best efforts—at incredibly diverse sites, such as Bay Harbor (reminiscent of Scottish links), Hawkshead (like Pine Valley), Shepherds Hollow (the Carolina sandhills), and Red Hawk (everything in one).

Best Course: Bay Harbor

You won't forget: Cart wheeling down the 350-foot high "Dune Climb" at the Sleeping Bear Dunes National Lakeshore.

Average cost to play: Varies. This trail is a do-it-yourself job.

877-872-4524, arthurhillstrail.com

HAWAII

HAWAII

MAUI
LANA'I
OAHU
MAUNA LEA AND MAUNA LANI

MAUI

Need proof that PGA Tour players are spoiled? Watch the Mercedes Championship in Maui. Only the previous year's champs can play, last place earns more than the national average income, and the scene is so chilled out that even Vijay Singh logs more beach time than range time. But Maui is more than a pretty start to the Tour each January. With its constant sunshine, black lava hazards, and the Pacific framing almost every hole, it's the perfect place to spoil yourself. There are four great destinations here—two each on Maui and the more sedate neighboring island of Lana'i—and while it's a healthy trek from east of the Mississippi, the golf more than justifies the journey.

WHERE TO PLAY

KAPALUA RESORT

Plantation: 7,263 yards, par 73, 142/75.2
Bay: 6,600 yards, par 72, 138/71.1
Greens fee: $185–$295 (Plantation);
$155–$210 (Bay)
808-669-8044, kapaluamaui.com

TOP 100 YOU CAN PLAY

The Plantation course is home to the PGA Tour's opening Mercedes Championship and has one of the most scenic finishing holes outside of Pebble Beach. Rolling through big meadows and forests of Norfolk pine, Plantation's wide-open fairways play tough only when the wind blows. To play the downhill 663-yard 18th, the longest hole on the PGA Tour, "hit as long a drive as you can, and favor the right side, which feed shots to the hole," says Fred Funk, who plays the Mercedes Championship each January. The nearby 6,600-yard Bay Course was designed by Arnold Palmer and Frances Duane and lacks the dramatic elevation changes that define Plantation. It rolls through tropical foliage until reaching Oneloa Bay on the 357-yard 4th, which has a kidney-shaped green perched above the rocky shoreline, and the 205-yard 5th, where you have to carry 100 yards of crashing waves. The main challenge is the wind whipping off the water.

WAILEA GOLF CLUB

Gold: 7,078 yards, par 72, 137/73.4
Emerald: 6,825 yards, par 72, 130/71.1
Blue: 6,765 yards, Par 72, 129/72.2
Greens fee: $160–$190 (Gold); $160–$190 (Emerald); $125–$185 (Blue)
808-875-7450, golfbc.com

The Gold hugs the slopes where the dormant Haleakala volcano meets the Pacific, about a 45-minute drive from Kahului Airport on Maui's southwestern shore. Home to the Champions Tour Skins Game each February, this Robert Trent Jones Jr. design uses Haleakala's rocky lava beds to dramatic and punishing effect. Lava chutes cross five holes, but not the Gold's toughest, the 590-yard 7th, a sharp dogleg-right that dares long hitters to fly two deep bunkers at the corner. Clear those and you're still left with a long iron into a heavily bunkered green with more ridges than the volcano. The Emerald course offers sensory overload for golfers-cum-horticulturalists. Thousands of flowers—firecracker plants, morning glories, and birds of paradise—line the wide, rolling fairways. The golf isn't bad either. Two fun par fours—the 392-yard 10th and the 332-yard 17th—curve around a lake lined by lava and share a long, multitiered green. The aqua pinches both fairways on the approach, but there's enough dry land to stay dry. The best hole is the finisher, which starts at the course's highest point and curves 553 yards downhill (and mercifully downwind) to a butterfly-shaped green. Built by Jack Snyder in 1972, the Blue course is closer to the ocean than its siblings and affords the same views, which is reason enough to check it out. But this is a true resort track: it lacks strategic tests, and homes and condominiums line many fairways.

WHERE TO STAY

The **Four Seasons Resort Maui** is just minutes from Wailea's courses. The poolside cabanas (left) turn lazy lounging into high art. Rooms start at $395 a night. **808-874-8000, fourseasons.com/maui** •• The **Ritz-Carlton at Kapalua Resort** has 548 guest rooms and the white sands of D.T. Fleming Beach are a quick stroll away. Rooms start at $325. **808-669-6200, ritzcarlton.com** •• **Kapalua Villas** have kitchens and washer/dryers, and are a good choice for families and foursomes. Rates start at $209 per person a night for a one bedroom. **808-545-0018, kapaluavillas.com**

WHERE TO EAT

Ferraro's Bar e Ristorante at the Four Seasons serves rustic Italian cuisine and fresh-caught fish on an open-air terrace above the beach. **808-874-8000, fourseasons.com/maui** •• **Sansei**, a bustling, casual sushi joint on South Kihei Road, flavors the freshest fish you'll find with tropical ingredients. Don't miss the mango crab salad hand roll or the savory and delicate miso butterfish. **808-931-6286, sanseihawaii .com** •• The **Banyan Tree** at the Ritz-Carlton Kapalua doesn't just take hotel cuisine to a

new level; it offers some of the most inspired and innovative food you'll find anywhere. **808-669-6200, ritzcarlton.com** •• **David Paul's Lahaina Grill**, about a 15-minute drive south of Kapalua on Lahainaluna Road in Lahaina, has a lively bar, a deep wine cellar, and an award-winning restaurant. **808-667-5117, lahainagrill.com** •• **I'O (808-661-8422, iomaui.com)** and **Pacific'O**, sleek open-air restaurants overlooking the harbor in Lahaina serve fresh seafood with Pacific Rim flair. **808-667-4341, pacificomaui.com**

LOCAL KNOWLEDGE

The 10,000-foot peaks of the dormant **Haleakala Volcano** are an hour from Wailea up the steep Haleakala Highway. Fit golfers should hike down toward the barren crater for a closer look at one of the world's most unusual ecosystems. Be sure to save juice for the trek back up. **808-572-4400, nps.gov/hale** •• Stop at the **Maui Winery** on Route 37 afterward for a taste of pineapple wine and grab lunch across the street at the **Ulupalakua Ranch Store**, which serves elk burgers, vegetarian taro burgers, and a mean Kahlua barbecue pork sandwich. **877-878-6058, mauiwine.com** ••

Maui's coral reefs are full of colorful marine life. **Friendly Charters** provides snorkeling gear, breakfast, lunch, and drinks on its five-hour morning tour of Molokini, a tiny crescent shaped island, and Turtle Town, home to hundreds of sea turtles. At the Maalaea Harbor Slip about 15 minutes from Wailea. Adults: $88, Children: $58 plus tax. **808-244-1979, mauisnorkeling.com** •• If someone tells you to see **the blowhole**, it's not an insult. About 10 miles north of Kapalua on Route 30, a short hike leads to one of Maui's natural wonders—a hole in the rocky shoreline that creates a natural waterspout.

GETTING THERE

Kahului Airport, about midway between Wailea and Kapalua, is served by 10 airlines, including Delta, United, Continental, American, and Air Canada. **hawaii.gov/dot/airports/maui/ogg/**

WHEN TO GO

The weather is great—75 and sunny—all year. Visit from December to April to see humpback whales making their annual migration north.

Hole 4 at Wailea (Blue Course), Maui, Hawaii

LEARN THE LINGO

On Maui you don't wave to others with a flat palm. Instead, curl your right index, middle, and ring fingers under, keeping the thumb and pinky outstretched. Rotate your wrist twice, and you've just made the universal sign for "Hang loose!"

Hole 1 at Wailea (Emerald Course), Maui, Hawaii

LANA'I
Although it's just seven miles from Maui, for most of the 20th century Lana'i was little more than a Dole pineapple plantation. (Dole owner David Murdock still owns 98 percent of the island.) Today it is home to two luxury golf resorts, one set on the cliffs above gorgeous white sand beaches, the other 2,500 feet above sea level in a misty pine forest.

WHERE TO PLAY

THE CHALLENGE AT MANELE
7,039 yards, par 72, 135/73.7
Greens fee: $190–$225
808-565-2222, manelebayhotel.com

TOP 100 YOU CAN PLAY

Set above Hulopo'e Bay, the well-manicured Challenge follows the dramatic contours of the rocky coastline. Jack Nicklaus perched three holes atop 150-foot cliffs more suited to paragliding than golf. The 202-yard 12th, which jumps a huge chasm from tee to green, is so stunning that Bill and Melinda Gates were married here.

THE EXPERIENCE AT KOELE
7,014 yards, par 72, 141/75.3
Greens fee: $185
808-565-4653, lodgeatkoele.com

When ocean views start to feel routine, try this mountain track designed by Greg Norman and Ted Robinson. The front nine runs through former pineapple fields and around a couple heavily landscaped lakes, but the back nine is the real stunner. It winds through forests of eucalyptus and pine, peeks out over the north end of the island toward the neighboring island of Molokai on the 15th, and then drops 250 feet from tee to green on the 390-yard 17th before requiring a 130-yard carry over a carp-filled lake on the fun par-three 18th.

WHERE TO STAY

The **Four Seasons Resort Lana'i at Manele Bay** is a five-minute shuttle ride from the Challenge and has a great beach. The **Lodge at Koele**, just eight miles away, also has a cool 18-hole putting course. Rooms in both resorts start at $395. **800-321-4666, islandoflanai.com**

WHERE TO EAT

The **Challenge at Manele** clubhouse serves up the best mahi mahi along with panoramic ocean views. **808-565-2230, manelebayhotel.com** •• **Ihilana** in the Four Seasons Manele Bay serves Italian fare infused with fresh seafood and accented with island ingredients. **808-565-2000, manelebayhotel.com**

LOCAL KNOWLEDGE

The Lodge at Koele's **Pine Sporting Clays and Archery Range** is a 14-station sporting clay course with a skeet field, a compact sporting range, an archery range, and an air-rifle range in a landscape of deep gulches and ravines, pampas grass, and groves of Australian pine. **800-321-4666, lodgeatkoele.com** •• The **beach at Manele Bay** is a perfect base for snorkeling, lounging, light hiking, and Spinner-dolphin watching. •• Stroll through the shops and casual restaurants in postage-stamp-sized Lana'i City, founded in 1924 for Dole Pineapple workers. •• Walking through the awe-inspiring, colorful geological formations at **Garden of the Gods** in the highlands is like taking a lunar stroll.

GETTING THERE

Island Air has flights to Lana'i Airport from Honolulu and Maui (**800-323-3345, islandair.com**). Or try a 45-minute ferry ride from Lahaina Harbor in Maui. Reservations recommended on Lana'I Expeditions Ferry. $52 round trip. **800-695-2624, go-lanai.com**

WHEN TO GO

The island has a desert climate but gets cool with passing clouds in the higher elevations. Whale-spotting is ideal from December to April. The Dole Pineapple Festival over 4th of July weekend is a good time to experience Lana'i City Culture.

THE CARD WRECKER: **EXPERIENCE AT KOELE** NO. 17, 390 YARDS, PAR 4

You feel like the king of the world on this 250-foot-high tee, but a royal drive is required to avoid the hazards. Even Jack Nicklaus has been fooled by the left-to-right trade winds: During an exhibition with Greg Norman, he put five balls in the lake before finding the fairway. Koele director of golf Doug Stephenson explains how to avoid a Bear-like meltdown:

"Most players can hit 3 wood here because of the elevation. Aim left, in line with the cart path; the wind will bring the ball back to center. On the second shot, the green is elevated, so hit one club longer. It also has three tiers—if the pin is in the back-right, and you're on the right side of the fairway, don't try to hit over the tree. Go for the middle."

Hole 4 at The Challenge at Manele, Lana'i, Hawaii

Hole 17 at Turtle Bay
(Palmer), Oahu, Hawaii

OAHU

Kauai is the Garden Island. Maui is the Valley Island. Hawaii is the Big Island, and Oahu—well, Oahu is the Layover Island, with most seasoned travelers using Honolulu Airport as a hub on their way to the other lush rocks in the mid-Pacific. But while Waikiki may deserve its rep as a tourist trap, Oahu gets a bad rap. Surfers know the north shore is Lani (heaven), and golfers should take note. The Turtle Bay Resort on the island's northernmost tip promises an authentic island experience right here on Oahu.

WHERE TO PLAY

TURTLE BAY RESORT

Fazio: 6,535 yards, par 72, 131/71.2
Palmer: 7,199 yards, par 71, 143/74.4
Greens fee: $115–$155 visitors (Fazio);
$145–$175 (Palmer)
800-293-8574, turtlebayresort.com

The Fazio course (George, not Tom) debuted with the original resort and played host to Arnold Palmer, Gary Player, Sam Snead, and Chi Chi Rodriguez in the inaugural Senior Skins Game in 1988. Four years later, the back nine closed to accommodate construction of a new Arnold Palmer–Ed Seay track, but money matters hampered the reopening of the full Fazio for 10 years. Now with a new inward nine, the Fazio is the friendlier of the two courses: fairly flat with ample greens and bunkers that are as lenient as a favorite uncle. Still, when the trade winds blow—at times upwards of 35 mph—all bets are off. The Palmer course is in danger of being nicknamed the Irwin course given that Hale has won all three Turtle Bay Championships since the Champions Tour started coming here in 2001. The course bends like a horseshoe around the 100-acre Punaho'olapa Marsh. Following a linkslike front side, the back nine delves deep into a jungle. Hard to know what kind of mood the usually affable Arnie was in when he sketched this track because there are some spots where the design can be so punitive they ought to add a penal-code page to the yardage book.

WHERE TO STAY

In 1972, Del Webb opened a resort on Kuilima Point that went on to fly the flags of Hyatt and then Hilton before its current incarnation as **Turtle Bay Resort**. More impressive than the $60 million renovation investment undertaken in 2003 are the resort's 880 acres and five and a half miles of coastline. The overhaul added a new spa, spruced up the 401 rooms and suites and 42 deluxe beach cottages—each sporting an ocean view—and breathed desperately needed new life into the only resort on Oahu with 36 holes of tournament-caliber golf. Rooms from $400, suites from $600, cottages from $850. **800-203-3650, turtlebayresort.com**

WHERE TO EAT

Three miles east of Turtle Bay along Kamehameha Highway in Kahuku is the graffiti-scrawled **Giovanni's Original White Shrimp Truck**, which serves up absurdly tasty fresh shrimp. Choose from garlic scampi, hot and spicy or lemon and butter, each $11 for 1/4 pound of shrimp and two scoops of rice. Half-plates are $6. **808-293-1839** •• Try one (or more) of **Lei Lei's** famous mai tais next to the Turtle Bay pro shop. Lei Lei's serves up the best golf club grub on this or any island—save for the Spam sushi. It's so good that locals come to the resort to eat. **800-239-2662, turtlebayresort.com**

LOCAL KNOWLEDGE

Surfing and golf have more in common than you might think. Both require a proper stance and precise timing, and both are best learned with a good teacher, such as Hans Hedemann, a former pro champion turned entrepreneur with six namesake surf schools on Oahu, including one right at Turtle Bay. Two-hour lessons: $150 for one person, $125 per person for two people, $75 per person for three or four people. Equipment included. **808-924-7778, hhsurf.com** •• For post-round relaxation try the kukui and macadamia nut oil massage at the new **Spa Luana**. **808-447-6868, turtlebayresort.com**

GETTING THERE

Honolulu International Airport, served by more than 20 airlines, is Hawaii's largest airport. **honoluluairport.com**

WHEN TO GO

There's no best time for a golf trip to Oahu, as the weather is fairly stable—and warm and sunny—all year. November through April is considered the rainy season, but the showers are brief.

MAUNA LEA AND MAUNA LANI

In the mid-1750s, around the time the Scottish forefathers gave birth to a new golf club called the Royal & Ancient, a *keiki* ("baby" in Hawaiian) entered the world on the rugged west coast of Hawaii's Big Island. The child would become a king, Kamehameha the Great. He would unify all the islands and be hailed a visionary (albeit a vicious one, but you can't conquer an archipelago without handing out some lumps). It's highly doubtful that Kamehameha ever envisioned emerald fairways splayed across the lava rock of his beloved Kohala coast, but the myriad attractions that inspired the king—dramatic landscapes, beautiful beaches, limpid waters teeming with fish—are still there.

WHERE TO PLAY

HAPUNA GOLF COURSE

6,875 yards, par 72, 136/73.3
Greens fee: $120–$145
808-882-5400, hapunabeachhotel.com

Designed by another beloved king, Arnold Palmer, and Ed Seay, this course plays mostly uphill and into morning trade winds on the front nine. Hapuna preys on your Napoleon complex. Take the 3rd hole, a 545-yard par five, where a smooth drive, an easy mid-iron and 100-yard pitch set up a birdie putt. But you didn't really fly all this way to lay up, did you? It's the same game at the 10th, a 372-yard sharp dogleg-left. The play is 3-wood then short iron, but here on Fantasy Island it's like the old Larry Bird vs. Michael Jordan commercial—fly the bunker, over the jacaranda tree, onto the narrowest strip of fairway. Nothing but lava.

MAUNA KEA GOLF COURSE

7,124 yards, par 72, 142/75.3
Greens fee: $150–$210
808-882-5400, hapunabeachhotel.com

TOP 100 YOU CAN PLAY

Robert Trent Jones Sr.'s Mauna Kea design does not make you wait for drama. Resist premature exhilaration at the 3rd hole, a 210-yard carry over a cove. The back tee is at 261; take enough club to reach Maui. The best holes on the back are the 555-yard 17th, marked by zigs, zags, humps, and bumps, and the finisher, a 428-yarder dipping into a gaping maw that begs you to swing as hard as you can. (Any goof can hit the fairway on the second try.)

MAUNA LANI

North: 6,913 yards, par 72, 136/73.2
South: 6,938 yards, par 72, 133/72.8
Greens fee: $140–$205
808-886-6655, maunalani.com

The North course was built on an ancient flow of pahoehoe, the smooth, braided lava that resembles twisted taffy. Many holes are lined by imposing kiawe trees, like the one found in the middle of the first fairway. The 421-yard dogleg-right carries the No. 3 handicap, providing a stout start. On the 401-yard 4th hole there's a clear view of Mauna Kea, the tallest mountain on Earth, topping Mount Everest when measured from its base beneath the ocean, and the hole features a tee shot over an archaeological preserve now filled with Pro-V1s. The South course, which hosted the Senior Skins Game for a decade, is carved across the relatively recent—16th-century—Kaniku flow, amid sharp, scraggly a'a lava. Pack your camera for the South's two boffo par threes along the ocean: the 214-yard 7th and the epic 15th, 196 yards over Iliilinaehehe Bay (say that three times fast).

WHERE TO STAY

 Mauna Kea (Mountain of White) was Kohala's first great resort. Built in 1965 by hotelier Laurance Rockefeller, it faces the Big Island's most stunning beach. A pretty sister property, the **Hapuna Beach Prince Hotel**, arrived in the 1990s, along with the Hapuna Golf Course. Mauna Kea Beach Hotel rooms from $390; Hapuna Beach Prince Hotel rooms from $370. **888-977-4623, princeresortshawaii.com** ● ●

 Ten minutes down the Queen's Highway is the **Mauna Lani** (Mountains Reaching Heaven) **Resort**, home to the **Mauna Lani Bay Hotel & Bungalows**, completed in 1983 and one of Hawaii's most beautiful resorts. Rooms from $430. **800-367-2323, maunalani.com** ● ● Classy and tranquil, the **Fairmont Orchid**, opened in 1990, exudes a serene sophistication, but it's just not the Mauna Lani. Rooms from $329. **808-885-2000, orchid-maunalani.com**

WHERE TO EAT

Thai curries and local lobster are highlights of menu at the elegant **Batik** restaurant at Mauna Kea. **808-882-5810, princeresortshawaii .com** ● ● You won't want to miss the oyster bar—or the regional cuisine—at the Hapuna Beach Prince Hotel's **Coast Grille**. **808-880-3192, princeresortshawaii.com** ● ● Some consider **Merriman's**, which serves locally caught fish (don't miss the wok-charred ahi), to be one of the Big Island's best restaurants. **808-885-6822, merrimanshawaii.com** ● ● The delectable architectural presentations at **Daniel Thiebaut** in Waimea are almost as colorful as the restaurants vintage-Hawaii setting. **808-887-2200, danielthiebaut.com**

LOCAL KNOWLEDGE

Each month, under the light of a rising moon, **Mauna Lani's historian**, Danny Akaka, hosts a night of native music, dance, and storytelling beside the oceanfront Eva Parker Woods cottage and Kalahuipua'a's seven fabled fish ponds. A 50-year-old father of five, Akaka is an instant friend, whose infectious passion embodies the Aloha spirit. **808-885-6622, maunalani culture.org** ● ● For three decades, the family-owned **Fair Wind Cruises** has trawled tourists out to snorkel in the crystalline waters of Kealakekua Bay. Morning cruises include everything from coffee and pastries to a barbecue lunch to diving masks with corrective lenses for spectacled customers. **800-677-9461, fair-wind.com** ● ● Hawaiian singer Nino Kaai fronts the trio **Lawakua** on weeknights at the Fairmont Orchid's Brown's Beach House. Kaai's silky vocals produce a perfect rendition of "Over the Rainbow/What a Wonderful World." **808-885-2000, orchid-maunalani.com**

GETTING THERE

Kona International Airport on the northwest coast is the Big Island's largest airport, with 12 international carriers and 3 inter-island carriers. The much smaller Hilo International Airport on the east coast is served by four inter-island airlines. **hawaii.gov/dot/airports/hawaii/**

WHEN TO GO

Any time is the right time for warm, sunny days.

THE TIPPING POINT

From the parking valets to the caddie master, you'll encounter more outstretched palms at a golf resort than an election candidate during primary season. But if you still rely on a laminated cheat sheet to figure out how much to leave the waitress at Cracker Barrel, you could use a few tips on how to tip well. We asked two gratuity gurus at Whistling Straits Resort—general manager Steve Friedlander and vice president of hospitality Alice Edland—how much coin is enough.

YOUR CADDIE

"We recommend a gratuity of $30 or more per golf bag if the caddie exceeded your expectations, $20 to $30 per bag if the caddie met your expectations, and no tip if the caddie did not meet your expectations," says Friedlander. "This is an extremely rare situation and sometimes happens when a golfer plays poorly and blames the caddie for his misfortune on the course." Call the course in advance to see what the guidelines are.

BAG-DROP GUYS

A $2 to $5 gratuity is appropriate when the attendant has cleaned your clubs or recovered personal items you inadvertently left in your cart or the locker room, according to Friedlander. If the attendant provides exceptional service, then increase the gratuity to $5 to $10.

BEER-CART ATTENDANT

You wouldn't stiff the bartender at your local saloon, so don't do it on the course either. Friedlander says the snack-cart attendants should be given a similar gratuity to a waiter in a restaurant: 15 to 18 percent of the total cost of the order. Increasingly, resorts are adding a gratuity to on-course orders, so be sure to ask if the tip is covered.

PARKING VALET

"At most golf courses, a $1 to $2 tip is appropriate," Edland advises. "There are few courses where parking is a challenge, so it's just to recognize the service. At a hotel or restaurant, I consider how difficult parking is going to be and tip between $3 and $5."

BELLHOP

"I only tip when a bellhop brings my bags to my room," Edland says. "If they tell me about the hotel, explain features of the room, and offer to hang up clothes, I'll tip $5. If they drop the bags in the room, I'll tip $1 per bag."

MAID SERVICE

Edland says a good guide is $2 to $3 per night if you have good service. On a brief trip, leave something at the end of the stay. For longer stays at a resort, tip every day—it will pay off.

CANADA

BRITISH COLUMBIA

ONTARIO

PRINCE EDWARD ISLAND

BANFF
OKANAGAN VALLEY

MUSKOKA GOLF TRAIL

PRINCE EDWARD ISLAND

BANFF

BANFF The Canadian Rockies are a lot like Charlize Theron—pretty in pictures but mind-blowing in person. A 90-minute drive west of Calgary, Banff is easier to reach than you think and provides as dramatic a backdrop for golf as exists on the planet. Not to be overlooked is the fact that the U.S. dollar goes farther north of the border, ensuring that a golf trip to Banff will be as affordable as it is memorable. Now, that's a real Rocky Mountain high.

WHERE TO PLAY

FAIRMONT BANFF SPRINGS GOLF COURSE

7,083 yards, par 71, 140/73.8
Greens fee: CAN$125–$200
403-762-6801, fairmont.com/banffsprings

This was the first course in the world to cost more than $1 million when designer Stanley Thompson unveiled it in 1928. The investment has paid off handsomely. Fused with the surrounding terrain rather than imposed upon it, the course can be resort-friendly for casual duffers or downright wicked for the more competitive player. Every hole is picturesque, but No. 4, a 199-yard downhill par three with a greenside glacier pool, is downright dazzling. The tee shot over the Bow River at the 480-yard par-four 15th is also unforgettable. The Fairmont also boasts a 3,357-yard, par-36 nine-hole course.

SILVERTIP GOLF RESORT

7,173 yards, par 72, 153/74.1
Greens fee: CAN$119–$160
877-877-5444, silvertipresort.com

Fifteen minutes east of Banff, the Les Furber–designed course is a wild child. Golfers have their hands full trying to keep control over rollicking holes characterized by uneven lies, humpy-lumpy greens, and climate-changing elevation swings—it's a 600-foot drop from the highest point at the 9th tee to the lowest at the 13th green. The fun starts at the first hole, a roiling, 559-yard, par-five dogleg-right with a forced carry over water. There is little let-up leading up to the home hole, a 444-yard par four that rates the No. 2 handicap, although a creek and fairway bunker are all but unreachable off the tee.

STEWART CREEK GOLF CLUB

7,195 yards, par 72, 130/73.3
Greens fee: CAN$125–$175
877-993-4653, tsmv.ca

More forgiving than Silvertip but no less fun, Stewart Creek opened in 2000 and is the first of two planned courses at Three Sisters Mountain Village. The Three Sisters mountain range overlooks the golf course and offers enchanting target lines along the way, but hookers and slicers need not fear: there is barely a man-made mound anywhere on the course, and the fairways are mercifully wide, most notably on the opening holes. All bets are off when you step onto the tee at No. 18, an altitude-aided 530-yard par five that is reachable.

THE CARD WRECKER: **FAIRMONT BANFF SPRINGS COURSE** NO. 10, 220 YARDS, PAR 3

This hole only ranks as the 14th most difficult on the course, but trust us—its bite is much worse than its bark. The bunkers flanking the left of the green are punishing, and water runs all the way up the front and to the right. The only consolation is that the green is relatively flat. We asked Doug Wood, the director of golf at Fairmont Banff Springs, how to play it.

His plan to survive the potential horrors of No. 10: "The key to playing "Little Bow" is to hit enough club. The hole requires a carry of 200 yards, usually into a crosswind. Any shot short of the green will find the water. The perfect shot would be a fade aimed at the left bunker, which takes the water out of play."

Hole 14 at Fairmont Banff
Springs, Banff, Canada

WHERE TO STAY

Built in 1888 as a retreat for Canadian Pacific Railway passengers, the Euro-inspired baronial castle **Fairmont Banff Springs** is at once a landmark and an experience. Although it is hard to fathom a 770-room hotel exuding intimacy, the Fairmont Banff Springs's coziness belies its mammoth size. The quaint town of Banff is an easy walk or a quick trolley ride from the hotel, but the resort has it all, from a world-class spa to 12 restaurants and lounges. Sunsets are best enjoyed from the terrace with a camera in one hand and a cocktail in the other. Rooms from $255*. **800-257-7544, fairmont.com/ banffsprings**

WHERE TO EAT

Highlights of the **Fairmont Banff Springs'** many food offerings include the gluttonous lunch buffet in the **Bow Valley Grill**, where the dessert case is a meal unto itself. Secluded in the woods is the Hansel & Gretelesque **Waldhaus Cottage**, with a formal dining room upstairs and the more relaxed and family-friendly Pub below serving authentic Bavarian fare, such as venison ragout, wiener schnitzel, and assorted fondues. Don't miss the Toblerone chocolate fondue. **fairmont.com/banffsprings** ●● In town,

Melissa's is a breakfast favorite famous for its eggs benedict with Canadian back bacon. **403-762-5511, melissasrestaurant.com** ●● **Earls** is an upscale epicurean institution in Canada's western provinces and is now making inroads in the U.S. Go early. Not only is it very popular, but everything on the menu is so tantalizing you'll need the extra time to decide. **403-762-4735, earls.ca**

LOCAL KNOWLEDGE

Knock 'em dead in the resort's Canadian **five-pin bowling alley**. You get three flings with a ball the size of a large coconut to topple five pins arranged in a V, with scoring based on which pins fall, not the total number. It's a hoot, especially after a few Labatts. **403-762-6892, fairmont.com/banffsprings** ●● Hoof it up to scenic **Lake Louise**. Thirty-seven miles up the highway from Banff, the limpid emerald water backed by towering Victoria Glacier resembles a Hollywood movie set and is an idyllic spot to enjoy a hike, canoe trip, ride a horse, or have a picnic. **877-482-6555, lakelouise.com** ●● **Rocky Mountain Raft Tours** offers one- and two-hour trips rafting down the Bow River and shoves off right below the Banff Springs hotel. No roiling whitewater, just a leisurely

bob alongside Tunnel Mountain, the Hoodoos, and majestic Mount Rundle. **403-762-3632, banfflakelouise.com** ●● A two-hour drive—but a world away—is the **Columbia Icefield** on the boundary of Banff and Jasper National Parks. Hop a ride (in shirt sleeves in the summer!) on an all-terrain SnoCoach for a fun and informative 90-minute spin on a glacier that is five times the size of Manhattan. **877-423-7433, columbiaicefield.com** ●● **Bikers** can choose from four guided rides ranging from easy to aggressive, with the entry-level one-hour tour covering three miles out and back along the Vermillion Lakes.

GETTING THERE

Calgary International Airport is a one-and-a-half-hour drive to Banff. It's four and a half hours from New York City, three and a half from Dallas, and three from Chicago, San Francisco, and Los Angeles. **403-735-1200, calgaryairport.com**

WHEN TO GO

June through September are ideal months for golf.

*All prices Canadian dollars.

WORTH THE DRIVE

Jasper Park Lodge is about a four-hour drive from Banff along a highway that redefines the word scenic. The resort is the sister property of Banff Springs and home to another Stanley Thompson–designed gem. The 903-acre resort feels like a laid-back luxury summer camp with log cabins and cedar chalets dotting the banks of Lac Beauvert. The 6,663-yard Jasper Park Lodge Golf Club is a par 71, but you should be happy if you can shoot its age: it celebrates its 80th birthday this year. *Rooms from* CAN$329, *Greens fee:* CAN$149 *resort guests.* 800-257-7544, *fairmont.com/jasper*

OKANAGAN VALLEY

OKANAGAN VALLEY Canadians are often thought of as a bunch of wheat-thrashing, lumber-cutting nice folks who spend their summers mending snowshoes. It isn't true. Any self-respecting Canadian can mend a pair of snowshoes in a weekend. What the continent's cohabitants are less known for are outstanding golf courses and world-class wines. British Columbia's Okanagan Valley is a place where you can sample both, and take in some awe-inspiring scenery at the same time. Located 200 miles northeast of Seattle, the Okanagan Valley is an undiscovered Napa North. It offers some of Canada's top-ranked golf courses and is quickly becoming one of the country's major golf destinations. A wide variety of layouts will challenge and please any golfer, with most courses centrally located in and around the lakeside city of Kelowna.

WHERE TO PLAY

GALLAGHER'S CANYON

6,802 yards, par 72, 123/72.2
Greens fee: CAN$85–$110
250-861-4240, gallagherscanyon.com

Another of western Canada's top courses, Gallagher's provides a classic test of course-management skills. Tree-lined layout has rolling fairways and well-guarded greens.

HARVEST GOLF CLUB

7,109 yards, par 72, 128/72.9
Greens fee: CAN$85–$105
250-862-3103, harvestgolf.com

Impeccably maintained and set amid working apple orchards and vineyards, Harvest tempts golfers with ample landing areas for tee shots. Approach shots are played to undulating greens.

OKANAGAN GOLF CLUB

Quail: 6,891 yards, par 72, 136/72.8
Bear: 6,900 yards, par 72, 133/71.1
Greens fee: CAN$85–$95
800-446-5322, golfokanagan.com

This muni offers two excellent courses. The Bear, a Jack Nicklaus Golden Bear Design opened in 1998, is a playable course offering both links-style and tree-lined fairways leading to bunkered, tiered greens. The Quail, opened in 1994, is a tighter track featuring multitiered fairways carved into a pine forest.

PREDATOR RIDGE

Osprey: 3,512 yards, par 35
Red Tail: 3,578 yards, par 36
Peregrine: 3,566 yards, par 36
Greens fee: CAN$85–$105
250-542-3436, predatorridge.com

From the moment you crest the ridge overlooking the course, you'll find yourself firmly in the hands of golf gods. However, you'll need your A-game to avoid a day in purgatory on this sprawling 27-hole links/mountain track.

WHERE TO STAY

Grand Okanagan Lakefront Resort has 320 rooms, with lake, city, or mountain views. Rates from $159*. **800-465-4651, grandokanagan .com** •• **Predator Ridge Resort** has fairway cottages and a craftsman-style Lodge & Spa. Rates from $185*. **250-542-9404, predatorridge.com**

WHERE TO EAT

Eateries are as varied as the golf. Local favorites include **Earls on Top (250-763-2777)** and **Milestone's (milestonesrestaurants.com).** Many wineries have their own restaurants and are worth a visit, including **Mission Hill (250-768-7611, missionhillwinery.com)** and **Quail's Gate (800-420-9463, quailsgate.com).**

LOCAL KNOWLEDGE

Although the night scene in valley is fairly quiet, **Lake City Casino** in downtown Kelowna at the Grand Okanagan Lakefront Resort features a full range of slots and gaming tables. If you're in the mood for a ride on the wild side, the OK Corral has a mechanical bull. **800-465-4651, grandokanagan.com** •• The Okanagan Valley boasts more than 25 **wineries**, ranging from small estates to large-scale operations that offer award-winning wines and spring and fall wine festivals. **360-604-1205, winesnw.com** •• Nearby **Okanagan Lake**, which stretches for more than 90 miles through the valley, offers numerous water sports. Alternatively, a peaceful balloon ride or back-country fishing trip may help restore your game.

GETTING THERE

The Okanagan Valley is nearly equidistant—about 260 miles—from both Vancouver to the west and Spokane to the south. Calgary is about 380 miles to the east. The regional Kelowna International Airport is served by flights from Seattle, Vancouver, Calgary, and Toronto. **kelowna.ca**

WHEN TO GO

An April-to-October golf season makes it possible for the energetic traveler to tee it up, ski, horseback ride, and tour a winery all in one (hectic) day. Mid-April through June and September through October are the best bets for cooler temperatures and quieter times.

*All prices Canadian dollars.

For information on packages, contact Okanagan Golf Association. golfokanagan.com.

MUSKOKA GOLF TRAIL

MUSKOKA GOLF TRAIL Two hours north of Toronto, Ontario, is the "cottage country" known as Muskoka. It is said that the last person who was disappointed by the region was surely a farmer. Peeking through the area's thin layer of topsoil is the Canadian Shield, the main block of the earth's crust underlying North America. The Shield, more than 3 billion years old, has for decades put designers and developers alike between a rock and a hard place. But enterprising architects, notably Toronto–based Tom McBroom, believe rock can provide beauty, character, and strategic nuance in golf design. No longer must bedrock be treated like a bad family secret, best covered up and forgotten. In capable hands, the Shield, selectively power-washed and used to create harmony between a course and its surroundings, can be a compelling design element. Case in point: the six venues on the newly formed Muskoka Golf Trail.

WHERE TO PLAY

BIGWIN ISLAND GOLF CLUB

7,166 yards, par 72, 136/74.4
Greens fee: CAN$150–$190
800-840-4036, bigwinisland.com

An exclusive high-society getaway in the 1920s, Bigwin Island, accessible via a five-minute ferry ride, sank into ruin more than 30 years ago but has been revived by the current owners. They hired Canadian designer Doug Carrick to superimpose a new course on the site of an overgrown Stanley Thompson layout. Carrick utilized some of the original corridors, but the course unveiled in 2001 is entirely his own creation. Built on rolling, wooded land with minimal rock in sight, the course offers plenty of challenge from the back tees but is never overbearing from the forward markers. Large, flashed-face bunkers filled with reddish-pink sand offer resistance to scoring, but Bigwin is mostly about majestic views. Mount the back tee at the par-four 6th for one of the grandest scenes in Canadian golf: a panorama of beautiful Lake of Bays and its forested islands.

DEERHURST HIGHLANDS

7,011 yards, par 72, 140/74.5
Greens fee: CAN$125–$160
705-789-6411, deerhurstresort.com

Tucked away on the shores of Peninsula Lake outside Huntsville, Highlands is the course that put Muskoka on the golf map. Sculpted from a forested granite ridge, the course, laid out in 1990 by McBroom and Bob Cupp, was the first in the area to embrace hills, cliffs, creeks, and wetlands. A wilderness tour de force with giddy 100-foot drops from tee to fairway, the Highlands is one of the most exacting courses in Ontario from the tips. Not only is the terrain rugged, but 14 of the topsy-turvy greens have at least two levels. The finish, with water in play on the final five holes, is nerve-wracking.

MUSKOKA BAY CLUB

7,367 yards, par 72
Greens fee: NA
866-361-7529, muskokabay.com

Muskoka Bay, which opened in the summer of 2006, is heavily wooded (though many of the fairways are generous), dotted with lakes (only a few of which come into play), and framed by exposed rock, which runs down and across the fairways. There's also plenty of elevation change.

THE RIDGE AT MANITOU

6,815 yards, par 72, 141/72.9
Greens fee: CAN$210
416-407-8014, ridgeatmanitou.com

Access to the Thomas Broom–designed Ridge at Manitou is restricted to members and guests of the Inn at Manitou. The course meanders through meadowland and forest and makes use of plentiful rock outcroppings. In the words of McBroom: "The Ridge at Manitou is an adventure where each hole affords a unique encounter with nature. Holes twist and turn through the forest. The rock that accents many holes reminds us that golf at its best is an experience in which you are integrated into the landscape."

Hole 11 at Taboo Golf
Course, Muskoka Golf
Trail, Canada

THE ROCK

6,545 yards, par 70, 144/72.4
Greens fee: CAN$84–$149
705-765-7625, therockgolf.com

This Nick Faldo layout at Minett Landing on Lake Rosseau is a compact course marked by narrow corridors and more than 75 flashed-face bunkers. Granite outcrops—ample portions of the Shield—come into play at more than half the holes. Small, undulating greens and the chipping areas that embrace them compensate for the relative lack of space.

TABOO GOLF COURSE

7,174 yards, par 71, 146/75.2
Greens fee: CAN$110–$195
800-461-0236, tabooresort.com

Set on Lake Muskoka in Gravenhurst, Taboo is paved through rock. Played from an incorrect set of tees, this stunning Ron Garl layout can be as troublesome as its name. Garl, a scratch golfer with a flair for showmanship, built a brawny track carved from a thick forest of conifers and birch. Taboo skirts streams and ponds and offers a postcard view of the lake, but mostly it showcases the Shield. Garl had little choice: no amount of dynamite could have rearranged the rock. To his credit, there isn't a forced or indifferent hole on the course.

WHERE TO STAY

Muskoka Golf Trail packages are offered by **Ultimate Golf Vacations**. The trail promotes various programs at several resorts. **800-465-3034, ultimategolf.ca** • • Reopened in 1999 after a major facelift, the all-suite **Delta Rocky Crest Resort** property has 65 units. Golf packages from $139* per person, per night. **877-814-7706, deltahotels.com** • • New or renovated lodge rooms, suites, condos, and 18 cottage chalets are available at **Taboo Resort**. Packages from $177*. **800-461-0236, tabooresort.com** • • **Deerhurst Resort**, an 800-acre resort complex, has a wide array of accommodations. Two-night packages from $177*, five nights from $842*. **800-461-4393, deerhurstresort.com** • • Set on 850 acres overlooking Fairy Lake, **Delta Grandview Resort** dates to 1911. Room rates from $149*. **705-789-4417, deltahotels.com** • • The **Delta Sherwood Inn** offers 49 charming cottage-style accommodations in the quaint village of Port Carling. Room rates from $175*. **705-765-3131, deltahotels.com** • • On the rocky shore of Manitouwabing Lake, the 35-room **Inn at Manitou** is surrounded by forest. Guests have access to the Ridge at Manitou. Rates from $220*. **705-389-2171, manitou-online.com**

WHERE TO EAT

Savor local ingredients and grilled seafood, meats, and poultry in an elegant setting at **Riverwalk** in Bracebridge. **705-646-0711, riverwalkmuskoka.com** • • Enjoy Asian and Mediterranean–influenced fare in **Aroma's** sophisticated Soho-esque setting. The steak and frites panini is not to be missed at lunch. **705-788-5160, aromadining.ca** • • It can feel like you're walking into a sitcom at the family-run **Blondies** in Gravenhurst, but the eclectic food is as serious as good-eating gets. **705-687-7756, blondiesrestaurant.ca**

LOCAL KNOWLEDGE

Learn about the area's wild critters and see live moose, wolves, bears, and eagles at the 100-acre **Muskoka Wildlife Centre** in Gravenhurst. **705-689-0222, muskokawildlifecentre.com** • • There are several options for touring the **Muskoka Lakes**. The Segwun is a historic steamship **(705-687-6667, segwun.com)**. Sunset Cruises offers a sail on a 1920s restored yacht **(705-645-2462, sunsetcruises.ca)**. And the 300-passenger Lady Muskoka **(705-646-2628, ladymuskoka.com)** offers brunch and candlelight tours. • • Take a guided hike through mature hardwood forests and have a picnic lunch on the beaches of Beausoleil

Island in **Georgian Bay Islands National Park**. **705-526-9804, parkscanada.gc.ca/gbi** • • Santa spends his summers on the Muskoka River in Bracebridge, don't cha know? **Santa's Village** sports amusement-park rides, including Santa's Express Train and Rudolph's Rollercoaster. **705-645-2512, santasvillage.com** • • Well-known performers often visit the historic **Gravenhurst Opera House**. **705-687-5550, gravenhurst.ca**

GETTING THERE

The Muskoka region is an hour-and-a-half to two hours by car north of Toronto.

WHEN TO GO

Prime golf conditions start in mid-April and run through mid-November. The scenery in the fall is spectacular, and the courses aren't as packed with tourists as in the summer months.

*All prices Canadian dollars.

For information on additional courses, attractions and dining, call 1-800-267-9700 or visit discovermuskoka.ca.

PRINCE EDWARD ISLAND Imagine a million-acre garden comprising a patchwork of glistening streams, lakes, and pine forests. Add 25 courses carved from gently rolling farmlands and you have Prince Edward Island (PEI). Often described as Canada's best-kept secret, Prince Edward Island sits in the Gulf of St. Lawrence on Canada's eastern seaboard, the island is separated from the mainland of New Brunswick and Nova Scotia by the Northumberland Strait. Since it was linked to the mainland in 1997 by a nine-mile bridge, visitors to the island have doubled and so has the number of courses.

WHERE TO PLAY

BRUDENELL RIVER GOLF COURSE

Brudenell River: 6,591 yards, par 72, 131/72.0
Dundarave: 7,284 yards, par 72, 139/76.2
Greens fee: CAN$30–$70 (Brudenell River);
CAN$35–$80 (Dundarave)
800-235-8909, golflinkspei.com

With six par threes, six par fours and six par fives, the Robbie Robertson–designed River has become one of the island's most popular resort courses since its opening in 1969. Fairways are wide open but water comes into play on the majority of holes. Brudenell has hosted several Canadian Tour events and in 2000 was home to the Lorie Kane Island Challenge—Canada's first women's skins game. Designed by Michael Hurdzan and Dana Fry, the challenging Dundarave was opened in 1999 and plays in a tranquil setting through pine forests and around the wide Brudenell River.

THE EAGLES GLENN

6,785 yards, par 72, 138/73.4
Greens fee: CAN$60–$75
866-963-3600, eaglesglenn.com

One of the best new courses on the island, located at Cavendish Beach and designed by Graham Cooke, the links-style Eagles Glenn has matured rapidly, playing over rivers and natural lakes to manicured greens. The sculpted fairways offer some challenging lies, and large, fast, undulating greens offer several demanding pin positions.

FOX MEADOW GOLF & COUNTRY CLUB

6,836 yards, par 72, 127/73.2
Greens fee: CAN$50–$60
877-569-8337, foxmeadow.pe.ca

The closest new course to the island's capital, Fox Meadow is seven minutes from the center of Charlottetown. This Rob Heaslip resort course plays across hilly terrain, with wide fairways, big greens, and elevated tees that provide wonderful views across the harbor. Fox Meadow is a favorite among cruise ship passengers.

GLASGOW HILLS RESORT & GOLF CLUB

6,915 yards, par 72, 134/73.8
Greens fee: CAN$60–$75
902-621-2200, glasgowhills.com

Opened in 2002, this Les Furber design plays over rolling terrain. The fairways are lined with trees yet still offer spectacular views of the surrounding countryside because of several elevated tees on the back nine.

THE LINKS AT CROWBUSH COVE

6,903 yards, par 72, 148/75.2
Greens fee: CAN$40–$90
800-235-8909, golflinkspei.com

If you have time to play only one course on PEI, this should be it. Designed by Thomas McBroom, Crowbush Cove is probably the toughest course on the island and features tight fairways, fast greens, long carries over water, and several holes played alongside the ocean where strong winds can come into play.

WHERE TO STAY

Delta Prince Edward Hotel is located on the waterfront in the center of the island's capital from where most courses can be reached within 90 minutes by car. Golf packages start at $84*. **902-566-2222, deltahotels.com** • • **Rodd Crowbush Golf and Beach Resort** has rooms and cottages overlooking one of the island's finest oceanfront courses. Rooms from $136*. **902-961-5600, rodd-hotels.ca** • • **Rodd Brudenell River** has rooms, cottages, and cabins around a 45-hole golf resort, which includes Dundarave, Brudenell River, and a nine-hole layout used by the Canadian Golf Academy. Rooms from $99*. **902-652-2332, rodd-hotels.ca**

WHERE TO EAT

Fresh seafood is available in abundance throughout the island with huge oysters, mussels, scallops, and succulent lobster topping the menus. Try **Dalvay by the Sea**, a Victorian mansion at Dalvay Beach.

902-672-2048, dalvaybythesea.com • • **The Dunes Café** overlooks a water garden in a tranquil country setting at Brackley. **902-672-2586, dunesgallery.com** • • **The Inn at St. Peters** serves fresh seafood at St. Peters Bay. **902-961-2135, innatstpeters.com**

LOCAL KNOWLEDGE

There are miles of deserted **red sand beaches**, as well as scenic hiking and biking trails, national parks, fishing, and kayaking. **gov.pe.ca/visitorsguide** • • Follow the well-marked trails in Cavendish leading to the original **Green Gables** house, the setting for the children's classic novel *Anne of Green Gables*. **gov.pe.ca/greengables** • • Renting a car is essential to get the most from the island. **Discount Car Rental** picks up from all Charlottetown hotels. **800-264-8909, discountcar.com**

GETTING THERE

PEI is about 1,000 miles northeast of Toronto and 650 miles northeast of Boston. Air Canada and Northwest airlines fly to the island's Charlottetown Airport **(flypei.com)**. Halifax International Airport on Nova Scotia is a scenic three-plus-hour drive away. **hiaa.ca**

WHEN TO GO

For half of the year the island is covered in snow, surrounded by ice floes and battered by biting winds. When spring arrives, however, the island undergoes a complete transformation, and by May the golfing season is in full swing. Most courses are open until the end of October, with ideal playing conditions between June and September and stunning colors of autumn foliage in October.

*All prices Canadian dollars.

See peiplay.com, golfpei.com, and travelcanada.ca for more information.

Hole 8 at The Links at Crowbush Cove, Prince Edward Island, Canada

CODE OF THE ROAD

Planning a road trip shouldn't mean budgeting as much for tickets as you do for greens fees. Throw the sticks in the trunk and follow these five tips to feel like the king of the road—even if you're desperately trying to check your e-mail at every rest stop—and prevent your trip from going south (unless that's the direction you're headed).

SUSS OUT SMOKEY

Avoid making deposits in the local sheriff's coffers with **speedtrap.org**, which lists Smokey's favorite spots to lie in wait while you're hustling to the next tee time. Organized by state, it also includes an extensive list of local traffic attorneys.

RADAR ALERTS

Cobra's latest radar detector, the XRS9930 ($220), sports a large color screen that allows you to read alerts easily, a SmartPower function that shuts the unit down when you turn off your car's ignition, and even a Voice Alert feature to bark out warnings ("Watch out for that tree!"). **cobra.com**

GRIDLOCK ALERT

Put Pioneer's AVIC-Z1 $2,250 navigation system in your dashboard and you'll have a car that's smarter than you are. The seven-inch, color touch-screen keeps you abreast of everything from traffic alerts to directions to the nearest Chili's. **pioneerelectronics.com**

ROADSIDE ASSIST

Do you keep all your information on a laptop or a PDA? When your info gadget self-destructs during a trip, get **rescuecom.com (1-800-Rescue7)** on the horn. Within an hour, a computer tech will be on site. Prices range from $90 to $180 depending on the level of the emergency.

TALK BACK

Pick up some inside knowledge from the boys in the big rigs with a Uniden PC780Elite CB radio ($100). Here's a brief lesson in trucker lingo: "alligator" means a blown tire and "bear cave" has nothing to do with grizzlies—it's a police station. **uniden.com**

CARIBBEAN & MEXICO

CARIBBEAN

BARBADOS
BERMUDA
PUERTO RICO

MEXICO

LOS CABOS
PUERTO VALLARTA
CANCUN

BARBADOS

BARBADOS When Tiger Woods chose Sandy Lane for his wedding in the fall of 2004, he was just the latest luminary to seek sanctuary at the famed Barbados resort. Chances are that you didn't receive an invite to the nuptials (ours was lost in the mail, too), but here's another reason to visit: The Green Monkey, a course by Tom Fazio that opened in 2004, was the most anticipated Caribbean debut since Teeth of the Dog more than 30 years ago.

WHERE TO PLAY

BARBADOS GOLF CLUB

6,697 yards, par 72, 124/71.0
Greens fee: $85
246-428-8463, barbadosgolfclub.com

Built in 1974, Barbados Golf Club remained largely beneath the radar until a refurbishment five years ago by architect Ron Kirby raised its profile. Numerous water hazards and coral-waste bunkers give the course character without being unduly punishing.

THE GREEN MONKEY

7,343 yards, par 72, 134/76.7
Greens fee: $300
246-444-2500, sandylane.com

Carved from a former quarry, the Green Monkey was named for the Bajan monkeys that roam the property. You'll marvel at the par threes as among the most spectacular and challenging collection of short holes you've ever played. The green at the 198-yard 8th is perched atop the quarry walls, while the 11th plummets down between them, although its length—270 yards from the tips, 175 from the next closest tee box—makes it an uphill battle for most. The swirling wind around the quarry only adds to the difficulty. There are, undoubtedly, some architectural purists who will loudly bemoan the fact that the soaring rock walls that give the Green Monkey much of its visual appeal are the designer's conceit—Fazio had his design team gouge the contours here from the quarry. But most visitors won't consider that a point worth debating when they stand on the tee at No. 16 and take in the challenge—226 yards downhill to a green fronted by bunkers and backed by a pond (see Card Wrecker below).

THE CARD WRECKER: THE GREEN MONKEY NO. 16, 226 YARDS, PAR 3

The signature hole—it even has the iconic green monkey carved into a greenside bunker—is a downhill par three, but short isn't the word for it. We asked Padraig Harrington, a regular visitor, for tips on how to tame the Monkey: "The 16th at the Green Monkey is a magnificent hole, set in a quarry against a lake. The tee shot is played from an elevated tee. Doubt is put in the mind when you get to this hole as the wind swirls, gusts and sometimes stops down in the quarry, making it difficult to select the right club. Ideally the shot should draw off the right hand bunker and feed towards the left-hand side of the green, where most of the pins would be located."

ROYAL WESTMORELAND
GOLF & COUNTRY CLUB

6,870 yards, par 72, 130/74.4
Greens fee: $150–$225
246-422-4653, royal-westmoreland.com

This Robert Trent Jones Jr. design was indisputably the best course on the island until the Green Monkey opened. It's still a terrific layout and has hosted European Senior Tour events. Former Masters champion Ian Woosnam lives part of the year on the 18th hole and says this course is one of his favorites anywhere.

SANDY LANE COUNTRY CLUB

7,060 yards, par 72, 132/74.7
Greens fee: $175–$220
246-444-2500, sandylane.com

Like other fine sibling courses—the Valley Course at Royal Portrush and the New Course in St. Andrews—Sandy Lane Country Club suffers from its proximity to a track that deservedly takes the spotlight. Fazio designed the Country Club in 2001, and it holds its own with any other course on the island, even if it doesn't quite rise to the level of the Green Monkey. Despite that, the layout is not without its challenges. The fairways are generous on almost every hole, and the potential for losing golf balls is limited. It can seem like a fairly bland resort course, but when the wind picks up, you'll understand why those fairways are so wide. The Country Club is all about angles: You might get a lot of free passes off the tee, but if you find yourself playing approach shots from the wrong places, you'll be scratching your head as if it's trigonometry class all over again.

WHERE TO STAY

Located in St. James, 35 minutes from Grantley Adams International Airport, **Sandy Lane Resort** combines classic style and modern amenities. (Everything in your room, from the shades to the lights, is controlled from a bedside panel.) The Spa at Sandy Lane is extensive. The Golfer's Tonic massage will put a spring in your spikes. A stay here doesn't come cheap—rooms start at $1,100 a night—but the service reflects that. (The staff will stop by the beach to spritz you with Evian water.) If you want to do things the way Tiger Woods does, rent the private villa. It holds 14 people—and you'll need them all to split the tab. Rates can get up to $25,000 per night. **246-444-2000, sandylane.com**

WHERE TO EAT

Sandy Lane's ultra-chic seafront eatery **L'Acajou** has great Caribbean haute cuisine. The wine list will cheer even choosy oenophiles. **246-444-2000, sandylane.com** •• Don't leave your plate unattended at Sandy Lane's casual **Bajan Blue**, because the birds will steal your food. And with good reason—Bajan Blue serves first-rate island fare. **246-444-2000, sandylane.com** •• You won't find any place with a more appealing ambiance than **Palm Terrace**, where the French cuisine has a distinctly Caribbean flair. **246-422-5555, fairmont.com** •• Located a couple of miles from Sandy Lane, the charming **Olives Bar & Bistro** has superb Mediterranean fare—and air conditioning. **246-432-2112**

LOCAL KNOWLEDGE

The Scotland District on the Atlantic coast echoes Cruden Bay more than the Caribbean. •• **Harrisons Cave** has stalactites and stalagmites, and underground lakes. **246-438-6640, harrisonscave.com** •• Visit the **Caribbean Cigar Company** to see how they turn out 4,000 puffers a week. **246-437-8519** •• **Graeme Hall Nature Sanctuary** has the island's largest lake, and dive-bombing birds reside in the aviary. **246-435-9727, graemehall.com** •• **Mount Gay Rum** is the world's oldest, dating from 1703. Call your tour and tasting a $6 history lesson. **246-425-8757, mountgayrum.com** •• Hop on the submarine at **Atlantis Adventures** in Bridgetown. **246-436-8929, goatlantis.com**

GETTING THERE

Grantley Adams International Airport is a four-and-a-half-hour flight from New York and three and a half hours from Miami. **gaia.com.bb**

WHEN TO GO

The average daily high temperature year-round is between 82 degrees and 86 degrees.

BERMUDA

Golfers may be forgiven for thinking that Bermuda is all about colorful shorts, a sun-loving strain of grass, and a mysterious triangle. But this 21-square-mile British colony has eight ocean-side courses that are as easily accessible as Florida for most travelers. And unlike the Sunshine State, there's not a theme park or retirement village in sight. Bermuda's volcanic terrain isn't an ideal canvas for golf, but the charms that drew such writers and artists as Mark Twain and Georgia O'Keeffe also lured architects Charles Blair Macdonald and Devereux Emmett. The fishhook-shaped main island is so narrow—not wider than two miles across—that almost every course offers views of the Atlantic. That's as true of the municipal Ocean View Golf Club as of the exclusive Mid Ocean Club. And "private" doesn't mean "inaccessible" in Bermuda, as it does in the U.S. Even members' clubs will welcome visitors on certain days. Have your hotel call to arrange tee times.

WHERE TO PLAY

PORT ROYAL GOLF COURSE

6,561 yards, par 71, 135/71.1
Greens fee: $132
441-234-0974, bermudatourism.com/golf

Port Royal is Bermuda's longest track, a Robert Trent Jones Sr. gem on the main island's southern end. The views are so good that locals are only half joking when they refer to Pebble Beach as "the Port Royal of the West." But there's no snobbery with that attitude: Port Royal is about as stuffy as your local muni, with a modest clubhouse and friendly staff. Shutterbugs who like to snap photos during a round will find no shortage of distractions on the back nine. The 15th hole is next to the ruins of a naval battery fort, and the 176-yard 16th is one of the most famous holes on the islands. Tee shots that fall short disappear into Port Royal's version of the Bermuda Triangle—a gaping cliff-top chasm.

MID OCEAN

6,520 yards, par 71, 135/72.8
Greens fee: $210
441-293-0330
themidoceanclubbermuda.com

The country's best course, this 1921 Macdonald design looks like a New England transplant, except for the flora. The 433-yard fifth wasn't Macdonald's first Cape Hole—that honor belongs to the 14th at National Golf Links in New York, for those keeping track at home—but it might be his toughest, a terrific risk-reward proposition. Cut off as much aqua as you dare on this dogleg left, or face a long-iron approach to a narrow, foot-print-shaped green that is heavily contoured and flanked by bunkers. "If you don't play this course every day, these greens can really give you headaches," warns assistant pro Chris Garland. The final two holes are stunning: a 200-yard Redan–style par three into the prevailing wind and a 421-yarder with bunkers to the left and a sheer drop to the Atlantic on the right. It's no surprise that Mid Ocean is Bermuda's answer to Bel Air Country Club. Members include New York's billionaire mayor Michael Bloomberg and Hollywood actor Michael Douglas.

TUCKER'S POINT GOLF CLUB

6,361 yards, par 70, NA/NA
Greens fee: $185
441-298-6970, tuckerspoint.com

Built in 1931 by Charles Banks, Tucker's Point sits above an egg-shaped basin created by a volcanic explosion 100 million years ago. Banks used doglegs and blind shots to squeeze the layout into the hilly terrain, but six new holes were built by Roger Rulewich in 2002 as part of a $12 million course redesign. Rulewich has softened its edges with wider fairways and greens that don't unduly punish errant shots. The track is fun and playable, with—no surprise—superb views over Castle Harbor and Harrington Sound. Two back-nine par fours take proper advantage of the landscape. The 425-yard 13th drops from an elevated tee to a tight fairway; miss it and you'll have a hard time hitting a green fronted by a sprawling bunker. Redemption is possible at the 310-yard 17th, with its wide fairway and large, flat green.

BELMONT HILLS GOLF CLUB

6,100 yards, par 70, NA/NA
Greens fee: $103
441-236-6400, belmonthills.com

A 25-minute drive southwest of Mid Ocean in Warwick, this Golden Age course recently underwent an extreme makeover to turn Devereux Emmett's nearly featureless design into a bumpy, heavily bunkered romp. The challenge is issued at the start: The 318-yard first drops through a tree-lined corridor to a shallow double green that it shares with the 10th. Bunkers and palm trees await go-for-broke golfers. The 167-yard 17th also plays downhill toward the Great Sound to a green that's ringed with bunkers.

RIDDELL'S BAY GOLF AND COUNTRY CLUB

5,794 yards, par 70, 121/66.9
Greens fee: $145
441-238-1060, riddellsbay.com

A short drive down Middle Road, Riddell's Bay was built by Emmett in 1922, shortly before he crafted Congressional Country Club near Washington, D.C. It is the island's flattest and shortest regulation course, with narrow fairways and tiny greens. The only trouble comes on holes 8, 9, 10, and 12, where you must flirt with the surf. Don't expect to feel the adrenaline pumping anywhere else. Small changes were made to toughen this track, but even the introduction of three-inch rough last year stirred the status-quo-loving members.

ST. GEORGE'S GOLF COURSE

4,043 yards, par 62, 103/61.7
Greens fee: $46–$65
441-297-8353

This public track on Bermuda's northernmost point is routed around the historic Fort St. Catherine, but its paltry length places it in the lower orders. Same with Ocean View Golf Course near Hamilton, a scrappy-but-charming nine-holer (2,940 yards) with the vistas its name promises. This is the best place to find a little Nassau action, especially on Friday afternoons when the locals blow off work.

WHERE TO STAY

There is only one resort here where golfers can stay and play: the 593-room **Fairmont Southampton**, an iconic pink behemoth perched on the cliffs at the southern curve of the main island. The hotel has an entertaining 2,684-yard, 18-hole executive course that bobs and weaves through steep hills overlooking the ocean and the Great Sound. The greens are superbly conditioned, and the constant breeze means this diminutive layout can serve as handy preparation for Bermuda's regulation tracks. The Fairmont was renovated in 2003 (Hurricane Fabian had sheared off its roof) and is within 30 minutes of the islands' best courses: Mid Ocean, Tucker's Point, Port Royal, and Belmont Hills. Rates from $219. **441-238-8000, fairmont.com/southampton**

WHERE TO EAT

Stop at the **Swizzle Inn** on Blue Hole Hill near the airport for a sip of the local drink, the rum swizzle, made with dark and gold rum and fresh fruit juices. **441-293-1854, swizzleinn .com** • • The **Hog Penny Restaurant and Pub** in Hamilton serves hearty English fare, such as bangers and mash and fish and chips. **441-292-2534, hogpennypub.com** • • **Little**

Venice, also in Hamilton, is great for authentic Italian, which can be enjoyed on a lovely terrace. **441-295-3503, littlevenice.bm** • • At the **Riddell's Bay clubhouse** you can sample Bermuda's famous sherry-infused fish chowder. **441-238-1060, riddellsbay.com** • • **Greg's Steakhouse** at Port Royal Golf Club serves up perfectly aged cuts. **441-234-6092** • • Don't miss the Fairmont Southampton's **Newport Room**, which offers four-star French in a setting resembling the cabin of a luxury yacht. Ahoy! **441-238-8000, fairmont.com/southampton**

LOCAL KNOWLEDGE

Front Street in the colorful capital of Hamilton offers the best in shopping and bar-hopping. Stop in at the great happy hours at **The Pickled Onion** (441-295-2263, thepickledonion .com) and **The Beach** (441-292-0219). • • Bermuda permits only one car per household for its 60,000 residents. That means there are no rental cars—scooters and taxis are the only options for visitors. Those unwilling to tackle the scooter will spend $4.80 for the first mile and $1.68 for each additional mile. (U.S. and Bermuda dollars are interchangeable). On the plus side, many cabbies are golfers who will offer local knowledge.

GETTING THERE

Bermuda's six connected islands are about a two-hour flight from Atlanta, Boston, Charlotte, Miami, New York City, Philadelphia, and Washington, D.C., all of which have nonstop flights. Fares have typically been expensive during the off-season (about $400), but discount carrier USA 3000 **(877-872-3000, usa3000airlines.com)** now flies from Baltimore and Newark for $129. **bermudaairport.com**

WHEN TO GO

High season is from May to September. Temperatures range from 75 to 85 degrees; off-season temps seldom drop below 70. December and January are the wettest months, each averaging 17 days of rain. Hurricane season is June to November, with the big storms hitting every three years on average. Visit **bermudaweather.bm**

For more information, visit bermudatourism .com or call 800-BERMUDA.

PUERTO RICO At first, they sound like birds. When the sun sets and the evening wind cools the air, their chirps ring from every coconut palm, bush, and thatch of green, gaining steam as the sky darkens. They're coqui tree frogs—thumbnail-size, rarely seen, incredibly loud, and Puerto Rico's unofficial mascot. Their ko-kee song, like a chorus of mutant crickets, will later form the soundtrack for your memories of Puerto Rico, which these days can include good and diverse golf experiences. A visit to this 3,400-square-mile island isn't about playing 36 a day every day. It's about relaxing, sipping a piña colada, and enjoying the big things in life, like friendly people, good food, and the nightly coqui orchestra. Not that you can't play twice a day. Puerto Rico's top tracks are all clustered fairly close together along its northern coast. Better yet, this Caribbean getaway is a quick flight from much of the continental U.S.

WHERE TO PLAY

COCO BEACH GOLF AND COUNTRY CLUB

Ocean: 3,519 yards, par 36
Lakes: 3,532 yards, par 36
Palms: 3,539 yards, par 36
Mountain: 3,520 yards, par 36
Greens fee: $130–$150
787-657-2000, cocobeachgolf.com

Along the northeastern coast of the island, Tom Kite and Bruce Besse collaborated on four nines at the 1,000-acre Coco Beach Resort. The Atlantic and El Yunque act as a backdrop to the Ocean and Lakes, where you'll never find an uneven lie or a big-breaking putt. Length, water and sand provide the danger here. The Palms course winds through protected palm and mangrove forests, with creeks, lakes, and vegetation creating ample hazards. The most intimidating hole is the par-three 4th. At 220 yards from the back, golfers must carry their tee shots 195 yards over a lake and creek to a small putting surface flanked by bunkers front and back. You'll need a good swing—and a few deep breaths. The newest course, the Mountain, will take you on a rolling good ride.

HYATT DORADO BEACH RESORT & COUNTRY CLUB

East: 7,000 yards, par 72, 140/75.7
West: 6,975 yards, par 72, 139/74.5
Greens fee: $125–$160
787-796-8961, doradobeach.hyatt.com

Dorado Beach's East and West, built by Robert Trent Jones and opened in 1958 and 1961, respectively, cut through the dense, lush vegetation of tropical forests and former citrus groves. Mature palms line their gently sloping fairways and pancake-flat greens. The East, host of 10 Champions Tour and two LPGA Tour events, has deeper bunkers and a few medium-size mammals buried beneath the putting surfaces. Its famous 525-yard, double-dogleg 4th zigzags right, then left, with lakes guarding both the corner and the green. A two-mile shuttle ride away, two formerly toothless Trent Jones tracks just got a $3 million overhaul.

EMBASSY SUITES DORADO DEL MAR BEACH AND GOLF RESORT

6,940 yards, par 72, 138/75.2
Greens fee: $87–$102
787-796-3070, embassysuites.com

Puerto Rico's native son Chi Chi Rodriguez lives 10 minutes east of the Hyatt near his 18-hole design at the Dorado del Mar Beach and Golf Resort. Houses reign in this tight course, built in 1998 with plenty more elevation change than you'll find at Dorado Beach. Get your camera ready on the 525-yard, dogleg-left 10th, which climbs 50 feet to a blind green teetering above the ocean. After crossing a lake twice on the 510-yard 18th hole, you may not feel up to reenacting Rodriguez's celebratory sword dance.

WESTIN RIO MAR

River: 6,945 yards, par 72, 135/74.5
Ocean: 6,782 yards, par 72, 132/73.8
Greens fee: $100–$165 (guests),
$135–$190 (non-guests)
888-627-8556, westinriomar.com

A 30-minute drive west on Route 3 to Rio Grande takes you to more merciful (read flat) tracks. The Westin Rio Mar owns 500 acres on the Atlantic, where guests enjoy 12 restaurants, a mile-long beach, and two entirely different golf courses. Opened in 1997, the River course is as tough as its designer Greg Norman, with small greens and winding fairways crisscrossed by the Mameyes River. The fickle trade winds and mounded, bunker-ringed greens set the challenge on the gentler Ocean course, designed by George and Tom Fazio and opened in 1974.

EL CONQUISTADOR

6,746 yards, par 72, 134/73.1
Greens fee: $165–$190
800-468-8365, elconresort.com

The resort's Arthur Hills–designed course, opened in 1993, is a roller-coaster ride with 200 feet in elevation change, tight, undulating fairways, and ever-changing trade winds. Although just 6,746 yards from the back, it's not your typical, easygoing resort track. The trouble starts on No. 1, a 395-yard dogleg-right with sweeping views of the 3,500-foot peaks of El Yunque rain forest to the southwest and the ocean to the north. You'll be distracted for just a second, as the hole demands a precise tee shot to a landing area 75 feet below, with dense brush to the left and a 30-foot drop-off to the right. The key to managing "El Con," as locals call it, is to leave your driver in the bag and keep the ball in play.

Hole 6 at Coco Beach (Lakes), Puerto Rico

WHERE TO STAY

Perched on 300-foot-high cliffs where the Atlantic Ocean and Caribbean Sea meet, an hour's drive east of San Juan near the port town of Fajardo, the **El Conquistador's** theatrical setting was used in the 1964 James Bond movie *Goldfinger*. Check into the new **Las Casitas Village**, where you'll find spacious Spanish-style villas with balconies and full kitchens. They are close to the resort's golf course and Golden Door Spa and are quieter than the 750-room main resort. Each villa has its own butler, available 24 hours to help with everything from unpacking bags to procuring those coladas. Rooms at the main resort from $139. Rooms at the Casitas from $375. **866-317-8932, elconresort.com** • • Relaxation sets in upon check-in at the **Hyatt Dorado Beach**, 45 minutes west of the capital city in Dorado, where waves crash beyond the open-air lobby and Coco the parrot screeches "Hello" to visitors. If you can pry yourself from the strategically placed hammock outside your beachfront room, four on-site courses await. Rooms from $298. **800-633-7313, doradobeach.hyatt.com**

WHERE TO EAT

Chef Victor Cruz serves Caribbean-influenced fare in the **Coco Beach clubhouse**. Pair his melon martini with the buffalo rib eye in a potato crust, served with mango salsa. **787-657-2000, cocobeachgolf.com** • • El Conquistador's intimate **Le Bistro** serves Puerto Rican cuisine (fresh fish, fried plantains) with a French twist—and great *mojitos*. (Ask veteran bartender Edward Rodriguez to give you a *mojito*-making lesson and a taste of his own fruity liqueur, called Morocco.) **787-863-1000, elconresort.com** • • For a more casual setting, head into Fajardo and try cabana-style **Calizo's**, which serves $3 Presidentes, pitchers of sangria and piña coladas, as well as six kinds of fish paired with your choice of six sauces. • •

Just 45 minutes from Dorado Beach, Old San Juan offers vibrant nightlife. Make two stops on Fortaleeza Street—**Dragonfly (787-977-3886)** for mouthwatering tapas and the **Parrot Club (787-725-7370)** for inspired Caribbean cooking and fruity tropical drinks. • • Make a mandatory lunch stop at one of the **roadside stands** on Route 3, where a dollar buys a crispy corn fritter filled with seasoned beef, pork, or chicken. Greasy and delicious.

LOCAL KNOWLEDGE

More than 240 species of plants and trees decorate El Yunque, a 28,000-acre tropical rain forest, which is just a 30-minute drive west of the Wyndham El Conquistador. Stop at the visitors' center for a map, and take a 30-minute hike to La Mina Falls, where you can cool off under 65-degree waters. **welcome.topuertorico.org** • • Looking for some gaming action and a cigar? Head for the wood-paneled Old World-style lobby bar and casino of the **El San Juan** on Isle Verde Avenue in San Juan, where a special stand sells freshly rolled stogies on weekends. **787-791-1000** • • Because

of the Wyndham El Conquistador's cliff-side setting, **Palomino Island**, a 15-minute ferry ride east, serves as the resort's private beach. Surrounding coral reefs protect dozens of species of tropical fish, making for colorful snorkeling. **561-447-5300, elconresort .com** • • The local version of Scotch-tasting is just a scenic 20-minute drive east of Dorado Beach, along the coast. You can smell the burnt sugarcane from the parking lot of the **Bacardi Rum Factory**, which has views across the water to Fort San Felipe in Old San Juan. A 90-minute tour relives the colorful history of Caribbean rum-making, topped by free tastes. The Bacardi Reserva has a smooth, smoky flavor best savored straight, like a good scotch. **787-788-8400, bacardi.com**

GETTING THERE

San Juan Airport is just three and a half hours from New York and four and a half from Dallas.

WHEN TO GO

Average temperatures are steady year-round—between 83 and 85 degrees.

Hole 3 at Coco Beach (Ocean), Puerto Rico

LOS CABOS

Mexico's premier model for high-end golf is found at the tip of Baja California Sur in Los Cabos (The Capes), the designated name for a 20-mile coastal corridor bookended by San Jose del Cabo (a quaint colonial town) and Cabo San Lucas (a party-hearty Margaritaville). As a destination, Los Cabos, located 1,000 miles south of San Diego, has enough first-rate layouts and deluxe hotel rooms to put it on an equal footing with Hawaii, Scottsdale, or Palm Springs. Once a rustic, sleepy hideaway at land's end favored by retired pirates and fishermen in search of trophy marlin, Los Cabos, in the span of 10 years, has reinvented itself as a golf getaway.

WHERE TO PLAY

PALMILLA RESORT

Ocean: 3,434 yards, par 36
Mountain: 3,602 yards, par 36
Arroyo: 3,337 yards, par 36
Greens fee: $245
01152-624-146-7000
oneandonlyresorts.com

Home to 27 holes of Jack Nicklaus–designed golf, Palmilla Resort is the facility that set the stage for growth in Los Cabos. In a box-shaped canyon set against by stark brown peaks in the Sierra de la Laguna range, Nicklaus created a core 18 in 1992 (the Mountain and Arroyo nines) on terrain that would have given Butch Cassidy and the Sundance Kid pause for thought. Palmilla was the first course in the hemisphere to combine ocean, mountain, and desert scenery—imagine Tucson with the Sea of Cortez at its feet. Nicklaus routed holes around long waste bunkers, irrigation ponds, and deep, boulder-strewn arroyos, with five sets of tees providing admirable versatility. Slim landing pods beckon from spiny vegetation on this target-style gem, and several holes call for do-or-die forced carries, but Palmilla overall exhibits excellent playability. The Ocean nine, added in 1999, features a 600-foot elevation change from the 1st tee to the 6th green, carrying players from the mountains to the sea. Palmilla's tile-roofed clubhouse, offering panoramic views of cactus forests, deep arroyos, and the distant sea, is magnificent.

CABO DEL SOL

Ocean: 7,075 yards, par 72, 147/74.5
Desert: 7,124 yards, par 72, 144/74.3
Greens fee: $220–$350 (Ocean);
$165–$220 (Desert)
866-231-4677, cabodelsol.com

TOP 100 IN THE WORLD

Debuted in 1994, the Ocean Course is a thrilling test of golf currently ranked 73rd on GOLF MAGAZINE's Top 100 Courses in the World. It's a seaside masterpiece worth crossing a continent to play. Intent on producing the "Pebble Beach of the Baja," Nicklaus routed big-time holes across gently sloping land creased by shallow arroyos and backdropped by rugged mountains. Giant cardon cacti and granite rock outcrops frame several greens. Like Pebble, the look is natural and unforced. From the tips, there are several death-or-glory shots to be played across Bahia de las Ballenas (Whale Bay), though staggered tees put most of the danger out of harm's way. In 2001 the Desert Course, a Tom Weiskopf design routed in mountain foothills high above the Ocean course, opened to immediate acclaim. And while the layout lacks a hole on the ocean, all 18 serve up a view of the sea. Shoehorning holes into rugged desert terrain crisscrossed by arroyos and staked out by twisted terote and palo blanco trees, Weiskopf produced a masterful design calling for a few semi-blind drives and approach shots that have kept players coming back for more.

CABO REAL RESORT

Cabo Real Golf Club:
6,988 yards, par 72, 140/74.1
El Dorado Golf Course:
7,050 yards, par 72, 143/74.4
Greens fee: $180–$260
877-795-8727, caboreal.com

In addition to the Robert Trent Jones Jr.–designed Cabo Real Golf Club, a Jekyll-and-Hyde design with holes chiseled into the mountains balanced by flatter holes routed along the shore, Eduardo Sanchez-Navarro, heir to the Corona beer fortune and developer of the Cabo Real resort, contracted Nicklaus to build a course to rival Cabo del Sol. Opened in 1999, El Dorado, with six ocean holes, is every bit the equal of the Ocean Course. This multitheme course occupies a pair of valleys divided by a giant hill of rock, with holes transitioning from giant arroyos, cardon cacti, and decomposed granite to dunelike formations. The finish—the par-three 17th calls for a brave shot to a green with crashing waves behind it, and the par-four 18th skirts the seashore—is unforgettable.

THE RAVEN AT CABO SAN LUCAS COUNTRY CLUB

7,220 yards, par 72, 138/75.4
Greens fee: $119–$169
888-328-8501, golfincabo.com

This is the only course in Los Cabos with a view of El Arco, the famous rock formations that mark land's end. A semiprivate course laid out by Roy Dye in 1994, this sturdy layout, the region's longest, compares favorably to a Scottsdale–area course, with fairways paved through the desert.

WHERE TO STAY

Palmilla was the best resort course in Mexico right from the first day it opened. All 172 rooms, decorated with handcrafted Mexican accents, face toward the sea and have a balcony or patio. Rates from $450. **866-829-2977, oneandonlyresorts.com** •• Eduardo Sanchez-Navarro, heir to the Corona beer fortune, developed **Cabo Real Resort** in the late 1980s with three miles of beachfront as its centerpiece. The property has seven hotels: Melia Cabo Real, Melia San Lucas, Casa del Mar, Hilton Los Cabos, Dreams, Las Ventanas al Paraiso, and the Westin Regina. Rates from $179. **877-795-8727, caboreal.com** •• The family-friendly **Los Cabos Golf Resort**, home to the Raven at Cabo San Lucas Country Club, has two pools, and one to three-bedroom suites with patios and balconies. Rates from $188. **877-461-3667, golfincabo.com** •• A four-year-old resort roosting on 17 lush acres at the tip of the Baja California Peninsula over the wave-beaten bays of the Sea of Cortez, **Esperanza** (Hope) is small (56 suites) and intimate (the concierge will know your name and your brand of chewing gum). The suites are earth-toned casitas with four-poster beds. Rates from $125. **866-311-2226, esperanzaresort.com** •• **Cabo del Sol** resort has two hotel properties. The charming and colorful **Sheraton Hacienda del Mar** sits on a private beach and has 270 rooms, more than 120 with ocean views. Rates from $250. **888-672-7137, cabodelsol.com** The elegant **Fiesta Americana Grand** has 267 rooms on 33 acres of beachfront property. Rates from $210. **800-FIESTA1, cabodelsol.com**

WHERE TO EAT

Head to Sammy Hagar's huge bar and restaurant, **Cabo Wabo**, for a shot of home-made tequila and fresh seafood. **624-143-1188, cabowabo.com** •• Don't miss the salsa bar at **Felix's**; the owner has reputedly collected more than 1,200 salsa recipes in his travels. **624-143-4290, felixcabosanlucas.com** •• Locals love **Mocambo's** for its fresh seafood, reasonable prices, and huge portions (prepare to share). **624-143-6070** •• Wave off the cart girl at **Cabo del Sol's Ocean Course** and wait for the "tacos at the turn," where a private taqueria from Cabo San Lucas sells its wares, among them Cabo's best fried-fish tacos that beat the clubhouse sandwich any day of the week. **800-386-2465, cabodelsol.com** •• The outdoor restaurant at Esperanza resort, **La Palapa**, serves Cabo's best ceviche. **866-311-2226, esperanzaresort.com**

LOCAL KNOWLEDGE

You can't visit Cabo without booking a **deep-sea fishing excursion** for yellowfin (many area restaurants are happy to prepare your fresh catch). Try a daytrip with Fishing International (Solmar Fleet). **800-950-4242, fishinginternational.com**

GETTING THERE

San Jose del Cabo International Airport receives more than 150 flights a week, including from Delta, America West, American, and Continental.

WHEN TO GO

November to May is the peak season for golf.

PUERTO VALLARTA Located on the Pacific coast of Mexico on the same latitude
as Hawaii, Puerto Vallarta is a multifaceted destination known for its cobblestone streets, fine restaurants, and perfect weather. Until recently, golf was not a major part of the local tourism equation, but with five courses opened since 2000, Puerto Vallarta is beginning to rival Los Cabos as a golf destination.

WHERE TO PLAY

VISTA VALLARTA

Nicklaus Course:
7,073 yards, par 72, 136/74.3
Weiskopf Course:
6,993 yards, par 72, 136/73.4
Greens fee: $163 (Nicklaus); $153 (Weiskopf)
01152-332-290-0030, vistavallartagolf.com

ClubCorp, the American golf development firm, hired Jack Nicklaus and Tom Weiskopf to build a pair of courses on an upcountry site 15 minutes from the hotel zone. The Nicklaus Course, host to the 2002 World Golf Championships–EMC World Cup, is routed across heaving land nearly 500 feet above sea level. Several of the holes push up against the foothills of the Sierra Madre, the rugged spine of mountains that dominates Mexico's interior. Giant ficus trees, tall palms, and sloping hillsides frame the fairways, with arroyos and creeks in play throughout. The course gives players plenty to think about on the greens, which have more contours than a deep-fried taco. On the lower end of the complex, Tom Weiskopf was handed a rugged, densely vegetated parcel marked by rock-strewn arroyos and meandering creeks. Weiskopf retained many specimen trees in his routing by positioning holes on long ridges above vegetation-choked ravines. The short, sporty front nine is marked by two memorable par fives, notably the 534-yard 8th, which plays from an elevated tee over a watery arroyo to a broad fairway, the target a lone palm at the base of a hill. The brawnier back nine opens with the longest par five at the facility, but its standout hole is the spectacular 15th. This hole plays anywhere from 124 to 181 yards and calls for a trans-arroyo tee shot to a deep, bilevel green set above a tawny, exposed bluff and staked out by bunkers large and small. There is no fairway—an all-or-nothing shot must be played.

EL TIGRE GOLF COURSE

7,239 yards, par 72, 133/74.5
Greens fee: $110
866-843-5951, eltigregolf.com

Located in Nuevo Vallarta, a burgeoning resort area north of the city, this Robert von Hagge–Rick Baril creation, named for a caged Bengal tiger behind the 17th tee, is a well-groomed, relatively flat course swept by breezes and hemmed by 42 acres of lakes, as well as a meandering creek and dozens of well-placed bunkers. The final three holes are among the toughest in Mexico. The 18th is a bruiser—621 yards from the tips, into the teeth of the wind, water up the left side.

FOUR SEASONS GOLF CLUB
PUNTA MITA

7,014 yards, par 72, 131/72.9
Greens fee: $185
01152-329-291-6000
fourseasons.com/puntamita

Routed in all directions across a narrow neck of land, the Jack Nicklaus–designed Punta Mita (Tip of the Arrow) has portions of five holes set along the Pacific, with an additional three holes skirting Banderas Bay. Its optional par-three hole, No. 3B, plays to a natural island green in the sea. The core 18 is not only intact, but it also remains the best-conditioned resort course in Mexico. Landscaped with 1,800 palms and framed throughout by dunelike mounds and vast waste bunkers, Punta Mita is one of the most cleverly plotted layouts Nicklaus has ever built. Forward tees put the holes well within reach of free-swinging holidaymakers. The course is open only to guests of the Four Seasons.

Hole 9 at Vista Vallarta
(Nicklaus), Puerto
Vallarta, Mexico

WHERE TO STAY

At the head of Banderas Bay, 45 minutes north of Puerto Vallarta, is the **Four Seasons Resort Punta Mita**, which occupies nearly 1,500 acres on a spear-shaped peninsula set between the Pacific and the Sierra Madre foothills. Opened in 1999, the resort quickly became one of Mexico's most idyllic getaways. Rates from $450. **01152-329-291-6000, fourseasons .com/puntamita** • • The pretty **CasaMagna Marriott Resort** sits on Banderas Bay and markets packages for Vista Vallarta and other area courses. Rates from $119. **01152-322-226-0000, marriott.com** • • The **Paradise Village Resort**, home to El Tigre Golf Course, is a 490-suite property with a fine beach. Rates from $137. **866-843-5951, paradise village.com**

WHERE TO EAT

The Four Seasons Punta Mita has two fine restaurants worth checking out. The casual, thatched-roofed **Ketsi Restaurant & Bar** (*ketsi* means "fish" in the local Huichol language)

provides lovely Pacific Ocean views and serves tropical cocktails, seafood, sandwiches, Mexican specialties, and light options for lunch. The **Aramara Restaurant & Bar** serves "Chino Latino" cuisine—a melding of Latin American and Asian flavors. On Saturdays, try the tequila-pairing menu every Saturday as part of their tequila night. **01152-329-291-6000, fourseasons.com/puntamita** • • You'll feel you've discovered a true find if you dine at the charming, intimate **El Arrayan** in Puerto Vallarta's Old Town, which highlights traditional regional recipes. **01152-322-222-7195, elarrayan.com.mx** • • The gorgeous views of Puerto Vallarta from the **Vista Grill's** contemporary dining room almost rival the European-Mexican cuisine, which is served with a modern flare. **01152-322-222-3570, vistagrill.com**

LOCAL KNOWLEDGE

The **Church of Our Lady of Guadaloupe**, built starting in 1929, is filled with hand-carved columns and decorative embellishments. It's also the focal point of a 12-day festival, the fiesta de Guadaloupe, each December. On Calle Hidalgo, one block east of Zocalo in downtown Puerto Vallarta. • • Speed demons can fly over the **El Eden rain-forest canopy** and see waterfalls and jungle life on zip lines that go up to 50 miles per hour. **866-217-9704, puertovallartatours.net** • • Enjoy the pristine, powdery beaches and coastal hiking trails near the fishing village of Boca de Tomatlon, about 20 minutes south of downtown Puerto Vallarta.

GETTING THERE

Flights from Chicago, Dallas/Fort Worth, Denver, Houston, Los Angeles, Minneapolis/ St. Paul, New York, Phoenix, San Antonio, San Diego, San Francisco, Seattle/Tacoma, and St. Louis arrive regularly at Puerto Vallarta-Ordaz International Airport.

WHEN TO GO

November to May is the peak season for golf.

CANCUN

CANCUN Cancun is a household name among Mexican destinations, especially for those seeking an island-style sun, surf, and golf holiday. Quintana Roo, the state in which Cancun is located, is the only place in Mexico with a Caribbean shoreline.

WHERE TO PLAY

MOON SPA & GOLF CLUB

Jungle: 3,599 yards, par 36
Lake: 3,602 yards, par 36
Dunes: 3,602 yards, par 35
Greens fee: $250
01152-998-881-6088, palaceresorts.com

This Jack Nicklaus 27-hole layout raised Cancun's golf profile significantly when it was built in the early 2000s. Created to harmonize with the site's lush vegetation, the design is flanked by dense jungle, a series of natural wetlands, and strategically placed bunkers. Among the signature holes is the sixth, a short, driveable par four; the 17th, a devilish little par three that plays to an island green; and the grand par-four 18th, a 445-yarder that calls for a carry over water from the tee.

THE GOLF CLUB AT PLAYACAR

7,144 yards, par 72, 148/NA
Greens fee: $180
01152-998-881-6088, palaceresorts.com

This Robert von Hagge layout opened in 1994. With a slope rating of 148 from the tips, the broad-shouldered course, routed around nearly 200 Mayan ruins, offers one of the stiffest tests of golf in Mexico. Laid out on a limestone plateau, the golf course weaves around sinkholes used by the ancient Mayans to collect rainwater. Guests of Palace Hotels have access to Playacar.

COZUMEL COUNTRY CLUB

6,734 yards, par 72, 133/72.2
Greens fee: $149
01152-987-872-9570
cozumelcountryclub.com.mx

The Cancun area's most intriguing venue is the Nicklaus Design Group's course on Cozumel, a rocky little island east of the Yucatan peninsula. Cozumel is known primarily for its superb scuba diving, but the sports focus on the island changed in 2001 when Cozumel Country Club, the island's first course, made its debut. Chiseled from coral rock, the layout is hemmed in by red mangroves, expansive wetlands, and shallow coral canyons.

WHERE TO STAY

All-inclusive golf packages for Playacar and Moon Spa & Golf Club are available at **Moon Palace**, a giant 2,103-room property where 80 percent of the accommodations have Caribbean views and all have balconies and jacuzzi tubs. Rates from $332. **01152-998-881-6000, palaceresorts.com** • • Just across the street from Cozumel Country Club, the all-inclusive, beachfront **Melia Cozumel** has 147 rooms with terraces and balconies, more than a third of which overlook the Caribbean. Rates from $205. **01152-987-872-9870, meliacozumel .solmelia.com** • • The 50-room **Playa Azul Golf & Beach Hotel Cozumel** offers access to the Cozumel Country Club. Rates from $140. **01152-987-872-0043, playa-azul.com**

WHERE TO EAT

Guidos on Avenue Rafael E. Melgar in Cozumel serves inspired Euro-Italian-Mexican cuisine in an al fresco setting. **guidoscozumel .com** • • Set in the charming courtyard of one of Cozumel's most beautiful colonial buildings, **Pancho's Backyard** serves mean margaritas and delectable Mexican fare. **52-987-872-2141, loscincosoles.com/panchosbackyard** • • **Pepe's Grill**, also on Avenue Rafael E. Melgar in Cozumel, is the place to find the heat, and we're not talking about extra spicy salsa: The meat and seafood here are grilled and flambéed to perfection. **52-987-872-0213** • • With its sculpture garden and award-winning cuisine based on family recipes, **La Habichuela** is the perfect place in Cancun for a romantic dinner under the stars. **52-998-884-3158, lahabichuela.com/english/index.php** • • Looking for a big juicy steak? Or maybe spit-barbequed pork or lamb? Head to the rustic, casual Argentinean steakhouse **Cambalache**, in Cancun's Forum by the Sea Mall. **52-998-883-0897, grupocambalache.com/cancun1.stm**

LOCAL KNOWLEDGE

You can ride horseback, snorkel, swim, kayak, and speedboat in **Tres Rios Ecopark**. **800-714-3643, tres-rios.com** • • Kids at heart can enjoy the waterslides and rides at two Cancun waterparks: The smaller **Parque Nizuc (01152-998-881-3000, parquenizuc .com)** has a "dolphin trainer for a day" program, and **Aquaworld (01152-998-848-8327, aquaworld.com.mx)** has waverunner snorkeling tours • • The **Coco Bongo** club is the heart of Cancun's crazy, college-kid nightlife. **01152-998-883-5061,cocobongo.com.mx** • • **Las Ruinas del Rey** are an ancient piece of Mayan history, dating to the 2nd or 3rd century B.C., in the heart of Cancun's main hotel zone drag. **01152-998-883-2080**

GETTING THERE

Cancun International Airport is accessible from most major cities in the U.S. and Canada.

WHEN TO GO

November through April is the peak season for golf.

CRISIS MANAGEMENT

Travel emergencies won't ruin your golf trip—if you plan for them.

It only takes one wrinkle—a lost passport or missing luggage—to turn your golf trip from a fiesta into a fiasco. Once you've settled the basics of your trip (where to play and stay), spend time preparing for the most common emergencies that can spoil things, especially if you're traveling overseas. "Take a preventative approach," says Amy Ziff, Travelocity's advice columnist. "Preparing ahead of time will allow you to mitigate any problems that arise." Here are five potential problems and how you can soften their bite.

LOST PASSPORT

Make two photocopies of your passport. Leave a copy at home with a friend and take the other copy with you, stored separately from your passport. Make a note of the location and phone number of the U.S. embassy at your destination. If you have a copy of your passport, the embassy should be able to issue you a replacement within 24 hours.

STOLEN WALLET

Don't carry any more than two credit cards and dump all those gift cards you've been carrying around since Christmas. There's also no need to stuff your money clip with Benjamins—even the most remote locations have ATMs.

MISSING BAGS

If you arrive ready to play but your clubs are still circling the airport, alert the airline immediately. Waiting more than 24 hours might mean your claim is dismissed. Pack a change of clothes in your carry-on to avoid having to recycle your underwear. Less than 2 percent of bags never turn up.

MEDICAL MISHAP

Many insurance policies don't cover you if you fall ill outside the U.S. If you have a chronic illness, ask your insurer in advance if you're covered. Investing in travel insurance is smart if you're prone to sickness, but be sure to find an insurer with a B+ rating or better.

MISSED FLIGHT

We all like to squeeze in another nine holes before departure, but the airline won't be understanding if you miss your flight. Tip No. 1: Don't book the last flight of the day. Miss it and you'll be spending the night in a motel with a bed that takes quarters. Tip No. 2: Be nice to the airline folks. They can be invaluable.

AUSTRIA

FRANCE

IRELAND

ITALY

PORTUGAL

SCOTLAND

SPAIN

THE ALPS

BIARRITZ

DUBLIN

EMILIA ROMAGNA

THE ALGARVE
ESTORIL AND SINTRA

ST. ANDREWS AND FIFE

COSTA DEL SOL

THE ALPS

Fill your lungs with the fresh mountain air of the Austrian Alps. The scenery and the golf courses are enough to make the heart sing; Tirol in the heart of the Austrian Alps has twelve courses set against a dramatic mountain backdrop. The mountainous region of Kitzbühel is a popular ski destination but in the summer months from May to October the lower slopes play host to a different ball game.

WHERE TO PLAY

GOLFCLUB SEEFELD-WILDMOOS
6,424 yards, par 72, NA/NA
Greens fee: €63
43-669-160-66-060, seefeldgolf.at

Set in the Nature Reserve of Wildmoos, this is one of the most beautiful golf courses in the Austrian Alps, but a course for mountain goats—sportingly demanding, narrow, and difficult to estimate. There are no golf carts.

GOLFCLUB WILDER KAISER
6,687 yards, par 72, 123/NA
Greens fee: €65
43-5358-4282, wilder-kaiser.com

Golfclub Wilder Kaiser offers 27 holes that roll through a valley near the snow-capped Kitzbüler Horn mountain range. Good practice facilities.

GOLFCLUB EICHENHEIM
6,479 yards, par 71, 126/71.1
Greens fee: €82
43-5356-66615, eichenheim.at

Eichenheim has some superb holes with elevation changes, including the signature 12th, which demands an accurate drive over a 200-foot precipice onto the fairway below.

WHERE TO STAY
The Kaiser in Tirol is situated in the pretty village of Scheffau just five minutes from Wilder Kaiser. Facilities include a well-stocked wine cellar and an indoor pool with integrated whirlpool and jetstreams. Five nights with breakfast €495 per person. hotel-kaiser-in-tirol.com

LOCAL KNOWLEDGE
The Seefeld Festival of Lights in August is a sight to be seen. The village is decked out with thousands of candles, and there are fireworks in the late evening. •• Visit the Seekirchl chapel, which is the emblem of the region. •• Go hiking in the Karwendel Alpine Park and Wetterstein mountain range. •• Take a drive and stop off for a beer at one of the region's traditional villages with cobbled streets and cosy bars.

GETTING THERE
Fly into Salzburg. Ryanair offers budget rates within Europe. 43-0900-210240, ryanair.com

WHEN TO GO
Late April to September is the peak time for golf.

MW Golf (43-0870-7469668, MW-golf.co.uk) has five-night packages at the Poll guest house, a five-minute walk from the town of St. Johann, including flights and two rounds for €425 per person. The Golf Alpin Card (golf-alpin.at) offers five green fees for €240 from 33 Golf Alpin partner clubs in Austria and is available at all golf club participants and partner hotels.

BIARRITZ With 10 terrific courses within 20 kilometers, the elegant resort of Biarritz is ideal for a winter break under a sunny sky.

WHERE TO PLAY

SEIGNOSSE GOLF HOTEL

6,293 yards, par 72, NA/NA
Greens fee: €52–70
335-5841-6830, golfseignosse.com

Designed by the American Robert Von Hagge, Seignosse is a great test of golf that will satisfy the demanding player. On a hilly estate covering 175 acres, the 18 holes thread their way through pines and over water hazards blending delicately into the landscape. This exceptional course attracts golfers to devote their passion to their favourite sport. It's a magnificent setting for an exceptional course; Seignosse ranks among Europe's finest courses.

GOLF DE CHIBERTA

6,215 yards, par 70, NA/NA
Greens fee: €65
335-5963-8320

If you are staying in the Aquitaine region, don't miss this course, which was designed in 1927. There are very few real French links, and this is one of them. The sandy soil makes for easy walking, greens are good and the hazards clearly visible. But the greatest challenge here is when the wind is blowing. The club is closed on Thursdays from mid-September through April.

MOLIETS

18 Hole Course: 6,728 yards, par 72, 133/73.7
9 Hole Course: 2,076 yards, par 31
Greens fee: €42–€60 (18 hole);
€15–€25 (9 hole)
335-5848-5465, golfmoliets.com

Golf de Moliet is one of the most beautiful French golf courses and ranks among Europe's finest. You find this Robert Trent Jones Sr. masterpiece situated between the ocean and the forest. Being enthusiastic about the magnificent combination between the forest protected by the Landes de Gascogne and the Atlantic Ocean, the architect gave his best to create these wonderful 27 holes, four of which are laid out in the dunes. Here the player can test all his talents in magnificent nature. Everybody can experiment according to his and her level.

ARCANGUES

6,719 yards, par 72, NA/NA
Greens fee: €40–€60
335-5943-1056

Very close to Biarritz, this course by Ronald Fream extends throughout 80 hectares (198 acres) of oak trees and meadows around the village of Arcangues and its chateau. The clubhouse is situated on the top of a hill facing south. A great variety of playing situations and varying landscapes make for an interesting game.

LE PHARE

5,859 yards, par 69, NA/NA
Greens fee: €40–€70
335-5903-7180

Built in 1888, Le Phare is the second established golf course in France. It was originally created to meet the demands of English clients. Situated practically in the town, this course has also the advantage of never being tiring. From various spots you will enjoy magnificent views of the ocean. It is a very pleasant and enjoyable course with 70-some bunkers and excellent greens.

WHERE TO STAY

The most glamorous play to stay is the **Hotel du Palais**, which overlooks the ocean and is two minutes from the town center, casino, and Le Phare golf course. Winter rates from €260 per room per night. **335-5941-6400, hotel-du-palais.com** • • The **Crowne Plaza** is a smart, newer hotel with spacious rooms close to the town center. Rooms from €70 per night. **335-5901-1313, crowneplaza.co.uk** • • If you prefer to stay in a golf hotel, **Seignosse** has rooms from €53. **335-5841-6840, golfseignosse.com**

LOCAL KNOWLEDGE

Biarritz has been popular for surfing since the 1950s. A **Surf Festival** is hosted in July, and in April the town hosts the **Biarritz Maider Arosteguy** competition, which attracts the biggest surfing talent in Europe. • • The game of **pelote**, the fastest ball sport in the world, hails from the Basque region and is worth watching. • • Check into the **Ilbiarritz** golf training center, which has targets in the center of a circular practice area mimicking the hazards you would encounter on a course. Place your bets at the **casino**.

GETTING THERE

The Biarritz–Anglone–Bayonne airport accepts direct flights from many European cities, as well as connecting flights through Lyon. **biarritz .aeroport.fr/flights.html**

WHEN TO GO

July and August is considered high season for golf, but March through October can be just as enjoyable.

For tourist information visit biarritz.tm.fr.

DUBLIN When the Ryder Cup was contested in 2006 at the K Club near Dublin, it demonstrated the difference between a great golf course and a great venue. The plush retreat is without equal as a tournament site—it was easily accessible and neither players nor officials had to step outside the walls of the estate—but the golf course is more Port St. Lucie than Portmarnock. Let your trip to Ireland be a mix of reality and fantasy: Sure, play the course where the Ryder Cup was fought. But start your journey at the course where it should have been played, 75 miles north of the K Club at the finest links Ireland has to offer.

Hole 3 at Royal County Down, Dublin, Ireland

WHERE TO PLAY

ROYAL COUNTY DOWN

Championship: 7,181 yards, par 71, NA/NA
Greens fee: €80–€124
353-28-4372-3847, royalcountydown.org

TOP 100 IN THE WORLD

If Ryder Cup venues were decided less on economics and more on the merits of golf courses, we'd all have gotten a lot more familiar with Royal County Down in 2006. Located 40 minutes drive south of Belfast in Newcastle, Northern Ireland, County Down is the highest ranked Irish track on GOLF MAGAZINE's Top 100 Courses in the World at No. 9. First laid out by Old Tom Morris in 1889, it is often cited for its appealing setting at the foot of the Mourne Mountains next to Dundrum Bay. But its not just aesthetics—County Down is simply one of the finest courses you'll ever play. The routing switches direction so frequently that the entire layout seems to swirl in the breeze, and with every turn you're presented with a battery of shot options. There's only one constant: miss the fairway and par flutters away on that ever-present wind. Visitors are welcome every day except Wednesday and Saturday.

THE K CLUB

Palmer Course: 7,337 yards, par 72, NA/76
Greens fee: €150
353-1601-7200, kclub.ie

The K Club in Straffan, County Kildare, has a number of things going for it: service that is second to none, immaculate conditioning, great food, proximity to the airport.... Are the positives stretching a little thin? The Palmer Course (yes, *that* Palmer designed it) here is not without merit. There are a handful of fine match play holes that were a great stage for drama at the 2006 Ryder Cup, most notably the 606-yard, par-five 7th (often played as No. 16 in tournaments, it's a double-dogleg with a green fronted by a stream) and the 537-yard, par-five 18th, where the green juts into a lake. But the only thing that exceeds expectations is the greens fee, which is more than $400, for the equivalent of an average Florida resort course, without the weather. Based purely on the panache of hosting the Ryder Cup, it is the most expensive round of golf in Ireland. However pleasant a visit here may be, you could throw a stone and hit a better course that costs a fraction of the price. And you wouldn't even have to aim carefully.

THE CARD WRECKER: **THE K CLUB** NO. 16, 395 YARDS, PAR 4

It's the shortest par four on the course, but according to Ryder Cup hero Paul McGinley, it has the most potential to have you reaching for the Jamesons. The Dublin native tells you how to survive it. Paul McGinley gives advice on how to play it: "No. 16 has an island fairway and an island green. How to play it? Well, keep your ball dry. It's the most visually intimidating hole, so beware of driver off the tee—hit something that can get you in the fairway. With an island green, you have to commit to your approach shot and really go after it, or you're all wet."

PORTMARNOCK GOLF CLUB

7,321 yards, par 72, NA/NA
Greens fee: €190
353-1846-2634, portmarnockgolfclub.ie

TOP 100 IN THE WORLD

Curving along a stretch of coastline on the Howth peninsula just 12 miles from downtown Dublin, Portmarnock has played host to a dozen Irish Opens and is No. 43 on GOLF MAGAZINE's list of the Top 100 Courses in the World. If Dublin's traffic weren't so bad, you could make it from the tarmac to the first tee in 15 minutes. There are three nines—Yellow, Red, and Blue, with the latter two combined to make up the championship course. Portmarnock's fairways are lined with tall, wispy grass that makes finding wayward shots fairly easy, although playing from there is anything but. The real bite is in the pot bunkers, which swallow inaccurate approach shots, and the wind that whips off the Irish Sea. Arnold Palmer has said that No. 15, a 174-yarder hard along the sea, is his favorite par-three anywhere. The only surprise is that Arnie could pick one among a plethora of great holes.

COUNTY LOUTH GOLF CLUB

6,936 yards, par 72, NA/NA
Greens fee: €115–€135
353-41-988-1530
countylouthgolfclub.com

Located in Drogheda, County Louth—also known as Baltray—is widely considered one of Ireland's best, and most underappreciated, links, although it did receive some long overdue attention in 2004 when it hosted the Irish Open. Less wildly contoured than some of its more famous brothers, and lacking the awe-inspiring scenery associated with golf here, it is nonetheless an understatedly brutal course. There are three par fives in the opening six holes, a stretch where the variety of shots required is matched only by the punishment inflicted when you fail to execute. Some locals will tell you Baltray has the best bunkering on the island. You can only hope that you are able to take their word for it.

WHERE TO STAY

The hotel at the **K Club** ranks as one of the finest in Ireland. Rates from €238. **353-1601-7279, kclub.ie** •• There are few more impressive buildings in Northern Ireland than the **Slieve Donard Hotel**, which sits at the front gate of Royal County Down. Rooms start at £145. **44-284-3721066, hastingshotels.com**

WHERE TO EAT

The **Byerley Turk** at the K Club offers superb French cuisine with an Irish flair. The roasted rack of Wicklow lamb and the seafood starters are enough to make you forget the greens fee. **353-1601-7200, kclub.ie** •• Just off the main highway between Belfast and Dublin, seven miles north of Dundalk, is **Fitzpatricks**. The

comfortable inn has a well-deserved reputation for serving some of the finest food in the area. **353-42-937-6193, fitzpatricks-restaurant.com**

LOCAL KNOWLEDGE

It's a short drive from Royal County Down up into the **Mourne Mountains**, one of the most scenic locales on the island. **mournemountains.com** •• One of Ireland's top visitor attractions is between County Down and the K Club. **Newgrange** is a megalithic tomb built about 3200 B.C. The one-acre mound is flanked by 97 decorated stones, and the inner passage leads to a chamber that is perfectly lit for 17 minutes by the sun on the Winter Solstice. Historians believe it took 300 men 20 years to build. •• Find out how Ireland's greatest

export is made—and sample some—at the **Guinness Brewery** in Dublin. **353-1408-4800, guinness-storehouse.com**

GETTING THERE

Continental Airlines offers direct flights from Newark International Airport to both Belfast and Dublin. Royal County Down is a 30-minute drive from Belfast International Airport. The K Club is 40 minutes drive from the airport in Dublin.

WHEN TO GO

Go from May to October, when the average high temperature never drops below 57 degrees.

EMILIA ROMAGNA
The Italians have a passion for the finer things in life—excellent food and wine, beautiful architecture, and sleek sports cars, but now the Italians have discovered a new passion: golf. With ten 18-hole courses, Emilia Romagna has one of the largest concentrations of courses in Italy, making the region an exciting golf destination. This area of northern Italy, whose green rolling hills are dotted with villas and castles, is recognized as the gastronomic heart of Italy. The clubhouses are often located in castles, old country houses, mansions, or restored farmhouses and serve gourmet lunches and dinner.

WHERE TO PLAY

CROARA COUNTRY CLUB
6,610 yards, par 72, 128/70.9
Greens fee: €55
39-052-397-7105, emiliaromagnagolf.com

A few kilometers from Piacenza in a particularly beautiful valley setting, this is a challenging course with elevated views. Host to the first Women's Italian Open, the tree-lined fairways place a limit on how often you can take a driver out of the bag, unless you are a straight hitter. The Trebbia River comes into play on a few of the holes. The fairways are quite narrow, lined with oaks, poplars, and black locusts, and when the river comes into play you will need to focus on your course-management skills. If you get a chance, visit the medieval village and the castle of Rivalta, which is two kilometers from the course.

GOLF CLUB CASTELL'ARQUATO
6,706 yards, par 73, 124/71.8
Greens fee: €50
39-052-389-5544

Golf Club Castell'Arquato, designed by Henry Cotton and Harvey Penick, is in an area of outstanding natural beauty close to the picturesque village of Castell'Arquato. There are plenty of elevated tees to provide spectacular views. There is also a hotel on site.

GOLF CLUB LA ROCCA
6,623 yards, par 71, 129/71.5
Greens fee: €60
39-052-183-4037, emiliaromagnagolf.com

Established in 1985, La Rocca is one of the oldest courses in Emilia Romagna and also one of the most difficult. The course rises up over the hills that dominate Parma, winding through woods and around artificial lakes. You'll need to make sure that your game is up to scratch to make a decent score here.

MODENA GOLF & COUNTRY CLUB
7,801 yards, par 72, 131/73.6
Greens fee: €60
modenagolf.it

Designed by Bernhard Langer, this 27-hole course in Colombaro di Formigine that was once host to the Italian Open is one of Italy's toughest layouts. The greens are huge, which will test your short game skills, and the five lakes will test your accuracy.

GOLF CLUB MATILDE DI CANOSSA

6,540 yards, par 72, 134/73.0
Greens fee: €45
39-052-237-1295
web.tiscali.it/golfcanossa/index2.htm

This course in San Bartolomeo enjoys many panoramic views of the Matildic Lands just outside the historic city of Reggio Emilia. The natural slopes and the Quaresimo stream that comes into play on a few of the holes create a challenge.

GOLF CLUB BOLOGNA

6,641 yards, par 72, 126/72.4
Greens fee: €60
39-051-969-100, golfclubbologna.it

Designed by Henry Cotton and John D. Harris in 1959 and updated in 2000 by Peter Alliss, this is one of Italy's finest courses. Rolling through hills and plains, the course sweeps through majestic countryside and has hosted a number of professional competitions. The club restaurant has been nominated among the best top-10 club restaurants in Italy on more than one occasion. The course is situated in the Torrente Sillaro valley near the renowned spa.

ADRIATIC GOLF CLUB CERVIA

6,808 yards, par 72, NA/NA
Greens fee: €57
39-054-992-786, golfcervia.com

Close to the ocean, this is a tough championship course. The first nine holes stretch through a pine forest, and the second nine are more open, with salt lakes coming into play on several of the holes. An additional nine holes opened in late 2003.

RIMINI GOLF CLUB

6,514 yards, par 72, 123/69.7
Greens fee: €60
39-054-167-8122, riminigolf.com

Situated in a beautiful location in the peaceful Valmarecchia Park, Rimini has a stunning backdrop of Mount Carpegna and has hosted the European Challenge Tour. The numerous bunkers and lakes are certain to keep you on your toes. The course has excellent practice facilities, including a golf academy and a covered-bay driving range.

RIOLO GOLF & COUNTRY CLUB

6,715 yards, par 72, 129/72
Greens fee: €40–€50
39-054-674-035, riologolf.it

This course is in a stunning setting with a background of a dramatic chalk vein carved into the hills. Test your game on the contrasting flat and sloping lies and hope you can hit over the ravines, which are a unique feature of the course.

GOLF CLUB LE FONTI

7,067 yards, par 72, 126/71.9
Greens fee: €50–€60
39-051-695-1958, golfclublefonti.it

Located near a famous health spa, this lengthy course gently undulates through the pretty Torrente Sillaro valley. Leave time to enjoy something to eat at the locally renowned clubhouse.

WHERE TO STAY

The Riviera Golf Club Resort is close to the sea and a lively marina. The resort's course is bound by the river and the hills and offers a relaxing and peaceful nine holes. There are good practice facilities, including a 27-hole putting green and covered-bay driving range. Rates from €150. **39-054-1347329** • • Golf and spa packages can be arranged at the **Grand Hotel Terme Riolo** in Ravenna. The Art-Nouveau–designed hotel has its own thermal baths. Rates from €65. **39-054-671041, grandhoteltermeriolo.com** • • If you like to combine a city break with golf, then the beautiful historic city of Bologna makes a perfect base. Stay at the **Hotel Metropolitan**, in the heart of Bologna, which offers great value golf breaks and is only a few minutes from the city's prestigious boutiques and traditional restaurants. Rates from €70. **39-512-29393, hotelmetropolitan.com** • • The 162-room **Holiday Inn** is on the outskirts of Bologna and only 10 minutes from Golf Club Bologna, one of Italy's most historic courses. Rates from €63. **877-465-4329, ichotelsgroup.com**

LOCAL KNOWLEDGE

Car lovers must visit the **Ferrari Autodrome** at Imola, east of Bologna, which is home to the San Marino Grand Prix. • • If you prefer to stay by the sea, base yourself on the **Adriatic Coast** and soak up the sun on the 110 kilometers of sandy beach. Cervia, a historic center that gained its wealth from the cultivation of salt, has a wide, clean beach and has been awarded the Blue Flag. Rimini is a popular center with everything: beaches, nightlife, and culture. In the evening the city center and the seafront bustle with activity. • • After a round, there is nothing more soothing to the back and legs than a trip to the spa. Emilia Romagna is famous for its **thermal springs**. The waters, which contain sodium chloride, iodide, bromide, sulphur, and sodium, are reputed to be excellent for the skin and general health. There are more than 20 spas you can check into and let your aches and pains be massaged away so that you will be raring to tackle the next 18 holes. • • Indulge in delicious freshly **sliced ham from Parma**, Parmigiano Reggiano cheese from Casina, balsamic vinegar from Modena, porcini mushrooms and truffles from the Bolognese Apennines, and cherries from Vigola. Tortellini has also historically been linked with the region. A Parma speciality is *anolini*—light pasta parcels stuffed with minced beef, breadcrumbs, and parmesan cheese served in a beef broth. *Zampone*, leg of pork, and mortadella sausage are delicious served with tasty potatoes, beans, and onions, washed down with a fine red or white Lambrusco from the hills between Reggio and Modena. • • The locals embrace their fine foods by throwing festivals where visitors and locals crowd the village streets to enjoy local music and sample local produce at the stalls. The **Feast of Wine** takes place on the third Sunday in May. August in Casina brings the **Fiera del Parmigiano Reggiano**, a celebration of the famed cheese.

GETTING THERE

The nearest airports are Bologna, Milan, and Rimini. Fly into Milan to discover the historic north and into Bologna for the beaches of the Adriatic Coast.

WHEN TO GO

July and August are peak travel months, but tee times might be harder to get. Be sure to plan ahead and be willing to go in September.

GOLF PACKAGES:
Emilia Romagna Golf can organize tee times, transfers, and accommodations at 28 hotels. All you need to do is book the flights. Seven nights' bed-and-breakfast accommodation in a three-star hotel and five green fees are available from €440. **39-54-4973340, emiliaromagnagolf.com.**

THE ALGARVE

The Algarve is full of testing championship tracks that are perfectly in tune with their environment. From the salt marshes of the Ria Formosa Natural Park to the limestone cliffs in the west, the Algarve is home to 27 full-length courses stretched along 150 kilometers of some of the most beautiful coastline imaginable. Natural beauty apart, the Portuguese themselves are responsible for their tireless work in keeping their courses well manicured. Despite the lack of rain, they manage to maintain their layouts to arguably the highest standard in Europe. New courses such as Victoria and Boavista incorporate lakes to help keep them a lush green, but it's the dry climate that attracts so many golfers eager to escape the winter and play a round without having to wear layers of sweaters and waterproofs.

WHERE TO PLAY

SAN LORENZO

6,799 yards, par 72, 128/72.2
Greens fee: €125
353-289-396533

One of the region's most stunning layouts, San Lorenzo is abundant with wildlife, especially during the winter, when the wetlands provide a home for migratory birds. From the back tees, the course challenges long hitters, and from the forward tees it offers plenty of exciting mid- and short-iron approaches to spectacular greens. On the par-three 5th the course really comes into its own. From the tee you see a putting surface that appears to have nothing beyond it but the crisp blue Atlantic. It's an optical illusion that gives you a flavor of what's to come, and the four holes that follow are breathtaking. Hugging the water's edge, they demand pinpoint accuracy from tee to green. The course then heads inland until the 17th, where San Lorenzo sets up a sensational finish. The penultimate hole features water all the way up the left side, and at the last hole, longer hitters are tempted into driving across a lake to a narrow sliver of fairway in order to get the best route into a semi-island green.

QUINTA DA RIA

6,557 yards, par 72, 120/NA
Greens fee: €90
351-281-950580, quintadariagolf.com

This is probably the best course in the eastern Algarve, and since it opened in 2002, it has placed the previously overlooked region between Faro and the Spanish border on the golf map. Located in the Ria Formosa Natural Park, the course has a particularly peaceful atmosphere. The holes are gently undulating, and the sea can be glimpsed on many holes on the back nine. The fairways look forgiving off the tee, but there is more trouble than meets the eye. Thousands of olive, almond, and carob trees provide the fairways with definition.

Hole 17 at San Lorenzo,
The Algarve, Portugal

SALGADOS

6,649 yards, par 72, 117/72.5
Greens fee: €63
351-289-583030, nexus-pt.com/salgados

Salgados is located on a flat stretch of land running along the Atlantic coast. There's a conspicuous absence of trees, leaving this links layout exposed to the perils of the sea breeze. But a complete lack of housing on the edge of the fairway makes it a breath of fresh air. Carved out of the salt marshes, Salgados has the largest number of water features of any course on the Algarve—the wet stuff comes into play on 14 holes. The par-five 6th has a large lake sweeping along the entire right side of the fairway, which, combined with the menacing rough on the left, makes the hole particularly tough. And there's no let-up at the 7th, a long par four playing 454 yards into the wind.

BOAVISTA

6,598 yards, par 71, NA/NA
Greens fee: €45–€65
351-282-000111, boavistagolf.com

This is the perfect course for mid to high handicappers, who will find the fairways a challenge without being overly demanding. The hilly layout offers superb views towards Lagos and the sea. Some of the elevated tees provide an ego boost for the shorter hitter, since the fairways tend to be firm and the ball can roll for miles. Remember, however, that for every hill you descend there's another that needs to be climbed, so Boavista is also a test of stamina and fitness. The par-four 5th demands a drive uphill but the second shot is critical; the designer has sneakily incorporated a line of trees that can block your path to the green. The showstopper is the 191-yard, par-three 6th; it plays across a ravine–you'll do well to par it.

QUINTA DO LAGO

North: 6,699 yards, par 72, NA/NA
South: 7,071 yards, par 72, 138/74.6
Greens fee: €45
351-289-390700, quintadolagogolf.com

Previously known as Ria Formosa because of its proximity to the famous natural park, this upmarket resort boasts two 18-hole courses, and many famous European soccer players have second homes here. Both courses weave around the estate, and the odd luxury villa occasionally encroaches onto the edge of the fairway. The signature hole is the South's par-three 15th, which measures 219 yards and requires you to launch your ball over a huge lake. The green is set in a semicircle of umbrella pines and is reachable by a wooden bridge. The North course requires both strength and accuracy, especially on the tough par fives.

VICTORIA

7,105 yards, par 72, 122/72.4
Greens fee: €80–€150
351-289-320100, vilamoura.net

This Arnold Palmer design opened in 2004 and is the newest addition to the Vilamoura fold. This long-awaited layout played host to the WGC–Algarve World Cup in 2005 and, as would be expected from a championship course, the holes are long. In fact the course is one of the longest in Portugal. But don't be afraid if you're not a big hitter; five different sets of tees make it suitable for all abilities. Palmer has designed Victoria to reward players who take on the numerous lakes and cleverly placed bunkers. The fairways are fairly flat, although mounds and waterfalls have been integrated to create added interest. The most notable stretch is from holes 11 to 13, where water encroaches on all three fairways; stray offline and you'll be looking at bogey at least. The 14th has two fairways; you can either play it safe and send the ball straight down the middle or, if you're feeling brave, take on the water in an effort to make birdie. And if you haven't run out of balls as you leave the 17th green, the grand finale could wipe you out of ammunition. The closing hole has more water than fairway.

VILA SOL

Prime: 3,544 yards, par 36
Challenge: 3,384 yards, par 36
Prestige: 3,367 yards, par 36
Greens fee: €70–€100
351-289-300529, vilasol.pt

The original 18-hole layout at Vila Sol was opened in 1991 and a year later played host to the Portuguese Open. It has remained one of the most popular destinations on the Algarve. The three nine-hole loops here provide interesting and varied tests. Prime and Challenge make up the premier 18, with two nines differing slightly in character. The former is longer, protected by intimidating water hazards, and tests your ability with the driver. The Challenge loop is defined by tall pine trees and places a premium on accuracy. Perhaps the most memorable hole at Vila Sol is the par-three 15th on the Challenge, which plays just under 200 yards. From the elevated tee, the tree-framed green is a superb sight.

VILAMOURA (OLD)

6,817 yards, par 73, 126/72.3
Greens fee: €95–€120
351-289-310341, vilamoura.net

Opened in 1969, this course has twice hosted the Portuguese Open and is widely regarded as the "must-play" track in the Vilamoura area. The front nine features some easy par fours, but the holes get progressively longer and harder on the way home, with the 550-yard 16th only reachable for the long (and straight) hitters. The par threes, all unique in design, provide realistic birdie opportunities but only if you club correctly. Built in and around the hillside, the natural contours and plentiful pine trees combine to demand accuracy, especially on dogleg holes such as the 7th, 11th, and 17th.

PINE CLIFFS

2,427 yards, par 33
Greens fee: €74 (18 holes)
351-289-500377, pinecliffs.com

Pine Cliffs is only a nine-holer, but don't be put off from making the effort to come and play this delightful layout. The course winds its way through swathes of pine trees and along awe-inspiring red cliffs overlooking the sea. The course is perhaps best known for its stunning par-three 9th hole, which is played over a deep ravine and nicknamed the Devil's Parlor. Anything other than a well-struck tee shot here will see you reaching for another ball. The rest of the course places a premium on accuracy over power (although the 440-yard 8th will test even big hitters), but you'll often need to be on the correct side of the fairway for a clear sight of the green.

PENINA

Championship: 6,862 yards, par 73, 131/73.7
Resort: 3,267 yards, par 36
Academy 2,025 yards, par 36
Greens fee: €100 (Championship); €45 (Resort); €30 (Academy)
351-282-420223, lemeridien.com/Portugal

Set in a peaceful 360-acre estate midway between Lagos and Portimao, Penina's Championship course was the handiwork of the late Henry Cotton, who lived in the area for many years. It's relatively flat, but this hasn't stopped it from providing a stern, nine-time test for the Portuguese Open. More than 360,000 trees and shrubs were planted during construction, and these now-mature specimens give the course its modern definition, along with the strategically placed water hazards.

VALE DO LOBO

Royal: 6,604 yards, par 72, NA/NA
Ocean: 6,338 yards, par 72, NA/NA
Greens fee: €155 (Royal); €145 (Ocean)
351-289-353465, valedolobo.com

Home to one of the most beautiful holes in golf—the par-three 16th on the Royal Course—Vale do Lobo has long been a favorite with British golfers. Vale do Lobo hosted the Portuguese Open in 2002, and both its Royal and Ocean courses have undergone recent alterations. Some of the greens have been enlarged and several new bunkers and lakes have been added. Most of the greens are well protected, and the undulating fairways are narrow and lined with umbrella pines, meaning that consistent straight hitting is crucial. From the back tees the Royal course is a very stiff test, doubtless a reason why Tour pro Jarmo Sandelin has made his home at this impressive venue.

WHERE TO STAY

Arguably the Algarve's most luxurious base, the Sheraton–run **Pine Cliffs** sits on a majestic spot overlooking the Atlantic. From luxurious rooms in the main hotel to the excellent golf suites that overlook the course, there is something for everyone. With a stunning beach, an excellent "Porto Pirata" kids club and off-course attractions such as tennis and mini-golf, the resort is popular with families. However, the nine restaurants, including the new Piri Piri steak house, which specializes in flame-grilled treats, and tranquil child-free zones make Pine Cliffs equally perfect for couples. Then there's the course and the golf academy, which feature a huge outdoor driving range, chipping green, bunker area, and two putting greens. Rates from €180. **351-289-500100, pinecliffs.com** • • **Vila Sol** offers modern luxury in Vilamoura. The hotel has 198 spacious rooms, including 49 suites featuring ultra-modern bathrooms and huge beds. For families and groups, one- to three-bedroom apartments are available in the Vila Sol Village, a short walk from the main building. The spa is beautifully designed (don't miss the scalp and aromatherapy massages). Beach lovers can catch the mini-bus to the Vila Sol Beach Club where water sports are offered, as well as a restaurant where you can enjoy freshly grilled fish. There are also two upmarket restaurants in the hotel—L'Olive, which serves Mediterranean cuisine, and the sophisticated

Green Pines. Rates from €120. **351-289-320375, vilasol.pt** • • Just 20 minutes from Lagos, toward the western edge of the Algarve, lies the **Parque da Floresta Golf and Leisure Resort**. This sizeable development set high in the hills can be windy, although this can be a relief in the summer. Accommodations are scattered throughout the resort in the form of apartments, town houses, and detached villas, some of which overlook the course. Also on offer are a spa, diving center, tennis, horseback riding, a children's club, and a selection of five restaurants. The course is not one of the region's must-play facilities, but it makes full use of the elevated terrain; the fairways wind through valleys, and some of the tee boxes perch on the tops of hills. Rates from €86. **351-282-690007, vigia-resorts.com** • • Situated in the heart of Vilamoura, **Dom Pedro Golf** is known as a golfer's hotel and feels like an extension of the grill room. A complimentary shuttle bus runs to all the courses in Vilamoura, so car rental isn't necessary. Rates from €124. **351-289-300700, dompedro.com**

LOCAL KNOWLEDGE

Thanks to a new motorway that extends from its west to its eastern tip, the Algarve is an easy region to explore. The fading elegance of **Tavira** in the east is worth a day trip. Moorish influence is evident in this historic, whitewashed town, where some of the buildings are brightly clad with painted ceramic

tiles. The countryside here is gentle and full of orange groves but becomes more mountainous near Spain, which is easily accessible via a suspension bridge. The Algarve coastline varies dramatically. In the west the beaches are more peaceful, and it is possible to find a secluded cove in which to relax and soak up the sun after a round. To the east of Faro the sandy beaches are reachable across the salt marshes and are edged by dunes. • • Head to the **marina at Vilamoura** in the evening, sit outside a café, and watch the world go by. Here you'll be spoiled for choice. If the Portuguese seafood doesn't tempt you, then you can choose from Mexican, Chinese, or Indian cuisine. Lagos in the west also has a great nightlife and plenty of bars for those who have the energy to live it up after a hard day on the course.

GETTING THERE

Faro is considered the gateway to Algarve. More than 30 carriers fly into te Faro Airport. **ana-aeroportos.pt**

WHEN TO GO

Golf can be enjoyed year round on the Algarve; even in summer the fairways are fanned by a refreshing Atlantic breeze.

ESTORIL AND SINTRA
The Algarve may have the majority of the courses in Portugal, but Lisbon has seven good reasons to visit. Lisbon is one of Europe's best value cities and provides a vibrant nightlife and enough sights and attractions to satisfy the hungriest of culture vultures. To the west of Lisbon lies the mountainous and unspoiled Sintra National Park, which is home to five courses. The hills that roll through the National Park create the perfect terrain for golf.

WHERE TO PLAY

PENHA LONGA
Atlantic: 6,881 yards, par 72, 119/71
Monastery: 2,820 yards, par 35
Greens fee: €90–€120 (Atlantic);
€33–€45 (Monastery)
351-219-249011, caesarparkpenhalonga.com

Robert Trent Jones Jr.'s 27 holes at Penha Longa use elevation changes to maximum impact with some mighty downhill tee shots. The views across the Sintra Mountains are superb. The Atlantic course has hosted the Portuguese Open.

BELAS
6,954 yards, par 72, 126/74.9
Greens fee: €75–€86
351-219-626640, belasgolf.com

Also tucked away in the hills lies Belas, which has some tough holes. They are a great deal of fun, but if you are wayward off the tee, you will find it difficult to score.

ESTORIL GOLF CLUB
Championship: 5,791 yards, par 69, 125/NA
Blue: 5,186 yards, par 68, 118/NA
Greens fee: €57
351-214-680176

Built in 1945, Estoril is one of the area's oldest clubs and still retains a traditional air of the heady days when plus-fours on the course and a tweed jacket for the bar were required. The Championship course is set above the Atlantic and runs through eucalyptus, pine, and mimosa trees.

OITAVOS
6,979 yards, par 71, 134/73.8
Greens fee: €150
351-214-860600
quintadamarinha-oitavosgolfe.pt

The region's newest course, Oitavos has a modern, sparkling chrome-and-glass clubhouse overlooking a links course that looks as if it dates back to the Victorian era but only opened at the turn of this century. The open fairways gently roll over hummocks and dunes with views of the Atlantic. Like most links, the course plays much harder than it looks.

QUINTA DA MARINHA
6,371 yards, par 71, 117/70.1
Greens fee: €44–€88
351-214-860100, quintadamarinha.com

On the prestigious Quinta da Marinha estate you'll find an excellent course and hotel. The 13th is a great hole with views of the ocean behind the green, followed by a par three across a ravine. Water also comes into play on some of the holes to keep you on your toes.

WHERE TO STAY

Hotel Estoril Eden in the heart of the bustling harbor town of Estoril has three nights with two rounds from €265 per person. Rates from €84. **351-214-667600, hotel-estoril-eden.pt** ●● **Caesar Park Penha Longa** is a luxurious golf hotel with golf and spa packages. Rates from €180. **351-219-249011, caesarpark penhalonga.com** ●● **Quinta da Marinha** is set in a prestigious resort with a golf course on site. This is the place to stay if you want the benefit of having the fairway on your hotel doorstep. Rooms from €160. **351-214-860100, quintadamarinha.com**

LOCAL KNOWLEDGE

Tucked away on the peaks of the Serra da Sintra mountains are two enchanting palaces waiting to be discovered. The **Palácio Nacional de** Sintra was a summer retreat for the Portuguese royal family and the charming **Palácio da Pena** was built in the 19th century for Queen Maria II. ●● Fishing is an important industry in Portugal. The harbors along the Estoril and Sintra coast are full of ancient and weather-beaten boats traditionally painted in bright colors so they are recognizable at sea. ●● The local restaurants buy daily from the fish markets in Cascais, ensuring that the fish is among the best you will have ever tasted. Feast on the nation's favorite dish, *bacalhau* (dried salted cod), or grilled sardines and mouthwatering shellfish. Some of the food, such as *cozido à Portuguesa*, which literally translates as "boiled Portuguese," consists of unidentifiable pieces of meat with potatoes, carrot, and cabbage and is best left for the adventurous.

GETTING THERE

Dozens of carriers fly into Lisbon Airport, including British Airways, US Airways, and Continental. **ana-aeroportos.pt**

WHEN TO GO

Peak season is July through the end of September, but the best time to go for lower rates and less of a crowd is April through June.

For more information about the region, visit estorilsintragolf.net.

Hole 6 at Penha Longa (Atlantic), Estoril and Sintra, Portugal

ST. ANDREWS AND FIFE

Every golfer needs to pay a visit to St. Andrews before sinking life's final putt. Some golf pilgrimages are prohibitively expensive to be a regular pleasure or too exclusive to be more than a fantasy. But for golfers armed with a sense of history and a valid passport, the promise of golf is realized at St. Andrews. Nowhere else in the world can you walk in the spike marks of every legendary figure to have played the game. (Okay, so Hogan never played here, but he stands alone.)

WHERE TO PLAY

OLD COURSE

6,721 yards, par 72, 139/73.3
Greens fee: £59–£120
44-133-447-7036, standrews.org.uk

TOP 100 IN THE WORLD

The Old Course, host to 27 British Opens (the last in 2005), has defied time and technology to stand as a reminder of what golf was intended to be—a test of mind and body against nature. Its greatness comes from its purity; there are no island greens, railroad ties, or dawdling duffers (the rangers enforce pace of play with a cheery firmness that brooks no dispute). You could play the Old Course for the remainder of your days and it would never get old.

NEW COURSE

6,625 yards, par 71, 125/71.9
Greens fee: £28–£57
44-133-447-7036, standrews.org.uk

The New Course is "new" only by St. Andrews standards. It opened in 1895 to accommodate an influx of golfers arriving on the then freshly laid railway. Edinburgh civil engineer W. Hall Blyth designed the holes, which Old Tom Morris spent 15 months building by hand. The New has hosted the prestigious Links Trophy and past Open Championship qualifying founds, and is, according to some, a fairer test of accuracy and imagination than the Old. The front nine offers more scoring opportunities, but if the wind kicks up, you can kiss a low number goodbye. The closing hole is a punishing 408-yarder that sports five of Old Tom's original six bunkers. Like a stepsister who deserves better, the New is to the Old as Spyglass Hill is to Pebble Beach.

KINGSBARNS GOLF LINKS

7,126 yards, par 72, 136/73.2
Greens fee: £125–£150
44-133-4460860, kingsbarns.com

TOP 100 IN THE WORLD

From the town of St. Andrews, take the five-mile drive along the A917, to one of Fife's newest and best courses. Kingsbarns, opened in 2000, is the ideal of links golf played within sight and sound of the sea. Every hole on this stretch of coast plays with a sea view, and the sound of waves crashing onto rocky shore intensifies the links experience. Kingsbarns is long but more a test of strategy than muscle. The 15th, a 212-yard par three, is the most spectacular hole. The tee is shielded from the wind by a forest, while the ball must carry 200 yards across rocks and surf to find the sanctuary of the green.

Hole 18 at St. Andrews
(Old Course), St. Andrews,
Scotland

Hole 7 at Kingsbarns,
St. Andrews, Scotland

ST. ANDREWS STEAL

There is one true bargain to be found in St. Andrews—the three-day ticket. For a little more than the cost of one round on the Old Course, a three-day ticket (£130 at press time) covers unlimited play on consecutive days on all Links Trust courses except the Old. The price drops to about £120 in low season (November-March). Tickets must be purchased from the starter on the first day you wish to play and are not available in advance. *For details, visit standrews.org.uk.*

JUBILEE COURSE

6,742 yards, par 72, 124/71.3
Greens fee: £28–£57
44-133-447-7036, standrews.org.uk

Tee times at the Jubilee are easier to obtain than any of St. Andrews Links Trust's other full-length courses—not because it's the least regarded, but because it's the most feared. Originally a 12-holer designed for beginners and women, St. Andrews' third course opened in 1897. After a deal was struck with the neighboring rifle and artillery range, six holes were added in 1905. Scottish architect Donald Steel revamped the layout in 1988, leaving just two original holes intact and elevating the Jubilee to a championship-caliber course worthy of a 2004 Scottish Amateur qualifier. Its proximity to the sea means the Jubilee often takes the brunt of bad weather, making holes like the 188-yard 13th play anywhere from a short iron to a driver depending on Mother Nature.

DUKE'S COURSE

7,271 yards, par 72, 127/73.5
Greens fee: £50–£95
44-133-447-4371, oldcoursehotel.co.uk

Owned by the Old Course Hotel and set to the west of St. Andrews, Duke is a monster designed by five-time British Open champion Peter Thomson. It is long and difficult, with tree-lined fairways and impenetrable swathes of gorse, but the views down over St. Andrews Bay are breathtaking.

ST. ANDREWS BAY GOLF RESORT AND SPA

Devlin: 7,049 yards, par 72, NA/NA
Torrance: 7,037 yards, par 72, NA/NA
Greens fee: £45–£95
44-133-483-7000, standrewsbay.com

At the St. Andrews Bay resort you can play the Devlin and the Torrance courses. The Devlin is considered the better course as each hole plays untouched by other golf traffic, often along dramatic cliff tops with views of St. Andrews, whereas the Torrance holes tend to run alongside each other out and back to the hotel.

LUNDIN GOLF CLUB

6,371 yards, par 71, 129/71.1
Greens fee: £45–£60
44-133-332-0202, lundingolfclub.co.uk

James Braid designed this superb seaside links course on the shores of the Firth of Forth in Lundin Links. The fairways dip and roll between banks of coarse sea grasses, and the greens are usually firm and true. The upper holes have spectacular panoramic views across Largo Bay to Edinburgh and North Berwick. Lundin is an Open Championship qualifying course and has hosted the World Senior Professional Championship.

LEVEN LINKS

6,506 yards, par 71, 119/70
Greens fee: £40–£65
44-133-342-8859, leven-links.com

Leven is separated from Lundin by only a dry stone wall, which was erected in 1868 when the land was split and two clubs were formed. Like Lundin, Leven has served as an Open Championship qualifying venue. Overlooking Largo bay, Leven winds through sand hills and bents. Golfers here are playing over one of the oldest golfing grounds in the world: Leven Golf Club began to play as early as 1846.

EDEN COURSE

6,195 yards, par 70, NA/NA
Greens fee: £17–£34
44-133-447-7036, standrews.org.uk

Because of its popularity with the St. Andrews townspeople, Harry S. Colt's 1914 design is, other than the Old, the toughest St. Andrews Links Trust tee time to obtain.

STRATHTYRUM COURSE

5,620 yards, par 69, NA/NA
Greens fee: £11–£23
44-133-447-7036, standrewos.org.uk

A short ego-booster by Donald Steel that the St. Andrews Links Trust opened in 1993. There are only 15 bunkers on the layout.

BALGOVE COURSE

1,520 yards, par 30
Greens fee: £7–£10
44-133-447-7036, standrews.org.uk

Built by the St. Andrews Links Trust in 1972 to encourage junior play. Redesigned in 1993.

LANDING YOUR OLD COURSE TEE TIME

The Old Course is run by the Links Trust and is open to the public, but the demand for tee times means that getting on isn't always easy. Here's how to earn your date with destiny at the Old.

The Basics: The Old Course opens at 6:30 AM Monday through Saturday (May through August) and at first light the rest of the year. The course is closed on Sundays.

Know Your Number: A valid handicap index card is required when you arrive for your tee time. The limit is 24 for men and 36 for women.

Plan early: On the first Wednesday of September, the Links Trust begins accepting reservations for the following year. "Be as quick as you can, they fill up within two weeks," says Links Trust spokesman Paul Kirkcaldy. E-mail the details of up to eight golfers (name, home club, and handicap) to reservations@standrews .org.uk or fax to 011-44-1334-477036.

List preferred dates: You can request two times per day, but from April through October one of those rounds must be played on another of the Trust's six courses. Provide details for one person in your group whom the Links Trust can contact.

The Lottery: Half of the annual tee times are assigned in a daily lottery ballot, providing a last shot for golfers without a reservation. Pairs can enter the lottery for next-day times in person at the starter's shack or by calling 011-44-1334-466666 before 2 PM. Lottery results are drawn at 4 PM and posted at several locations in town.

Just Show Up: Singles can't enter the lottery, but they can arrive early at the starter's hut to be slotted in where possible during the day. The wait could be minutes or hours. Check in with the concierge at some of the smarter hotels in town; they often have the next day's tee sheet and know just how many single slots remain.

Old Course Experience: Book a vacation package with the Old Course Experience, which owns exclusive overseas selling rights to Old Course tee times. Golfers stay in the town's best hotels and are guaranteed a start on the Old, usually between 9 AM and 11 AM. 44-1334-479050, oldcourse-experience.com

Bargain Hunt: Local hotels and guest houses are also allotted tee times and are the best place to find bargains. Check out the options—from the quaint Albany Hotel (£112 to £169 per person, per night) to the West Park House (£51 to £61 per person per night)—at stayinstandrews.co.uk. Check "Special Offers" for information on the Links Trust Winter Package: a guaranteed round on the Old Course and meal vouchers, for £99 per person December through March, accommodations not included.

FIND THE RIGHT MAN FOR YOUR BAG

St. Andrews' caddie manager Rick MacKenzie offers the inside dope on hiring the right bagman for your loop around the Old Course.

Do first-time visitors need a caddie?
"When the wind is blowing, it's said, 'the sheep hold on to the gorse with their teeth!' Imagine how difficult it is for visitors. Yes, take a caddie."

How do visitors hire a caddie? And how much does it cost?
"You can request a caddie in advance or on the day. We have a fixed caddie fee of £35 [$65] and £25 [$47] for trainee caddies."

What about tipping?
"I'd say 10 to 15 pounds [$19 to $28]."

What should a golfer expect from his caddie?
"A friend once said, 'Caddying is not brain surgery, it's far more complicated.' They are at times a companion, guide, psychologist, history teacher, storyteller, and valet all rolled into one. We have approximately 180 regular caddies, including 13 females. The stereotypical image of the rough-hewn drunk is long gone."

What's the most important piece of advice you would offer visiting golfers?
"Never hire a caddie with hiccups!"

WHERE TO STAY

The luxurious **Old Course Hotel** overlooks the "Road Hole" on the Old Course. Rates from £250. **44-133-4474371, oldcoursehotel .kohler.com** •• The lovely, chateau-like **St. Andrews Bay Hotel Resort and Spa**, which has stunning vistas of St. Andrews and two fine courses, is a quick drive to the Old Course. Rates from £215. **44-133-4837000, standrewsbay.com** •• A fixture on the Old Course's 18th fairway since 1887, **Rusacks Hotel** has been remodeled to include every modern convenience. Rates from £115. **44- 150-6815142 (International)** or **888-892- 0038 (U.S.), macdonaldhotels.co.uk** •• See **stayinstandrews.co.uk** for a variety of bed-and-breakfasts and small hotels with guaranteed tee times on the Old Course.

LOCAL KNOWLEDGE

Explore the ruins of **St. Andrews Castle**, which dates back 800 years. Visitors can crawl around the dungeon underground tunnels from the siege of 1546. •• In **St. Andrews Cemetery**, you'll find the gravesites of Old and Young Tom Morris. Be sure to also climb to the top of **St. Rule's Tower** for stunning views. •• **Auchterlonies** golf shop, just yards from the Old Course's 18th green, has Old Course souvenirs and continues to craft hickory- shafted clubs. **auchterloniesofstandrews.co.uk** •• Also nearby the Old Course, the **British Golf Museum** tells the story of golf from the middle ages to the present. **44-133-4460046, britishgolfmuseum.co.uk** •• Diets be damned. Bring on the fish and chips at **Kinness Fry Bar**. **44-133-4473802, kfb-standrews.co.uk**

GETTING THERE

Both Edinburgh and Glasgow accept plenty of international flights. Edinburgh is an 85-mile drive, and Glasgow is 55 miles away. There is also train service from London's Kings Cross Station to Leuchars, which is five miles from St. Andrews.

WHEN TO GO

"Nae rain, nae wind, nae golf," the Scots say, so don't expect fine weather. Pack for all seasons, no matter when you go. April has the least rainfall (1.6 inches), July is the hottest month (average high: 65 degrees), and May has the most sunny days. Local clubs, tournaments, and members of the R&A are allotted a chunk of tee times, so always call the Links Trust or visit standrews.org.uk before booking a trip. Also, you might want to avoid November through February, when golfers must hit off mats in the fairways to protect the course.

COSTA DEL SOL

COSTA DEL SOL The Costa del Sol stretches along the southwest coast of Spain, where Europe meets Africa and the Atlantic Ocean merges with the Mediterranean Sea. The area is renowned as a holiday destination, as many tourists are attracted by the wonderful weather and the beaches. But the quality of golf available in the region is also a draw. The town of Sotogrande, home to the world-renowned Valderrama and Sotogrande courses, is synonymous with golf, with more than 40 courses in the region.

WHERE TO PLAY

CLUB DE GOLF VALDERRAMA

6,556 yards, par 71, 142/NA
Greens fee: €290
34-956-791200, valderrama.com

TOP 100 IN THE WORLD

Valderrama is the number-one course on the European continent. Host of the 1997 Ryder Cup, it has impeccable greens, wonderful fairways dotted with old cork trees, olive trees, flower beds, and skillfully placed white sand bunkers. The 4th is the most beautiful hole, which ends on a raised green with a waterfall close by. The 8th commands all your concentration to master the trees lining the fairway and a green completely protected by bunkers. From the 15th you will enjoy magnificent views. You have to go around a slope and a hill before reaching the long, shaped green, which slopes at the rear. The 6th, a par three is surrounded by no fewer than six bunkers! The 11th, a par five of 550 yards, slopes to the right so that the green is not visible.

SOTOGRANDE CLUB DE GOLF

6,807 yards, par 72, 135/73.1
Greens fee: €160
34-956-795029, golfsotogrande.com

Sotogrande, located in the province of Cádiz, is on nearly 8,400 acres of rolling grassland and cork forest rising gently from one of the Mediterranean's fine beaches to the foothills of the Sierra de Almenara, with the Guadiaro River winding through. The name Sotogrande is a combination of the two Spanish words—*soto*, a riverside meadow abundant with trees and other vegetation, and *grande*. Both the 18-hole championship course and its accompanying par-three links were designed and built by Robert Trent Jones Sr., his first European courses. There's practically no rough, but because of the strategically placed bunkers and water hazards, golfers must prepare to assume the offensive from the first tee.

LA RESERVA DE SOTOGRANDE

7,325 yards, par 72, NA/NA
Greens fee: €150
34-956-785252, sotogrande.es

La Reserva has been created primarily as a members' club (the initiation fee is about €60,000), but tee times are available to visitors. The course winds its way through two deep valleys that meet to form a Y where the 8th green and 9th hole run parallel—and the results are spectacular. The rolling terrain offers a series of elevated tees, which tempt you to blast the ball into the wide blue yonder, and gives you a wonderful sense of being in the middle of nowhere with only the birds for company. The highlight on the homeward stretch is the downhill par-five 15th with its stunning views of the Mediterranean Sea equaled by the approach to a narrow green perched on the edge of a lake. La Reserva is a great design from start to finish, but its most endearing quality is that it is challenging without being too severe, thereby allowing players of all standards to have an enjoyable experience.

SANTANA GOLF AND COUNTRY CLUB

6,203 yards, par 72, NA/NA
Greens fee: €65–€80
34-951-062562, santanagolf.com

Santana, situated near Fuengirola, is set among avocado, orange, lemon, and olive trees. Santana is a relaxed experience, with wide fairways and inviting greens that make it ideal for players of all abilities. Standout holes are the 175-yard par-three 2nd (watch out for the water protecting the green) and the par-five 4th, where your approach shot is fired onto a putting surface enclosed by tall trees.

FLAMINGOS GOLF

6,412 yards, par 72, NA/NA
Greens fee: €99
34-952-889150, flamingos-golf.com

In the hills above Marbella lies Flamingos Golf, which has held a European seniors tour event. This beautifully kept course was designed by former European Tour pro Antonio Garrido. Water comes into play with dramatic effect on several holes.

LA CALA

Campo America: 6,187 yards, par 73, 138/72.7
Campo Asia: 6,458 yards, par 72, NA/NA
Campo Europa: 6,555 yards, par 71, 119/71.7
Greens fee: €45–€70
34-952-669033, lacala.com

La Cala, a resort with 54 holes of excellent golf, is next door to Santana. All three courses are quite different in character and offer a refreshing contrast for the visiting golfer. Campo America is more difficult than the shorter Campo Asia, but both tracks demand accuracy making club selection vital on approach shots. The third course, Camp Europa, plays in and around the River Ojen, and there are plenty of water hazards to focus your attention. Completing the impressive and comprehensive golf set-up at La Cala is a six-hole par-three academy course and a David Leadbetter Golf Academy, so if your swing is not quite on song there is help at hand.

Hole 15 at Valderrama,
Costa del Sol, Spain

SAN ROQUE CLUB

Old Course: 7,078 yards, par 72, NA/NA
New Course: 7,222 yards, par 72, NA/NA
Greens fee: €155 (Old); €120 (New)
34-956-613030, sanroqueclub.com

The Old Course was created in 1990 and designed by Dave Thomas. The front nine is played through cork oak forests, while the back nine is laid out across rolling hills, where water creates an extra hazard on the closing holes. The New Course, designed by Perry Dye and Seve Ballesteros, has some great holes, particularly early on the first nine, which has a Scottish feel. The 3rd plays uphill to a green surrounded by linkslike pot bunkers, while the 4th is an excellent par three where anything left will disappear into a deep ravine. The 5th is a short par-four downhill—simple if you hit a straight drive, but a nightmare if you stray off the narrow fairway.

ALMENARA

6,723 yards, par 72, 134/NA
Greens fee: €57–€77
34-902-181-836

Play golf at Almenara, a beautiful 27-hole layout on the Sotogrande estate, after 4:30 P.M. and you'll make huge savings on the regular green fees. Twilight golf for two people costs €100, including a buggy, until July 31.

WHERE TO STAY

Of minimalist design, the **NH Sotogrande** has clean lines and an abundance of natural light. Rates from €100. **34-956-695-444, nh-hotels .com** •• **NH Almenara Golf-Hotel & Spa** has rooms ranging from €140 to €224. **34-956-582-000, nh-hotels.com** •• A member of the Leading Small Hotels of the World group, the charming **Villa Padierna** is located northwest of Marbella. Rooms from €300. **34-952-889-150, hotelvillapadierna.com** •• If you want a golf and spa break, the **Gran Hotel Elba Estepona & Thalasso Spa** fits the bill. Rooms from €120. **34-952-809-200, elbaestepona .com** •• If you want to be closer to the nightlife of Marbella and Puerto Banus, the **Westin La Quinta** is a great hotel option. The hotel itself is superb and there are 27 holes of quality golf packed with trees, water hazards, and undulating terrain. Rates from €169. **34-952-762-000, westin.com/laquinta** •• The **Golf Hotel Guadalmina** is another good option if you want to stay at a golf resort within striking distance of Marbella and Puerto Banus. The hotel has two 18-hole courses and direct access to the adjoining beach. Rates from €130. **34-952-882-211, hotelguadalmina.com** •• For a hotel right in the center of Marbella, the **Hotel El Fuerte** is geared up to the needs of golfers and has direct access to the beach. Rates from €134. **34-952-920-000, fuertehoteles.com**

LOCAL KNOWLEDGE

Away from the fairways, there is also much to savor here for those looking for a taste of Spanish culture. Due to its strategic position, fertile soil and fantastic weather, the **Andalusia** region has attracted many civilizations across the centuries, and thanks to this, it has become an area of fascinating diversity and history. The Costa del Sol is no exception. With a wide variety of restaurants serving delicious fresh seafood, local dishes, and lovely hams and cheeses, there's as much to whet your appetite off course as there is on course.

GETTING THERE

Iberian (**Iberia.com**), Easyjet (**easyjet.co.uk**), Monarch (**flymonarch.co.uk**), Excel (**xl.com**), and British Airways (**ba.com**) fly to Malaga. Or fly into Gibraltar, which is closer to Sotogrande.

WHEN TO GO

Tourists can take their pick of two great times to visit. The weather peaks in March, April, and May but is also ideal for golfing in September, October, and November.

PERFECT THE BUDDY SYSTEM

Five tips to planning the perfect trip with your pals

There are as many types of buddy trips—from a party weekend in Myrtle Beach to a marathon fortnight in Ireland—as there are pitfalls that can sour the experience. We asked the folks at Golf Zoo, a travel agency that arranges golf vacations, for five keys that will guarantee a friction-free trip—and insure that you're all still friends when you get home.

GET THE RIGHT MIX

Choose people who play well with others. Not everybody's idea of a good time is a $100 Nassau or milking a case of Budweiser until 4 A.M. (Hard to believe, we know.) Invite like-minded souls who can enjoy the whole trip.

RETHINK THAT HOTEL

If your group consists of a couple of foursomes, splitting the cost of a condo or golf villa is often more affordable than renting individual hotel rooms. And you don't have to plead with the kitchen staff to fire up the grill for a late-night snack.

PLAN AHEAD

If you want prime tee times at popular courses, you will need to reserve them months in advance. Or you can use a package provider with access to those tee times. Planning ahead will also help you score cheap airfares.

BE FLEXIBLE

Some courses offer reduced rates for late morning and early afternoon tee times. This won't work if your group insists on squeezing in 36 holes a day, but at least the party animals will get more time to sleep off the previous night's effects.

DON'T ASSUME THE BEST

If a deal sounds too good to be true—"Seven days in St. Andrews for $99!"—it probably is. Read the fine print. And find out in advance if you can pre-book replay rounds; don't assume a tee time will be available when you get there.

Hole 5 at Pinehurst
No. 8, The Sandhills,
North Carolina

GOLF MAGAZINE'S **GOLD AND SILVER MEDAL RESORTS** Since 1988 GOLF MAGAZINE has ranked the finest retreats in the United States based on the golf, the service, the amenities, and the overall luxury of the experience. Starting with our 10th ranking in 2006, we asked readers to share their opinions and experiences on our Web site, golf.com. Based on that input, as well as that of our own experts, these 75 Gold and Silver medalists constitute the most authoritative ranking of America's best golf resorts.

GOLD MEDALISTS

Gold Medal Resorts are indicated throughout the book by this symbol:

The American Club
Kohler, Wisconsin

Medal History: Gold medalist since 1992

Why It's Worth It: Two reasons: the golf and the facilities—yes, *those* facilities. Kohler's justly famed bathroom fixtures—like the whirlpool bath, where you'll have more jets shooting at you than a fleeing Taliban—are standard issue here. You'll need that luxurious soak after battling the resort's Straits course at Whistling Straits (No. 28 on our Top 100 Courses in the U.S.), which hosted the 2004 PGA Championship. Whistling's Irish course and two more at Blackwolf Run make this resort a dairy-land queen. **800-344-2838, destinationkohler.com**

Bandon Dunes Golf Resort
Bandon, Oregon

Medal History: Debuted as a Gold medalist in 2002

Why It's Worth It: The Lodge at Bandon Dunes doesn't have a spa or any other bells and whistles, just comfortable beds, nice food, and good drink. Bandon is about golf the way Scotland is—in fact, you'd swear you were there if it weren't for the good showers. It's the only resort where you can play three of GOLF MAGAZINE's Top 100 Courses in the U.S. Pacific Dunes (No. 8) and Bandon Dunes (No. 40) sit cheek by jowl on stunning ocean-side cliffs; located more inland, Bandon Trails (No. 47) opened in June and sealed Bandon's

standing as the best pure golf destination in America. **888-345-6008, bandondunes.com**

The Boulders Resort & Golden Door Spa
Carefree, Arizona

Medal History: One of only five resorts to win Gold in each GOLF MAGAZINE ranking

Why It's Worth It: Carefree isn't just the hometown of the Boulders—it's an attitude that's reinforced at the Golden Door Spa, a 33,000-square-foot Sonoran Shangri-la that offers treatments like the Watsu, an underwater, "back to the womb" experience. Use it to recharge your batteries after a round at the two outstanding Jay Morrish–designed courses that hopscotch over arroyos and around cactuses, or to entertain your spouse while you play. **866-397-6520, theboulders.com**

The Broadmoor
Colorado Springs, Colorado

Medal History: Gold in all 10 rankings since 1988

Why It's Worth It: A new Jack Nicklaus course opens this year, bringing a neat symmetry to the Bear's history at the Broadmoor, where he won the U.S. Amateur in 1959. You'll also find a superb tree-lined test that bears the imprint of two titans of design—Donald Ross and Robert Trent Jones Sr.—a storied roster of guests (from presidents to Bob Hope), 11 restaurants, and an extensively renovated spa

that includes a Serenity Shower, a $100,000 contraption with 18 showerheads that adapts to your body shape. **866-837-9520, thebroadmoor.com**

Coeur d'Alene Resort
Coeur d'Alene, Idaho

Medal History: Longtime Silver medalist, elevated to Gold in 2000

Why It's Worth It: Complimentary massages on the practice tee and bunker rakes that pop from the ground at the push of a button are signs of just how white-glove the service is here. Golfers are ferried from the resort to the course via mahogany water taxi, and it's another short boat ride to the most famous hole here, the floating green at No. 14. **800-688-5253, cdaresort.com**

Four Seasons Resort Aviara
Carlsbad, California

Medal History: Moved from Silver to Gold in 2004

Why It's Worth It: This southern California hilltop retreat has just added the MATT System—that's Motion Analysis Technology by TaylorMade—at its Aviara Golf Academy, the only place west of the Mississippi where you'll find it. Get club-fitted like the pros as nine cameras monitor your swing, and then test that knowledge on the watery Arnold Palmer course, which tiptoes around a lagoon. **800-819-5053, fourseasons.com/aviara**

Four Seasons Resort Hualalai

Ka'upulehu-Kona, Hawaii

Medal History: Debuted as a Gold in 2000

Why It's Worth It: Every room sports ocean views in the shadow of the Hualalai volcano. This resort epitomizes the idea of going with the flow. (Don't worry, the volcano hasn't popped in almost 205 years.) The closest you'll get to hot rocks is the signature massage in the highly regarded spa. The Nicklaus–designed course—home of the Champions Tour's season opener—has fairways that cut through black lava before reaching a grand finale alongside the ocean. **800-819-5053, fourseasons.com/hualalai**

Four Seasons Resort Lana'i at Manele Bay

Lana'i, Hawaii

Medal History: Seven consecutive Gold awards

Why It's Worth It: Formerly known as the Manele Bay Hotel, this was a longtime Gold medalist even before the Four Seasons brand took over last year. The result is a ramping up in service (such as personalized check-in) and amenities (Evian spritzes and chilled towels at the remodeled pool area). The existing Nicklaus course doesn't need much work—the cliff-top setting is so dramatic that Bill Gates chose to get married on the tee at No. 12. **800-819-5053, fourseasons.com/manelebay**

Four Seasons Resort Scottsdale at Troon North

Scottsdale, Arizona

Medal History: Debuted Gold in 2002

Why It's Worth It: You can't get more at one with the Sonoran Desert this side of a tent and sleeping bag—every room has a balcony or patio overlooking the desert landscape. The resort's Cowboy Campfires—nighttime stories of the Old West from a cowboy crooner—almost match the entertainment value of the two courses at Troon North, both of which are on our Top 100 Courses You Can Play: the Tom Weiskopf–Jay Morrish Monument (No. 21) layout and Pinnacle (No. 64), a solo Weiskopf effort. **800-332-3442, fourseasons.com/scottsdale**

Grand Wailea Resort

Maui, Hawaii

Medal History: Elevated to Gold in 2000, Silver before that

Why It's Worth It: With tropical oceanfront settings and jagged lava hazards, the Gold (home of the Champions Tour Skins game), Blue, and Emerald courses are the jewels here, but the real bauble for guests is the Spa Grande, where you can get massaged and scrubbed with everything from seaweed to sea shells to sand wedges. Okay, we made that last one up, but the rest is true. Kids will love the 2,000-foot-long Wailea Canyon Activity Pool. **800-888-6100, grandwailea.com**

The Greenbrier

White Sulphur Springs, West Virginia

Medal History: Gold since 1988

Why It's Worth It: The Greenbrier's genteel old-world feel is epitomized by the daily tradition of afternoon tea and cookies, accompanied by music. (This is one of the resort's more recent traditions—it started in 1931.) You'll feel like landed gentry at leisure with such amenities as skeet shooting, falconry, and off-road driving. The Greenbrier course hosted the 1979 Ryder Cup, and the Old White course, designed by C.B. Macdonald, is nearing the end of a major restoration. Sam Snead made his final ace here on the 18th hole in 1995. The most interesting bunker on the property is the 112,000-square-foot underground fortress designed to house Congress in the event of a Cold War incident (that is, a nuclear attack). The renovated bunker reopens to tours this spring. **800-453-4858, greenbrier.com**

The Homestead

Hot Springs, Virginia

Medal History: Only once, in 2000, has the resort been less than Gold standard.

Why It's Worth It: The Homestead is older than the Republic. And the resort is celebrating its 240th birthday by restoring the superb Cascades course—No. 56 on GOLF MAGAZINE's Top 100 Courses in the U.S.—to its original 1923 design by William Flynn, who also created Shinnecock Hills. Cascades reopens in May. The Old Course has been touched up too, but still retains the oldest continuously used first tee in the U.S. (in use since 1892). Other attractions include the Lower Cascades course (by Robert Trent Jones Sr.) and the original Sam Snead's Tavern. **800-838-1766, thehomestead.com**

Inn & Links at Spanish Bay

Pebble Beach, California

Medal History: Medalist since 1988; this is its fifth Gold medal.

Why It's Worth It: An outstanding new restaurant has elevated Spanish Bay to equal status with its sister property, the Lodge at Pebble Beach. The homemade pasta at Peppoli is matched only by the Pacific views. You can feast on the golf, too. The Links—designed by Robert Trent Jones, Tom Watson, and Sandy Tatum—is more Monterey than Muirfield (it's a little too well manicured), but the course offers a testing trot alongside the Pacific and a stirring prep for the other courses you have access to, Pebble Beach and Spyglass Hill. **800-654-9300, pebblebeach.com**

Kauai Marriott Resort & Beach Club

Kauai, Hawaii

Medal History: Solid Gold since 1998

Why It's Worth It: The golf here shows the first stirrings of the Bear—two early Jack Nicklaus designs that can still maul you, most notably the Kiele layout, which is No. 78 on our Top 100 Courses You Can Play. More modern (but no less important) means of relaxation at this resort are Marriott's new beds, the pillows and comforters on which feature more feathers than a chicken farm. **800-220-2925, marriott.com**

Kiawah Island Golf Resort

Kiawah Island, South Carolina

Medal History: After 8 Silvers Kiawah finally gets its Gold.

Why It's Worth It: In the summer of 2005, Kiawah opened the South's finest new hotel, the Sanctuary at Kiawah Island. The resort—just 21 miles from Charleston—finally has accommodations to match its Gold Medal golf, most notably Pete Dye's Ocean Course, the 1991 Ryder Cup venue. Twin sweeping staircases off the lobby suggest a formal *Gone with the Wind* elegance but the comfort level is pure Southern charm. The resort has also just broken ground on a new clubhouse at the Ocean course. **800-576-1570, kiawah resort.com**

Lake Las Vegas Resort
Henderson, Nevada
Medal History: Moved from Silver in 2004 to Gold
Why It's Worth It: This diamond in the desert is growing as fast as nearby Las Vegas. (The Strip is only 17 miles away.) The property includes two superior hotels—a Hyatt Regency and a Ritz-Carlton—with a 400-room Loews hotel on the way. Also in the works is Rainbow Canyon, a new Tom Fazio layout that will complement the existing pair of diverse but riotously entertaining courses: Nicklaus' strategically demanding lakeside layout Reflection Bay and Tom Weiskopf's Falls course, which climbs high into the barren hills, where the hazards include scowling mountain sheep. **702-567-1234 (Hyatt) or 702-567-4700 (Ritz), lakelasvegas.com**

The Lodge at Koele
Lana'i, Hawaii
Medal History: Made the leap to Gold in 2004
Why It's Worth It: Thanks to a takeover by the Four Seasons, the already swank Lodge promises upgrades in 2006. Guests already can enjoy amenities such as an archery range and a sporting clay course, along with nice touches like the pineapple cider at check-in. The real thrill, however, is the Experience, the Ted Robinson–Greg Norman golf course, where the tee shot at No. 17 plummets into the deepest gorge on the island. **800-321-4666, lodgeatkoele.com**

The Lodge at Pebble Beach
Pebble Beach, California
Medal History: A perennial Gold
Why It's Worth It: You just won't find a more storied public-access course in the U.S. The Lodge is just a lag putt from the first tee and 18th green, and nothing beats that feeling of drawing back your room shades to see the whales in Stillwater Cove looking back at you. A post-round beer in the Tap Room is a rite of passage. **800-654-9300, pebblebeach.com**

Mauna Lani Resort
Kohala Coast, Hawaii
Medal History: Has never dropped from the Gold podium in 18 years
Why It's Worth It: There are two luxury properties on site, the Mauna Lani Bay Hotel & Bungalows and the Fairmont Orchid, both of which are perched on a pristine, white sand beach. Both the North and South courses are breezy island layouts that are more soothing to play than nerve-wracking, so you can't use golf as an excuse for the signature massage in a secluded hale, a traditional grass-thatched Hawaiian hut. 800-323-7500, maunalani.com

Pinehurst Resort
Pinehurst, North Carolina
Medal History: Eight consecutive Golds
Why It's Worth It: The century-old Carolina hotel is always keeping itself in the game. In 2006 the resort completed phase one of a major room renovation that includes deluge rain showerheads and ultra-soft luxury bedding. You have eight courses to choose from. The big daddy is No. 2, the 2005 U.S. Open venue, but Nos. 4 and 8 also earn spots on our Top 100 Courses You Can Play. With 144 holes, even grumpy Grandpa will find one course to like. **800-487-4653, pinehurst.com**

Princeville Resort
Kauai, Hawaii
Medal History: Gold since 1994
Why It's Worth It: It's the little touches that make a difference at Princeville, a member of

the exclusive Luxury Collection resorts. Recent innovations include "In Room Aromatherapy," providing guests with a relaxing fragrance from the indigenous maile vine. Each room also has been fitted with a large privacy window, which turns from opaque to clear at the touch of a button. The Prince Course, by Robert Trent Jones Jr., climbs and dives across heaving terrain and is No. 20 on our Top 100 Courses You Can Play. **800-826-4400, princeville.com**

Sea Island Resort
Sea Island, Georgia
Medal History: Gold since 1992
Why It's Worth It: The resort's famed waterfront Cloister Hotel underwent an extreme makeover, which culminated with an unveiling in the spring of 2006. The resort has been a haven for the well-heeled for 75 years. (President Bush's parents honeymooned here, which is why he chose it as the venue of the 2005 G8 Summit.) The luxury Lodge at Sea Island lets you walk from your room to the pro shop in less time than it takes to lace up your spikes. The dunes-strewn Seaside Course is the best of the three options and ranks No. 95 on our Top 100 Courses in the U.S. **800-732-4752, seaisland.com**

Sunriver Resort
Sunriver, Oregon
Medal History: Gold since 2002
Why It's Worth It: Sunriver is not a couch spud's resort. You can ski and play golf on the same day. The best of the three courses is Bob Cupp's Crosswater layout, with par fives that are longer than the buffet line at an Overeaters Anonymous convention. When you're done with that, ride a canoe down the Deschutes River or tackle the ropes course. Kids will enjoy Fort Funnigan, with its petting zoo and daily activities. The Owl's Nest bar serves up some of the best microbrews in the Pacific Northwest. **800-801-8765, sunriver-resort.com**

Walt Disney World Resort

Orlando, Florida

Medal History: This is Mickey's sixth Gold to go with two Silvers.

Why It's Worth It: There are 99 holes here—and almost as many hotels and price points—with more thrills for the family than you can shake a wand at. Three courses by Joe Lee (the best of which is the recently refurbished Magnolia track, which hosts the PGA Tour's Funai Classic) and contributions from Tom Fazio and Pete Dye round out a magical kingdom for golfers. Disney's latest thrill ride, *Expedition Everest—Legend of the Forbidden Mountain*, opens this spring and gives you an excuse for a golf trip under the guise of generous parenting. **407-934-7639, disneyworld.com**

Williamsburg Inn

Williamsburg, Virginia

Medal History: Has fallen short of Gold only once since 1988

Why It's Worth It: Founded as a retreat for John D. Rockefeller Jr., the inn received a major facelift four years ago that involved reducing the number of rooms from 100 to 62 so they could be enlarged, refinishing the original antique furniture, and adding a tea room. The white-glove service will inspire you to keep up with the Joneses, and you can do that at the Golden Horseshoe golf club, where you'll find tracks by Robert Sr. and his son Rees. Kids under 15 can play the Spotswood Course free with a parent. **800-447-8679, colonialwilliamsburg.com**

SILVER MEDALISTS

Silver Medal Resorts are indicated throughout the book by this symbol:

Amelia Island Plantation
Amelia Island, FL
aipfl.com
888-261-6161

The Balsams
Dixville Notch, NH
thebalsams.com
800-255-0600

Barton Creek Resort
Austin, TX
bartoncreek.com
800-336-6158

Boyne Highlands
Harbor Springs, MI
boynehighlands.com
800-462-6963

The Breakers
Palm Beach, FL
thebreakers.com
888-273-2537

Doral Golf Resort & Spa
Miami, FL
doralresort.com
800-713-6725

Fairmont Scottsdale Princess
Scottsdale, AZ
fairmont.com/scottsdale
800-257-7544

Fairmont Turnberry Isle
Miami, FL
fairmont.com/turnberryisle
800-257-7544

Four Seasons Resort & Club Dallas at Las Colinas
Dallas, TX
fourseasons.com
800- 257-7544

Grand Cypress Resort
Orlando, FL
grandcypress.com
877-330-7377

Grand Geneva Resort & Spa
Lake Geneva, WI
grandgeneva.com
888-392-8000

Grand Hyatt Kauai
Kauai, HI
hyatt.com
800-233-1234

Grand View Lodge
Nisswa, MN
grandviewlodge.com
800-432-3788

Horseshoe Bay Resort
Horseshoe Bay, TX
horseshoebaytexas.com
800-531-5105

Hotel Hershey
Hershey, PA
hersheyresorts.com
717-533-2171

Hyatt Regency Hill Country Resort & Spa
San Antonio, TX
hyatt.com
800-233-1234

Hyatt Regency Resort & Spa at Gainey Ranch
Scottsdale, AZ
hyatt.com
800-233-1234

Hyatt Tamaya Resort & Spa
Santa Ana Pueblo, NM
hyatt.com
800-233-1234

The Inn at Bay Harbor
Bay Harbor, MI
innatbayharbor.com
800-462-6963

Inn at Palmetto Bluff
Bluffton, SC
palmettobluffresort.com
866-706-6565

JW Marriott Desert Springs
Resort & Spa
Palm Desert, CA
desertspringsresort.com
800-331-3112

Kapalua Resort
Maui, HI
kapaluamaui.com
800-527-2582

Keystone Resort
Keystone, CO
keystoneresort.com
877-753-9786

Kingsmill Resort
Williamsburg, VA
kingsmill.com
800-832-5665

La Quinta Resort & Club
La Quinta, CA
laquintaresort.com
800-598-3828

Lodge at CordeValle
San Martin, CA
cordevalle.com
877-255-2626

Lodge at Torrey Pines
La Jolla, CA
lodgetorreypines.com
858-453-4420

The Lodge & Spa at Cordillera
Edwards, CO
cordillera-vail.com
800-877-3529

The Lodge at Ventana Canyon
Tucson, AZ
thelodgeatventanacanyon.com
800-828-5701

Loews Ventana Canyon Resort
Tucson, AZ
loewshotel.com
520-299-2020

Makena Resort/Maui Prince Hotel
Maui, HI
princeresortshawaii.com
866-774-6236

Mauna Kea Resort
Kohala Coast, HI
maunakeabeachhotel.com
866-774-6236

Nemacolin Woodlands
Resort & Spa
Farmington, PA
nemacolin.com
800-422-2736

Ojai Valley Inn & Spa
Ojai, CA
ojairesort.com
888-697-8780

Omni Tucson National
Tucson, AZ
tucsonnational.com
520-297-2271

Palm Coast Resort
Palm Coast, FL
palmcoastresort.com
800-654-6538

The Phoenician
Scottsdale, AZ
thephoenician.com
800-888-8234

Pine Needles Lodge/Mid Pines Inn
Southern Pine, NC
pineneedles-midpines.com
800-747-7272

Ritz-Carlton Golf Resort
Naples, FL
ritzcarlton.com
800-241-3333

Ritz-Carlton at Half Moon Bay
Half Moon Bay, CA
ritzcarlton.com
800-241-3333

Ritz-Carlton Lodge
Reynolds Plantation
Greensboro, GA
reynoldsplantation.com
800-826-1945

Sandestin Golf & Beach Resort
Destin, FL
sandestin.com
800-622-1038

Sawgrass Marriott Resort
Ponte Vedra Beach, FL
sawgrassmarriott.com
800-457-4653

Sea Pines Resort
Hilton Head Island, SC
seapines.com
888-807-6873

Shanty Creek Resort & Club
Bellaire, MI
shantycreek.com
800-678-4111

Treetops Resort
Treetops Village, MI
treetops.com
888-873-3867

Westin Innisbrook Resort
Palm Harbor, FL
westin-innisbrook.com
877-752-1480

Westin La Cantera
San Antonio, TX
westinlacantera.com
210-558-6500

Westin La Paloma Resort
Tucson, AZ
westinlapalomaresort.com
520-742-6000

Westin Mission Hills
Rancho Mirage, CA
starwoodhotels.com
800-228-3000

Hole 9 at Bay Harbor
(Quarry), North Michigan

GOLF MAGAZINE'S TOP 100 COURSES YOU CAN PLAY

1   **Pacific Dunes**
Bandon, OR $75–$240

2   **Pebble Beach Golf Links**
Pebble Beach, CA $425–$450

3   **Kiawah Island Resort (Ocean Course)**
Kiawah Island, SC $196–$305

4   **Whistling Straits**
Haven, WI $325

5   **Bandon Dunes**
Bandon, OR $75–$240

6   **Pinehurst No. 2**
Pinehurst, NC $275–$375

7   **Bethpage State Park (Black)**
Farmingdale, NY $41–$102

8   **Shadow Creek**
North Las Vegas, NV $500

9   **Spyglass Hill**
Pebble Beach, CA $300–$330

10   **Bandon Trails**
Bandon, OR $75–$240

11   **TPC at Sawgrass (Stadium)**
Ponte Vedra Beach, FL $214–$350

12   **Pasatiempo Golf Club**
Santa Cruz, CA $150–$197

13   **Blackwolf Run (River)**
Kohler, WI $189–$214

14   **Kapalua Golf Club (Plantation)**
Kapalua, Maui, HI $295

15   **Harbour Town Golf Links**
Hilton Head Island, SC $135–$270

16   **Sea Island Golf Club (Seaside)**
St. Simons Island, GA $170–$250

17   **World Woods (Pine Barrens)**
Brooksville, FL $40–$150

18   **The Homestead (Cascades)**
Hot Springs, VA $210–$261

19   **Cuscowilla**
Eatonton, GA $89–$150

20   **Princeville Resort (Prince), Princeville**
Kauai, HI $75–$175

21   **Troon North (Monument)**
Scottsdale, AZ $75–$295

22   **Cog Hill (No. 4)**
Lemont, IL $135

23   **Mauna Kea**
Kohala Coast, HI $150–$210

24   **Red Sky Ranch (Norman)**
Wolcott, CO $175–$225

25   **Caledonia Golf & Fish Club**
Pawleys Island, SC $80–$190

26   **Bulle Rock**
Havre de Grace, MD $145

27   **Arcadia Bluffs**
Arcadia, MI $75–$180

28   **Taconic**
Williamstown, MA $145

29   **PGA West (Stadium)**
La Quinta, CA $55–$235

30   **Paa-Ko Ridge**
Sandia Park, NM $57–$89

31   **Bay Harbor (Links/Quarry)**
Bay Harbor, MI $109–$199

32   **Dancing Rabbit (Azaleas)**
Philadelphia, MS $55–$99

33   **Challenge at Manele Lanai City**
Lanai, HI $190–$225

34   **Crosswater at Sunriver**
Sunriver, OR $105–$160

35   **Black Mesa**
La Mesilla, NM $59–$82

36   **We-Ko-Pa Golf Club**
Fort McDowell, AZ $70–$195

37   **Pumpkin Ridge (Ghost Creek)**
Cornelius, OR $50–$150

38   **Trump National Los Angeles**
Rancho Palos Verdes, CA $195–$300

39   **Cascata**
Boulder City, NV $350–$550

40   **Linville Golf Club**
Linville, NC $95

41   **Torrey Pines (South)**
La Jolla, CA $140–$205

42   **The Links at Spanish Bay**
Pebble Beach, CA $240–$270

43   **Reynolds Plantation (Great Waters)**
Greensboro, GA $125–$195

44   **Arnold Palmer's Bay Hill Club (Championship)**
Orlando, FL $205

45   **Pine Needles Lodge & Golf Club**
Southern Pines, NC $140–$175

46   **Dunes Golf & Beach Club**
Myrtle Beach, SC $160

47   **Longaberger**
Nashport, OH $125

48   **Golden Horseshoe (Gold)**
Williamsburg, VA $155

49   **Wynn Las Vegas**
Las Vegas, NV $500

50   **Wild Horse Golf Club**
Gothenburg, NE $34.80–$52.75

51   **Karsten Creek**
Stillwater, OK $250

52   **The Greenbrier (Greenbrier)**
White Sulphur Springs, WV $185–$350

53   **May River Course at Palmetto Bluff**
Bluffton, SC $240

54   **Reflection Bay at Lake Las Vegas**
Henderson, NV $110–$270

55   **The Harvester GC**
Rhodes, IA $45–$65

56   **Quarry at Giants Ridge**
Biwabik, MN $45–$75

57   **Coeur d'Alene Resort**
Coeur d'Alene, ID $200–$250

58   **Wolf Creek GC**
Mesquite, NV $85–$185

59   **Troon North (Pinnacle)**
Scottsdale, AZ $75–$295

60   **Reynolds Plantation (Oconee)**
Greensboro, GA $135–$260

61	**Atunyote at Turning Stone Resort** Verona, NY $150–$200		81	**The Broadmoor (East)** Colorado Springs, CO $145–$180	
62	**Hawktree GC** Bismark, ND $50–$60		82	**Capitol Hill (Judge)** Prattville, AL $65–$67	
63	**The General at Eagle Ridge** Galena, IL $80–$165		83	**Rustic Canyon** Moorpark, CA $35–$67	
64	**Shenandoah at Turning Stone** Verona, NY $80–$125		84	**Old Works** Anaconda, MT $29–$57	
65	**The Glen Club** Glenview, IL $125–$155		85	**Cambrian Ridge (Sherling/Canyon)** Greenville, AL $35–$57	
66	**CordeValle** San Martin, CA $85–$315		86	**DarkHorse** Auburn, CA $45–$79	
67	**Pine Hill** Pine Hill, NJ $79–$99		87	**Grayhawk GC (Talon)** Scottsdale, AZ $50–$225	
68	**Barton Creek (Fazio Foothills)** Austin, TX $135–$240		88	**Westin Innisbrook (Copperhead)** Palm Harbor, FL $100–$235	
69	**Barton Creek (Fazio Canyons)** Austin, TX $135–$240		89	**Boulders Club (South)** Carefree, AZ $75–$290	
70	**Grand National (Lake)** Opelika, AL $40–$62		90	**Grand Bear** Saucier, MS $89–$135	
71	**La Quinta Resort (Mountain)** La Quinta, CA $50–$190		91	**Sugarloaf** Carrabassett Valley, ME $75–$115	
72	**Pinehills (Nicklaus)** Plymouth, MA $60–$100		92	**Lakewood Shores (Gailes)** Oscoda, MI $43–$62	
73	**WeaverRidge** Peoria, IL $73–$83		93	**Beechtree** Aberdeen, MD $70–$95	
74	**Branson Creek GC** Hollister, MO $48–$94		94	**Forest Dunes** Roscommon, MI $75–$125	
75	**Whistling Straits (Irish)** Haven, WI $53–$196		95	**Barefoot Resort (Love)** North Myrtle Beach, SC $75–$155	
76	**Deacon's Lodge** Breezy Point, MN $60–$106		96	**St. Ives Resort (Tullymore)** Stanwood, MI $82–$95	
77	**Belgrade Lakes** Belgrade Lakes, ME $50–$130		97	**Lake of Isles (North)** North Stonington, CT $95–$175	
78	**Ocean Hammock** Palm Coast, FL $215–$285		98	**Doral (Blue)** Miami, FL $145–$295	
79	**Links at Lighthouse Sound** Bishopville, MD $65–$179		99	**Pinehurst (No. 8)** Pinehurst, NC $200–$250	
80	**Lakota Canyon Ranch** New Castle, CO $75–$85		100	**Gold Mountain Golf Complex (Olympic)** Bremerton, WA $35–$63	

GOLF MAGAZINE'S TOP 100 COURSES YOU CAN PLAY (RANKED BY STATE)

ALABAMA

70 Grand National (Lake)
Opelika $35–$57

82 Capitol Hill (Judge)
Prattville $65–$67

85 Cambrian Ridge (Sherling/Canyon)
Greenville $35–$57

ARIZONA

21 Troon North (Monument)
Scottsdale $75–$295

36 We-Ko-Pa Golf Club
Fort McDowell $45–$160

59 Troon North (Pinnacle)
Scottsdale $75–$295

87 Grayhawk GC (Talon)
Scottsdale $50–$225

89 Boulders Club (South)
Carefree $75–$290

CALIFORNIA

2   Pebble Beach Golf Links
Pebble Beach $425–$450

9   Spyglass Hill
Pebble Beach $300–$330

12 Pasatiempo Golf Club
Santa Cruz $150–$197

29 PGA West (Stadium)
La Quinta $55–$235

38 Trump National Los Angeles
Rancho Palos Verdes $195–$300

41 Torrey Pines (South)
La Jolla $105–$135

42 The Links at Spanish Bay
Pebble Beach $240–$270

66 CordeValle
San Martin $85–$315

71 La Quinta Resort (Mountain)
La Quinta $50–$190

83 Rustic Canyon
Moorpark $35–$67

86 DarkHorse
Auburn $45–$79

COLORADO

24 Red Sky Ranch (Norman)
Wolcott $175–$225

80 Lakota Canyon Ranch
New Castle $75–$85

81 The Broadmoor (East)
Colorado Springs $145–$180

CONNECTICUT

97 Lake of Isles (North)
North Stonington $95–$175

FLORIDA

11 TPC at Sawgrass (Stadium)
Ponte Vedra Beach $214–$350

17 World Woods (Pine Barrens)
Brooksville $40–$150

44 Arnold Palmer's Bay Hill Club
(Championship)
Orlando $205

78 Ocean Hammock
Palm Coast $215–$285

88 Westin Innisbrook (Copperhead)
Palm Harbor $100–$235

98 Doral (Blue)
Miami $145–$295

GEORGIA

16 Sea Island Golf Club (Seaside)
St. Simons Island $170–$250

19 Cuscowilla
Eatonton $89–$150

43 Reynolds Plantation (Great Waters)
Greensboro $125–$195

60 Reynolds Plantation (Oconee)
Greensboro $135–$260

HAWAII

14 Kapalua Golf Club (Plantation)
Kapalua, Maui $295

20 Princeville Resort (Prince)
Princeville, Kauai $75–$175

23 Mauna Kea
Kohala Coast $150–$210

33 Challenge at Manele
Lanai City, Lanai $190–$225

IDAHO

57 Coeur d'Alene Resort
Coeur d'Alene $125–$225

ILLINOIS

22 Cog Hill (No. 4)
Lemont $135

63 The General at Eagle Ridge
Galena $80–$165

65 The Glen Club
Glenview $125–$155

73 WeaverRidge
Peoria $73–$83

IOWA

55 The Harvester GC
Rhodes $45–$65

MAINE

77 Belgrade Lakes
Belgrade Lakes $50–$130

91 Sugarloaf
Carrabassett Valley $75–$115

MARYLAND

26 Bulle Rock
Havre de Grace $145

79 Links at Lighthouse Sound
Bishopville $65–$179

93 Beechtree
Aberdeen $70–$95

MASSACHUSETTS

28 Taconic
Williamstown $145

72 Pinehills (Nicklaus)
Plymouth $60–$100

MICHIGAN

27   Arcadia Bluffs
     Arcadia $75–$180

31   Bay Harbor (Links/Quarry)
     Bay Harbor $109–$199

92   Lakewood Shores (Gailes)
     Oscoda $43–$62

94   Forest Dunes
     Roscommon $75–$125

96   St. Ives Resort (Tullymore)
     Stanwood $82–$95

MINNESOTA

56   Quarry at Giants Ridge
     Biwabik $45–$75

76   Deacon's Lodge
     Breezy Point $60–$106

MISSISSIPPI

32   Dancing Rabbit (Azaleas)
     Philadelphia $55–$99

90   Grand Bear
     Saucier $89–$135

MISSOURI

74   Branson Creek GC
     Hollister $48–$94

MONTANA

84   Old Works
     Anaconda $29–$57

NEBRASKA

50   Wild Horse Golf Club
     Gothenburg $34.80–$52.75

NEVADA

8   Shadow Creek
     North Las Vegas $500

39   Cascata
     Boulder City $350–$550

49   Wynn Las Vegas
     Las Vegas $500

54   Reflection Bay at Lake Las Vegas
     Henderson $110–$270

58   Wolf Creek GC
     Mesquite $85–$185

NEW JERSEY

67   Pine Hill
     Pine Hill $79–$99

NEW MEXICO

30   Paa-Ko Ridge
     Sandia Park $57–$89

35   Black Mesa
     La Mesilla $59–$82

NEW YORK

7   Bethpage State Park (Black)
     Farmingdale $41–$102

61   Atunyote at Turning Stone Resort
     Verona $150–$200

64   Shenandoah at Turning Stone
     Verona $80–$125

NORTH CAROLINA

6   Pinehurst (No. 2)
     Pinehurst $275–$375

40   Linville Golf Club
     Linville $95

45   Pine Needles Lodge & Golf Club
     Southern Pines $140–$175

99   Pinehurst (No. 8)
     Pinehurst $200–$250

NORTH DAKOTA

62   Hawktree GC
     Bismark $50–$60

OHIO

47   Longaberger
     Nashport $125

OKLAHOMA

51   Karsten Creek
     Stillwater $250

OREGON

1   Pacific Dunes
     Bandon $75–$240

5   Bandon Dunes
     Bandon $75–$240

10   Bandon Trails
     Bandon $75–$240

34   Crosswater at Sunriver
     Sunriver $105–$160

37   Pumpkin Ridge (Ghost Creek)
     Cornelius $50–$150

SOUTH CAROLINA

3   Kiawah Island Resort (Ocean Course)
     Kiawah Island $196–$305

15   Harbour Town Golf Links
     Hilton Head Island $135–$270

25   Caledonia Golf & Fish Club
     Pawleys Island $80–$190

46   Dunes Golf & Beach Club
     Myrtle Beach $160

53   May River Course at Palmetto Bluff
     Bluffton $240

95   Barefoot Resort (Love)
     North Myrtle Beach $75–$155

TEXAS

68   Barton Creek (Fazio Foothills)
     Austin $135–$240

69   Barton Creek (Fazio Canyons)
     Austin $135–$240

VIRGINIA

18   The Homestead (Cascades)
     Hot Springs $210–$261

48   Golden Horseshoe (Gold)
     Williamsburg $48–$155

WASHINGTON

100 Gold Mountain Golf Complex (Olympic)
     Bremerton $35–$63

WEST VIRGINIA

52   The Greenbrier (Greenbrier)
     White Sulphur Springs $185–$350

WISCONSIN

4   Whistling Straits
     Haven $325

13   Blackwolf Run (River)
     Kohler $189–$214

75   Whistling Straits (Irish)
     Haven $53–$196

GOLF MAGAZINE'S THRIFTY 50 COURSES
THE 50 BEST U.S. COURSES FOR $50 OR LESS

ALDEEN GOLF CLUB
Rockford, IL
7,131 yards, par 72, 130/74.2
Greens fee: $45
888-425-3336, aldeengolfclub.com

With few elevation changes, Aldeen relies on other features to resist scoring: cleverly positioned moguls, auto-bogey bunkers, imposing trees, and dense rough. Aldeen demands both strategy and heroism—the latter at No. 8, a 203-yard, island-green par three that makes the 17th at Sawgrass look like a breeze.

AMANA COLONIES GOLF COURSE
Amana, IA
6,820 yards, par 72, 136/73.3
Greens fee: $50
800-383-3636, amanagolfcourse.com

This killer layout built within the Amana Colonies, a religious site on the National Register for Historic Places, was cut from 300 acres of solid timber. Unlike almost all of the surrounding land, it features natural elevation changes that create tricky lies, and blind shots from the lush fairways. The 18th calls for a drive out of a tree-lined chute to the fairway below, then an approach shot up a steep hill.

BIG CREEK GOLF & COUNTRY CLUB
Mountain Home, AR
7,320 yards, par 72, 135/76.0
Greens fee: $45
870-425-0333, bigcreekgolf.com

Big Creek sits on a fairly flat site (for the Ozarks), but its breathtaking mountain views won't let you forget where you are. Despite its lack of trees, the course keeps play exciting with long, fescue-lined holes and perplexing greens. There are a few breathers thrown in, but you'll find that holes 7, 8, and 9, a trio of bruising par fours, earns its nickname—the Gauntlet.

BIG MOUNTAIN GOLF
Kalispell, MT
7,015 yards, par 72, 72.5/121
Greens fee: $49
800-255-5641, golfmt.com

Previously called Northern Pines, the course remains essentially unchanged since its debut in 1996. Two-time U.S. Open champion Andy North and design partner Roger Packard kept it real: wide fairways, tough approach shots, and fair, fast greens. The back nine ambles alongside the Flathead River, with the tee shot on 14 requiring a nail-biting carry that would unnerve local boy Evel Knievel.

BLACK MESA GOLF CLUB
La Mesilla, NM
7,307 yards, par 72, 141/73.9
Greens fee: $50
505-747-8946, blackmesagolfclub.com

Architect Baxter Spann said of Black Mesa, "more than any other project, I eagerly anticipated every trip I made to this course." Golfers can understand why. Located north of Santa Fe, the layout features a routing that carpets the land between rough sandstone peaks. Deceptive target areas, blind shots, narrow chutes, and 150 bunkers give Spann's track a wild and strategic feel.

BUFFALO DUNES MUNICIPAL GOLF COURSE
Garden City, KS
6,774 yards, par 72, 127/72.1
Greens fee: $20
620-276-1210, garden-city.org/golfcourse

Buffalo Dunes isn't long, but its severe undulations will test shotmaking and creativity. And with soft, sandy soil muting roll and the wind normally blowing at 10 to 20 mph, you won't pine for a 7,000-yard layout. Lush fairways provide a contrast to the bordering sagebrush and native Kansas grasses. Locals simply call it "the gunch."

BUFFALO RUN GOLF COURSE
Commerce City, CO
7,411 yards, par 72, 129/74.5
Greens fee: $39
303-289-1500, buffalorungolfcourse.com

Formerly a flat, treeless buffalo ranch, this Keith Foster design is dotted with humps and hollows. There is little development to block the wind, so you'll need clever ground play to find Foster's slick greens. Ponds and streams protect several greens, but the 8th is guarded by a six-foot-deep buffalo "waller," where bison once wallowed.

CHICKASAW POINTE GOLF RESORT
Kingston, OK
7,085 yards, par 72, 125/74.5
Greens fee: $45
866-602-4653
oklahomagolf.com/pages/golf7.html

Chickasaw Pointe perches atop bluffs overlooking 93,000-acre Lake Texoma, providing stunning water views on 15 holes. Surprisingly, it's not water but the trees lining every hole that are the course's main defense. They are marked as lateral hazards to keep play moving. Hidden swales in the landing areas will either advance your ball or create awkward lies.

DEVIL'S THUMB GOLF CLUB
Delta, CO
7,176 yards, par 72, 132/72.9
Greens fee: $35
970-874-6262, deltagolf.org

The name refers to a rock that juts from the northwest portion of the property, which itself rises 500 feet above the remote town of Delta. The course is a treeless ribbon of mounded and hollowed fairways, which repeatedly climb to the tops of ridges, then dive into valleys. Bunkers and native grass areas catch errant drives.

DRAPER VALLEY GOLF CLUB
Draper, VA
7,070 yards, par 72, 127/73.5
Greens fee: $45
866-980-4653, drapervalleygolf.com

Highway engineer Harold Louthen, who helped build the Beltway in Washington, D.C., was a one-course wonder who completed Draper Valley in 1992. Off the tee, it's an open design, but your uphill and downhill approach shots will need to be precise. The old clubhouse, built about 1775, was home to the Draper family, whose liberated and popular daughters helped it earn the nickname "Bachelor's Retreat."

EAGLESTICKS GOLF CLUB
Zanesville, OH
6,508 yards, par 70, 120/70.1
Greens fee: $50
800-782-4493, eaglesticks.com

Transformed by Mike Hurdzan from a horse farm into a compact course set on fewer than 140 acres, Eaglesticks still manages to offer hole-to-hole seclusion. Its lush, rolling landscape provides few even lies, and the rough can get lose-your-ball thick. Sections of the farm's wooden corncrib now serve as footbridges over rocky streams, evoking the Zanesville of a century ago.

THE FORT GOLF COURSE
Indianapolis, IN
7,148 yards, par 72, 139/74.5
Greens fee: $50
317-543-9597
golfus.com/thefort/home.htm

Just eight miles from dead-flat downtown Indianapolis lies a topographical aberration, a delightfully undulating, heavily wooded course by Pete Dye. The Fort combines its natural defenses with those Dye is known for: forced carries for better players, pins best accessed with a cut or draw, and a great balance of holes.

GOLD MOUNTAIN GOLF COMPLEX
Bremerton, WA
7,073 yards, par 72, 131/73.5
Greens fee: $35–$63
360-415-5432, goldmt.com

Gold Mountain is the epitome of the scenic, unspoiled Pacific Northwest, but its beauty is more than skin deep. A smart layout emphasizing accurate shots into the contoured greens, it's as thought-provoking as it is visually inspiring. The guy trailing in the final match of the 2006 U.S. Amateur Public Links Championship will have plenty to consider at the almost-driveable par-four 18th.

THE GOLF CLUB AT FLEMING ISLAND
Orange Park, FL
6,801 yards, par 71, 136/72.7
Greens fee: $49
888-244-9167, flemingislandgolf.com

This Jacksonville–area stunner was designed by Bobby Weed, a Pete Dye protégé who also worked on several TPC courses. That experience served him well at Fleming Island, where Weed transformed a flat site into the wide-open, mounded front nine and the wooded, marshy back nine. The contoured edges of his greens repel mediocre shots.

GOLF CLUB AT YANKEE TRACE
(CHAMPIONSHIP COURSE)
Centerville, OH
7,139 yards, par 72, 136/74.1
Greens fee: $47
800-438-4654, yankeetrace.org

Yankee Trace rolls gently, but its manicured fairways produce tighter than normal lies. Running your ball up to the greens is no problem, although stopping it on these 12-Stimpers can be. From 1999 to 2003, the course hosted the Nationwide Tour's Dayton Open, and its everyday conditions vary little from tournament shape.

GRAY PLANTATION
Lake Charles, LA
7,196 yards, par 72, 137/75.0
Greens fee: $50
337-562-1663, graywood.net

Considered by many to be one of Louisiana's top five courses, Gray Plantation is a delicate mix of Southern charm and Cajun fire. On many early holes, architect Rocky Roquemore provided generous landing areas between towering pines and 60 acres of lakes, ponds, and streams. Later on, however, there are several forced carries, including approaches to island greens at the 6th and 17th.

HAWK RUN GOLF COURSE
Findlay, OH
7,155 yards, par 72, 132/74.4
Greens fee: $40
877-484-3429, redhawkrun.com

Fortunately for golfers, designers Arthur Hills and Steve Forrest were able to devote 250 of this development's 350 acres to the golf course. Red Hawk Run keeps you guessing: Fairway bunkers make landing areas appear narrower than they are; the thick native areas swallow offline drives; and the unpredictable wind plays havoc with approach shots.

HAWKTREE GOLF CLUB
Bismarck, ND
7,085 yards, par 72, 137/75.2
Greens fee: $60
888-465-4295, hawktree.com

Known for dramatic designs, Jim Engh took what was virtually the only land within hundreds of miles that had natural elevation changes and made the most of them. At times you're perched atop gigantic mounds that make even the longest holes look drivable. At others you're down in quiet valleys. The wind is often so severe that the Hawktree staff suggests playing different tees from hole to hole.

LASSING POINTE GOLF COURSE
Union, KY
6,720 yards, par 71, 132/72.2
Greens fee: $37
859-384-2266, boonecountyky.org

Much of this track's appeal comes from an idyllic location of natural hilly and flat areas, affording player-friendly fairways. Lassing Pointe also boasts some of the largest and best-conditioned greens in the area—one of which, on the 18th, is 101 yards long—plus plenty of water hazards, tall native grasses and 63 well-placed bunkers.

THE LINKS AT HIAWATHA LANDING
Apalachin, NY
7,104 yards, par 72, 133/74.4
Greens fee: $45
607-687-6952, hiawathalinks.com

You can get to this superb course in three hours from New York City . . . with a tailwind, that is. Known for its challenge and impeccable conditioning, the Links calls for no forced carries or blind shots, but drives must be threaded through narrow corridors of bunkers and fescue. The par-five 18th is a great closer, reachable in two if you can carry the pond that runs up the left side.

THE LINKS OF NORTH DAKOTA
Williston, ND
7,092 yards, par 72, 128/75.1
Greens fee: $50
701-568-2600, thelinksofnorthdakota.com

Here's a real-life "field of dreams" that includes fescue so lethal it spawned a local drop-where-it-entered rule. Nearly 90 cavernous bunkers and eye-tearing wind off Lake Sakakawea make every round feel like the British Open. Elevation changes are benign except for the 100-foot drop on the par-three 17th, but the playing angles and passageways are cause for contemplation.

THE MOORS GOLF & LODGING
Milton, FL
6,828 yards, par 70, 126/72.9
Greens fee: $47
800-727-1010, moors.com

The Moors has been a Champions Tour stop for the past decade, hosting the Blue Angels Classic (formerly the Emerald Coast Classic). The mostly treeless landscape, mounding, and 80-plus bunkers impart the appearance of a links. Add a bit of wind, and you've got a minefield ahead of you, although on most holes there is a safe route to the green.

NORTHWOOD GOLF COURSE
Rhinelander, WI

6,724 yards, par 72, 140/73.1

Greens fee: $34

715-282-6565, northwoodgolfclub.com

Northwood's holes are so insulated by dense forest that you could play naked without fear of embarrassment. While the fairways are generous, the towering trees are more like maximum-security prison than plain old jail. Bunkers are placed on the far side of doglegs to catch balls from running too far. Here being in the rough is bliss.

OGLEBAY RESORT (JONES COURSE)
Wheeling, WV

7,001 yards, par 71, 137/72.1

Greens fee: $42

800-752-9436

oglebay-resort.com/speidel.htm

One of Robert Trent Jones's first public projects, the pride of Oglebay became the 11-year home of the LPGA's Wheeling Ladies' Classic soon after it opened in 1971. Finding the proper landing areas off the tee is a must if you want a flat lie, which helps when playing to the elevated, well-bunkered greens.

OLD SILO GOLF CLUB
Mount Sterling, KY

6,977 yards, par 72, 139/74.5

Greens fee: $49

859-498-4697, oldsilo.com

The middle of Kentucky horse country is an intriguing place for Aussie Graham Marsh's first U.S. design. Marsh made the most of it: Old Silo features stacked rock, lone fairway trees, and 96 well-placed bunkers. The 6th hole offers a view of the namesake silo, followed by a 90-foot drop to the fairway and a creek in front of the green.

OLD WORKS
Anaconda, MT

7,705 yards, par 72, 133/76.0

Greens fee: $41

406-563-5989, oldworks.org

This Jack Nicklaus Signature course built atop a Federal EPA Superfund cleanup site makes golden use of the Bear's design expertise. The holes make the best use of the land's natural elevation changes while guiding you past embedded remains of a former copper smelter. Nicklaus filled the bunkers with black coal slag, a byproduct of the copper smelting process.

PACIFIC GROVE MUNICIPAL GOLF COURSE
Pacific Grove, CA

5,732 yards, par 70, SLP/RTG

Greens fee: $38

831-648-5777, ci.pg.ca.us/golf/default.htm

Bag your 3-iron and replace it with a camera. Every hole on the back nine at Pacific Grove, designed in 1960 by Pebble Beach architect Jack Neville, has a view of Monterey Bay. Most are framed by white-sand dunes and gnarled cypress trees. Neville's narrow fairways and tiny greens are hemmed in by those same cypresses, as well as pines and oaks. Play it safe when you can.

PAPAGO GOLF COURSE
Phoenix, AZ

7,068 yards, par 72, 132/73.3

Greens fee: $35

602-275-8428

ci.phoenix.az.us/sports/papago.html

Much of Papago's appeal comes from its traditional parkland style, a unique look in an area filled with desert golf. Here golfers encounter 20 to 30 yards of rough before tiptoeing through the cacti. Instead of rugged canyons or arroyos, they are treated to an unbroken trail of green fairways populated by mature palm, eucalyptus, and pine trees.

PIÑON HILLS GOLF COURSE
Farmington, NM

7,249 yards, par 72, 139/73.9

Greens fee: $38

505-326-6066

fmtn.org/depts/parks/golf/phills.html

This bargain track sits on land that looks untouched since the beginning of time; the fairways run alongside otherworldly landforms, snake around huge rock outcroppings, and bound over deep canyons. The greens are large, fast, and multitiered, making three-, four-, and even five-putts common. The rare occasion of slow play, however, is usually caused by picture taking.

PIPER GLEN GOLF CLUB
Springfield, IL
6,985 yards, par 72, 132/73.5
Greens fee: $33
217-483-6537, piperglen.com

Piper Glen makes the most of its hilly site, with stands of 200-foot oaks and a creek running throughout. You won't find boring, flat greens here, to the delight of the Midwestern clientele. In fact, the greens are so exciting and the terrain so distinctive that golfers from as far away as St. Louis gladly drive 90 miles to tee up.

PRAIRIE HIGHLANDS GOLF COURSE
Olathe, KS
7,066 yards, par 72, 129/74.5
Greens fee: $49
913-856-7235, prairiehighlands.com

Prairie Highlands is expertly integrated into a rolling landscape with course conditions said to be the best in the Kansas City area. In fact, local pros often drop by just to use the true-rolling practice green. Some landing areas lean back toward the tees, minimizing roll. The clubhouse is a funky, post-modern gem.

RADISSON GREENS
Baldwinsville, NY
7,010 yards, par 72, 134/74.2
Greens fee: $37
315-638-0092, radissongreens.com

By 1978, when Radisson Greens was finished, Robert Trent Jones was no longer able to make many site visits to his projects, but his talented associates stepped in. Nevertheless, at more than 7,000 tree-lined yards, Radisson Greens has more than its share of the classic Jones bite. Why the $37 greens fee? Until recently, Syracuse had more golf courses than the locals could play. Even now, the course's Web site says that tee times are only "recommended."

THE RAWLS COURSE
Lubbock, TX
7,207 yards, par 72, 126/73.2
Greens fee: $42
806-742-4653, texastechgolf.ttu.edu

Tom Doak turned an old cotton field into the rounded, mounded home of the Texas Tech golf team. The surrounding topography of canyons and mesas is as forceful and imposing as is the West Texas wind. Innovative and tricky, Doak's design could potentially frustrate golfers into imitating Tech basketball coach Bobby Knight's outbursts.

RIVERDALE (DUNES)
Brighton, CO
7,067 yards, par 72, 129/72.1
Greens fee: $40
303-659-6700, riverdalegolf.com

The site of the 1993 U.S. Amateur Public Links Championship, this Pete and Perry Dye creation 20 miles northeast of Denver is a wily layout. Twelve holes play along or across water, and 10 bottomless pot bunkers stand ready to claim errant shots. The fairways are wide, but beware the tall fescue, which turns a breathtaking shade of gold in the fall.

ROCK HOLLOW GOLF CLUB
Peru, IN
6,944 yards, par 72, 132/74.0
Greens fee: $45
765-473-6100, rockhollowgolf.com

Built on a former gravel quarry mined by the family of PGA Tour player Chris Smith, this layout was hollowed out 30 to 40 feet below ground. Impressive elevation changes, unique land shapes, and, of course, lots and lots of rocks contribute to a decidedly un-Hoosier landscape. The addition of mature trees and vegetation creates distinct environments to play through...and over.

RUSTIC CANYON GOLF COURSE
Moorpark, CA
6,900 yards, par 72, 128/73.3
Greens fee: $50
805-530-0221, rusticcanyongolfcourse.com

Surrounded by the rugged walls of a desert canyon and lined with native grasses, cactus, and wildflower beds, Rustic Canyon would look at home in the Australian Outback. Subtle ripples and rolls unlock the best paths to the greens, which are encircled by close-cropped collection areas. For average players, this creates welcome shot options, for better players, indecision.

SANTA ANA GOLF CLUB
(TAMAYA/CHEENA COURSE)
Santa Ana Pueblo, NM
7,239 yards, par 71, 132/74.1
Greens fee: $42
505-867-9464, santaanagolf.com

Sloping greens are the focal point at this lush oasis within the Santa Ana Pueblo tribe's 77,000 acres of sacred desert. Stimpmeter readings up to 10 mean that on some greens players struggle just to two-putt. Clever mounding lines the fairways and offers plenty of friendly kicks, saving errant shots from the waist-high desert brush.

SHENNECOSSETT GOLF COURSE
Groton, CT
6,562 yards, par 71, 122/71.5
Greens fee: $40
860-445-0262, town.groton.ct.us/
depts/parksrec/shenny.asp

Shennecossett's first four holes were built in 1898, but Donald Ross later got his hands on the place—and it remains the only public course in the state that he designed. In 1997 the town of Groton, which owns the course, built three new holes overlooking the Thames River and Long Island Sound, turning a perennially solid muni into one of the deals of the century.

SOUTHERN HILLS GOLF CLUB
Hawkinsville, GA
6,741 yards, par 72, 134/72.7
Greens fee: $22
478-783-0600, southernhillsgolf.com

This hilly site in central Georgia wouldn't grow cotton or peanuts, but grass took to Southern Hills like gravy on biscuits. Today the course is known for its near-perfect conditioning. A thinking man's layout, it winds around creeks, trees, and bunkers. The back nine opens with a short par 4 and a go-for-it par five—a green light to go low.

SPIRIT HOLLOW GOLF COURSE
Burlington, IA
7,021 yards, par 72, 129/73.6
Greens fee: $45
319-752-0004, spirithollowgolfcourse.com

Just a few 3-woods from the Mississippi River, Spirit Hollow winds through stacks of 100-year-old trees and 40- to 80-foot elevation drops. These features are integrated into visually intimidating holes that actually play with compassion. A service-oriented staff takes food and drink orders via cart-mounted GPS and delivers the goods on the course.

STONEBRIDGE GOLF CLUB
Rome, GA
6,835 yards, par 72, 128/73
Greens fee: $32
706-236-5046, romestonebridge.com

Architect Arthur Davis designed a third of Stonebridge's holes with some type of carry—water, mounds, marshes, or green-fronting bunkers—amid the tall pines and gentle hills that characterize the course. Davis likes to include an island-type feature in his designs, and here it's on No. 9, a 550-yarder with two peninsula fairways and bunkers that bedevil the entire right side.

THE SUMMIT GOLF CLUB
Cannon Falls, MN
7,022 yards, par 72, 138/74.6
Greens fee: $40
507-263-4648, summitgolfclub.com

Thanks to holes that drop 100 feet, tree-lined chutes, and rock ledges dotting fairways and greens, first-timers often rush to tell their friends about one of the Midwest's most stunning courses. But the Summit is more than scenic. Its two closing holes have dramatic forced carries—across a valley on No. 17 and then over a pond on No. 18.

THE TENNESSEAN GOLF CLUB
Paris, TN
7,183 yards, par 72, 136/74.6
Greens fee: $35
866-710-4653, tennesseangolfclub.com

A Keith Foster–designed roller coaster, the Tennessean was cut from a dense forest that provided cover for thousands of critters and a least one moonshine still or two. The holes scramble up and down the steep terrain, calling for shots that must avoid rock outcroppings, chasms and creeks. You'll find two streams on the monster 630-yard 15th hole.

TEXARKANA GOLF RANCH
Texarkana, TX
7,370 yards, par 72
Greens fee: $24
903-334-7401, hankhaney.com

GOLF MAGAZINE Top 100 Teacher Hank Haney charges more than $350 for a lesson, yet a round at his latest golf ranch costs little more than a good Texas T-bone. The course cuts through woodlands surrounding Bringle Lake, with eight exciting holes along its shoreline. The par-three 5th even has a natural island green—234 yards from the tee.

TOKATEE GOLF CLUB
McKenzie Bridge, OR
6,806 yards, par 72, 126/72.0
Greens fee: $39
800-452-6376, tokatee.com

Tokatee is a Chinook word meaning "place of restful beauty," and on the course you feel miles (or centuries) away from city life. A few wide-open holes lead players into the majestic trees, and the rest of the easy-walking layout, completed in 1969, remains true to its rugged roots. Rough-hewn hills serve as the backdrops for many greens.

TWISTED GUN GOLF COURSE
Wharncliffe, WV
7,015 yards, par 72, 124/73.1
Greens fee: $30
304-664-9100, twistedgungolf.com

To build the mountainous coalfield region's first 18-hole course two miles up on a mountaintop, the developers blew the top off a peak. The resulting crater was filled in with 80 million cubic yards of dirt. Twisted Gun is a firm and fast track, relying mainly on wind, tall grass, and mesmerizing views to create a memorable challenge.

VALLEY VIEW GOLF COURSE
Layton, UT
7,147 yards, par 72, 127/73.2
Greens fee: $24
801-546-1630, golfingutah.com/valleyview

The clubhouse and 9th and 18th holes occupy a plateau overlooking the Wasatch Mountains; the rest of the holes are routed through a valley with a menacing creek never too far away. Valley View's challenges include elevated tees, sidehill lies, and demanding shots. Less precise players can survive out here, too, mainly because the rough won't eat you alive.

WAILUA GOLF COURSE
Lihue, HI
6,981 yards, par 72, 129/73.3
Greens fee: $44
808-241-6666

Despite being built a few holes at a time, Wailua hangs together well. Many holes dogleg around stands of stalwart palm and pine trees, but Wailua is otherwise wide open, allowing Hawaii's legendary trade winds to challenge golfers. Perhaps the best thing about the course is its local, laid-back feel— something the big Hawaiian resorts can't match.

WILD HORSE GOLF CLUB
Gothenburg, NE
6,865 yards, par 72, 125/73.0
Greens fee: $35
308-537-7700, playwildhorse.com

A windswept, treeless beauty, Wild Horse strikes a perfect balance between modern manicuring and natural ruggedness. The challenge is playing to the weak side of the cavernous bunkers, landing the ball short of lightning-fast greens and, above all, avoiding the three-foot-high native grass. The entire project was completed for just $1.5 million, and that includes $500,000 to build the clubhouse.

WILLINGER'S GOLF CLUB
Northfield, MN
6,809 yards, par 72, 150/74.4
Greens fee: $42
952-440-7000, willingersgc.com

Garrett Gill, a prolific Midwestern architect, transformed this secluded site from a tree nursery into two distinct nines. The front side is flatter but demands carries over water, wetlands, and sand. The back is wooded and offers dramatic elevation changes, but its hazards are mostly aesthetic. Don't expect a lot of extras here; this is golf, pure and simple.

GOLF MAGAZINE'S 25 BEST GOLF SCHOOLS

Academy of Golf Dynamics
Austin, TX; Colorado Springs, CO
Price: $995–$1,050*
$1,325 (lodging)
800-879-2008
golfdynamics.com

Arnold Palmer Golf Academy
Orlando, FL
Price: $641–$855
800-523-5999
apga.com

Butch Harmon School of Golf
Las Vegas, NV
Price: $2,900–$5,100
(no commuter rates available)
702-777-2444
butchharmon.com

Craft-Zavichas Golf School
St. George, UT;
Pueblo and Denver, CO
Price: $850–$995
800-858-9633
czgolfschool.com

Dana Rader Golf School
Charlotte, NC
Price: $695–$750
704-542-7635
danarader.com

Dave Pelz Scoring Game Schools
45 clinic locations including:
Boca Raton, FL; Cordillera, CO;
Homestead, MI; Napa and
Palm Springs, CA; Reynolds
Plantation, GA
Price: $2,375–$2,490
512-263-7668
pelzgolf.com

David Leadbetter Golf Academy
Champion's Gate, FL
Price: $900–$3,000
888-633-5323
davidleadbetter.com

Dr. David Wright's Golf Schools
Mission Viejo, Fallbrook, and
Indio, CA
Price: $1,395
888-620-4653
mindunderpar.com

Extraordinary Golf
Carmel and Palm Springs, CA
Price: $1,490
800-541-2444
extraordinarygolf.com

Golf54
Phoenix, AZ
Price: $1,295–$1,495
602-482-8983
golf54.com

Golf Schools of Scottsdale
Scottsdale, AZ; Quechee, VT
Price: $510–$995
800-356-6675
azgolfschool.com

Grand Cypress Academy of Golf
Orlando, FL
Price: $1,350–$1,915
800-790-7377
grandcypress.com

Innisbrook Troon Golf Institute
Palm Harbor, FL
Price: $800
727-942-5283
golfinnisbrookresort.com

Jim McLean Golf Schools
La Quinta, CA; Miami and
Weston, FL; Williamsburg, MI;
Bahamas
Price: $995–$3,950
800-723-6725
jimmclean.com

**Kip Puterbaugh's Aviara
Golf Academy**
Carlsbad, CA
Price: $1,650
800-433-7468
aviaragolfacademy.com

Kostis/McCord Learning Center
Scottsdale, AZ
Price: $1,995–$2,295
480-502-2656
kostismccordlearning.com

Martin Green Golf Academy
Panama City Beach and West
Palm Beach, FL; Albuquerque,
NM; New York, NY
Price: $1,435
800-814-7824
mgga.net

McGetrick Golf Academy
Denver, CO
Price: $700
800-494-1818
mcgetrick.com

Phil Ritson–Mel Sole Golf School
Pawleys Island, SC; Atlanta, GA;
Wilmington, NC; Kansas City,
MO; Ellicottville, NY; Malinalco,
Mexico
Price: $395–$595
800-624-4653
ritson-sole.com

Pinehurst Golf Advantage School
Pinehurst, NC
Price: $1,425–$2,240
(no commuter rate available)
866-291-4427
pinehurst.com

Pine Needles Learning Center
Southern Pines, NC
Price: $1,295–$2,095
(no commuter rate available)
800-747-7272
pineneedles-midpines.com

Resort Golf Schools
Scottsdale, Phoenix and
Tucson, AZ; Las Vegas, NV;
Naples and St. Augustine, FL
Traveling school visits 25 cities.
Price: $525–$795
888-373-7555
resortgolf.com

Rick Smith Golf Academy
Gaylord, MI; Naples, FL
Price: $1,475–$2,200
800-444-6711 ext.2485
treetops.com

Todd Sones Impact Golf
Vernon Hills, IL;
St. Augustine, FL
Price: $495 (one-day school)
847-549-8678
toddsones.com

Tradition Golf School
Pawleys Island, SC
Price: $399–$459
800-397-2678
traditiongolfschool.com

*Price ranges are the commuter rate for a
three-day school unless otherwise noted.

291

GOLF MAGAZINE'S **TOP 100 COURSES IN THE U.S.**

1   Pine Valley, Clementon, NJ
Crump/Colt (1918)

2   Cypress Point, Pebble Beach, CA
Mackenzie (1929)

3   Augusta National, Augusta, GA
Mackenzie/Jones (1932)

4   Shinnecock Hills, Southampton, NY
Toomey/Flynn (1931)

5   Pebble Beach GL, Pebble Beach, CA
Neville/Grant (1919), Egan

6   Sand Hills GC, Mullen, NE
Coore/Crenshaw (1995)

7   Merion (East), Ardmore, PA
H. Wilson (1912)

8   Pacific Dunes, Bandon, OR
Doak (2001)

9   Oakmont, Oakmont, PA
Fownes (1903)

10 Pinehurst (No. 2), Pinehurst, NC
D. Ross (1903–35)

11 National GL of America, Southampton, NY
Macdonald (1911)

12 Seminole, North Palm Beach, FL
D. Ross (1929), D. Wilson

13 Crystal Downs, Frankfort, MI
Mackenzie/Maxwell (1929)

14 San Francisco GC, San Francisco, CA
Tillinghast (1915)

15 Prairie Dunes, Hutchinson, KS
Maxwell (1935–56)

16 Winged Foot (West), Mamaroneck, NY
Tillinghast (1923)

17 Fishers Island, Fishers Island, NY
Raynor (1917)

18 Oakland Hills (South), Bloomfield, MI
D. Ross (1917), R.T Jones Sr.

19 Bethpage (Black), Farmingdale, NY
Tillinghast (1935), Rees Jones (1998)

20 Chicago GC, Wheaton, IL
Macdonald (1895), Raynor

21 The Country Club (Open), Brookline, MA
W. Campbell (1895), Flynn, Rees Jones

22 Riviera, Pacific Palisades, CA
Thomas/Bell (1926)

23 Muirfield Village, Dublin, OH
Nicklaus/Muirhead (1974)

24 Oak Hill (East), Rochester, NY
D. Ross (1926), R.T. Jones Sr., G. & T. Fazio

25 Baltusrol (Lower), Springfield, NJ
Tillinghast (1922), R.T. Jones Sr.

26 Olympic (Lake), San Francisco, CA
Reid (1917), Whiting, R.T. Jones Sr.

27 Southern Hills, Tulsa, OK
Maxwell (1935)

28 Whistling Straits (Straits), Haven, WI
Pete Dye (1998)

29 TPC at Sawgrass (Stadium), Ponte Vedra, FL
Pete Dye (1981)

30 Los Angeles CC (North), Los Angeles, CA
Thomas (1921)

31 The Golf Club, New Albany, OH
Pete Dye (1967)

32 Medinah (No. 3), Medinah, IL
Bendelow (1928), Collis, Packard

33 Kiawah Island (Ocean), Kiawah Island, SC
Pete Dye (1991)

34 Harbour Town, Hilton Head Island, SC
Dye/Nicklaus (1969)

35 Quaker Ridge, Scarsdale, NY
Tillinghast (1926), R.T. Jones Sr.

36 Winged Foot (East), Mamaroneck, NY
Tillinghast (1923)

37 Inverness, Toledo, OH
D. Ross (1919), G. & T. Fazio, Hills

38 Maidstone, East Hampton, NY
W. & J. Park (1891), Tucker

39 Garden City GC, Garden City, NY
Emmet (1898), Travis

40 Bandon Dunes, Bandon, OR
D. Kidd (1999)

41 Friar's Head, Baiting Hollow, NY
Coore/Crenshaw (2003)

42 Shoreacres, Lake Bluff, IL
Raynor (1919)

43 Scioto, Columbus, OH
D. Ross (1916), D. Wilson

44 Somerset Hills, Bernardsville, NJ
Tillinghast (1917)

45 Congressional (Blue), Bethesda, MD
Emmet (1924), R.T. Jones Sr., Rees Jones

46 Shadow Creek, North Las Vegas, NV
T. Fazio/Wynn (1989)

47 Bandon Trails, Bandon, OR
Coore/Crenshaw (2005)

48 Trump National, Bedminster, NJ
T. Fazio (2004)

49 Spyglass Hill, Pebble Beach, CA
R.T. Jones Sr. (1966)

50 Camargo, Cincinnati, OH
Raynor (1921)

51 Ocean Forest, Sea Island, GA
Rees Jones (1995)

52 East Lake, Atlanta, GA
Bendelow (1910), D.Ross, Cobb, Rees Jones

53 Wade Hampton, Cashiers, NC
T. Fazio (1987)

54 Colonial CC, Fort Worth, TX
Bredemus (1935), Maxwell

55 Peachtree, Atlanta, GA
R.T. Jones Sr./Bob Jones (1948)

56 Cascades (Upper), Hot Springs, VA
Flynn (1923)

57 The Honors Course, Ooltewah, TN
Pete Dye (1984)

58 Valley Club of Montecito, Santa Barbara, CA
Mackenzie/Hunter (1928)

59 Yeamans Hall, Hanahan, SC
Raynor (1925), Doak

60 Torrey Pines (South), La Jolla, CA
W. Bell (1926), Rees Jones (2001)

61   Cherry Hills, Englewood, CO
     Flynn (1923)

62   Olympia Fields (North), Olympia Fields, IL
     Park (1922)

63   Baltimore CC (Five Farms E.), Timonium, MD
     Tillinghast (1926), Silva

64   Briar's Creek, Johns Island, SC
     Rees Jones (2002)

65   Plainfield, Plainfield, NJ
     D. Ross (1920)

66   World Woods (Pine Barrens), Brooksville, FL
     T. Fazio (1993)

67   Hazeltine National, Chaska, MN
     R.T. Jones Sr. (1962), Rees Jones

68   Baltusrol (Upper), Springfield, NJ
     Tillinghast (1923), Rees Jones

69   Piping Rock, Locust Valley, NY
     Macdonald/Raynor (1913)

70   Myopia Hunt Club, So. Hamilton, MA
     Leeds (1896)

71   Pasatiempo, Santa Cruz, CA
     Mackenzie (1929)

72   Kittansett, Marion, MA
     Hood (1923)

73   Trump International, West Palm Beach, FL
     Jim Fazio (1999)

74   Pete Dye GC, Bridgeport, WV
     Pete Dye (1994)

75   Milwaukee CC, River Hills, WI
     Colt/Alison (1929)

76   Forest Highlands, Flagstaff, AZ
     Weiskopf/Morrish (1988)

77   Yale University, New Haven, CT
     Macdonald (1926)

78   Long Cove, Hilton Head Island, SC
     Pete Dye (1981)

79   Desert Forest, Carefree, AZ
     Lawrence (1962)

80   Double Eagle, Galena, OH
     Weiskopf/Morrish (1991)

81   Newport CC, Newport, RI
     W. Davis (1894), Tillinghast, D. Ross

82   Bel-Air CC, Los Angeles, CA
     Thomas/Bell (1926)

83   The Creek, Locust Valley, NY
     Macdonald/Raynor (1925)

84   Cascata, Boulder City, NV
     Rees Jones (2000)

85   Black Diamond (Quarry), Lecanto, FL
     T. Fazio (1987)

86   Holston Hills, Knoxville, TN
     D. Ross (1927)

87   Canterbury, Cleveland, OH
     Strong (1922)

88   Firestone (South), Akron, OH
     R.T. Jones Sr. (1959), Nicklaus

89   Crooked Stick, Carmel, IN
     Pete Dye (1964)

90   The Bridge, Bridgehampton, NY
     Rees Jones (2002)

91   Ridgewood (West/East), Paramus, NJ
     Tillinghast (1929)

92   Calusa Pines, Naples, FL
     Fry (2003)

93   Bellerive, Creve Coeur, MO
     R.T. Jones Sr. (1959)

94   Wannamoisett, Rumford, RI
     D. Ross (1916)

95   Sea Island (Seaside), St. Simons Island, GA
     Colt/Alison (1928), Lee, T. Fazio

96   Interlachen, Edina, MN
     Watson (1910), D. Ross, R.T. Jones Sr.

97   Atlantic GC, Bridgehampton, NY
     Rees Jones (1992)

98   Lehigh, Allentown, PA
     Toomey/Flynn (1928)

99   Salem CC, Peabody, MA
     D. Ross (1926)

100 Blackwolf Run (River), Kohler, WI
     Dye (1988)

GOLF MAGAZINE'S TOP 100 COURSES IN THE WORLD

1   Pine Valley, Clementon, NJ
Crump/Colt (1918)

2   Cypress Point, Pebble Beach, CA
Mackenzie (1929)

3   St. Andrews (Old Course),
St. Andrews, Scotland
(15th century)

4   Augusta National, Augusta, GA
Mackenzie/Jones (1932)

5   Shinnecock Hills, Southampton, NY
Toomey/Flynn (1931)

6   Pebble Beach, Pebble Beach, CA
Neville/Grant (1919), Egan

7   Muirfield, Gullane, Scotland
T. Morris (1891), Colt, Simpson

8   Sand Hills GC Mullen, NE
Coore/Crenshaw (1995)

9   Royal County Down,
Newcastle, Northern Ireland
T. Morris (1889), Dunn,Vardon

10   Royal Melbourne (Composite),
Melbourne, Australia
Mackenzie/Russell (1926)

11   Merion (East), Ardmore, PA
H. Wilson (1912)

12   Royal Portrush (Dunluce),
Portrush, Northern Ireland
Colt (1929)

13   Pacific Dunes, Bandon, OR
Doak (2001)

14   Oakmont, Oakmont, PA
Fownes (1903)

15   Royal Dornoch, Dornoch, Scotland
T. Morris (1886), Sutherland, Duncan

16   Ballybunion (Old), Ballybunion, Ireland
Murphy (1906), Simpson, Gourlay

17   Turnberry (Ailsa), Turnberry, Scotland
P. M. Ross (1906)

18   Pinehurst (No. 2), Pinehurst, NC
D. Ross (1903–35)

19   National Golf Links of America,
Southampton, NY
Macdonald (1911)

20   Kingston Heath, Melbourne, Australia
Soutar (1925), Mackenzie

21   Carnoustie (Championship),
Carnoustie, Scotland
Robertson (1842), Park, Braid

22   Seminole, North Palm Beach, FL
D. Ross (1929), D. Wilson

23   Crystal Downs, Frankfort, MI
Mackenzie/Maxwell (1929)

24   San Francisco GC, San Francisco, CA
Tillinghast (1915)

25   Prairie Dunes, Hutchinson, KS
Maxwell (1935–56)

26   Winged Foot (West), Mamaroneck, NY
Tillinghast (1923)

27   Cape Kidnappers, Hawke's Bay,
New Zealand
Doak (2004)

28   Fishers Island, Fishers Island, NY
Raynor (1917)

29   Oakland Hills (South), Bloomfield, MI
D. Ross (1917), R.T. Jones Sr.

30   Bethpage (Black), Farmingdale, NY
Tillinghast (1936), Rees Jones (1998)

31   Royal Birkdale, Southport, England
Lowe (1889), Hawtree/Taylor

32   Royal St. George's, Sandwich, England
Purves (1887), Mackenzie, Pennink

33   Chicago GC, Wheaton, IL
Macdonald (1895), Raynor

34   New South Wales, La Perouse, Australia
Mackenzie (1928)

35   Hirono, Kobe, Japan
C. Alison (1932)

36   The Country Club (Open) Brookline, MA
W. Campbell (1895), Flynn, Rees Jones

37   Riviera, Pacific Palisades, CA
Thomas/Bell (1926)

38   Muirfield Village, Dublin, OH
Nicklaus/Muirhead (1974)

39   Oak Hill (East), Rochester, NY
D. Ross (1926), R.T. Jones Sr., G. & T. Fazio

40   Royal Troon (Old), Troon, Scotland
Fernie (1878), Braid

41   Casa de Campo (Teeth of the Dog),
La Romana, Dominican Republic
Pete Dye (1971)

42   Baltusrol (Lower), Springfield, NJ
Tillinghast (1922), R.T. Jones Sr.

43   Portmarnock, Portmarnock, Ireland
G. Ross/Pickeman (1894), Hawtree

44   Olympic (Lake), San Francisco, CA
Reid (1917), Whiting, R.T. Jones Sr.

45   Southern Hills, Tulsa, OK
Maxwell (1935)

46   Sunningdale (Old), Sunningdale, England
W. Park (1901), Colt

47   Woodhall Spa, Woodhall Spa, England
Hotchkin/Hutchison (1905)

48   Whistling Straits (Straits), Haven, WI
Pete Dye (1998)

49   Barnbougle, Bridport, Tasmania, Australia
Doak (2004)

50   TPC at Sawgrass (Stadium), Ponte Vedra, FL
Pete Dye (1981)

51   Los Angeles CC (North), Los Angeles, CA
Thomas (1921)

52   Royal Lytham & St. Annes,
St. Annes on Sea, England
Lowe (1886)

53 The Golf Club, New Albany, OH
Pete Dye (1967)

54 Royal Adelaide, Adelaide, Australia
Gardiner (1904), Mackenzie

55 Medinah (No. 3), Medinah, IL
Bendelow (1928), Collis, Packard

56 Kiawah Island (Ocean), Kiawah Island, SC
Pete Dye (1991)

57 Morfontaine, Senlis, France
Simpson (1927)

58 Kauri Cliffs, Kerikeri, New Zealand
David Harman (2000)

59 Harbour Town, Hilton Head Island, SC
Dye/Nicklaus (1969)

60 Quaker Ridge, Scarsdale, NY
Tillinghast (1926), R.T. Jones Sr.

61 Winged Foot (East), Mamaroneck, NY
Tillinghast (1923)

62 Inverness, Toledo, OH
D. Ross (1919), G. & T. Fazio, Hills

63 Maidstone, East Hampton, NY
W. & J. Park (1891), Tucker

64 Garden City, Garden City, NY
Emmet (1898), Travis

65 Kingsbarns, St. Andrews, Scotland
K. Phillips (1999)

66 Loch Lomond, Luss, Scotland
Weiskopf/Morrish (1994)

67 Lahinch, Lahinch, County Clare, Ireland
T. Morris (1893), Gibson, Mackenzie

68 Ganton, Ganton, England
T. Dunn (1891), Colt, Cotton

69 Bandon Dunes, Bandon, OR
D.Kidd (1999)

70 Valderrama, Sotogrande, Spain
R.T. Jones Sr. (1975)

71 Cape Breton Highlands (Links),
Ingonish, Nova Scotia, Canada
Thompson (1935), Cooke

72 Royal Liverpool, Hoylake, England
G. Morris/Chambers (1869), Pennink

73 Cabo del Sol, Los Cabos, Mexico
Nicklaus (1994)

74 Friar's Head, Baiting Hollow, NY
Coore/Crenshaw (2003)

75 Shoreacres, Lake Bluff, IL
Raynor (1919)

76 Scioto, Columbus, OH
D. Ross (1916), D. Wilson

77 Somerset Hills, Bernardsville, NJ
Tillinghast (1917)

78 Cruden Bay, Cruden Bay, Scotland
Fowler/Simpson (1926)

79 Congressional (Blue), Bethesda, MD
Emmet (1924), R.T. Jones Sr., Rees Jones

80 Kawana (Fuji), Kawana, Japan
C. Alison/Fujita (1936)

81 Durban CC, Durban, South Africa
Waters/Waterman (1922), Hotchkin

82 St. George's, Islington, Ontario, Canada
Thompson (1929), Robinson

83 Shadow Creek, North Las Vegas, NV
T. Fazio/Wynn (1989)

84 Hamilton CC (West/South), Ancaster,
Ontario, Canada
Colt (1914), Rees Jones

85 Wentworth (West), Virginia Water, England
Colt/Morrison (1924)

86 Bandon Trails, Bandon, OR
Coore/Crenshaw (2005)

87 Trump National, Bedminster, NJ
T. Fazio (2004)

88 Spyglass Hill, Pebble Beach, CA
R.T. Jones Sr. (1966)

89 Camargo, Cincinnati, OH
Raynor (1921)

90 Ocean Forest, Sea Island, GA
Rees Jones (1995)

91 European Club, Brittas Bay, Ireland
Ruddy (1992)

92 Walton Heath (Old), Tadworth, England
Fowler (1904)

93 East Lake, Atlanta, GA
Bendelow (1910), D. Ross, Rees Jones

94 Tokyo GC, Sayama-City, Japan
Ohtani (1940)

95 Nine Bridges, Jeju Island, South Korea
Fream (2001)

96 Wade Hampton, Cashiers, NC
T. Fazio (1987)

97 Colonial CC, Fort Worth,TX
Bredemus (1935), Maxwell

98 Peachtree, Atlanta, GA
R.T. Jones Sr./Bob Jones (1948)

99 Cascades (Upper), Hot Springs, VA
Flynn (1923)

100 Naruo GC, Osaka, Japan
Crane (1904), C. Alison

GOLF.COM USER RATINGS

Visitors to golf.com and golfcourse.com can rank courses they have visited. Each course gets a score from 1 to 5, with 5 being the highest, in the following categories: condition, pace, service, value, and overall experience. The scores are then averaged to give a final user rating. To rate the courses you have played, go to golfcourse.com. Following are golf.com user ratings for many of the courses in this book. Courses for which ratings are unavailable do not appear in the following list.

NEW ENGLAND

MASSACHUSETTS

The Berkshires
Crumpin-Fox Club 4.5
Wahconah Country Club 4.7
Taconic Golf Club 4.7

Cape Cod
Waverly Oaks Golf Club 4.2
Pinehills Golf Club: Nicklaus 3.5, Jones 3.6
The Country Club at New Seabury:
　Dunes 3.0, Ocean 4.8
Farm Neck Golf Club 4.9
Mink Meadows Golf Club 5.0
Olde Barnstable Fairgrounds Golf Course 4.5
Captains Golf Course: Port 4.1
Cranberry Valley 3.5
Cape Cod National Golf Club 4.7
Highland Links 4.2

RHODE ISLAND

Newport
Green Valley Country Club 3.7
Exeter Country Club 4.1
Triggs Memorial Golf Course 3.6

VERMONT

The Equinox in Manchester
Gleneagles Golf Course 3.7
Stratton Mountain Country Club:
　Forest/Lake 3.4, Lake/Mountain 3.7,
　Mountain/Forest 4.5
Rutland Country Club 4.7
Tater Hill Golf Club 2.9

MID-ATLANTIC

NEW JERSEY

Atlantic City
Blue Heron Pines Golf Club:
　West 3.9, East 4.0
Shore Gate Golf Club 3.6
Seaview Marriott Resort & Spa:
　Bay 3.6, Pines 3.8
Sand Barrens Golf Club: North/South 3.8,
　South/West 4.2, West/North 3.8
McCullough's Emerald Golf Links 3.6
The Links at Brigantine Beach 4.2

NEW YORK

Lake Placid
Saranac Inn Golf Club 4.4
Lake Placid Resort & Golf Club:
　Links 3.5, Mountain 4.3
Whiteface Club & Resort 3.3
Craig Wood Golf Course 4.1

Long Island
Montauk Downs 4.4
Long Island National Golf Club 3.9
The Links at Shirley 3.9
Tallgrass Golf Club 4.2

PENNSYLVANIA

Laurel Highlands
Nemacolin Woodlands Resort:
　Mystic Rock 4.0, Woodlands Links 2.7
Seven Springs Mountain Resort:
　Mountaintop 4.2
Hidden Valley Resort 3.5

VIRGINIA

Williamsburg
Golden Horseshoe Golf Club:
　Gold Course 4.4, Green 4.4
Kingsmill Golf Club & Resort:
　River 4.1, Plantation 3.9
The Colonial Golf Course 4.1

Virginia Beach
The Signature at West Neck 4.4
Heron Ridge Golf Club 4.0
Bay Creek Golf Club: Palmer 4.9, Nicklaus 4.0
TPC at Virginia Beach 4.1

WEST VIRGINIA
The Greenbrier: Greenbrier Course 4.9,
　Old White Course 4.2, Meadows Course 4.5

WASHINGTON, D.C.
East Potomac Golf Course:
　Red 4.0, White 3.0, Blue 3.3
Rock Creek Golf Course 2.5
Langston Golf Course 3.3
Whiskey Creek Golf Club 4.0
P.B. Dye Golf Club 3.7
Raspberry Falls Golf & Hunt Club 3.6

SOUTH

ALABAMA

Robert Trent Jones Golf Trail
Hampton Cove: Highlands 3.4, River 3.5
The Shoals:
　Fighting Joe 4.8, The Schoolmaster 4.3
Silver Lakes: Backbreaker/Mindbreaker 4.3,
　Heartbreaker/Backbreaker 4.5, Mindbreaker/
　Heartbreaker 4.8
Oxmoor Valley: Valley 4.0, Ridge 4.6

Grand National: Links 4.7, Lake 4.6

Capitol Hill: Judge 4.3, Senator 4.5,
   Legislator 4.1

Cambrian Ridge: Canyon/Loblolly 3.8,
   Loblolly/Sherling 2.5, Sherling/Canyon 4.5

Highland Oaks: Highlands/Marshwood 3.8,
   Magnolia/Highlands 3.9, Marshwood/
   Magnolia 2.8

Magnolia Grove: Crossings 3.7, Falls 4.1

FLORIDA

The First Coast

Amelia Island Plantation: Ocean Links 4.1

The TPC of Sawgrass: Stadium 3.9, Valley 4.7

Sawgrass Country Club: East/South 5.0

Windsor Parke Golf Club 4.1

Hyde Park Golf Club 3.3

Orlando

Victoria Hills Golf Club 4.5

Walt Disney World Resort: Eagle Pines 3.9,
   Osprey Ridge 4.4, Palm 4.2, Magnolia 3.7,
   Lake Buena Vista 4.2, Oak Trail 4.4

Grand Cypress Resort: East/North 4.5,
   North/South 4.9, South/East 5.0

The Legacy Club at Alaqua Lakes 4.3

Timacuan Golf and Country Club 4.1

Orange County National:
   Panther 4.7, Crooked Cat 4.6

Mystic Dunes 3.9

Champions Gate:
   National 4.2, International 4.4

Bay Hill Club & Lodge 4.3

Metrowest Golf Club 4.2

North Shore Golf Club 3.9

The Emerald Coast

Sandestin Resort: Burnt Pine 4.4,
   Raven 4.2, Baytowne Golf Club 3.8

Kelly Plantation Golf Club 4.5

Regatta Bay Golf Course 4.5

Camp Creek Golf Club 4.9

Windswept Dunes 4.6

Naples

The Rookery at Marco 4.5

Hammock Bay 3.3

Tiburon Golf Club: Black: 4.2, Gold 3.9

Naples Grande Golf Club 5.0

GEORGIA

Sea Island

The Seaside Course 4.9

The Plantation Course 4.4

The Retreat Course 4.7

Savannah

Crosswinds Golf Club 4.5

Club at Savannah Harbor 4.3

Wilmington Island Club 4.0

Southbridge Golf Club 4.4

The Woodyard at Savannah Quarters 4.5

LOUISIANA

New Orleans

Carter Plantation 4.3

TPC of Louisiana 4.2

Audubon Park Golf Course 3.3

English Turn 3.8

Money Hill Golf and Country Club 3.5

MISSISSIPPI

Northeastern Mississippi

Cherokee Valley Golf Club 4.2

Kirkwood National Golf Club 3.5

Mallard Pointe Golf Course 3.9

River Bend Links 3.9

Cottonwoods Course at Grand Casino 4.4

Big Oaks Golf Club 4.3

Old Waverly Golf Club 4.8

North Creek 3.1

NORTH CAROLINA

The Sandhills

Pinehurst Resort: No. 1 4.0, No. 2 4.2,
   No. 3 4.0, No. 4 4.5, No. 5 3.0,
   No. 6 4.5, No. 7 4.4, No. 8 4.3

Pine Needles 4.2

Mid Pines 4.4

Tobacco Road Golf Club 4.3

Bayonet at Puppy Creek 4.7

Little River Farm 4.2

Talamore Golf Resort 4.3

Hyland Hills Golf Club 4.3

SOUTH CAROLINA

Kiawah Island

The Ocean Course 4.8

Osprey Point 4.5

Turtle Point 4.3

Cougar Point 4.3

Oak Point 3.8

Myrtle Beach's South Strand

Caledonia Golf and Fish 4.7

True Blue 4.4

TPC of Myrtle Beach 4.3

Litchfield Country Club 2.5

River Club 4.2

Heritage Club 4.1

Pawleys Plantation Golf & Country Club 3.9

Willbrook Plantation 3.3

Tradition Club 4.2

Wachesaw Plantation East 2.9

MIDWEST

ILLINOIS

Chicago

Pine Meadow 3.5

Kemper Lakes Golf Club 3.8

Heritage Bluffs Public Golf Club 3.9

The Glen Club 3.6

Cantigny Golf Club:
   Lakeside/Hillside 4.3,
   Hillside/Woodside 4.0,
   Woodside/Lakeside 4.8

Village Links 3.6

Orchard Valley Golf Course 4.8

Thunderhawk Golf Club 4.2

Harborside International Golf Center:
   Port Course 4.2, Starboard Course 4.0

Bolingbrook Golf Club 4.6

MICHIGAN

Northern Michigan

Arcadia Bluffs Golf Course 4.4

Grand Traverse Resort: The Bear 4.5,
   Spruce Run 3.7, The Wolverine 3.8

Forest Dunes 4.6

Shanty Creek:
    Cedar River 4.6, Legend Course 4.2,
    Schuss Mountain 5.0, Summit 3.8
Bay Harbor Golf Club:
    Links 4.3, Preserve 3.7, Quarry 4.8
Boyne Higlands Resort and Country Club:
    Arthur Hills 4.0, The Heather 4.7,
    Donald Ross Memorial 4.0, The Moor 4.3
Lakewood Shores:
    Blackshire 4.1, Gailes 4.6, Serradella 3.8
Treetops Sylvan Resort:
    Premier 4.6, Masterpiece 4.4,
    Signature 4.3, Tradition 4.0
Marquette Golf Club: Heritage 4.5

MINNESOTA

Northern Minnesota

The Classic Course at Madden's on Gull Lake 5.0
Grand View Lodge: Deacon's Lodge 4.8,
    Preserve 4.8, Lakes/Woods 4.6,
    Woods/Marsh 5.0, The Garden 4.0
The Legacy Courses at the Craguns: Bobby 3.5
Ruttger's Bay Lake Lodge: Lakes 4.7
Izaty's Golf & Yacht Club: Black Brook 4.0

NORTH DAKOTA

The North Dakota Golf Trail

Hawktree Golf Club 4.9
The Links of North Dakota 4.8
Riverwood Golf Club 4.3
Prairie West Golf Course 4.0
Heart River Municipal Golf Course 4.6
Souris Valley Golf Club 4.1
Painted Woods Golf Course 5.0

WISCONSIN

Kohler

Brown Deer Golf Course 3.8
Blackwolf Run:
    River Course 4.7, Meadow Valleys 4.3
Whistling Straits: Straits 4.4, Irish 3.8

WEST

ARIZONA

Scottsdale–Phoenix

The Boulders: South 4.1, North 4.5
Grayhawk Golf Club: Talon 4.2, Raptor 4.1
The Raven Golf Club at Verrado 4.6
Talking Stick Golf Club: North 4.1, South 4.0
TPC Scottsdale: Stadium 4.1, Desert 3.8
Troon North Golf Club: Monument 4.4,
    Pinnacle 4.3
Vistal Golf Club 3.9
We-Ko-Pa Golf Club 4.5
Whirlwind Golf Club:
    Devil's Claw 3.8, The Cattail 4.3
Wildfire Golf Club: Faldo Championship 4.3,
    Palmer Signature 4.2

Tucson

The Gallery Golf Club 4.3
Golf Club at Vistoso 4.4
Tucson National: Orange/Gold 3.5
Ventana Canyon Golf Club:
    Canyon 3.9, Mountain 4.5
Westin La Paloma Resort: Canyon/Hill 4.7,
    Hill/Ridge 4.7, Ridge/Canyon 4.7

CALIFORNIA

Napa

Fountaingrove Golf & Athletic Club 4.6
Napa Golf Course at Kennedy Park 3.4
Silverado Resort: North 2.4, South 3.7
Sonoma Golf Club 4.9
Vintner's Golf Club 4.3

San Francisco to Pebble Beach

Harding Park Golf Course 3.7
Presidio Golf Course 3.2
Half Moon Bay Golf Links:
    Old Course 4.2, Ocean Course 4.2
Pasatiempo Golf Club 4.3
Pebble Beach Golf Links 4.3
Spyglass Hill 4.2
Links at Spanish Bay 4.4

San Diego

Aviara Golf Club 4.1
The Auld Course 3.8
Barona Creek Golf Club 4.2
The Encinitas Ranch Golf Course 4.0
The Grand Golf Club 3.0
La Costa Resort & Spa: North 3.5, South 3.1
Maderas Golf Club 4.6
The Riverwalk Golf Course: Mission/Friars 3.0,
    Friars/Presidio 2.6, Presidio/Mission 3.1
Torrey Pines Municipal Golf Course:
    North 3.6, South 3.7

Palm Springs

Desert Willow Golf Resort: Firecliff 4.4
La Quinta Resort & Club: Mountain 4.1
Marriott's Shadow Ridge Resort 4.7
PGA West Stadium Course 4.1

COLORADO

Vail Valley

Club at Cordillera: Summit 4.8, Valley 2.3,
    Mountain 4.5, Short 4.0
Cotton Ranch Golf Club 4.5
Eagle Ranch Golf Course 3.0
Red Sky Golf Club:
    Greg Norman 5.0, Tom Fazio 5.0
Sonnenalp Golf Club 4.4
Beaver Creek Golf Course 3.1
Vail Golf Club 4.3

NEVADA

Las Vegas

Shadow Creek Golf Club 4.7
Primm Valley Golf Club: Lakes 4.6, Desert 4.5
Bali Hai Golf Club 3.8
Lake Las Vegas Resort: Reflection Bay 4.2

TEXAS

San Antonio

Pecan Valley Golf Club 3.7
La Cantera Golf Club: Palmer 4.0, Resort 4.1
Hill Country Golf Club 4.2
Silver Horn Golf Club 4.5
Cedar Creek Golf Course 3.8

Quarry Golf Club 4.0
Bandit Golf Club 4.5
Golf Club of Texas 3.7

Houston

Redstone Golf Club 4.0
Magnolia Creek:
    England 4.3, Ireland 4.4, Scotland 4.7
BlackHorse Golf Club: North 4.1, South 3.7
Cypress Wood Golf Club:
    Cypress 4.0, Tradition 4.5

UTAH, MONTANA, IDAHO, AND WYOMING

Salt Lake City to Anaconda

Old Works Golf Course 4.8
Fairmont Hot Springs Resort 2.0

Salt Lake City to Sun Valley

Sun Valley Resort Golf Course 4.1
Elkhorn Resort 4.7
Bigwood Golf Club 4.0

Salt Lake City to Jackson Hole

Jackson Hole Golf & Tennis Club 3.6
Teton Pines Country Club & Resort 4.0

NORTHWEST

IDAHO

Coeur d'Alene

Circling Raven Golf Club 4.9
The Coeur d'Alene 4.1
Hidden Lakes Golf Resort 4.6

MONTANA

The Flathead Valley

Eagle Bend Golf Club: Championship 4.7
Whitefish Lake Golf Club: South 4.0, North 4.3
Buffalo Hill Golf Course:
    Championship 4.1, Cameron Nine 4.2
Meadow Lake 4.4
Polson Country Club:
    Eighteen 3.0, Olde 4.3
Mission Mountain Country Club 4.5
Village Greens Golf Course 5.0
Glacier View Golf Club 5.0

OREGON

Bandon Dunes

Pacific Dunes 4.8
Bandon Dunes 4.7
Bandon Trails 4.8

Bend and Sunriver

Sunriver Resort: Crosswater 4.6,
    Meadows 4.5, Woodlands 5.0
Widgi Creek 4.1
Lost Tracks Golf Club 4.1
Eagle Crest:
    Ridge 3.0, Resort 4.0, Mid Iron 4.3
Aspen Lakes 4.3
Black Butte Ranch:
    Big Meadow 4.7, Glaze Meadow 4.4
Quail Run Golf Course 3.8

Portland

Pumpkin Ridge: Ghost Creek 4.4
Heron Lakes:
    Great Blue 4.3, Greenback 3.5
Langdon Farms 3.8
The Reserve Vineyards & Golf Club:
    South 4.6, North 3.7

WASHINGTON

Seattle

Gold Mountain Golf Complex:
    Olympic 4.8
McCormick Woods Golf Course 4.5
Trophy Lake Golf & Casting 4.1
Golf Club at Newcastle:
    Coal Creek 3.3, China Creek 3.8
Washington National Golf Club 4.1
Druids Glen Golf Club 3.3
West Seattle Golf Course 3.3

HAWAII

Maui

Kapalua Resort:
    Plantation 4.2, Bay 4.1, Village 3.5
Wailea Golf Club:
    Gold 4.8, Emerald 4.7, Blue 3.8

Lana'i

The Challenge at Manele 4.4
The Experience at Koele 4.3

Oahu

Turtle Bay Resort: Fazio 3.7, Palmer 4.1

Mauna Lea and Mauna Lani

Hapuna Golf Course 3.9
Mauna Kea Golf Course 4.3
Mauna Lani: North 4.2, South 4.5

CANADA

Banff

Fairmont Banff Springs Golf Course 4.7
Silvertip Golf Resort 4.5

Muskoka Golf Trail

Deerhurst Highlands 4.5

Prince Edward Island

Brudenell River Golf Course:
    Brudenell River 4.5, Dundarave 4.3
The Eagles Glenn 4.3
Fox Meadow Golf & Country Club 4.0
Glasgow Hills Resort & Golf Club 4.8
The Links at Crowbush Cove 5.0

Okanagan Valley

Gallagher's Canyon 4.8
Harvest Golf Club 4.3
Okanagan Golf Club: Quail 4.3, Bear 3.7
Predator Ridge:
    Osprey 4.7, Red Tail 4.6, Peregrine 4.0

CARIBBEAN AND MEXICO

Puerto Rico

Hyatt Dorado Beach Resort & Country Club:
    East 4.4, West 4.0
Embassy Suites Dorado del Mar Beach
    and Golf Resort 4.2
Westin Rio Mar: River 4.1, Ocean 4.3
Wyndham El Conquistador 4.2

Page numbers in **bold** refer
to photographs.

Adriatic Golf Club Cervia, 253
air travel, 97
Alabama, 56–60, **57, 59,** 194
Algarve, Portugal, The, 255–59, **256**
Almenara, 270
Alps, The, 246
Amelia Island Plantation, 64
American Club, 273
Anaconda, MT, 166
Arcadia Bluffs Golf Course, 104
Arcangues, 247
architects, big-name, bargain tracks
   by, 24–27
Arizona, 119, 122–33, **124–25,**
   129, 131, 132, 273, 274
Arizona National, 119, 130
Arizona State University, 119
Arkansas, 194
Arthur Hills Michigan Golf Trail, 195
Aspen Lakes, 185
Atlantic City, NJ, 30–31, **32–33**
Audubon Golf Trail, 194
Audubon Park Golf Course, 83
Auld Course, The, 139
Austria, 246
Aviara Golf Club, 139

Balgove Course, 266
Bali Hai Golf Club, 150
ballparks, courses near, 144
Bandit Golf Club, 163
Bandon Dunes, 182
Bandon Dunes Golf Resort, 179–83,
   180–81, 273
Bandon Trails, 182
Banff, Canada, 212–14, **213**
Barbados, 226–28, **227**
Barbados Golf Club, 226
bargain courses, 24–27, 284–90
Barona Creek Golf Club, 139, **141**
baseball, 144
Bay Creek Golf Club, 44, **45**
Bay Harbor Golf Club, 105, **278–79**
Bay Hill Club and Lodge, 7, **71,** 74
Bayonet at Puppy Creek, 88
Bear Creek Golf Course, 122

Bear Trace, 194
Beaver Creek Golf Course, 148
Belas, 260
Belmont Hills Golf Club, 230
Bend, OR, 184–86
Berkshires, The, 12–13
Bermuda, 229–31
Bethpage State Park, 24, 36, **36,** 52
Biarritz, France, 247–48
Big Mountain Golf Club, 176
Big Oaks Golf Club, 85
Bigwin Island Golf Club, 218
Bigwood Golf Club, 167
Birck Boilermaker Golf Complex, 119
Black Butte Ranch, 186
Blackhorse Golf Club, **160,** 161
Blackwolf Run, 117
Blue Heron Pines Golf Club, 30,
   32–33
Boavista, 257
Bolingbrook Golf Club, 103
Bologna Golf Club, 253
Boulders Resort & Golden Door Spa,
   122, 273
Boyne Highlands Resort and Country
   Club, 105, 109
Brigantine Beach, The Links at, 31
British Columbia, Canada, 194,
   212–16
Broadmoor, The, 273
Brown Deer Golf Course, 117
Brudenell River Golf Course, 221
buddy trips, 271
Buffalo Hill Golf Course, 177
Bulle Rock, 144
Bully Pulpit Golf Course, 114
Buncombe County Golf Course, 24
Butte, MT, 165, 166

Cabo del Sol, 235
Cabo Real Resort, 236
Cacapon Resort State Park, 24
Caledonia Golf and Fish Club, 94
California, 24, 25, 26, 53, 134–43,
   137, 141, 273, 274, 275
Cambrian Ridge, 58
Camp Creek Golf Club, 62
Canada, 194, 212–22, **213, 217,**
   219, 222

Cancun, Mexico, 241–42
Canoa Hills, 133
Canoa Ranch Golf Club, 133
Cantigny Golf Club, 102
Cape Cod, MA, 14–16
Cape Cod National Golf Club, 15
Capitol Hill, 58
Captains Golf Course, 15
Caribbean, 226–34, **227, 233, 234**
Carter Plantation, 82, **82**
Castell'Arquato Golf Club, 252
Cedar Creek Golf Course, 163
Challenge at Manele, The, 202, **203**
Championsgate, 74
Cherokee Valley Golf Club, 84
Chiberta, Golf de, 247
Chicago, IL, 100–3, **101, 102**
Circling Raven Golf Club, 174
Clemmons, NC, 53
Club at Cordillera, 145, **146–47**
Club at Genoa Lakes, 153
Club at Savannah Harbor, 76
Club de Golf Valderrama, 268, **269**
Coco Beach Golf and Country Club,
   232, **233, 234**
Coeur d'Alene, ID, 174–75, 273
Coeur d'Alene Resort, 174, 273
Cog Hill Golf and Country Club,
   100, **101, 102**
colleges, 119
Colonial Golf Course, 40
Colorado, 145–49, **146–47,** 273
Cordillera, Club at, 145, **146–47**
Costa del Sol, Spain, 268–70, **269**
Cotton Ranch Golf Club, 145
Cottonwoods Course at Grand
   Casino, 84
Cougar Point, 93
Country Club at New Seabury, 14
County Louth Golf Club, 251
Coyote Moon Golf Club, 155
Cozumel Country Club, 241
Craguns Resort on Gull Lake, 110, 111
Craig Wood Golf Course, 34
Cranberry Valley, 15
Croara Country Club, 252
Crosswinds Golf Club, 76
Crowbush Cove, The Links at, 221,
   222

Crumpin-Fox Club, 12
Cypress Wood Golf Club, 161

D'Andrea Golf Club, 157
Dayton Valley Golf Club, 153
Deerhurst Highlands, 218
Desert Willow Golf Resort, 142
Dragon at Gold Mountain, 155
Druids Glen Golf Club, 192
Dublin, Ireland, 249–51, **249**
Duke's Course, 265
Duke University, 119

Eagle Bend Golf Club, 176
Eagle Creek Golf Club, 27
Eagle Crest, 185
Eagle Ranch Golf Course, 145
Eagles Glenn, 221
East Potomac Golf Course, 47
Eden Course, 265
Edgewood Tahoe Golf Course,
   6, 153, **154**
Eichenheim, Golfclub, 246
El Conquistador, 233
Elkhorn Resort, 167
El Tigre Golf Club, 237
Embassy Suites Dorado Del Mar
   Beach and Golf Resort, 232
Emerald Coast, FL, 61–63, **62,**
   67, 69
emergencies, 243
Emilia Romagna, Italy, 252–54
Encinitas Ranch Golf Course, 139
English Turn, 83
Equinox Resort, Manchester Village,
   VT, 20–23, **21**
Escena Golf Club, 142
Esmeralda Golf Course, 175
Estoril, Portugal, 260–61, **261**
Estoril Golf Club, 260
Europe, 246–70
Exeter Country Club, 18
Experience at Koele, 202, 203, 275

Fairmont Banff Springs Golf Course,
   212, 213, **213**
Fairmont Hot Springs Resort, 166
Fife, Scotland, 262–67
First Coast, FL, 64–66

Flamingos Golf, 269

Flathead Valley, MT, 176–78

Florida, 25, 26, 53, 61–75, **62, 64, 67, 69, 71, 72–73, 74,** 276

Forest Dunes, 104

Forest Meadows Golf Resort, 24

Fountaingrove Golf & Athletic Club, 134

Four Seasons Golf Club Punta Mita, 237

Four Seasons Resort Aviara, 273

Four Seasons Resort Hualalai, 274

Four Seasons Resort Lana'i at Manele Bay, 274

Four Seasons Resort Scottsdale at Troon North, 274

Fox Meadow Golf & Country Club, 221

France, 247–48

French Lick Springs Resort, 52

friends, traveling with, 271

Gallagher's Canyon, 215

Gallery Golf Club, The, **129,** 130, **132**

Genoa Lakes, Club at, 153

George Wright Golf Course, 144

Georgia, 76–81, **79, 80,** 275

Glacier View Golf Club, 177

Glasgow Hills Resort & Golf Club, 221

Glen Club, 100

Glenn Abbey Golf Club, 144

Gleneagles Golf Course, 20, **21**

Golden Horseshoe Golf Club, 40

Gold Medal resorts, 273–76

Gold Mountain Golf Complex, 190

Golf Club at Newcastle, **191,** 192, **192**

Golf Club at Playacar, 241

Golf Club at Vistoso, 130

Golf Club at Whitehawk Ranch, 155

Golf Club Bologna, 253

Golf Club Castell'Arquato, 252

Golfclub Eichenheim, 246

Golf Club La Rocca, 252

Golf Club Le Fonti, 253

Golf Club Matilde di Canossa, 253

Golf Club of Texas, 163

Golfclub Seefeld-Wildmoos, 246

Golfclub Wilder Kaiser, 246

golf.com user ratings, 296–99

Golf de Chiberta, 247

golf schools, 291

Grand Casino, Cottonwoods Course at, 84

Grand Cypress Resort, 72, 75

Grand Golf Club, 140

Grand National, 58

Grand Traverse Resort, 104, 109

Grand View Lodge, 110, 111

Grand Wailea Resort, 274

Grayhawk Golf Club, 122, **124–25,** 126

Graysburg Hills Golf Course, 25

Greenbrier, The, 49–51, 274

Greenbrier Course, 49, **50**

Green Monkey, 226, **227**

Green Valley, AZ, 133

Green Valley Country Club, 18

Greg Norman Signature Course, Ritz-Carlton Golf Club, 72

Half Moon Bay Golf Links, 136

Hammock Bay, 68

Hampton Cove, 56

Hapuna Golf Course, 207

Harborside International Golf Center, 103

Harding Park Golf Course, 136

Harvest Golf Club, 215, **217**

Hawaii, 198–208, **199, 200–1, 203, 204–5,** 274, 275

Hawktree Golf Club, 114

Heart River Municipal Golf Course, 115

Hell's Point Golf Club, 44

Heritage Bluffs Public Golf Club, 100

Heritage Club, 95

Heron Lakes, 187

Heron Ridge Golf Club, 44

Hershey Country Club, 52

Hidden Lakes Golf Resort, 175

Hidden Valley Resort, 38, 39

Highland Links, 15

Highland Oaks, 59

Hill Country Golf Club, 162

Homestead, 274

Houston, TX, 160–61, **160**

Hyatt Dorado Beach Resort & Country Club, 232

Hyde Park Golf Club, 25, 65

Hyland Hills Golf Club, 89

Idaho, 165, **165,** 167–68, **168,** 174–75, 195, 273

Idaho Golf Trail, 195

Illinois, 52, 100–3, **101, 102**

Indian Canyon Golf Course, 174

Inn & Links at Spanish Bay, 138, 274

Ireland, 249–51, **249**

Ironhorse Golf Club, 144

Italy, 252–54

Izaty's Golf & Yacht Club, 111

Jackson Hole, WY, 165, 169–70

Jackson Hole Golf & Tennis Club, 169

James Braid Golf Trail, 195

Jubilee Course, 265

Kapalua Resort, 198

Karsten Creek, 119

Karsten Golf Course, 119

Kauai Marriott Resort & Beach Club, 274

K Club, 250

Kearney Hill Golf Links, 25

Keller Golf Course, 52

Kelly Plantation Golf Club, 61

Kemper Lakes Golf Club, 52

Kiawah Island Golf Resort, 91–93, **91,** 274–75

Kingsbarns Golf Links, 262, **264**

Kingsmill Golf Club & Resort, 40, **41**

Kirkwood National Golf Club, 84

Kohler, WI, **116,** 117–18, 273

La Cala, 269

La Cantera Golf Club, 162

La Costa Resort & Spa, 140

Lake Las Vegas Resort, 151, 275

Lake Placid, NY, 34

Lake Placid Resort & Golf Club, 34

Lakeridge Golf Course, 153, 156

Lake Tahoe, NV, **6,** 153–55, **154**

Lakewood Shores, 105

Lana'i, HI, 202–3, **203,** 274, 275

Lancaster, KY, 26

Langdon Farms, 187

Langston Golf Course, 47

La Quinta Resort & Club, 142, 143

La Reserva de Sotogrande, 268

La Rocca Golf Club, 252

Las Cruces, NM, 119

Las Vegas, NV, 150–52, **151**

Laurel Highlands, PA, 7, 38–39, **39**

Le Fonti Golf Club, 253

Legacy Club at Alaqua Lakes, 73

Legacy Courses at the Craguns, 110

Le Phare, 247

Leven Links, 265

Links at Brigantine Beach, The, 31

Links at Crowbush Cove, The, 221, **222**

Links at Shirley, The, 35

Links at Spanish Bay, 138, 274

Links of North Dakota, The, 114

Litchfield Country Club, 94

Little River Farm, 89

Lodge at Koele, The, 275

Lodge at Pebble Beach, The, 275

Long Island, NY, 35–37, **36**

Long Island National Golf Club, 35

Los Cabos, Mexico, 235–36

Lost Tracks Golf Club, 184

Louisiana, 26, 82–83, **82,** 194

Louisiana, TPC of, 82

Lundin Golf Club, 265

Lyman Orchards Golf Club, 25

McCormick Woods Golf Course, 190

McCullough's Emerald Golf Links, 31

Mackenzie Golf Course at Haggin Oaks, 25

Maderas Golf Club, 140

Madden's on Gull Lake, 110, 111, **112–13**

Magnolia Creek, 160

Magnolia Grove, 59

major venues, 52–53

Mallard Pointe Golf Course, 84

Manchester Village, VT, 20–23, **21**

Mark Twain Golf Course, 25

Marquette Golf Club, **108,** 109

Marriott's Shadow Ridge Resort, 143

Massachusetts, 12–16

Matilde di Canossa Golf Club, 253
Maui, HI, 198–99, **199, 200–1,** 274
Mauna Kea Golf Course, 207
Mauna Lani Resort, 207–8, 275
Mauna Lea, HI, 207–8
Maverick Golf Trail, 195
Mayfair Country Club, 26
Meadow Lake, 177
Meadows, 49
Metrowest Golf Club, 75
Mexico, 235–42, **238–39**
Michigan, 104–9, **106–7, 108,** 195,
 278–79
Mid-Atlantic region, 30–51
Mid Ocean, 229
Mid Pines, 88
Midwest, 100–118
Minnesota, 52, 110–11, **112–13**
Mission Mountain Country Club, 177
Mississippi, 84–85
Modena Golf & Country Club, 252
Moliets, 247
Money Hill Golf and Country Club, 83
Montana, 165, 166, 176–78
Montauk Downs, 35
Montaup Country Club, 18
Moon Spa & Golf Club, 241
Mount Pleasant Golf Course, 144
Muskoka Bay Club, 219
Muskoka Golf Trail, 218–20, **219**
Myrtle Beach, SC, South Strand of,
 94–96
Myrtle Beach, TPC of, 94
Mystic Dunes, 74

Napa, CA, 134–35
Napa Golf Course at Kennedy Park,
 134
Naples, FL, 67–68
Naples Grande Golf Club, 68
Natural State Golf Trail, 194
Nemacolin Woodlands Resort, 38,
 39, **39**
Nevada, **6,** 150–57, **151, 154,**
 158–59, 275
Newcastle, Golf Club at, **191,** 192,
 192
New Course at St. Andrews, 262
New England, 12–23

New Jersey, 30–31, **32–33,** 53
New Mexico State University, 119
New Orleans, LA, 82–83, **82**
Newport, RI, 17–19, **17, 19**
Newport National Golf Club, 17,
 17, 19
New York, 24, 25, 34–37, **36,** 52
NMSU Golf Course, 119
North Carolina, 24, 53, 86–90, **87,**
 89, 119, 195, 275
North Creek, 85
North Dakota, 114–15
North Shore Golf Club, 75
Northwest, 174–93

Oahu, HI, **204–5,** 206
Oakhurst Links, 49, **51**
Oak Point, 93
Ocean Course, 91, **91,** 92
Oitavos, 260
Okanagan Golf Club, 215
Okanagan Valley, Canada, 215–16,
 217
Oklahoma State University, 119
Old Course at St. Andrews, 262,
 263, 264, 266, 267
Olde Barnstable Fairgrounds Golf
 Course, 15
Old Greenwood, 157
Old Orchard Country Club, 144
Old Waverly Golf Club, 85
Old White, 49
Old Works Golf Course, 166
Ontario, Canada, 218–20, **219**
Orange County National, 74
Orchard Course at Newport National
 Golf Club, 17
Orchard Valley Golf Course, 102
Oregon, **8,** 179–89, **180–81, 188,**
 273, 275
Oregon Golf Association Course, 189
Orlando, FL, 70–75, **71, 72–73, 74,**
 276
Osprey Point, 92
Oxmoor Valley, 58

Pacific Dunes, 179, **180–81**
Painted Woods Golf Course, 115
Palmilla Resort, 235

Palm Springs, CA, 142–43
Papago Golf Course, 144
Pasatiempo Golf Club, 136
Pawleys Plantation Golf & Country
 Club, 95
P.B. Dye Golf Club, 48
Pebble Beach, CA, 53, 136–38,
 137, 274, 275
Pebble Beach Golf Links, 53, 137,
 137
Pecan Valley Golf Club, 53, 162
Penha Longa, 260, **261**
Penina, 258
Peninsula Golf Resort, 26
Pennsylvania, 7, 38–39, **39,** 52
PGA National Golf Course, 53
PGA West Stadium Course, 142, 143
Phoenix, AZ, 122–28
Pine Cliffs, 258
Pinehills Golf Club, 14
Pinehurst Resort & Country Club, 53,
 86–90, **87, 89,** 275
Pine Meadow, 100
Pine Needles, 88
Pit Golf Links, 88
planning a road trip, 223
Plantation Course, 78
Playacar, Golf Club at, 241
Polson Country Club, 177
Portland, OR, 187–89, **188**
Portmarnock Golf Club, 251
Port Royal Golf Course, 229
Portugal, 255–61, **256, 261**
Prairie West Golf Course, 115
Predator Bridge, 215
Presidio Golf Course, 136
Primm Valley Golf Club, 150
Prince Edward Island, Canada, 194,
 221–22, **222**
Prince Edward Island Golf Trail, 194
Princeville Resort, 275
Puerto Rico, 232–34, **233, 234**
Puerto Vallarta, Mexico, 237–40,
 238–39
Pumpkin Ridge, 187, **188**
Purdue University, 119

Quail Run Golf Course, 186
Quarry Golf Club, 163

Quinta da Marinha, 260
Quinta da Ria, 255
Quinta do Lago, 257

Raspberry Falls Golf & Hunt Club, 48
Raven at Cabo San Lucas Country
 Club, 236
Raven Golf Club at Verrado, 123, 126
Red Sky Ranch & Golf Club, 148
Redstone Golf Club, 160
Regatta Bay Golf Course, 61
Reno, NV, 153, 156–57, **158–59**
Republic Golf Club, 163
Reserve Vineyards & Golf Club, 189
Resort at Red Hawk, 156, **158–59**
Retreat Course, 78
Rhode Island, 17–19, **17, 19,** 27
Riddell's Bay Golf and Country
 Club, 230
Ridge at Manitou, 219
Ridgefield Golf Course, 26
Rimini Golf Club, 253
Riolo Golf & Country Club, 253
Ritz-Carlton Golf Club, 72
River Bend Links, 84
River Club, 95
Riverwalk Golf Course, 140
Riverwood Golf Club, 115
Robert Trent Jones Golf Trail, 56–60,
 57, 59, 194
Rock, The, 220
Rock Creek Golf Course, 47
Rookery at Marco, The, 67, **67, 69**
Ross Bridge, 58
Royal County Down, **249,** 250
Royal Westmoreland Golf & Country
 Club, 228
Rutland Country Club, 20
Ruttger's Bay Lake Lodge, 111

St. Andrews, Scotland, 262–67,
 263, 264
St. Andrews Bay Golf Resort and
 Spa, 265
St. George's Golf Course, 230
Salgados, 257
Salt Lake City, UT, 165–70
San Antonio, TX, 53, 162–64
Sand Barrens Golf Club, 31

Sandestin Resort, 61, **62**, 63
Sandhills, The, 86–90, **87**, **89**
San Diego, CA, 139–41, **141**
Sandy Lane Country Club, 228
San Francisco, CA, 136–38
San Ignacio Golf Club, 133
San Lorenzo, 255, **256**
San Roque Club, 270
Santa Maria Golf Club, 26
Santana Golf and Country Club, 269
Saranac Inn Golf Club, 34
Savannah, GA, 76–77
Sawgrass, TPC of, 64, **64**, 65
Sawgrass Country Club, 65
schools, golf, 291
Scotland, 195, 262–67, **263**, **264**
Scottsdale, AR, 122–28, **124–25**,
    274
Scottsdale, TPC of, 123, 126
Sea Island Resort, 78–81, **79**, **80**,
    275
Seaside Course, 78, **79**, **80**
Seattle, WA, 190–93, **191**, **192**
Seaview Marriott Resort & Spa,
    30, 53
Seefeld-Wildmoos Golfclub, 246
Seignosse Golf Hotel, 247
Seven Springs Mountain Resort,
    38, 39
Shadow Creek Golf Club, 150, **151**
Shanty Creek, 105
Sharp Park Golf Course, 26
Sheep Ranch, 182
shipping your clubs, 171
Shirley, The Links at, 35
Shoals, The, 56, **57**, **59**
Shore Gate Golf Club, 30
Signature at West Neck, **43**, 44
Silverado Resort, 134
Silver Horn Golf Club, 163
Silver Lakes, 56
Silver Medal resorts, 276–77
Silvertip Golf Resort, 212
Sintra National Park, 260–61, **261**
Sonnenalp Golf Club, 148
Sonoma Golf Club, 134
Sotogrande Club de Golf, 268
Souris Valley Golf Club, 115
South, 56–96

Southbridge Golf Club, 76
South Carolina, 91–96, **91**, 195,
    274–75
Spain, 268–70, **269**
Spanish Bay, Links at, 138, 274
Spyglass Hill, 137
Stewart Creek Golf Club, 212
Stonewater Golf Club, 144
Strathtyrum Course, 266
Stratton Mountain Country Club,
    2, 20, **22**
Strawberry Farms Golf Club, 144
Sunriver Resort, **8**, 184–86, **185**,
    275
Sun Valley, ID, 165, **165**, 167–68,
    168
Sun Valley Resort Golf Course, **165**,
    167, **168**
Swope Memorial Golf Course, 26
Sycamore Course at Eagle Creek Golf
    Club, 27

Taboo Golf Course, **219**, 220
Taconic Golf Club, 12
Talamore Golf Resort, 89
Talking Stick Golf Club, 123
Tallgrass Golf Club, 37
Tanglewood Park, 53
Tater Hill Golf Club, 23
Tennessee, 25, 194
Teton Pines Country Club & Resort,
    169, 170
Texas, 53, 160–64, **160**
thrifty 50 courses, 284–90
Thunderhawk Golf Club, 102
Tiburon Golf Club, 68
Timacuan Golf and Country Club, 73
tipping, 209
Tobacco Road Golf Club, 88
top 10 golf trails, 194–95
top 100 courses, 280–81
    ranked by state, 282–83
    in the U.S., 292–93
    in the world, 294–95
Torrey Pines Municipal Golf Course,
    140, 141
TPC at Virginia Beach, 45
TPC of Louisiana, 82
TPC of Myrtle Beach, 94

TPC of Sawgrass, The, 64, **64**, 65
TPC Scottsdale, 123, 126
Tradition Club, 95
Treetops Sylvan Resort, **106–7**,
    108, 109
Triggs Memorial Golf Course, 19, 27
Troon North Golf Club, 126
Trophy Lake Golf & Casting, 190
True Blue, 94
Tubac Golf Resort, 133
Tucker's Point Golf Club, 230
Tucson, AZ, 119, 129–33, **129**,
    131, **132**
Tucson National, 130, **131**
Turtle Bay Resort, **204–5**, 206
Turtle Point, 92

university courses, 119
University of Arizona, 119
University of Wisconsin, 119
University Ridge Golf Course, 119
Utah, 165–70

Vail Golf Club, 149
Vail Valley, 145–49, **146–47**
Valderrama Club de Golf, 268, **269**
Vale do Lobo, 258
Van Cortlandt Park Golf Course, 144
Vancouver Island Golf Trail, 194
Ventana Canyon Golf Club, 131
Vermont, **2**, 20–23, **21**, **22**
Victoria, 257
Victoria Hills Golf Club, 70
Vilamoura, 258
Vila Sol, 258
Village Greens Golf Course, 177
Village Links, 102
Vintner's Golf Club, 135
Virginia, 40–46, **41**, **43**, **45**, 195,
    274, 276
Virginia Beach, TPC at, 45
Virginia Beach, VA, 43–46, **43**, **45**
Vistal Golf Club, 126
Vista Vallarta, 237, **238–39**
Vista Verde Golf Course, 127
Vistoso, Golf Club at, 130

Wachesaw Plantation East, 95
Wahconah Country Club, 12

Wailea Golf Club, 198, **199**, **200–1**
Walt Disney World Resort, 70,
    72–73, **74**, 75, 276
Washington, 190–93, **191**, **192**
Washington, DC, 47–48
Washington Duke Inn & Golf Club,
    119
Washington National Golf Club, 192
Waverly Oaks Golf Club, 14
We-Ko-Pa Golf Club, 127
West, 122–70
Westin La Paloma Resort, 131
Westin Rio Mar, 233
West Seattle Golf Course, 193
West Virginia, 24, 49–51, **50**, **51**,
    274
Whirlwind Golf Club, 127
Whiskey Creek Golf Club, 48
Whiteface Club & Resort, 34
Whitefish Lake Golf Club, 176
Whitehawk Ranch, Golf Club at, 155
White Sulphur Springs, WV, 49, **50**,
    51, 274
Widgi Creek, 184
Wilder Kaiser Golfclub, 246
Wildfire Golf Club, 127
Willbrook Plantation, 95
Williamsburg, VA, 40–42, **41**, 276
Williamsburg Inn, 276
Wilmington Island Club, 76
Windsor Parke Golf Club, 65
Windswept Dunes, 62
Wisconsin, **116**, 117–18, 119, 273
Wolf Run Golf Club, 156
Wyoming, 165, 169–70

Acknowledgments

Thanks to GOLF MAGAZINE editor David Clarke for making this project possible, and to Lisa Freedman, for her tireless efforts to make sure the information in the book is accurate.

Editor: Charles Kochman
Designer: Binocular, New York
Production Manager: Jacquie Poirier

Library of Congress Cataloging-in-Publication Data
Golf magazine great getaways : the best of the best three-and four day golf trips / edited by Tara Gravel ; introduction by Arnold Palmer.
   p. cm.
  ISBN 13: 978-0-8109-9293-1 (flexi-bind)
  ISBN 10: 0-8109-9293-0 (flexi-bind)
  1. Golf courses—United States—Guidebooks. 2. Golf resorts—United States—Guidebooks. I. Gravel, Tara. II. Golf magazine.
  GV981.G654 2007
  796.352'060973—dc22

                 2006035558

Printed and bound in Hong Kong
10 9 8 7 6 5 4 3 2 1

Photograph Credits

Photographs courtesy of: Barona Valley Ranch Resort & Casino: 141; Bay Creek Golf Club: 45; Bay Hill Golf Club: 71; Blackhorse Golf Club: 160; Blue Heron Golf Club: 32–33; Carter Plantation: 82; Coco Beach Golf and Country Club: 233, 234; Cog Hill Golf and Country Club: 101, 102; Edgewood Tahoe Golf Course: 6, 154; Fairmont Banff Springs: 213; Four Seasons Resort Lana'i at Manele Bay: 203; The Gallery Golf Club: 129, 132; Grayhawk Golf Club: 124–125; The Greenbrier: 50; Kevin Frisch Resort & Golf Marketing: 106–107, 108, 278–279; Kiawah Island Golf Resort: 91, 92; Kingsbarns Golf Links: 264; Kingsmill Golf Club & Resort: 41; Madden's on Gull Lake: 112–113; Nemacolin Woodlands Resort: 39; Newport National: 17, 19; Oakhurst Links: 51; Pebble Beach Golf Links: 137; Pinehurst Resort: 87, 89, 272; Pumpkin Ridge: 188; Red Hawk Golf Club: 158–159; The Robert Trent Jones Golf Trail: back cover, 57, 59; Rock Resorts: 21; The Rookery at Marco: 67, 69; Sandestin Resort: 62; Shadow Creek Golf Club: 151; The Signature at West Neck: 43; Stratton Mountain Country Club: 2, 22; Sunriver Resort: 8, 185; Sun Valley Resort: 165, 168; Taboo Golf Course: 219; Tucson National: 131; Turtle Bay Resort: 204–205; Wailea Golf Club: 199, 200–201; Walt Disney World Resort: 72–73, 74.

Photographs by: Aidan Bradley: 249; Sam Greenwood: 79, 80; John and Jeannine Henebry: 217, 222; Mike Klemme/Golfoto: 227; Rob Perry: front cover, 191, 192; Wood Sabold: 180–181; Keiichi Sato: 146–147; Evan Schiller: 238–239; Fred Vuich: 36, 64, 116, 256, 261, 263, 269.

HNA
harry n. abrams, inc.
a subsidiary of La Martinière Groupe
115 West 18th Street
New York, New York 10011
www.hnabooks.com